T5-BAQ-318

Learning HTML 4.0

DDC Publishing, Inc.
275 Madison Ave.
New York, NY 10016-1161
techsupp@ddcpub.com
www.ddcpub.com

Author	Curt Robbins
Managing Editor	Susan Alcorn
Technical Editor	Amy Towery
Content Editor	Holly Nichols
Proofreader	Eileen Levandoski
Illustrator	Bill Vitucci
Piloter	Gus Biggelow

Legal Notice

About the Author

Curt Robbins is an Internet instructor and courseware developer. He teaches Internet classes, conducts Internet train-the-trainer sessions, presents seminars, and contributes to panel discussions in the United States and Canada. He can be reached at curt@quessing.com.

Mr. Robbins was previously the Webmaster for Northrop Grumman Corporation and the Senior Internet Instructor at Gestalt Systems in Herndon, Virginia. He is a member of the Internet Society, the American Society of Training and Development, the Society for Applied Learning Technology, the International Webmasters Association, and the HTML Writers Guild.

Mr. Robbins co-authored the first series of Internet courses in the United States between 1993-1994. His students have included those from NASA, Microsoft, Oracle, IBM, America Online, AT&T, the FBI, the CIA, the White House and Senate staffs, and members of the Washington Redskins football team.

Mr. Robbins develops custom Internet courseware titles for Microsoft, CompUSA, Micro Center, the FDIC, and the Maryland Bar Association. He has also developed special vertical market Internet courses for the pharmaceutical and travel industries as well as the legal profession.

Mr. Robbins is a native of Ohio and currently resides in Purcellville, Virginia. He attended Ohio State University, where he studied journalism and organizational psychology. Mr. Robbins is an active member of Rotary International and enjoys landscape photography and distance running.

Table of Contents

DDC Publishing • www.ddcpub.com

Course Setup

Installing the Student Files

The student files necessary for *Learning HTML 4.0* are archived on the Student Files CD-ROM. Follow these steps to install the student files:

1. Insert the Student Files CD-ROM into the appropriate drive on your computer.

2. Using Windows Explorer (file manager) or another file management utility, locate the files named HTML-1.EXE, HTML-2.EXE, and HTML-3.EXE and copy each of them to your Windows Desktop.

    ■   On the CD-ROM, select all of the files using <SHIFT> and right-click.

    ■   On the shortcut menu that appears, select **Copy**.

    ■   On your Desktop, be sure your mouse pointer is not on an icon or application and right-click.

    ■   Select **Paste**. This will copy the files from the Student Files CD-ROM to your Windows Desktop.

3. On your Desktop, double-click HTML-1.EXE.

4. The **WinZip Self-Extractor** dialog box will appear. Click the **Unzip** button.

5. If the files were decompressed and installed correctly, an alert box will appear that indicates this.

6. In the HTML-1 directory, double-click README.TXT. This will open the file in Notepad. <u>Carefully read the README.TXT file prior to taking or teaching this course.</u> Close Notepad after you have **<u>completely</u>** read README.TXT.

7. Repeat this process by double-clicking HTML-2.EXE and HTML-3.EXE.

All Student Files have been virus checked and are guaranteed virus-free upon release by the courseware developer *prior to entering the distribution channel*. The courseware developer is not responsible for virus infection that may occur as the result of customer or distribution channel manipulation.

Course Conventions

General Conventions

File and directory names	Indicated in all caps, Times Roman font: Open the file WEBPAGE.HTM and from the C:\HTML-1 directory.
HTML text to be typed in hands-on exercise	Indicated in bold Courier font: **`<TITLE>My Web Page</TITLE>`**
Web page hyperlinks	Indicated in bold and underlined: **This is a <u>hyperlink</u> to a Web page.**
New terms, text to be emphasized, Web page titles	Indicated in italic: Background colors are specified using *RGB codes*.
Icons, buttons, text fields, pulldown menus & menu items requiring student action	Indicated in bold: Click the **Back** button on the toolbar.

Internet Addresses

Uniform Resource Locator	Indicated in Courier font: `www.ddcpub.com`
E-mail address	Indicated in Courier font: `webmaster@ddcpub.com`

Web Browser Configuration

Web browser and version	MSIE 5.0*x* or Netscape Navigator 4.0*x*
Options ▶ Auto Load Images	✓ Selected
Options ▶ Show Toolbar	✓ Selected
Options ▶ Show Location	✓ Selected
Directory Buttons (Navigator)	⊘ Turned off
Links Toolbar (IE)	⊘ Turned off
Other browser settings	Browser defaults

DDC Publishing • www.ddcpub.com

Icon Legend

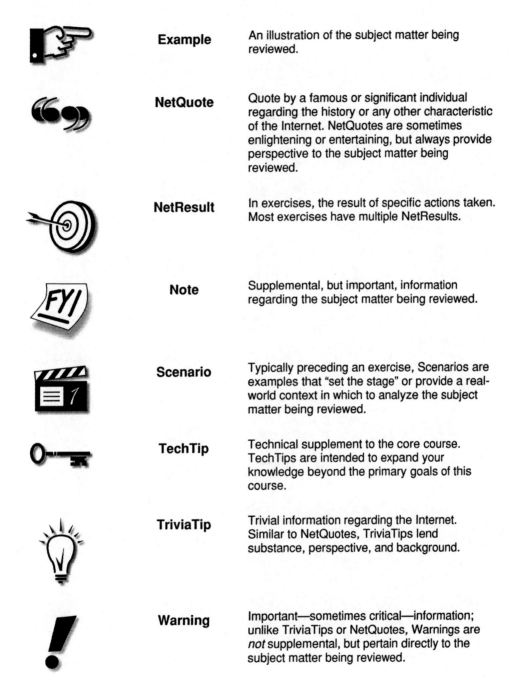

	Example	An illustration of the subject matter being reviewed.
	NetQuote	Quote by a famous or significant individual regarding the history or any other characteristic of the Internet. NetQuotes are sometimes enlightening or entertaining, but always provide perspective to the subject matter being reviewed.
	NetResult	In exercises, the result of specific actions taken. Most exercises have multiple NetResults.
	Note	Supplemental, but important, information regarding the subject matter being reviewed.
	Scenario	Typically preceding an exercise, Scenarios are examples that "set the stage" or provide a real-world context in which to analyze the subject matter being reviewed.
	TechTip	Technical supplement to the core course. TechTips are intended to expand your knowledge beyond the primary goals of this course.
	TriviaTip	Trivial information regarding the Internet. Similar to NetQuotes, TriviaTips lend substance, perspective, and background.
	Warning	Important—sometimes critical—information; unlike TriviaTips or NetQuotes, Warnings are *not* supplemental, but pertain directly to the subject matter being reviewed.

(This page intentionally left blank)

DDC Publishing • www.ddcpub.com

*"I'm going to put him back to bed in a minute, Carol.
I just need Jeffrey to check my HTML tags for errors…"*

Part 1:
HTML 4.0 Fundamentals
Creating Hypertext Web Pages

Part 1 Description

Welcome to *HTML 4.0 Fundamentals*, the first section in DDC's *Mastering HTML* series. This course is designed as a thorough and detailed introduction to the HyperText Markup Language—more commonly known as HTML. This course covers elements of HTML Specifications 3.2 and 4.0 as maintained by the World Wide Web Consortium.

Part 1 Objectives

This course is intended for people who want to learn to use HTML to create Web pages suitable for publishing via the Internet and viewing with a Web browser, such as Netscape Navigator/Communicator or Microsoft Internet Explorer.

- Hypertext and Hypermedia
- Hyperlinks (HTML anchors)
- HTML tag syntax and usage
- Tag attributes
- Lists (ordered and unordered)
- Character references (entity and numeric)
- Inline images
- Background colors, background patterns, and text colors
- <META> tag

Part 1 Setup

DDC's *HTML 4.0 Fundamentals* requires minimal PC configuration and setup. Three primary elements are required for this course: Web browser, text editor, and student files.

During this entire course, you (or your students) will toggle back and forth between your Web browser and your text editor as you create Web pages following the exercises in this course.

Required Software

Two software applications are required to take or teach this course:

- A Web browser (Netscape Navigator 4.0*x* or higher or Microsoft Internet Explorer (IE) 5.0*x* or higher recommended). Navigator can be downloaded from the Netscape Web site at www.netscape.com; Microsoft IE can be downloaded from Microsoft's Web site at www.microsoft.com/ie.

- A text editor (Microsoft Windows Notepad recommended). Notepad can be launched in Windows 95/98/2000 and Windows NT from the Start button on the task bar (choose **Programs ▶ Accessories ▶ Notepad**).

Lesson 1
What is HTML?

Lesson Topics

► Hypertext

► The HyperText Markup Language

► What is an HTML Document?

► HTML Document Structure

► HTML Document Characteristics

► Lesson 1 Summary

Hypertext

Hypertext is the method by which documents, files, and multimedia data are organized (by publishers), referenced, and navigated (by users) via the Internet's World Wide Web. The concept of hypertext can be traced back to the ideas of Dr. Vannevar Bush, science advisor to President Roosevelt.[1] The theory of hypertext was expanded during the 1960s and 1980s by Ted Nelson. Nelson coined the terms "hypertext" and "hypermedia" in 1965.

There are three primary objectives of hypertext information systems:

- to make available extremely large volumes of information from a wide variety of sources via a single medium (the World Wide Web);

- to make this body of information easy to navigate and to make specific data easy to locate;

- to allow you to explore and navigate this information via an arbitrary path of your choice.

Hyperlinks

A *hyperlink*, or link, is a visible navigational anchor in a hypertext document that refers (points) to another hypertext document or multimedia data object (audio file, video file). A hyperlink can refer to a different location in the same hypertext document or to a specific location in a different hypertext document. There is no limit to the number of hyperlinks that can be placed within an individual hypertext document, but each hyperlink can only point to a single document or multimedia data object.

Hypertext Publishing vs. Conventional Publishing

In conventional publishing, an author attempts to eliminate extraneous, supplemental, or "peripheral" information from a document via the editing process. In hypertext publishing, however, peripheral information need not be excluded; it may simply be relegated to a separate hypertext document or collection of documents that are accessible via hyperlinks.

Hypertext publishing creates an environment in which each user determines what information is central and important and what is peripheral or of minimal value. Some contemporary literary experts, such as Dr. George Landow of Brown University, believe that hypertext enables the user to play a part as an author. Although the user does not write the information presented, he or she is able to navigate his or her own path through a body of hypertext documents, viewing only that information that is of interest or subjective value.

---

[1] July 1945 *Atlantic Monthly* article "As We May Think."

Nonlinear Information

When reading a book or magazine article, information is displayed in a linear sequence and only makes sense if it is consumed in a specific, predefined order (progressing from page 1 to page 2 to page 3, and so forth).

If consumed in any other order, linear publications lose their meaning. By contrast, hypertext systems not only *allow* you to navigate through a hypermedia "space" following the path of your choice, but *require* you to do so to consume the available information.

The basis of hypertext is *nonlinear*, nonhierarchical, fluid, and "borderless" information. True hypertext publications do not offer or suggest any predefined path through a body of information. Modern tools for navigating hypertext information systems allow you to quickly revisit a previously viewed document in order to backtrack and, if you choose, select a different hyperlink available in that document.

Conventional vs. Nonlinear Publications

Many, but not all, paper-based publications also assume that the reader will consume the entire body of the text, as in the case of a novel, magazine article, or newspaper article. Reference materials, such as a dictionary, thesaurus, or encyclopedia, however, are designed to provide small pieces of valuable information quickly. Such publications are suitable for presentation in a hypertext format and navigated via hyperlinks.

"Many, perhaps most, writers have been frustrated by the problem of choosing a sequence for the ideas they are presenting. Any sequence is generally arbitrary, and what is right for one reader may be wrong for another."

— *Ted Nelson, inventor of hypertext and hypermedia, 1982*

Hypermedia

Hypermedia is the fusion of hypertext with multimedia files, such as audio, video, and animation. Hypermedia allows Web documents to include hyperlinks that can connect you to a variety of multimedia files, as well as specialized multimedia data, such as virtual reality environments and interactive applications.

A problem many users experience with hypermedia is the amount of time it takes to download multimedia files. Most Internet connections have technical limitations and relatively poor data transfer capabilities. Several new multimedia data formats for the Web have been developed to overcome these technical limitations. The most promising category of multimedia data is *streamed data*. Steaming applies to audio and video formats and makes these otherwise impractical multimedia formats consumable by the average user.

The HyperText Markup Language

The *HyperText Markup Language*, or HTML, is a network-based document scripting language that allows multimedia hypertext documents and related multimedia data to be authored, edited, published, referenced, and navigated via the World Wide Web.

HTML comprises four primary elements, or concepts:

- hypertext and hypermedia computer network-based publishing;

- a scripting language (HTML tag family);

- a software application to locate, download, interpret, and display Web data (Web browser, such as Netscape Navigator or Microsoft Internet Explorer);

- a Web-specific data transfer protocol (HyperText Transfer Protocol or HTTP).

Scripting Language

HTML is a *scripting language*.[2] It is a language for "scripting" documents (analogous to a playwright authoring the "script" of a play) that utilizes a family of syntactical elements called *tags*. These tags are interpreted by a Web browser and tell the browser what to display (content) and how to display it (format).

Thus, an HTML document (commonly called a Web page) is comprised of two discrete elements:

1. content (the words and images in the page); and

2. instructions (HTML tags that command a Web browser to display the content in a particular manner).

A scripting language is very different from a programming language. Programming languages—such as C++, Pascal, or Java—involve both application files and associated data files. HTML, on the contrary, is self contained; the instructions (HTML tags) and data (non-tag HTML document content) are contained within a single file (the HTML document).

---

[2] A scripting language is sometimes referred to as a *markup language*.

The HTML Specification

The official technical rules of HTML—including definitions and usage parameters of the complete tag set, tag attribute set, and character reference entities—are called the *HTML Specification*[3]. Since its introduction in 1992, the HTML Specification has evolved from version 1.0, to version 2.0, to version 3.2, to the current version 4.0.

The HTML Specification is maintained by the World Wide Web Consortium or W3C. The W3C, based in Cambridge, Massachusetts, has been instrumental in establishing and maintaining technical standards for the World Wide Web since 1994.

"Insisting on HTML 4.0 compliance now will preserve your free choice of suppliers of Web software, tools and applications well into the future. With HTML 4.0, any Web application can be vendor independent. There really is no excuse for tying yourselves or your partners to proprietary solutions."

— *Tim Berners-Lee, Director of the W3C, 1998*

HTML Extensions

Although the W3C publishes the official HTML Specification, both Netscape Communications Corporation and Microsoft Corporation—the manufacturers of the two leading Web browsers—frequently publish "extensions" to the HTML Specification. *Extensions* are tags, tag attributes, and character references proposed or published by any party or organization other than the W3C (typically a browser developer/manufacturer).

HTML extensions, by definition, are unofficial additions to the HTML Specification. Even so, many HTML extensions are extremely popular and are in use on millions of Web sites. However, because they deviate from the official HTML standard, these extensions create a lack in conformity and consistent interpretation of Web pages among available Web browsers.

For example, assume Microsoft Corporation introduces a new HTML tag that only the Microsoft Internet Explorer Web browser recognizes and can properly interpret. HTML scripters and webmasters who use this proprietary tag risk all non-Microsoft browsers misinterpreting and not properly displaying pages containing this unofficial tag. You should avoid proprietary HTML extensions unless they are recognized by both the current and the previous versions of *both* Netscape Navigator/Communicator and Microsoft Internet Explorer.

---

[3] The complete HTML 4.01 Specification can be downloaded from the W3C Web site at www.w3.org.

Web Browsers

Web browsers are software applications that run on client computers. In simplified terms, browsers do two things:

- interpret HTML documents;

- display HTML documents.

Despite the fact that HTML is a cross-platform, universal scripting language, browsers from different developers (Netscape and Microsoft) interpret and display HTML documents slightly differently. Sometimes the *same* version of the *same* browser on a different computer operating system (Windows, Macintosh, UNIX) will display a single HTML document differently.

"As computer CRT screens become more and more available, there is less and less reason for printing on paper. The costs of wood pulp and gasoline, the long lead times of editorship and production, the increasing divergence of specialized interests, and the lowering cost of computers with screens, of disk storage, and digital communications, all suggest this."

— *Ted Nelson, inventor of hypertext and hypermedia, 1982*

Discrepancies in HTML document interpretation and display are also apparent between different versions of the same browser for the same computer platform. As a result of the rapid evolution of the HTML Specification (as promoted by the W3C, Netscape, and Microsoft), later versions of any browser provide considerably more functionality and capability than earlier versions. Thus, HTML documents may be interpreted properly in the *latest* version of a browser but misinterpreted and improperly displayed in the *previous* version of the same browser for the same computer platform.

To ensure the most universal and correct interpretation and display of the pages you create among all users of the Web, always test your HTML documents by opening them in both the current and the previous versions of Netscape Navigator and Microsoft Internet Explorer.

While this testing is a time consuming process and requires you to have four Web browsers installed on your computer, it helps ensure the ability of as many Web users as possible to properly interpret your Web pages, saving you embarrassment and lost revenues.

HyperText Transfer Protocol

The *HyperText Transfer Protocol*, or HTTP, is a data communications protocol that operates in conjunction with the Internet's universal TCP/IP protocol. Technically speaking, HTTP is a sub-protocol of TCP/IP.

HTTP makes it possible for a single HTML document to be archived on any type of server computer and viewed using any type of client computer (Windows, DOS, Macintosh, UNIX) and any Web browser (Netscape Navigator, Netscape Communicator, Microsoft Internet Explorer, Opera). HTTP is the technical foundation that provides the true cross-platform capability of HTML. Basically, HTTP allows Web servers and Web browsers to communicate with one another.

Transfer Protocol

A *transfer protocol* is the method by which information is transferred between a server computer and a client computer across the Internet. The transfer protocol you specify in a link in an HTML document determines the type of server to which you are referring, be it a Web server, an FTP server, a news server (newsgroups, also called Usenet), or a mail server (e-mail).

The major transfer protocols used in HTML are listed in Table 1-1.

Transfer Protocol	Server Type	URL Syntax
FTP	FTP	ftp://ftp.domain.com
HTTP	Web	http://www.domain.com
MAILTO[4]	E-mail	mailto:username@domain.com
NEWS	Newsgroup (Usenet)	news://news.domain.com nntp://news.domain.com

Table 1-1: Major transfer protocols supported by Web browsers

---

[4] MAILTO is not a true transfer protocol, but instead a URL prefix that instructs a browser to automatically launch a user's default e-mail application and open a pre-addressed outgoing message, as you will learn during this course. Also note that MAILTO, unlike the other true protocols, lacks forward slashes.

What is an HTML Document?

HTML documents are files archived on Web servers that can be accessed by Internet users via Web browsers (Netscape Navigator, Microsoft Internet Explorer).

HTML documents:

- must be in ASCII file format[5];

- may be any byte count size;

- may assume either portrait, landscape, a combination of both, or other non-traditional layout schemes;

- may include two chief elements: 1) HTML script (tags, tag attributes, and character entities) and 2) non-HTML content (text, images, or multimedia data).

Information other than HTML script or non-HTML content should be avoided.

Creating HTML Documents

HTML documents can be created using any standard text editor, word processor, or HTML editor[6] (Microsoft FrontPage 2000[7], HotDog Pro, HoTMetaL PRO). The format of an HTML document must be ASCII text (sometimes called *plain text* or *DOS text*).

HTML documents not formatted in ASCII text will be partially or totally misinterpreted by a Web browser. Thus, before previewing HTML documents in a Web browser or uploading them to a Web server, remember to format them in ASCII format.

 When creating an HTML document with a word processor, be sure to save the file in ASCII format.

---

[5] ASCII format is also called *plain text* format or *DOS text* format.
[6] For more information regarding HTML editors, see Appendix F: *HTML Editors*.
[7] See DDC's *Mastering FrontPage 2000* Series for more information regarding Microsoft FrontPage.

 DDC Publishing • www.ddcpub.com

HTML Document Structure

Traditional desktop publishing and journalistic design and layout dictate three sections to a physical page: 1) a header; 2) a body; and 3) a footer. In Web publishing with HTML, however, only two sections make up a document.

A properly formatted HTML document contains two sections:

- Head section

- Body section

Head Section

The Head section of an HTML document provides browsers with specific logical data pertaining to the Web page, such as the document title. None of the information provided by an HTML author in the Head section of an HTML document appears in the viewing area of the Web browser.

Body Section

The Body section of an HTML document contains all of the information that is displayed in the browser. While some logical instructions are available that are scripted outside of the Body section in an HTML document, none of this information is visible by a user in the content area of the browser.

 "The overarching vision I propose, then, we might call a 'hyperworld'—a vast new realm of published text and graphics, all available instantly; a grand library that anybody can store anything in...with links...available as options to anyone who wishes to publish them."

— *Ted Nelson, inventor of hypertext and hypermedia, 1982*

HTML Document Characteristics

An HTML document must be properly formatted in order for any Web browser to interpret it correctly. To ensure correct formatting, HTML authors must understand the various characteristics of HTML documents.

White Space

Web browsers recognize no more than a single space between "content" words in an HTML document. Web browsers also ignore the following elements:

- line breaks;

- paragraph breaks;

- multiple non-breaking horizontal spaces.

The HTML script excerpt below, despite its formatting, produces the result shown in Figure 1-1. To force text to wrap or insert white space, specific tags must be used. The excerpt does not contain these tags, and thus most of the additional spaces and line breaks are disregarded in the browser. The Break tag and the Paragraph tag are among the tags that serve this purpose, both of which are covered in Lesson 2: *HTML Tags*.

```
This is an example of    standard u n f o r matted body te xt displayed
within
        an    HT ML document. In the      up  co ming exercises, you will
learn to use
Heading Level      tags to structure your Web pages and formatting
tags to format the text in your      Web pages.
```

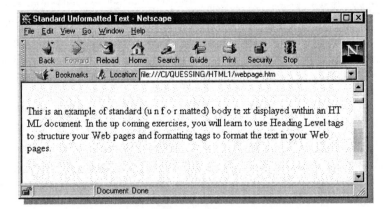

Figure 1-1: Result of poorly formatted script

Lesson 1 Summary

▶ HTML is a scripting language (sometimes called a *markup language*). Scripting languages differ substantially from programming languages.

▶ The official HTML Specification is maintained by the World Wide Web Consortium (W3C). The current version of the Specification is 4.0 and can be downloaded in a variety of file formats from the W3C's Web site at `www.w3.org`.

▶ HTML encompasses four primary technical elements: 1) hypertext and hypermedia publishing; 2) a scripting language; 3) a client software application to download, interpret, and display HTML documents; and 4) a Web-specific data transfer protocol (HTTP).

▶ HTML is a cross-platform scripting language. A document formatted in HTML can be viewed using any Web browser on any computer platform (DOS, Macintosh, UNIX, or Windows).

▶ Uniform Resource Locators (URLs) are the addressing scheme of Web pages and Web sites, and are a syntactical and technical conglomeration of the Web transfer protocol (HTTP), the server address, the directory path, and the file name. Some servers are configured to require only the transfer protocol and server name (`http://www.domain.com`) in order to access a Web page.

▶ Web browsers support several Internet transfer protocols. In addition to the HTTP protocol for HTML documents and related multimedia data available via the Web, popular browsers also support the FTP, MAILTO, and NEWS transfer protocols.

▶ An HTML document has two sections: a Head and a Body. The Head section traditionally contains only the title of the individual HTML document. The Body section contains the portion of the HTML document not contained in the Head section.

▶ HTML editors are valuable for those with a knowledge of HTML. They also help HTML authors to: 1) expedite the creation and editing of HTML documents, and 2) ensure the accuracy and validity of HTML script.

▶ Web browsers download, interpret, and display HTML documents. In sequence, browsers: 1) locate HTML documents; 2) download HTML documents; 3) interpret HTML documents; and 4) display Web pages.

Lesson 1 Quiz

Matching

___ 1. information with no pre-defined order   a. linear data

___ 2. visible navigation anchor   b. hypertext

___ 3. data that proceeds in a pre-defined order   c. hypermedia

___ 4. fusion of hypertext and multimedia   d. HTML

___ 5. linking organization scheme for files   e. hyperlink

___ 6. HyperText Markup Language   f. non-linear

Fill in the Blank

7. HTML is a type of _____ language.

8. The current version of HTML is _____ . The previous version was _____ .

9. Tags, tag attributes, and character references proposed or published by any party or organization other than the W3C are called _____ .

10. HTML code is interpreted by a Web _____ .

11. HTTP stands for _____ _____ _____ .

True or False?

T / F   12. Different services of the Internet feature different transfer protocols.

T / F   13. HTML documents must be in ASCII text format.

T / F   14. HTML documents cannot be created using a word processor.

T / F   15. ASCII text is also known as "DOS text."

T / F   16. Two primary sections of an HTML document are Head and Body.

T / F   17. White space must be invoked using special tags in HTML.

Lesson 2
HTML Tags

Lesson Topics

▶ What are HTML Tags?

▶ Document Section Tags

▶ Text Formatting Tags

▶ Layout Tags

▶ Logical Tags

▶ Lists

▶ Lesson 2 Summary

What are HTML Tags?

HTML *tags*, sometimes referred to as *markup tags*, are the coded instructions that accompany the plain text of an HTML document. The plain text of the HTML document (often called the "content" of the document)—in conjunction with the tags of the document—is interpreted by a Web browser and displayed as a Web page. Tags are the most basic elements necessary to create HTML documents for publication via the Web.

 For the purposes of this course, "HTML document" is the term used to describe the ASCII text document when it is being edited in a text editor or HTML editor. The HTML document is referred to as a "Web page" when it is interpreted by and displayed in a Web browser.

Tag Syntax

HTML tags have a precise syntax, as shown in Figure 2-1. It is essential to use the correct syntax when scripting HTML documents to avoid erroneous interpretation of HTML documents and incorrect display of Web pages by a Web browser. A tag is defined by:

- a left wicket;

- a tag element;

- an optional set of tag attributes;

- a right wicket.

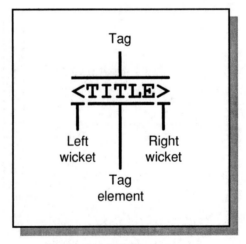

Figure 2-1: HTML tag syntax

Opening & Closing Tags

A tag is enclosed in a pair of angle brackets (the mathematical "less than" and "greater than" signs), commonly referred to by HTML authors as *wickets*. An opening tag begins with the left wicket (<) followed immediately by the tag element, and then the right wicket (>).

Closing tags differ from opening tags with the addition of a forward slash (/) that follows the opening wicket and precedes the tag element, as shown in Figure 2-2. The forward slash functions as a switch,[8] identifying the closing tag and differentiating it from the opening tag.

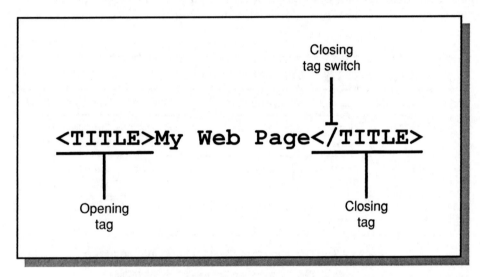

Figure 2-2: Opening and closing tag syntax

Empty vs. Non-empty Tags

All of the tags presented in this lesson were examples of *non-empty tags*. Non-empty tags are comprised of an opening tag and a closing tag, separated by the effected text. No spaces should occur between the opening tag and the first word of the affected text or the last word of the affected text and the closing tag. Conversely, *empty* tags do not occur in tag sets; instead, they stand alone as solitary elements.

The majority of the HTML tag family is comprised of non-empty tags.

---

[8] A switch is sometimes referred to as a *delimiter*.

Document Section Tags

The two major HTML document sections, the Head and Body, are created with the <HEAD> and <BODY> tags, respectively. Both <HEAD> and <BODY> are non-empty tag sets.

The Head section's primary function is to house the document Title tag, <TITLE>. <TITLE> must be nested within the opening and closing <HEAD> tags of each HTML document. The text between the opening and closing Title tags appears on the title bar of the client browser when the HTML document is interpreted and displayed.

Table 2-1 identifies and suggests usage of HTML tags that are placed outside of the Body section and that divide an HTML document into sections.

Tag	Elements Nested Within	Comment
<HTML>	Entire document contents	Defines an HTML document
<HEAD>	Title tag	All <META> information is placed in the <HEAD> area
<BODY>	Non-head document contents	All visible page data is placed in the <BODY> area
<TITLE>	Text to be displayed on browser title bar	Avoid ALL CAPS titles

Table 2-1: HTML tags that divide a page into sections

Head, Title, and Body Tags

All HTML documents begin with the HTML document definition tag, <HTML>, followed by the Head tag, <HEAD>. The Title tag, <TITLE>, is nested within the opening and closing <HEAD> tags. The <TITLE> tag determines the text that is displayed in the title bar of any browser that downloads and interprets the HTML document. After the closing Head tag, </HEAD>, the opening <BODY> tag is inserted.[9]

The latest versions of the Netscape Navigator and MSIE browsers do not require the <BODY> tag. However, in order to employ advanced Web page effects—such as background patterns, background colors, and text colors—the <BODY> tag must be included in the HTML document.

---

[9] The last two tags of any HTML document are the closing Body tag, </BODY>, and the closing HTML tag, </HTML>.

DDC Publishing • www.ddcpub.com

Exercise 2-1: Creating a New HTML Document

In this exercise, you will open an existing ASCII text document containing substantial content, but no HTML tags or attributes. Throughout the rest of this course, you will add tags, attributes, and minor content to this document in order to create a richly formatted Web page.

1. Launch a text editor (Microsoft Notepad is suggested).[10]

2. Open the file WEBPAGE.HTM from the HTML-2 folder on your Desktop.

3. With your cursor at the beginning of the document, type the following script:

```
<HTML>

<HEAD>
<TITLE><your name's> Practice Web Page</TITLE>
</HEAD>

<BODY>
```

4. Save the HTML document (**File ▶ Save** in Notepad).

5. Launch your Web browser.

6. Open the HTML document named WEBPAGE.HTM in your Web browser.

   - In Microsoft IE 5.0*x*, select **File ▶ Open ▶ Browse**, locate WEBPAGE.HTM in the HTML-1 folder on your Desktop and double-click it.

   - In Netscape Navigator/Communicator 4.0*x*, select **File ▶ Open Page ▶ Choose File**, locate WEBPAGE.HTM in the HTML-1 folder and double-click it.

[10] The Notepad executable file is NOTEPAD.EXE and is located in C:\WINDOWS\NOTEPAD.EXE in Windows 95/98/2000 and in C:\WINNT\NOTEPAD.EXE in Windows NT 4.0.

7. Compare the title bar that is displayed in your Web browser with that displayed in Figure 2-3. If they are not identical, check your HTML script against the script in Step 3.

HTML title

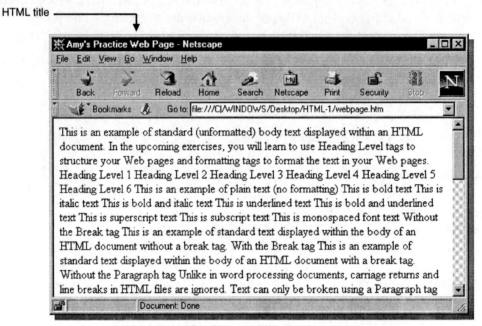

Figure 2-3: HTML title displayed in browser title bar

The text between the opening and closing Title tags ("<your name's> Practice Web Page") is case sensitive, and will be displayed *exactly* as it is typed. However, the browser ignores the case of the tags themselves. <TITLE> and <title> and <TiTlE> are all equivalent with respect to how this, or *any* tag element, will be interpreted by *any* browser.

It is recommended, however, that you use ALL CAPS when scripting tags because it increases the ease with which tags and non-tag HTML document content can be differentiated. Using ALL CAPS tags also makes it easier for you or another HTML scripter to edit your documents later (this is called script "readability").

Body Text

Body text is the non-formatted text of HTML documents that is displayed as standard text in Web pages. As previously mentioned, without the addition of text formatting tags, body text appears in Web pages as a continuous paragraph. Without layout tags, the only breaks in text occur between words and at the line wrap width (right margin) of the browser.

Exercise 2-2: Entering Standard Body Text

1. Switch applications to your text editor. Open WEBPAGE.HTM, if necessary.

2. Type the portion of the following script that appears in bold:

   This is an example of standard (unformatted) body text displayed within an HTML document. In the upcoming exercises, you will learn to use Heading Level tags to structure your Web pages and formatting tags to format the text in your Web pages. **Standard body text can be added to an HTML document simply by typing; no special tags are required. It's as easy as typing text into a word processing document.**

3. Save the HTML document (<ALT + F, S>).

4. Switch applications to your Web browser (<ALT + TAB>).

5. Reload the Web page (<CTRL + R> in both IE 5 and Navigator/Communicator).

6. Compare the screen that is displayed in your Web browser with Figure 2-4. They should appear nearly identical. If they are not identical, repeat the steps of this exercise, taking care to accurately type the script in Step 2.

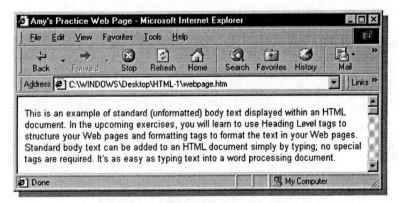

Figure 2-4: HTML default body text

Formatting of Tags

When downloading and interpreting HTML documents, a browser first recognizes a tag by its wickets. This is a process known as *parsing*. The browser displays the information between the opening and closing tags according to the format specified by the tag.

Although formatted differently, layouts 1, 2, and 3 below result in an *identical* interpretation and display in *any* browser.

Layout 1

```
<HEAD>
<TITLE>Amy's Practice Web Page</TITLE>
</HEAD>
```

Layout 2

```
<HEAD>
<TITLE>
Amy's Practice Web Page
</TITLE></HEAD>
```

Layout 3

```
<HEAD><TITLE>Amy's Practice Web Page</TITLE></HEAD>
```

 Clean formatting of tags is important, not to ensure proper interpretation of HTML script by the browser, but to make future editing of HTML script easier for the author(s).

 White space *within* individual tags and between opening and closing tags can confuse a browser and result in misinterpreted script. Avoid white space within a tag unless required (when using tag attributes).

Text Formatting Tags

HTML has a variety of tags available for changing the formatting of text blocks. The most fundamental style tags include those that bold, italicize, and underline text. Also available are tags for changing default proportional text to a monospaced (fixed) font and tags for creating superscript and subscript effects.

Multiple formatting tags can be applied to a single block of text. The use of multiple tags to modify a single block of text is referred to as *nesting*.

Heading Levels

Heading Levels are fundamental to HTML documents and help define overall document structure.

HTML currently specifies six levels of headings:

- <H1> (the largest)

- <H2>

- <H3>

- <H4>

- <H5>

- <H6> (the smallest)

Heading Level text is always formatted in bold, with white space inserted *before* and *after* the heading text. Additional formatting tags for paragraph breaks or line breaks are *not* recommended, and may cause problems when editing HTML script in the future.

The tags <H1> through <H6> are non-empty tag sets.

 Heading Level tags do not specify the *absolute* font size used by browsers to display Heading Level text. Instead, Heading Level tags collectively represent a *relative* text sizing scale.

Exercise 2-3: Using Heading Level Tags

1. Switch applications to your text editor.

2. Add the bold script (as shown below) to the text on your screen:

    ```
    <H1>Heading Level 1</H1>
    <H2>Heading Level 2</H2>
    <H3>Heading Level 3</H3>
    <H4>Heading Level 4</H4>
    <H5>Heading Level 5</H5>
    <H6>Heading Level 6</H6>
    ```

3. Resave the HTML document.

4. Switch applications to your Web browser.

5. Reload the Web page.

6. Compare the screen that is displayed in your Web browser with Figure 2-5. They should appear nearly identical. If they are not identical, repeat the steps of this exercise, taking care to accurately type the script in Step 2.

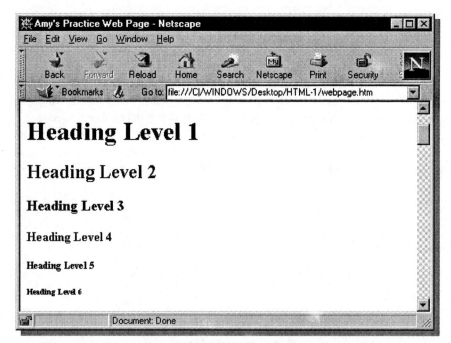

Figure 2-5: Text formatted with Heading Levels <H1> through <H6>

Bold <B>, Italic <I>, & Underline <U> Tags

Three of the most popular text formatting tags are the Bold tag, <B>, the Italic tag, <I>, and the Underline tag, <U>.

- All of these tags are non-empty tag sets.

- Bold formatting can also be applied using the <STRONG> tag.

- Italic formatting can also be applied using the <EM> (emphasis) tag.

Superscript <SUP> & Subscript <SUB> Tags

The Superscript tag, <SUP>, and the Subscript tag, <SUB>, were added to the HTML tag family in the 3.2 Specification.

- Both the <SUP> tag and the <SUB> tag allow text blocks to be formatted with more advanced text formatting attributes. Prior to Specification 3.2, such formatting was possible only with conventional word processing or desktop publishing applications.

- These tags are valuable in more sophisticated HTML documents, such as those containing equations, formulas, and footnotes.

- Both the <SUP> tag and the <SUB> tag are non-empty tag sets.

Teletype Font Tag <TT>

The Teletype tag, <TT>, is a new addition to the HTML tag family.

- The <TT> tag instructs the browser to display body text in a monospaced (sometimes called "fixed" or "fixed width") font.

- By default, browsers display body text in a pre-defined proportional (sometimes called "variable width") font (*Times New Roman* in both Navigator/Communicator and IE). The default proportional font and monospaced font are user-definable in both Navigator and IE.

- Navigator and IE by default display monospaced text in the *Courier New* font.

- The <TT> tag is a non-empty tag set.

Exercise 2-4: Adding Text Styles

1. Switch applications to your text editor.

2. Add the following script, as shown in bold, to your HTML document:

```
This is an example of plain text (no formatting)<P>
<B>This is bold text</B><P>
<I>This is italic text</I><P>
<B><I>This is bold and italic text</I></B><P>
<U>This is underlined text</U><P>
<B><U>This is bold and underlined text</U></B><P>
This is <SUP>superscript</SUP> text<P>
This is <SUB>subscript</SUB> text<P>
This is <TT>monospaced font</TT> text<P>
```

3. Save the HTML document.

4. Switch applications to your Web browser and reload the Web page.

5. Compare the screen that is displayed in your Web browser with Figure 2-6. If they do not appear nearly identical, repeat the steps of this exercise, taking care to accurately type the script in Step 2.

Figure 2-6: Text formatting tag effects

Layout Tags

Layout tags add "white space" to a Web page and affect the structure, spacing, or layout of a Web page. Layout tags give an HTML document the equivalent of soft returns and hard returns in word processing documents.

Layout tags are useful for:

- creating a user-friendly, eye-pleasing design and layout for Web pages

- breaking Web page text and overall pages into logical sections that convey significance and meaning to a Web user

Break Tag

The Break tag, <BR>, inserts a line break immediately following the <BR> tag, forcing text to the next line and justifying it to the left.

The <BR> tag is an empty tag.

Paragraph Tag <P>

The Paragraph tag, <P>, is used to mark the beginning of a new paragraph or block of text. Text immediately following the <P> tag is forced to the next line and left justified.

The <P> tag is an empty tag.

The difference between the <BR> and <P> tags is that the <P> tag inserts a line of white space before and after the line of text containing the <P> tag.

"I think there are certainly going to be lots of debates about the Internet. My hunch is that the First Amendment rights are going to prevail, and that in fact this is an astonishingly free country and pretty much intends to remain that way, and the Internet will just be one more expression of our freedom."

— *Newt Gingrich, Speaker of the U.S. House of Representatives, 1995*

Exercise 2-5: Inserting Line Breaks

1. Switch applications to your text editor.

2. Add the following script, as shown in bold, to your HTML document:

```
<H3>Without the Break tag</H3>

This is an example of standard text displayed within the body of an HTML
document

without a break tag (but with a break in the text).

<H3>With the Break tag</H3>

This is an example of standard text<BR>displayed within the body of an
HTML<BR>document with a break tag. <BR>
```

3. Save the HTML document.

4. Switch applications to your Web browser and reload the Web page.

5. Compare the screen that is displayed in your Web browser with Figure 2-7. If this is not nearly identical, repeat the steps of this exercise.

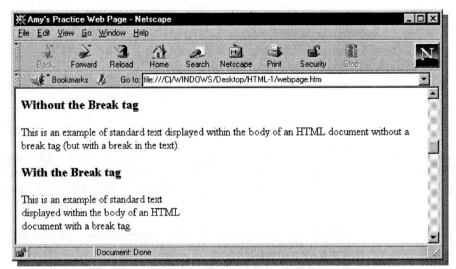

Figure 2-7: Line break inserted with the <BR> tag

Exercise 2-6: Inserting Paragraph Breaks

1. Switch applications to your text editor.

2. Add the following script, as shown in bold, to your HTML document:

```
<H3>Without the Paragraph tag</H3>

Unlike in word processing documents,
carriage returns and line breaks in HTML files are ignored.
Text can only be broken using a Paragraph tag or Break tag.

<H3>With the Paragraph tag</H3>

Unlike in word processing documents,<P>carriage returns and line breaks
in HTML files are ignored. Text can only<P> be broken using a Paragraph
tag or Break tag. <P>
```

3. Save the HTML document.

4. Switch applications to your Web browser and reload the Web page.

5. Compare the screen that is displayed in your Web browser with Figure 2-8. If they are not nearly identical, repeat the steps of this exercise.

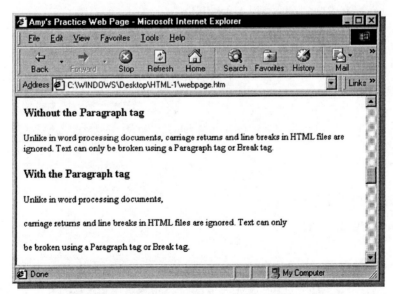

Figure 2-8: Paragraph break inserted with the <P> tag

Preformatted Tag <PRE>

The Preformatted tag, <PRE>, instructs the Web browser to display text exactly as it is typed in the HTML document, preserving the spacing between characters and overall formatting of the text. This tag is useful for presenting tabular data (rows and columns) quickly and easily (without creating an HTML table). The font used with the <PRE> tag is monospaced and appears different from the proportional font used to display body text.[11]

The <PRE> tag is a non-empty tag set.

Exercise 2-7: Preformatting Text

1. Switch applications to your text editor.

2. Add the following script, as shown in bold, to your HTML document:

```
<H3>Without the Preformatted Tag</H3>

        Ohio    Virginia    Texas    Georgia

1996    87          77          43       102

1997    41          59          92       116

<H3>With the Preformatted Tag</H3>

<PRE>
        Ohio    Virginia    Texas    Georgia

1996    87          77          43       102

1997    41          59          92       116
</PRE>
```

3. Save the HTML document.

4. Switch applications to your Web browser and reload the Web page.

---

[11] Web browsers have a default monospaced and proportional font used to display preformatted text. Most browsers allow you to customize fonts via a preferences dialog box.

5. Compare the screen that is displayed in your Web browser with Figure 2-9. If they are not nearly identical, repeat the steps of this exercise, taking care to accurately type the script in Step 2.

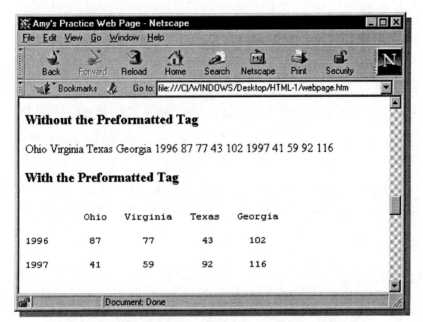

Figure 2-9: Preformatted text created with the <PRE> tag

Block Quote Tag <BLOCKQUOTE>

The Block Quote tag, <BLOCKQUOTE>, is useful for indenting blocks of text, and is commonly used for quotes and citations. This tag indents both the left and right margins.

Exercise 2-8: Indenting Text (or Creating Outquote Text)

1. Switch applications to your text editor.

2. Add the bold script (as shown below) to the text on your screen:

   <H2>Without the Blockquote tag**</H2>**

   This is an example of standard body text. The text extends all the way to the left margin and all the way to the right margin.

   <H2>With the Blockquote tag**</H2>**

   <BLOCKQUOTE>
   This is an example of standard body text with the Blockquote tag. Notice how the text is indented on both the left and the right.
   </BLOCKQUOTE>

3. Save the HTML document.

4. Switch applications to your Web browser and reload the Web page.

5. Compare the screen that is displayed in your Web browser with Figure 2-10. If they do not appear nearly identical, repeat the steps of this exercise.

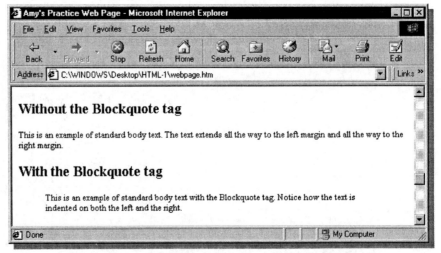

Figure 2-10: Text indented using the <BLOCKQUOTE> tag

Logical Tags

Logical tags are not directly interpreted and displayed in the user's browser. Logical tags are used in HTML to create a wide range of effects and HTML document characteristics. One of the most common logical tags is the Comment tag, <!-->.

Comment Tag <!-->

The Comment tag allows you to place text that you do not wish to have appear in the user's browser in an HTML document. The tag instructs the browser to not display comment text in the browser. The Comment tag is an empty tag.

The Comment tag has an unusual syntax. After the opening wicket is: 1) the exclamation character, which is followed immediately by 2) a dash[12], and then 3) a horizontal space. Any comment you want included in your HTML document is typed next. This text may be of any length or case. A horizontal space follows the comment text, followed by a second dash, and the closing wicket.

Exercise 2-9: Commenting HTML Script

1. Switch applications to your text editor.

2. Type the following script:

    ```
    <!-- This Web page was last updated on [today's date] by [your
    name]of [your organization] -->
    ```

3. Save the revised HTML document.

4. Switch applications to your Web browser and reload the Web page.

5. You should see no difference in the Web page after the Comment tag and comment text were added. If this tag or its accompanying text are displayed in the Web browser, a mistake has been made, and you should check your HTML script against Step 2.

HTML comment text is sometimes called *annotation text* or *remark text*.

---

[12] Grammatically speaking, a dash is created by typing two hyphens.

Lists

Lists are categorized as layout tags and are used to structure information so it may be more easily read and understood. There are two types of lists available in HTML:

1. unordered lists

2. ordered lists

Unordered Lists

The first type of list is an unordered list, commonly referred to as a "bullet" list. Each item in an unordered list is indented and preceded by a bullet. The Unordered List tag, <UL>, is used for unordered lists. The individual items in either an unordered or ordered list are preceded by the List Item tag, <LI>.

- The <UL> tag is a non-empty tag set;

- <LI> is an empty tag.

Ordered Lists

The second type of list is an ordered list, commonly referred to as a "numbered" list. An ordered list is identical to an unordered list with the exception that the items in the list are preceded by ordered, or "ranked," numbers instead of bullets. The Ordered List tag, <OL>, is used to create ordered lists. The individual items in an ordered list are also preceded by the <LI> tag.

- The <OL> tag is a non-empty tag set;

- <LI> is an empty tag.

"Don't try to attract users to your site by bragging about your use of the latest Web technology. You may attract a few nerds, but mainstream users will care more about useful content and your ability to offer good customer service."

— *Jakob Nielsen, Ph.D., Web user advocate and author, 1999*

Exercise 2-10: Creating Bullet and Numbered Lists

1. Switch applications to your text editor.

2. Add the following script, as shown in bold, to your HTML document:

    ```
    <H3>The Biggest States</H3>

    <UL>
    <LI>Alaska
    <LI>California
    <LI>Nevada
    <LI>Texas
    </UL>

    <H3>Morning Routine</H3>

    <OL>
    <LI>Turn off alarm
    <LI>Make coffee
    <LI>Take shower
    <LI>Shave
    <LI>Drink all of coffee
    <LI>Brush teeth
    <LI>Drive to the office
    </OL>
    ```

3. Save the HTML document.

4. Switch applications to your Web browser and reload the Web page.

5. Compare the screen that is displayed in your Web browser with Figure 2-11. If they are not nearly identical, repeat the steps of this exercise.

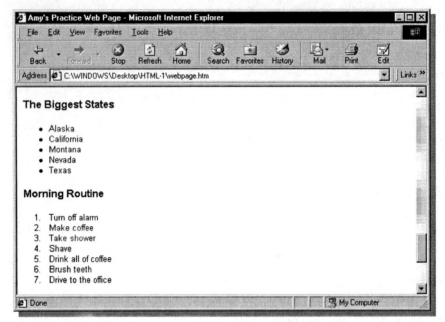

Figure 2-11: Bullet list and numbered list created with the <UL> and <OL> tags

 It is not necessary to insert a <BR> tag when using the <LI> tag. The <LI> tag by default moves the next list item to the following line.

Use of a <P> tag following an <LI> tag will create additional white space following the list item text.

Lesson 2 Summary

► HTML tags are the codes that provide instructions to a Web browser regarding the format, layout, content, and overall appearance of an HTML document. Following the tags' instructions, the browser translates the HTML document into a Web page.

► The two categories of HTML tags are empty and non-empty. Most HTML tags are non-empty.

► An HTML document Head section is defined using the <HEAD> tag; the body section is created with the <BODY> tag. Both <HEAD> and <BODY> are non-empty tags.

► Text formatting tags include the Heading Level tags, <H1>...<H6>, the Bold tag, <B>, the Italic tag, <I>, the Underline tag, <U>, the Superscript tag, <SUP>, the Subscript tag, <SUB>, and the Teletype Font tag, <TT>. All text formatting tags are non-empty tags.

► Headings levels are useful for adding structure to a Web page. There are six heading levels, all of which are non-empty tags. Heading Level 1, <H1>, offers the largest font. Heading Level 6, <H6>, is the smallest font.

► Layout tags allow you to add "white space" to your Web pages. Layout tags include the Break tag, <BR>, and the Paragraph tag, <P>.
 adds what in word processing jargon is called a soft return, or line break. <P> adds what is also called a hard return, or paragraph break. Both of these tags are empty tags.

► The Preformatted tag, <PRE>, allows you to instruct a browser to temporarily turn off interpretation of your HTML document. Thus, you can use no tags or character references between opening and closing <PRE> tags (unless you desire to display the uninterpreted tags to the user in the Web browser). <PRE> is a non-empty tag.

► The Block Quote tag, <BLOCKQUOTE>, is a method by which a text block can be indented on both the left and right. <BLOCKQUOTE> is a non-empty tag.

► The Comment tag, <!-->, allows you to "comment out" text in a Web page so that it will not be displayed to a user in the Web browser. Comment text is also called "annotated text" or "remark text."

► There are two types of lists: ordered and unordered. Ordered lists (also called numbered lists) are created using the <OL> tag in conjunction with the <LI> tag. Unordered lists (also called bullet lists) are created using the <UL> tag, also in conjunction with the <LI> tag.

Lesson 2 Quiz

Matching

___	1. commands interpreted by a Web browser	a.	ASCII text
___	2. examples of text formatting tags	b.	\<BODY\>
___	3. left wicket, tag element, right wicket	c.	tags
___	4. the visible "content" of a Web page	d.	\<H1\>, \<B\>
___	5. examples of layout tags	e.	tag syntax
___	6. HTML document	f.	\<P\>, \<BR\>

Fill in the Blank

7. Non-empty tag sets feature two types of tags: _____ tags and closing tags

8. A "switch" is sometimes referred to as a _____ .

9. Text between the opening and closing \<TITLE\> tags is case _____ .

10. _____ within individual tags and between opening and closing tags can confuse a browser and result in misinterpreted script.

11. Use the _____ tag to make text appear like it came from a typewriter, monospaced.

12. Each list item must be accompanied by a _____ tag.

True or False?

T / F   13. Empty tags do not occur in tag sets.

T / F   14. Closing tags are characterized by a backward slash "\".

T / F   15. The HTML title of a page appears on the browser Status Bar.

T / F   16. The majority of the HTML tag family is comprised of empty tags.

T / F   17. You can make text "invisible" using the Comment tag.

Lesson 3
Tag Attributes &
Character References

Lesson Topics

▶ Tag Attributes

▶ Character References

▶ Lesson 3 Summary

Tag Attributes

Tag attributes are elements (technically called *parameters*) that modify the effect of a tag. Technically, tag attributes provide additional instructions to a Web browser that modify or alter the browser's interpretation of the tag. Thus, tag attributes allow HTML authors to script more complex, sophisticated Web pages.

New versions of the HTML Specification from the W3C and new browser versions from Netscape and Microsoft typically include new attributes for existing tags. These new attributes often provide more power and flexibility than new tags. Thus, a tag that you do not find functional or useful with its current attributes may become appealing to you if new attributes are released in the future.

Attribute Syntax

Attributes are placed *within* tags, as shown in Figure 3-1. An attribute always follows a tag element in the *opening* tag of a non-empty tag set. Attributes must be separated from the tag element by a single space. *Do not* use multiple spaces to separate a tag from its associated attribute(s).

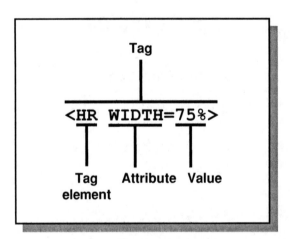

Figure 3-1: Tag attribute syntax

Not all HTML tags have attributes and some tags have multiple attributes. All attributes are tag-specific and *cannot arbitrarily be applied to other tags.*

Attribute Values

Attribute values cover a wide spectrum of functions and can be specified as:

- relative values (percentages or directions);

- absolute values (screen pixels or other units of measurement);

- author-supplied information (for example, data regarding an inline image or overall HTML document).

Values as Percentages or Numbers

Attribute values, when denoted as a percentage or value, have a specific range. This range, called the *attribute value range*, is tag-specific and depends entirely on the logical function of the attribute. The WIDTH attribute for the horizontal rule tag, <HR>, for instance, specifies the width of a horizontal rule in a user's browser. Because the rule can be no wider than the entire width of the browser, 100% is the top of the attribute value range and 0% is the bottom of the value range.

Required Attributes

Some tags, such as the Anchor tag, <A>, Image tag, <IMG>, and Font tag, <FONT>, require at least one attribute to function properly (establish validity) and to be correctly interpreted by a Web browser.

There are two categories of required attributes:

- specific, individual attributes;

- those attributes that are members of a specific tag's attribute family.

The syntax and value set specifications of required attributes are identical to that of non-required attributes.

 Many HTML novices mistakenly perceive required attributes as part of the tag element. This misperception often leads to the creation of closing tags containing the attribute as well as the tag. In many browsers, this mistake will negate the validity of the closing tag or the entire tag set.

Attribute Rules

The syntactical and related rules applying to tag attributes must be followed to establish and maintain HTML document validity.

Keep the following in mind when applying attributes to an HTML tag:

- some tags have no attributes;

- both empty and non-empty tags offer attributes;

- multiple attributes can be used with a single tag;

- multiple attributes of a single tag may be presented in *any order*;

- multiple attributes must be separated by a single space;

- some tags have *required* attributes;

- the same attribute may be applied to different tags; because the tags differ, so too may the value range of the attribute.

 If a single attribute has a value consisting of more than one word (separated by spaces), enclose the attribute value in quotation marks (`<IMG ALT="Image of a Porsche">`).

Without the quotation marks, the browser will recognize only the *first* word of the value.

DDC Publishing • www.ddcpub.com

Horizontal Rule Tag <HR> Attributes

The Horizontal Rule tag, <HR>, places a horizontal line called a *rule* in a Web page to provide structure and organization to the page. Beyond the structural (layout) and white space benefits, the <HR> tag is used largely for cosmetic purposes.

- <HR> is an empty tag;

- <HR> has four tag attributes associated with it; two of which have multiple value ranges;

- <HR> has no required attributes.

Multiple tag attributes may be used with the <HR> tag simultaneously. As with all tags, the order of the attributes is irrelevant (they must simply be separated by a space).

Table 3-1 displays the <HR> attributes and their associated values.

<HR> Attribute	Description	Value(s)
WIDTH	Length of rule	<ul><li>0-100% (percentage of page width) when % symbol directly follows value</li><li>Width of rule as measured in *pixels* (no logical value limits) when no % symbol follows value</li></ul>
SIZE	Height (thickness) of rule	Height of rule as measured in *pixels* (no logical value limits)
ALIGN	Alignment of rule relative to page margins	Left, center, right
NOSHADE	Solid color fill of rule (rather than traditional shadowed "groove")	None

Table 3-1: Attributes associated with the <HR> tag

You can add vertical white space to an HTML document by specifying a horizontal rule with a specific SIZE but a WIDTH of zero. For example, <HR WIDTH=0 SIZE=15> would provide vertical white space of 15 pixels.

Note: this trick will produce a small tick mark in place of the rule if you are using a dark background color or pattern.

Exercise 3-1: Inserting Horizontal Rules and Modifying Rule Formatting

1. Switch applications to your text editor. Open WEBPAGE.HTM, if necessary.

2. Add the bold script (as shown below) to the text on your screen:

```
<B>Default horizontal rule</B>
<HR><P>

<B>WIDTH=50%</B>
<HR WIDTH=50%><P>

<B>WIDTH=50%, ALIGN=left</B>
<HR WIDTH=50% ALIGN=left><P>

<B>WIDTH=75%, ALIGN=right, SIZE=10</B>
<HR WIDTH=75% ALIGN=right SIZE=10><P>
```

3. Save the HTML document.

4. Switch applications to your Web browser.

5. Reload the Web page.

6. Compare the screen that is displayed in your Web browser with Figure 3-2. If they are not nearly identical, repeat the steps in this exercise.

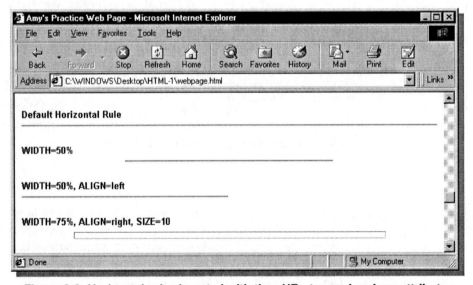

Figure 3-2: Horizontal rules inserted with the <HR> tag and various attributes

Font Tag <FONT> Attributes

The Font tag, <FONT>, introduced with HTML 3.2, allows you to change the size or color of Web page fonts. <FONT> is a non-empty tag; all text (from a single character to thousands of words) between the opening and closing tags is affected.

- <FONT> has three associated tag attributes, each of which has multiple value ranges

- <FONT> requires at least one attribute

The value range of the SIZE attribute is 1-7. These values can be specified as either *absolute* or *relative* values. To specify an absolute value, you must choose a number between 1 and 7 (<FONT SIZE=4>, for example). The relative value range is between –7 and +7, excluding 0 (<FONT SIZE=+4>).

The <FONT> attributes are outlined in Table 3-2.

<FONT> Attribute	Description	Values
SIZE	Text size	■ 1-7 (absolute values; no direct mapping to point or pixel sizes) ■ +1-7 / -1-7 (relative values; no direct mapping to point or pixel sizes)
COLOR	Text color	■ One of 16 color names (black, green, silver, gray, white, maroon, red, purple, fuchsia, lime, olive, yellow, navy, blue, teal, aqua) ■ RGB hexadecimal notation codes (see *Appendix D: RGB Color Codes*)
FACE	Text font	■ Any TrueType font name. This attribute defines a comma-separated list of font names in order of preference. ■ <FONT FACE="verdana,arial,impact">

Table 3-2: Attributes associated with the <FONT> tag

Exercise 3-2: Changing Font Size and Color

1. Switch applications to your text editor.

2. Add the bold script (as shown below) to the text on your screen:

```
<FONT SIZE=2>This is an absolute font size of 2</FONT>
<FONT SIZE=6>This is an absolute font size of 6</FONT>
<FONT SIZE=+3>This is a relative font size of +3</FONT>
<FONT SIZE=+5>This is a relative font size of +5</FONT>
<FONT SIZE=-5>This is a relative font size of -5</FONT><P>
```

3. Save the HTML document.

4. Switch applications to your Web browser.

5. Reload the Web page.

6. Compare the screen that is displayed in your Web browser with Figure 3-3. If they are not nearly identical, repeat the steps of this exercise, taking care to accurately type the script in Step 2.

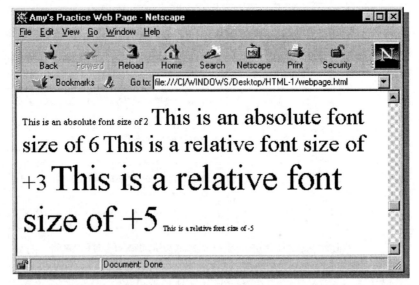

Figure 3-3: Text formatted with various absolute and relative font sizes

7. Modify the script you entered in Step 2 with the following bold script:

```
<FONT SIZE=2>This is an absolute font size of 2</FONT><BR>
<FONT SIZE=6>This is an absolute font size of 6</FONT><BR>
<FONT SIZE=+3>This is a relative font size of +3</FONT><BR>
<FONT SIZE=+5>This is a relative font size of +5</FONT><BR>
<FONT SIZE=-5>This is a relative font size of -5</FONT><P>

<FONT SIZE=+3 COLOR=green><B>This text is green</B></FONT><BR>
<FONT SIZE=+2 COLOR=red FACE=arial><B>This text is red and Arial
font</B></FONT><P>
```

8. Save the HTML document.

9. Switch applications to your Web browser.

10. Reload the Web page.

11. Compare the screen that is displayed in your Web browser with Figure 3-4. If they are not nearly identical, repeat the steps of this exercise, taking care to accurately type the script in Step 7.

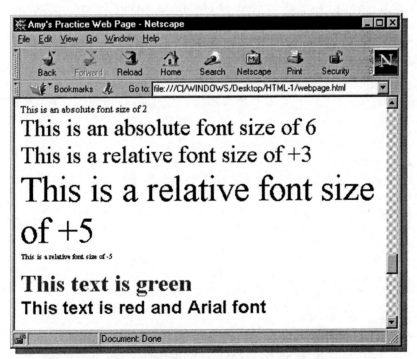

Figure 3-4: Text size and color modified with the <FONT> tag

Heading Level Tags <H1>-<H6> Attribute

HTML 3.2 introduced a single attribute for the Heading Level tag family. The attribute, ALIGN, has three values:

- ALIGN=**left**

- ALIGN=**center**

- ALIGN=**right**

Left is the default alignment for Heading Levels; therefore, use of the ALIGN=left attribute value is unnecessary.

 Many Web page design experts advocate using the <H2> heading tag, rather than the <H1> tag, as the "largest" tag. This creates a more subtle—yet still pronounced—effect for heading text. Because its font size is so large, the <H1> tag should be used sparingly.

Exercise 3-3: Changing Alignment of Heading Level Text

1. Switch applications to your text editor.

2. Add the bold script (as shown below) to the script you entered in the previous Heading Level exercise (see Exercise 2-3) to read as follows:

```
<H1>Heading Level 1</H1>
<H2 ALIGN=center>Heading Level 2</H2>
<H3>Heading Level 3</H3>
<H4>Heading Level 4</H4>
<H5 ALIGN=right>Heading Level 5</H5>
<H6>Heading Level 6</H6>
```

3. Save the HTML document.

4. Switch applications to your Web browser.

5. Reload the Web page.

6. Compare the previous Heading Level text with the current text. Note how the different ALIGN attribute values affected the justification of the heading text.

Character References

Character references, sometimes called *character entities*, are numeric or symbolic names for characters that can be incorporated into an HTML document. Character references may appear in two forms: 1) character *numeric* references and 2) character *entity* references.

Characters that can be represented by HTML character references include the following:

- copyright symbol (©)

- trademark registration symbol (®)

- degree symbol (°)

- accented character (tildes ~, umlauts ¨)

Character references have an exact syntax: reference elements are always preceded by an ampersand (&) and followed by a semicolon (;), as shown in Figure 3-5.

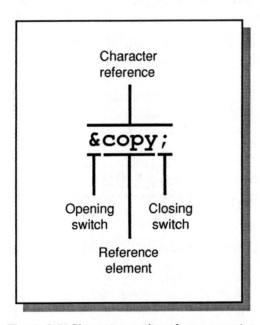

Figure 3-5: Character *entity* reference syntax

 Character entity references are *case sensitive*; they must be all lower-case. If the character entity element is specified in uppercase or mixed case, the browser will misinterpret it.

Character Number References

Character number references are specified using the same syntax as standard character references. The only exception between the two methods is the use of ANSI character numbers in character number references instead of entity references.

Syntax

Using the standard character reference syntax, substitute a pound sign (#) followed by an ANSI character number for the entity element.

Thus, a non-breaking horizontal space can be specified in two ways with identical results:

-

-

Like character entity references, character numeric references have an exact syntax: reference elements are always preceded by an ampersand (&) and followed by a semicolon (;), as shown in Figure 3-6.

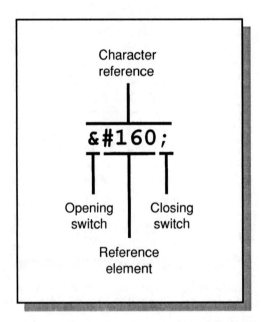

Figure 3-6: Character *numeric* reference syntax

The complete list of 216 ANSI characters that can be specified as HTML character entities is provided in Appendix C: *ANSI Character Set.*

DDC Publishing • www.ddcpub.com

Exercise 3-4: Using Character Entity References

1. Switch applications to your text editor.

2. Add the bold script shown below to the text in your HTML document:

```
<FONT SIZE=+1>Character Entity References</FONT><P>

<UL>
Copyright symbol &copy;<BR>
Registered symbol &reg;<BR>
Ampersand &amp;<BR>
Degree symbol &deg;<BR>
Quotation mark &quot;<P>
</UL>
I can even insert additional         horizontal
spaces<P>

<HR SIZE=4 WIDTH=50% ALIGN=left><P>
```

3. Save the HTML document.

4. Switch applications to your Web browser.

5. Reload the Web page.

6. Compare the screen that is displayed in your Web browser with Figure 3-7. They should appear nearly identical. If this is not the case, check your HTML script against Step 2.

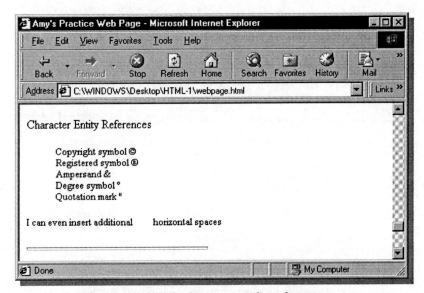

Figure 3-7: HTML character entity references

Exercise 3-5: Using Character Numeric References

1. Switch applications to your text editor.

2. Add the bold script shown below to the text in your HTML document:

```
<FONT SIZE=+1>Character Numeric References</FONT><P>

<UL>
Zero sum symbol &#216;<BR>
Legal section symbol &#167;<BR>
Percentage symbol &#137;<BR>
Japanese Yen symbol &#165;<BR>
Paragraph symbol &#182;<P>
</UL>

I can even insert additional         horizontal
spaces<P>

<HR SIZE=4 WIDTH=50% ALIGN=left><P>
```

3. Save the HTML document.

4. Switch applications to your Web browser.

5. Reload the Web page.

6. Compare the screen that is displayed in your Web browser with Figure 3-8. They should appear nearly identical. If this is not the case, check your HTML script against Step 2.

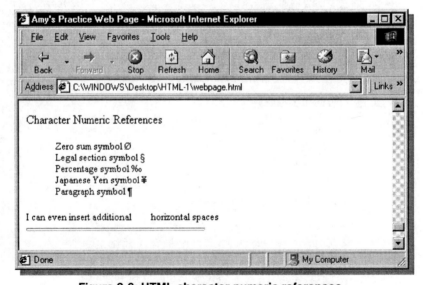

Figure 3-8: HTML character numeric references

Lesson 3 Summary

▶ The HTML scripting language is comprised of tags, tag attributes, and character entities.

▶ The manner in which a tag is interpreted by a Web browser can be manipulated using tag attributes. Attributes are specific to an individual tag. Not all tags have attributes, and many tags have multiple attributes. If available, multiple attributes can be used with a single tag.

▶ Attribute values cover a wide spectrum of functions and can be specified as relative values (percentages or directions), absolute values (screen pixels or other units of measurement), or author-supplied information (for example, data regarding an inline image or overall HTML document).

▶ The syntactical and related rules applying to tag attributes must be followed to establish and maintain HTML document validity, These rules include: 1) some tags have no attributes; 2) both empty and non-empty tags offer attributes; 3) multiple attributes can be used with a single tag; 4) multiple attributes of a single tag may be presented in any order; 5) multiple attributes must be separated by a single space; 6) some tags have required attributes, and 7) the same attribute may be applied to different tags; because the tags differ, so too may the value of range of the attribute.

▶ The <HR> tag has four attributes: width, size, align, and noshade.

▶ The <FONT> tag has three associated attributes, each of which has multiple value ranges. <FONT> requires at least one attribute.

▶ The family of Heading Level tags (<H1> through <H6>) has a single attribute: ALIGN. The values of ALIGN are left, center, and right.

▶ Character references, sometimes called character entities, enable HTML authors to add special characters to their Web pages, such as copyright symbols, degree signs, and foreign language characters. Character entities also ensure the proper interpretation of punctuation marks— such as quotation marks—by a Web browser.

▶ Character number references are specified using the same syntax as standard character references. The only exception between the two methods is the use of ANSI character numbers in character number references instead of entity references.

▶ 216 of the 256 symbols in the ANSI character set may be represented by a character entity using the standard character entity syntax. Substitute a pound sign (#) and the ANSI character number for the conventional character entity element. As with all character entities, a semi-colon must close the character entity.

Lesson 3 Quiz

Matching

___ 1. an attribute for the <HR> tag

a. single space

___ 2. character references

b. attributes

___ 3. modify the behavior of a tag

c. ©

___ 4.

d. symbols

___ 5. attribute shared by <HR> and <FONT>

e. WIDTH

___ 6. copyright symbol

f. SIZE

Fill in the Blank

7. Attributes are added directly after the _____ _____ of an HTML tag.

8. Multiple attributes in a single tag must be separated by a _____ .

9. You specify a specific typeface using the _____ attribute to the <FONT> tag.

10. There is a single attribute to the <H1> tag: _____ .

11. Numeric or symbolic names for characters that can be incorporated into an HTML document are called _____ _____ .

True or False?

T / F   12. All HTML tags have at least one attribute.

T / F   13. All attribute values are measured in percentages.

T / F   14. The syntax of an attribute is attribute element, equal sign, value.

T / F   15. Some HTML tags feature attributes that are required.

T / F   16. Multiple attributes can be used with a single tag.

T / F   17.   is identical in effect to .

Lesson 4
Inline Images &
Colors

Lesson Topics

▶ Inline Images

▶ GIF vs. JPEG: Which Format to Use?

▶ Incorporating Inline Images

▶ Background Images & Colors

▶ Lesson 4 Summary

Inline Images

One of the most appealing characteristics of Web publishing and HTML is the ability to incorporate images into Web documents to produce more visually appealing Web pages. These images, called *inline images*, allow HTML authors to create pages with rich page design and layout.

Web browsers are capable of displaying three image file formats:

- GIF (Graphics Interchange Format), DOG.GIF

- JPEG (Joint Photographic Experts Group), DOG.JPG

- PNG (Portable Network Graphics), DOG.PNG

GIF Image Format

The GIF image file format (pronounced "jif") is the most common image format found on the Internet. Introduced by CompuServe Inc. in 1987, the GIF format has gained popularity because the size (byte count [as opposed to pixel dimensions]) of GIF images is smaller than that of other image formats. There are two versions of the GIF format:

- 87a

- 89a

What makes the GIF image format smaller than other image file formats is the fact that it is an inherently compressed file format. Any graphics application or Web browser capable of opening and displaying GIF images has a built in GIF decoder that first decompresses the GIF image. The application then displays the decompressed GIF file.

 The GIF 89a format, a more robust and capable format, is preferred over the 87a format. For more information regarding Web graphics, see DDC's *Creating Web Graphics* course.

When stored, on a computer hard drive or other storage device (floppy disk, CD-ROM, etc.), GIF images are always in compressed form. GIF images are decompressed only for actual display or editing.

A downside of the GIF format is that it supports a maximum color depth of only 256 (8 bit). On the upside, however, GIF supports transparency (whereas JPEG does not), allowing GIF images to integrate seamlessly with colored and patterned backgrounds.

JPEG Image Format

The JPEG image format (pronounced "jay peg") has become increasingly popular with the growth of Web publishing. Although similar to the GIF format, the JPEG format has one distinct advantage over GIF: it can handle a maximum color depth of 16.7 million (24 bit).

The JPEG image format, like GIF, is an inherently compressed file format. JPEG images, however, offer greater compression ratios than GIF. Therefore, an image in JPEG format is smaller (requires less storage volume) than the same image in GIF format.

Lossy Format

The disadvantage of the JPEG format is that it is a lossy image format, meaning that the JPEG compression algorithm "loses" the quality of an image when it is converted to JPEG. However, the reduction in image quality is not very noticeable to the human eye because patches of similar colors are converted to a single "average" color. Because the human eye is more sensitive to variations in image *brightness* than variations in image *color*, it is tricked into thinking the compressed JPEG image is nearly identical to the original, non-compressed image (that resides in a different format than JPEG).

PNG Image Format

PNG (pronounced "ping"), or *Portable Network Graphics*, is a newcomer to the world of Web graphics formats. In 1998, the W3C[13], the premier standards body for the Web, released a specification recommendation for the PNG format. This format was hailed as a replacement for both GIF and JPEG images.

PNG is well suited for *both* graphics and photo-realistic images. This is a distinct advantage over GIF, which is better at representing graphics with large blocks of the same color (such as line art and cartoons). PNG is also superior to JPEG, which is better for photo-quality images with high color variance.

Advantages of PNG

PNG offers many advantages over the GIF and JPEG formats. Among these are 10-30% better *lossless* compression than GIF (depending on the composition of each particular image), 24-bit and 48-bit true color support (superior to JPEG, but creates images typically too large for the Web), two-dimensional interlacing for progressive display (current standards offer only one-dimensional interlacing), and 254 levels of alpha channel transparency (GIF offers only two levels of transparency).

---

[13] You can learn more about the W3C and its Web initiatives and standards at www.w3.org.

Disadvantages of PNG

Despite its advantages and overall superiority as a Web graphics format, PNG does have some disadvantages. PNG is not commonly used because it is only supported by more recent versions of major Web browsers. If your organization has standardized on a browser that supports PNG images, you can use PNG images on your intranet. At this time, it is not recommended that you use PNG images on an external Web site due to still significant numbers of people still using versions 3.0x and older of both major browsers.

Support for PNG images has been included in the following browser versions:

- Netscape Navigator 4.04 and more recent

- Microsoft Internet Explorer 4.0b1 (beta 1) and more recent

Never Completely Replace GIF

Even if the PNG format does become the default graphics and image file format of the Web and HTML, GIF will not become extinct. This is because PNG does not support animation. Thus, HTML scripters must continue using animated GIFs to place animation on their Web pages (or the PNG format will need to be revised to include animation capabilities). For a complete review of GIF animation, see DDC's *Creating Web Graphics*.

Comparing GIF, JPEG, & PNG

Users viewing Web pages are completely unaware of the format of the images they are seeing. However, it is important for you, as a Web publisher, to be very familiar with the characteristics of both image formats and to know the circumstances under which one format is more appropriate than the other.

Table 4-1 compares the characteristics of GIF, JPEG, and PNG image formats.

Attribute	GIF	JPEG	PNG
Maximum Color Depth	256	16.7 million	16.7 million+
Image Transparency	Yes (two levels)	No	Yes (254 levels)
Lossy Compression Scheme	No	Yes	No
Size of a 1153 KB BMP (bitmap format) photo-realistic image file when converted to…	300 KB	48 KB	764 KB

Table 4-1: GIF, JPEG, and PNG image formats compared

 DDC Publishing • www.ddcpub.com

GIF vs. JPEG: Which Format to Use?

Knowing the differences between the GIF and JPEG formats is important when deciding which format you should use for the image on your Web page. You should base your format choice on the type of graphic or image you plan to use.[14]

 Choosing between the GIF and JPEG format is not a question of "which format is better?"; it is a question of which format is best suited to handle the particular characteristics of an individual image.

The JPEG format was created for full-color (often called *true* color) or grayscale photo-realistic images. Scanned photographs and Kodak Photo CD images (files with a PCD file name extension) should be saved in JPEG format. Technically, any image with a large degree of color variance (typical of photo-realistic images) is best stored in the JPEG format.

The GIF image format, although capable of storing photo-realistic images not exceeding 256 colors in depth, is best for storing images with large areas of solid colors, such as clipart, cartoon-like images, and logos. Icons and bullets are typically comprised of few colors and little variation and thus are best stored in the GIF format.

Table 4-2 lists common image applications and the formats best suited to them.

Image Type	GIF	JPEG
Line drawings / clipart	✓	⊘
Cartoons & cartoon-like images	✓	⊘
Most non-photo-realistic images	✓	⊘
Images with a small number of distinct colors or shades of gray	✓	⊘
Photo-realistic color images	⊘	✓
Photo-realistic grayscale images	⊘	✓
Images intended to have greater than 256 colors or shades of gray	⊘	✓

Table 4-2: Comparison of GIF and JPEG format uses

---

[14] The PNG format has been excluded from this overview; it will be added when it becomes common.

Image Format Conversion

A plethora of freeware, shareware, and commercial graphics software is available for the purpose of converting an image that is improperly formatted. Whether the image should be converted to a different format, however, is determined, in large part, by its present format.

JPEG to GIF Only

Because JPEG is designed to handle images with greater than 256 color depth, converting a 256-color (or fewer) GIF image to JPEG format is not always a good idea. When converted to JPEG format, the image will remain 256 colors in depth; converting to JPEG does not mean that the number of colors in an image will increase. In extreme cases, images are the same size or *larger* after being converted from GIF to JPEG.

JPEG to GIF file conversion, however, is typically a safe path to follow. Remember that the image will automatically be dithered to only 256 colors when converted to GIF.

Conversion is simple and problem-free when you begin with a file in its original format (TIFF, EPS, BMP, PCD). Thus converting to either GIF or JPEG can be accomplished with no risk of image corruption and maximum compression of the file.

Image Conversion Rules

Observe the following rules when converting images between formats:

- Non-photographic images should generally be left in GIF format;

- Never convert black-and-white images (grayscale) from GIF to JPEG;

- When possible, use an original file for conversion to the desired destination format. "Original" formats include BMP, PCD, TIFF, EPS, and PSD.

Inline images with a color depth greater than 256 should rarely be used, especially in Web pages to be posted on an external Web server. Such images impose a bandwidth burden on dial-up modem clients attempting to download the pages containing the images. If scripting for an Intranet to which users are connected via speeds substantially higher than those of analog modems, true color images can be used.

Incorporating Inline Images

The Image tag, <IMG>, is simply a pointer, or reference, to an image file. When a user downloads a Web page, the HTML script instructs the browser to: 1) perform a separate download for the image and to 2) display it in a particular manner in the browser.

Image Tag <IMG>

The Image tag, <IMG>, is an empty tag with five commonly used attributes, as shown in Table 4-3.

Attribute	Description	Values	Necessary?
SRC	Short for "source"; SRC is the URL of the image file. It provides the location of the image to the user's browser.	Complete or partial URL	Yes
ALIGN	Allows text to be wrapped around the image.	■ left, center, right ■ top, middle, bottom	No
ALT	Short for "alternate"; if a user has turned off the display of graphics in the browser, ALT provides text describing the image. The ALT information also appears in a popup window when a user hovers the mouse pointer over the image.	Any text string	No
HSPACE	Adds space to both the left and right of the image, as measured in pixels.	1-100 (pixels)	No
VSPACE	Adds space to the top and bottom of the image, as measured in pixels.	1-100 (pixels)	No

Table 4-3: Attributes associated with the <IMG> tag

The ALT attribute requires text strings consisting of more than one word (separated by spaces) enclosed by quotation marks (ALT="Picture of German sports car").

Exercise 4-1: Adding an Inline Image

1. Switch applications to your text editor and open WEBPAGE.HTM (if necessary).

2. Type the following script that appears in bold:

```
<HR SIZE=4 WIDTH=50% ALIGN=left><P>
```

`<IMG SRC=tractor.jpg ALT="Frost Farm in Bucyrus, Ohio">``My trip to the` **`farm<P>`**

3. Save the HTML document.

4. Switch applications to your Web browser.

5. Reload the Web page.

6. Move your mouse pointer over the image. Note the popup text that appears. This displays the value for the ALT attribute.

7. Compare the screen that is displayed in your Web browser with Figure 4-1. If they are not similar, repeat the steps of this exercise, taking care to accurately type the script in Step 2. Note that, by default, the image aligns at the bottom of the adjacent text.

Figure 4-1: Inline image placed with the <IMG> tag

DDC Publishing • www.ddcpub.com

Exercise 4-2: Aligning an Inline Image to Vertical Middle

This exercise, and those that follow, teach you how to align inline images with body text using the ALIGN attribute. The ALIGN attribute is useful for wrapping text around images. Exercise 4-6 and Exercise 4-7 show you how to create a bullet list using the <IMG> tag as an alternative to using the <UL> list tag.

1. Switch applications to your text editor.

2. Edit the script you entered in Exercise 4-1 to appear as follows:

    ```
    <IMG SRC=mailpouch.jpg HSPACE=20 ALIGN=middle ALT="Barn north of
    Waverly, OH on Rt. 23">My trip to Ohio<P>
    ```

3. Save the HTML document.

4. Switch applications to your Web browser.

5. Reload the Web page.

6. Compare the screen that is displayed in your Web browser with Figure 4-2. If they are not nearly identical, repeat the steps of this exercise, taking care to accurately type the script in Step 2.

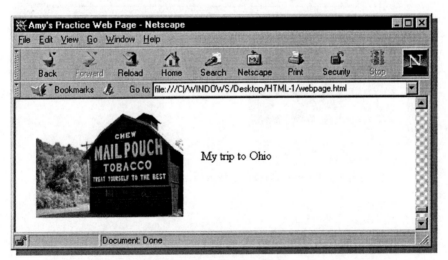

Figure 4-2: Inline image with ALIGN=middle and HSPACE=20

Exercise 4-3: Aligning an Inline Image to Vertical Top

1. Switch applications to your text editor.

2. Edit the script you entered in Exercise 4-2 to appear as follows:

```
<IMG SRC=mailpouch.jpg HSPACE=10 ALIGN=top ALT="Barn north of Waverly,
OH on Rt. 23">My trip to Ohio<P>
```

3. Save the HTML document.

4. Switch applications to your Web browser.

5. Reload the Web page.

6. Compare the screen that is displayed in your Web browser with Figure 4-3. If they are not nearly identical, repeat the steps of this exercise, taking care to accurately type the script in Step 2.

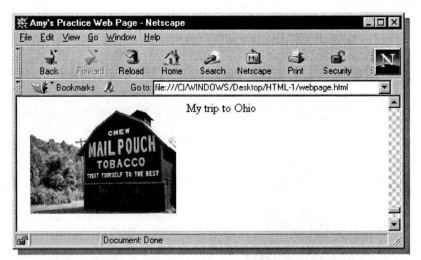

Figure 4-3: Image with ALIGN=top and HSPACE=10 attributes

Exercise 4-4: Aligning an Inline Image to Horizontal Right

1. Switch applications to your text editor.

2. Edit the script you entered in the previous Image tag exercise to appear as follows:

    ```
    <IMG SRC=mailpouch.jpg HSPACE=10 ALIGN=right ALT="Barn north of Waverly,
    OH on Rt. 23">My trip to Ohio<P>
    ```

3. Save the HTML document and switch applications to your Web browser.

4. Reload the Web page.

5. Compare the screen that is displayed in your Web browser with Figure 4-4. If they are not nearly identical, repeat Steps 2-4 of this exercise.

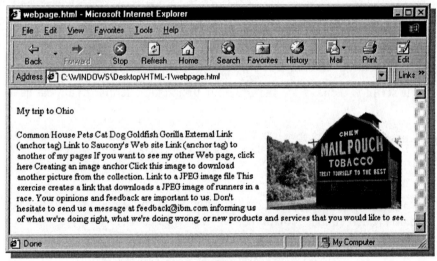

Figure 4-4: Inline image with ALIGN=right

6. Note the text that appears to the left of the image. There is an attribute to the <BR> tag that can force this text below the image.

7. Switch applications to your text editor.

8. Edit the script you entered in the previous Image tag exercise to appear as follows:

    ```
    <IMG SRC=mailpouch.jpg HSPACE=10 ALIGN=right ALT="Barn north of
    Waverly, OH on Rt. 23">My trip to Ohio<BR CLEAR=all>
    ```

9. Save the file. Switch applications to your Web browser and reload the Web page.

10. Compare the screen that is displayed in your Web browser with Figure 4-5. If they are not nearly identical, repeat Step 9.

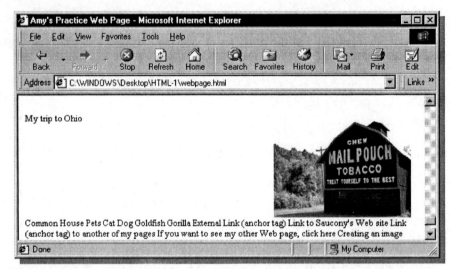

Figure 4-5: Text pushed below image with CLEAR=all attribute to the <BR> tag

11. Switch applications to your text editor.

12. Edit the script you entered in the previous Image tag exercise to appear as follows:

```
<IMG SRC=mailpouch.jpg HSPACE=10 VSPACE=15 ALIGN=right ALT="Barn north
of Waverly, OH on Rt. 23">My trip to Ohio<BR CLEAR=all>
```

13. Resave the file. Switch applications to your Web browser and reload the Web page. Compare the screen that is displayed in your Web browser with Figure 4-6.

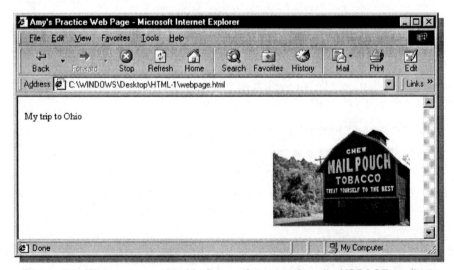

Figure 4-6: White space added below an image using the VSPACE attribute

Exercise 4-5: Horizontally Centering an Inline Image and Caption

1. Switch applications to your text editor.

2. Edit the script you entered in the previous exercise to appear as follows:

```
<CENTER>
<IMG SRC=plane.jpg VSPACE=15 ALT="Andrews Air Force Base, Greenbelt,
Maryland"><BR>The Air Show
</CENTER><P>
```

3. Save the HTML document.

4. Switch applications to your Web browser.

5. Reload the Web page.

6. Compare the screen that is displayed in your Web browser with Figure 4-7. If they are not nearly identical, repeat the steps of this exercise, taking care to accurately type the script in Step 2.

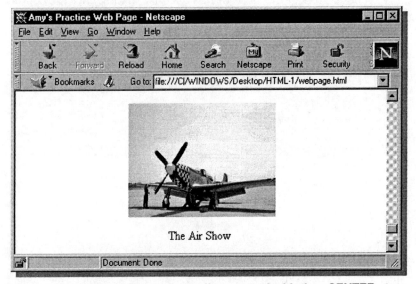

Figure 4-7: Inline image horizontally centered with the <CENTER> tag

Exercise 4-6: Creating a Bullet List with a GIF Image

1. Switch applications to your text editor. Open WEBPAGE.HTM, if necessary.

2. Add the bold script (as shown below) to the text on your screen:

```
<FONT SIZE=+2>Common House Pets</FONT><P>
<IMG SRC=bullet.gif>Cat<BR>
<IMG SRC=bullet.gif>Dog<BR>
<IMG SRC=bullet.gif>Goldfish<BR>
<IMG SRC=bullet.gif>Gorilla<P>

<HR SIZE=4 WIDTH=50% ALIGN=left><P>
```

3. Save the HTML document.

4. Switch applications to your Web browser.

5. Reload the Web page.

6. Compare the screen that is displayed in your Web browser with Figure 4-8. If they are not nearly identical, repeat the steps of this exercise, taking care to accurately type the script in Step 2.

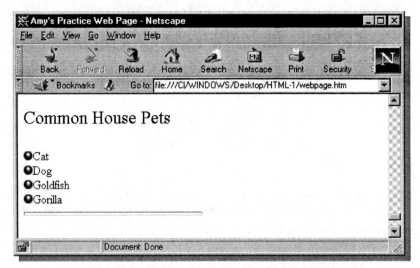

Figure 4-8: A bullet list created with an inline GIF image

Exercise 4-7: Refining a GIF Image Bullet List

1. Switch applications to your text editor.

2. Edit the GIF image bullet list script you entered in the previous exercise to appear as follows:

```
<FONT SIZE=+2>Common House Pets </FONT>

<BLOCKQUOTE>
<IMG SRC=bullet.gif HSPACE=6>Cat<BR>
<IMG SRC=bullet.gif HSPACE=6>Dog<BR>
<IMG SRC=bullet.gif HSPACE=6>Goldfish<BR>
<IMG SRC=bullet.gif HSPACE=6>Gorilla<P>
</BLOCKQUOTE>
```

3. Save the HTML document.

4. Switch applications to your Web browser.

5. Reload the Web page.

6. Compare the screen that is displayed in your Web browser with Figure 4-9. If they are not nearly identical, repeat the steps of this exercise, taking care to accurately type the script in Step 2.

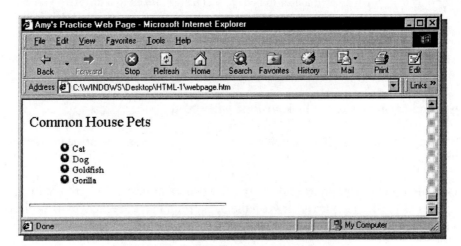

Figure 4-9: A *refined* GIF image bullet list

7. Compare Figure 4-8 with Figure 4-9. Note that the HSPACE attribute to the <IMG> tag added space between the bullet images and the adjacent text.

Background Images & Colors

You can easily enhance your Web pages using background images and colors. While easy to apply, such effects are often "overdone," distracting to users, or simply tacky.

Background Images

HTML allows a GIF or JPEG image to be used as a background "pattern" in a Web page. Users with large monitors running high resolution video drivers will see many more replications of the pattern than those with small monitors running at low resolution.

To fill the screen, the image is replicated to create the illusion of a cohesive background. This repeating pattern of the image file is called *tiling*. Once an image is designated by the HTML scripter, the browser automatically tiles it to form the background image.

Syntax

To designate a background in HTML, you use an attribute to the <BODY> tag. The background attribute is BACKGROUND=*image filename*. To prevent losing your image files, you should archive the background image file in the same directory as your HTML documents.

 It is typically good practice to use the same background on all the pages of a Web site. Different backgrounds on different pages of the same Web site may lead a user to believe that he has linked to a different Web site.

Not all images are suitable for background images and some may not be appropriate for the content of your Web page. When deciding on a background, you face two major challenges:

- finding an image that looks natural when tiled

- finding an image that contrasts well with body text and other page elements

A common mistake made by HTML scripters when including a background image in their Web pages is a lack of contrast between the background and the page text. Without such contrast, text will be difficult to read, thus decreasing the value of the Web page.

 "Trying to fix HTML is like trying to graft arms and legs onto hamburger."

— *Ted Nelson, inventor of hypertext, 1998*

Background Colors

For a simpler look, solid color may be specified as a background, rather than an image. Both background colors and text colors are specified using *RGB*[15] *codes*. See Appendix D: *RGB Color Codes* for a complete list of RGB codes.

`<BODY BGCOLOR=`*#RGB code*`>`

 For better contrast, when using darker background colors, change text color to a lighter color, such as white, cream, or yellow.

Text Colors

Text colors are specified with the TEXT attribute to the `<BODY>` tag. The same RGB codes used for background colors are used for TEXT values.

`<BODY TEXT=`*#RGB code*`>`

Table 4-4 lists the RGB codes for some popular colors. Note that an RGB code must always be preceded by a pound sign (#).

Color	RGB Code
Black	#000000
Blue	#0000FF
Gold	#CD7F32
Green	#00FF00
Gray	#C0C0C0
Orange	#FF7F00
Red	#FF0000
Silver	#E6E8FA
White	#FFFFFF
Yellow	#FFFF00

Table 4-4: RGB codes

---

[15] RGB stands for red, green, blue.

Exercise 4-8: Adding a Background Pattern

1. Switch applications to your text editor.

2. Edit the <BODY> tag script at the top of your HTML document with the following script:

```
<HEAD>
<TITLE><your name's> Practice Web Page</TITLE>
</HEAD>

<BODY BACKGROUND=whittile.jpg>
```

3. Save the HTML document.

4. Switch applications to your Web browser.

5. Reload the Web page.

6. Compare the Web page with Figure 4-10. The background pattern should appear. If not, repeat the steps of this exercise, taking care to accurately type the script in Step 2.

Figure 4-10: BACKGROUND attribute applied to the <BODY> tag

Exercise 4-9: Adding a Background Color

1. Switch applications to your text editor.

2. Edit the <BODY> tag script you typed in the previous exercise with the following script:

```
<HEAD>
<TITLE><your name's> Practice Web Page</TITLE>
</HEAD>

<BODY BGCOLOR=#4F4F2F>
```

3. Save the HTML document.

4. Switch applications to your Web browser.

5. Reload the Web page.

6. Compare the Web page with Figure 4-11. You should see a dark olive green background color. If not, repeat the steps of this exercise, taking care to accurately type the script in Step 2.

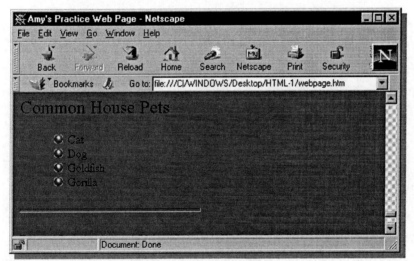

Figure 4-11: Poor contrast between background color and default body text

Exercise 4-10: Changing Text Color

1. Switch applications to your text editor.

2. Edit the <BODY> tag script you typed in THE previous exercise with the following script:

```
<HEAD>
<TITLE><your name's> Practice Web Page</TITLE>
</HEAD>

<BODY BGCOLOR=#4F4F2F TEXT=#FFFFFF>
```

3. Save the HTML document.

4. Switch applications to your Web browser.

5. Reload the Web page.

6. Compare the Web page with Figure 4-12. You should notice that the text is now white and has contrast against the dark background. If not, repeat the steps of this exercise, taking care to accurately type the script in Step 2.

Figure 4-12: Text color changed with TEXT attribute in the <BODY> tag

7. Remove the BGCOLOR and TEXT attributes from the <BODY> tag. This will return the text color to the default black and the background color to the default white.

Lesson 4 Summary

▶ The Image tag, <IMG>, is used to incorporate an image into a Web page.

▶ Web browsers support two image file formats: GIF and JPEG.

▶ Image files are separate from an HTML document. The <IMG> tag simply instructs a browser to locate, download, and properly display an image within a Web page.

▶ The <IMG> tag has various attributes, one of the most significant being ALIGN. VSPACE and HSPACE are also useful for configuring text and images beside each other.

▶ Small images that resemble bullets or icons may be employed in place of an unordered list (<UL> tag). They add a colorful, multimedia flair to a Web page.

▶ Various <IMG> tag attributes, especially the HSPACE attribute, may be used to refine a bullet list. Use of the <BLOCKQUOTE> tag will indent the list.

▶ GIF and JPEG images may be used to specify background patterns on Web pages. The image files are laid out as an overall pattern via a method called *tiling*. The tiling scheme is determined by the browser.

▶ An attribute, not a tag, designates an image as a background pattern. The BACKGROUND attribute to the <BODY> tag allows this.

▶ A solid color, rather than an image, may be specified as a background in Web pages. The background color is specified with the BGCOLOR attribute to the <BODY> tag.

▶ Text color may be changed by adding the TEXT attribute to the <BODY> tag. This is especially useful when the background color or pattern is dark and contrasts poorly with the default black body text.

▶ Both text and background colors are specified using a six-digit RGB (red, green, blue) color. The same RGB colors are used for both background colors and text colors. The RGB code is preceded by a pound sign (#). White, for example, is specified as #FFFFFF.

Lesson 4 Quiz

Matching

___ 1. compression scheme that loses quality   a. 16.7 million

___ 2. maximum color depth of GIF   b. GIF

___ 3. best format for line drawings, cartoons   c. lossy

___ 4. how HTML inserts inline images   d. 256

___ 5. maximum color depth of JPEG   e. JPEG

___ 6. best format for photo-realistic images   f. <IMG>

Fill in the Blank

7. You should not use images with a color depth of greater than _____ on your site.

8. Two valuable attributes to the <IMG> tag for adjusting white space around a graphic are _____ and _____ .

9. Background images, or patterns, are inserted into a document using the _____ attribute to the _____ tag.

10. Body text can be given a specific color using the _____ attribute.

11. Background colors are inserted using the _____ attribute to the _____ tag.

True or False?

T / F   12. The attribute value for <BODY TEXT=??> must be preceded by a #.

T / F   13. You should never convert black-and-white images from GIF to JPEG.

T / F   14. There are five attributes for the <IMG> tag.

T / F   15. PNG is a new graphics file format that is rarely used on the Web.

T / F   16. GIF employs a lossy compression scheme, but different from JPEG.

Lesson 5
Creating Hyperlinks

Lesson Topics

▶ Hyperlinks

▶ Anchor Tag Syntax

▶ Types of Anchors

▶ Lesson 5 Summary

Hyperlinks

Using HTML to create an unlimited number of non-linear links between Web pages is arguably the most powerful and dynamic feature of the Web. Hyperlinks, technically called *anchors* in HTML, are the navigational method of the Web and play a critical role in the hierarchical infrastructure of the Web.

Hyperlink Action Results

Hyperlinks, known commonly as *links*, allow a user to click on a highlighted text block, graphic, or image within a Web page to obtain one of the following three things:

- download a different Web page;

- advance from one location to another within a single Web page;

- automatically launch a user's e-mail application and open a new message addressed to a particular e-mail address;

- download a binary file or multimedia data object (MS Word file, Adobe Acrobat file, application executable file (EXE), compressed file (ZIP or SIT), audio, or video file, etc.).

 Links download Web pages or multimedia data objects from Web sites that can, geographically, be located anywhere in the world.

Hyperlink Formatting

A text hyperlink is a section of text that is specially marked—usually by underlining and the color blue—to indicate to the user that it is a link. Hypertext links can be created using any of the following page elements:

- inline images: images are denoted as links via a blue frame[16]

- body text: text is denoted as blue and underlined

Once clicked, a link of any type will change from blue to fuchsia (purple) to indicate that it has been visited. This function helps a user distinguish between visited and unvisited links.

---

[16] The <IMG> tag has an attribute called BORDER that—when set to 0 (BORDER=0)—will remove the blue frame from an image link.

Anchor Tag Syntax

The Anchor tag defines the *beginning* and *end* of a hyperlink. The Anchor tag, <A>, requires one attribute, typically HREF (hypertext reference). HREF bears its name because it refers to another Web page or Internet element (e-mail address, binary file residing on FTP server, etc.).

Figure 5-1 displays the syntax for the Anchor tag. This example references the home page of a Web site.

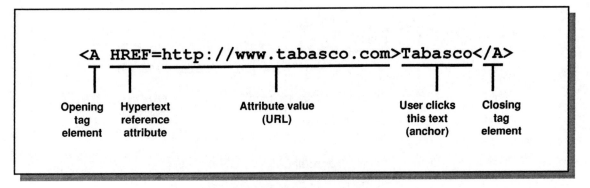

Figure 5-1: Anchor tag syntax

Four Types of Anchors

There are four primary types of hypertext anchors. Anchors can do the following:

1. Link to another Web page: reference other Web pages using the HREF attribute

2. Download a file: automatically download binary files residing on either Web or FTP servers (ftp:// transfer protocol for FTP servers; http:// protocol for Web servers)

3. Automatically generate an outgoing e-mail message: automatically launch user's e-mail application, open a new outgoing message, and address it to a specific e-mail address (MAILTO: URL prefix in attribute value)

4. Link to another section of the same Web page: reference another section of the same Web page (HREF & NAME attributes)

Detailed examples of these four types of anchors, including hands-on exercises, are presented throughout the remainder this Lesson.

Types of Anchors

Table 5-1 below lists the four primary types of hypertext anchors and the tags, attributes, and URL for each. Note that the anchor text that is displayed to a user in his or her browser is underlined. The destination of a NAME anchor is not underlined.

Action	Tags & Attributes	URL Syntax
Link to other Web page	■ Anchor tag (`<A>`) ■ `HREF` attribute ■ `http://` transfer protocol	`<A HREF=http://www.ibm.com>` `user clicks here</A>`

Download a file from a server	■ `<A>` tag
	
	■ `HREF` attribute
	
	■ `ftp://` transfer protocol
	
	■ `http://` transfer protocol
		■ Download file from Web server:
		
		  `<A HREF=http://www.ibm.com/`
		  `file.exe>user clicks here</A>`
		
		■ Download file from FTP server:
		
		  `<A HREF=ftp://ftp.ibm.com/`
		  `file.exe>user clicks here</A>`

Automatically generate an outgoing e-mail message (Also called a MAILTO anchor)	■ `<A>` tag ■ `HREF` attribute ■ `MAILTO:` URL prefix	`<A HREF=mailto:bob@ibm.com>` `user clicks here</A>`

Link to another section of the same Web page
 	
(Also called an "internal" link or a NAME anchor)
	■ `<A>` tag
	
	■ `HREF` attribute
	
	■ `NAME` attribute
		■ Link within a Web page:
		
		  `<A HREF=#porsche>click here`
		  `for Porsche section</A>`
		
		■ Link within a Web page target:
		
		  `<A NAME=porsche>Porsche`
		  `Section</A>`

Table 5-1: Tags, attributes, and URL syntax of primary types of anchors

"If documents can be reached and used on-line by anyone, all we need additionally is the ability to create links among them…to quote from them by direct excision."

— *Ted Nelson, inventor of hypertext and hypermedia, 1982*

Anchors That Link to Other Web Pages

The most common type of hypertext anchor is one that references (links to) another Web page. This standard type of anchor involves:

- the HREF attribute to the <A> tag;

- the http:// transfer protocol;

- exact URL address of the Web page to which you are referring.

To create an anchor that links to another Web page, you only have to know the basic syntax of this type of anchor and the exact URL address of the page to which you are referring.

Like other types of anchors, standard links can be presented to users as either standard body text or inline images. You will conduct a hands-on exercise in which you will use an inline image as an anchor later in this lesson.

Different Types of Standard Anchors

There are three types of standard anchors: text anchors, image anchors, and image maps. You will learn how to create text and image anchors in this course. The syntax for text and image anchors is identical; the only discrepancy is whether the user is presented with a text block or an inline image for the clickable anchor.

Syntax

The syntax of standard anchors that link to other Web pages is illustrated in the following example:

- You can obtain more information regarding the Eudora Pro e-mail application from the <A HREF=http://www.eudora.com>Eudora Web site</A>, maintained by QUALCOMM.

Common Uses

Standard hypertext anchors are used to provide a user with any type of link to another Web page at your Web site or another Web site. These types of anchors are the way in which you provide visitors to your Web site with a means of navigating your site or accessing outside resources.

As you will see in Lesson 6: *HTML 4.0 Tips & Tricks*, you can also have a standard anchor automatically launch a new browser window in which the referred Web page is displayed. This preserves the original Web page so you do not lose a visitor from your Web site and they can conveniently return to your site by closing the new window.

Exercise 5-1: Creating a Link to a Different Web Site

In this exercise, you will create the most common type of anchor: a standard hypertext link from one Web page to another. You will link from one of your pages to an outside Web page.

1. Switch applications to your text editor. Open WEBPAGE.HTM, if necessary.

2. Add the bold script (as shown below) to the text on your screen:

    \<FONT SIZE=+1\>External Link (anchor tag)**\</FONT\>\<P\>**

    \<A HREF=http://www.saucony.com\>Link to Saucony's Web site**\</A\>\<P\>**

3. Save the HTML document.

4. Switch applications to your Web browser.

5. Reload the Web page.

6. Compare the screen that is displayed in your Web browser with Figure 5-2. They should appear nearly identical. The text, Link to Saucony's Web site, should be underlined and blue (the common convention used by most browsers to denote a text anchor). If not, repeat the steps of this exercise, taking care to accurately type the script in Step 2.

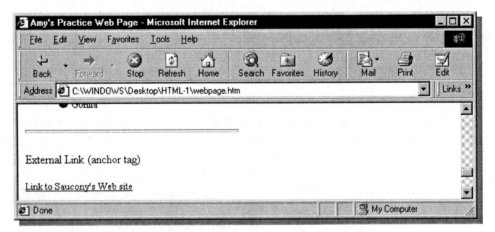

Figure 5-2: External link created with the \<A\> tag

7. Click the anchor you have just created entitled **Link to Saucony's Web site**. If you do not have a live Internet connection, your browser will display an error message.

DDC Publishing • www.ddcpub.com

Exercise 5-2: Linking Between Two Pages You Have Created

In this exercise, you will create an anchor that links to another Web page. Although this type of anchor is identical to the one you created in the previous exercise, this particular anchor will link from a page you have created to another page you have created (as opposed to an outside Web page owned and managed by someone else).

1. Switch applications to your text editor.

2. Add the bold script (as shown below) to the text on your screen:

    ```
    <H3>Link (anchor tag) to another of my pages</H3>

    If you want to see my other Web page, click <A
    HREF=linkto.htm>here</A><P>
    ```

3. Save the HTML document.

4. In your text editor, open LINKTO.HTM from the HTML-1 folder (this will close WEBPAGE.HTM).

5. Add the bold script (as shown below) to the text on your screen:

    ```
    <HTML>

    <HEAD>
    <TITLE>The Destination of My Anchor</TITLE>
    </HEAD>

    <BODY>

    <H2>It worked! My link is functional.</H2>

    <HR WIDTH=50% ALIGN=left><P>

    Congratulations to me! I just successfully created a hyperlink using a
    partial URL. Now I can use the Back button on the toolbar and I'll see
    that the anchor text on the referring Web page has turned fuchsia, an
    indication by the browser that the link has been "visited".

    </BODY>
    </HTML>
    ```

6. Save LINKTO.HTM.

7. Switch applications to your Web browser.

8. Reload the Web page (WEBPAGE.HTM).

9. Click the link **here**, as shown in Figure 5-3.

Figure 5-3: Internal link created with the <A> tag

10. The destination of the anchor (LINKTO.HTM) appears, as shown in Figure 5-4.

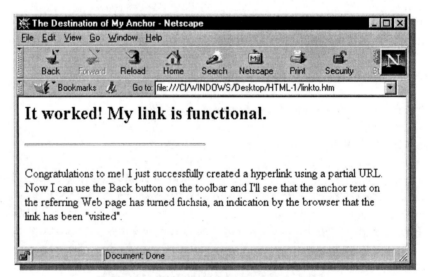

Figure 5-4: Destination of the internal link

Exercise 5-3: Creating an Image Anchor

In this exercise, you will create a standard hypertext anchor, but you will use an inline image for the clickable anchor instead of a text block.

1. Switch applications to your text editor. Open WEBPAGE.HTM, if necessary.

2. Add the bold script (as shown below) to the text on your screen:

    ```
    <H2>Creating an image anchor</H2>

    Click this image to download<BR>
    another picture from the collection.<BR>
    <A HREF=children.jpg><IMG SRC=pickup.jpg></A><P>
    ```

3. Save the HTML document.

4. Switch applications to your Web browser.

5. Reload the Web page.

6. Compare the screen that is displayed in your Web browser with Figure 5-5. They should appear nearly identical. The image of the pickup truck (PICKUP.JPG) should display a blue border, indicating that it is a hyperlink. If not, repeat the steps of this exercise, taking care to accurately type the script in Step 2.

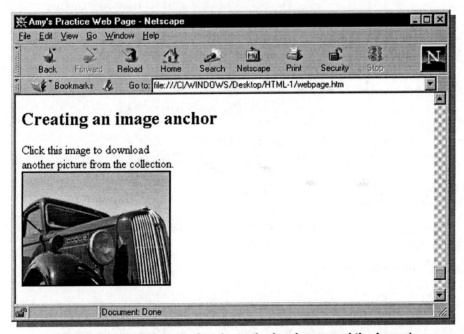

Figure 5-5: An image anchor (note the border around the image)

7. Click the image anchor. Another image should be downloaded and displayed, as shown in Figure 5-6. If the anchor does not function properly and the image file is not downloaded and displayed when the anchor is clicked, check your script against Step 2.

Figure 5-6: Image downloaded via an image anchor

8. Switch applications to your text editor.

9. Add the bold script (as shown below) to the text on your screen:

```
<H2>Creating an image anchor</H2>

Click this image to download<BR>
another picture from the collection.<BR>
<A HREF=children.jpg><IMG SRC=pickup.jpg BORDER=0></A><P>
```

10. Save the HTML document.

11. Switch applications to your Web browser. Click the **Back** button to return to your HTML document.

12. Reload the Web page.

You should notice that the image anchor no longer displays the blue border (but is still a functional hyperlink anchor). If not, repeat the steps of this exercise, taking care to accurately type the script in Step 9.

Anchors That Download Files

You can create links that download binary files from either Web servers or FTP servers. The only difference is the transfer protocol. You will learn how to create anchors that download files from FTP servers in an upcoming section of this Lesson.

The only difference between a standard anchor that links to another Web page and one that downloads a file from a Web server is that the file download URL must include the location and name of the file to be downloaded. Both types of anchors involve the HTTP transfer protocol. The `ftp://` transfer protocol is substituted when downloading files from an FTP server.

Syntax

The syntax of anchors that download files is as follows (the differences between the two types of file download anchors are presented in **bold** text).

- Download file from a Web server:

  Click `<A HREF=`**`http`**`://`**`www`**`.ibm.com/files/cobra.pdf>`here`</A>`
  to download an Adobe Acrobat (PDF) file containing the technical specifications
  of IBM's Aptiva SE7 (code named "Cobra") 450 MHz PC.

- Download file from an FTP server:

  Click `<A HREF=`**`ftp`**`://`**`ftp`**`.ibm.com/files/cobra.pdf>`here`</A>`
  to download an Adobe Acrobat (PDF) file containing the technical specifications
  of IBM's Aptiva SE7 (code named "Cobra") 450 MHz PC.

Common Uses

Anchors that download files can be employed to make files available on your Web site 24 hours a day, seven days a week. These files provide customer support, general product information, marketing and sales literature, technical specifications of products and services, technical support, etc.

Exercise 5-4: Creating a Link that Downloads a File

In this exercise, you will create a link that downloads a binary file from a Web server. To demonstrate the effectiveness of this type of link, you will download a JPEG image file that is automatically displayed by your browser. You must have a live Internet connection to complete this exercise.

1. Switch applications to your text editor and open WEBPAGE.HTM. Scroll to the bottom of the document.

2. Add the bold script (as shown below) to the text on your screen:

    ```
    <H2>Link to a JPEG image file</H2>

    This exercise creates a link that downloads a JPEG image of <A
    HREF=http://www.quessing.com/runners.jpg>runners</A> in a race.<P>

    <HR WIDTH=75% SIZE=6><P>
    ```

3. Save the HTML document.

4. Switch applications to your Web browser.

5. Reload the Web page. Your screen should appear similar to Figure 5-7.

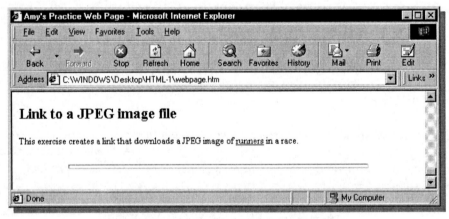

Figure 5-7: Link to download an image file

6. Click the **runners** link to download an image of hundreds of runners in Virginia who are very cold.

7. Compare the screen that is displayed in your Web browser with Figure 5-8. If they are not nearly identical, repeat the steps of this exercise, taking care to accurately type the script in Step 2.

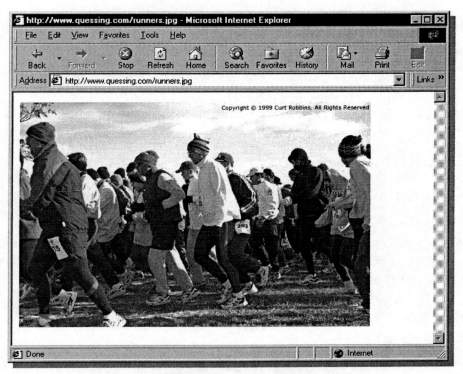

Figure 5-8: JPEG image file downloaded via a link

8. Press the **Back** button. This will return you to your HTML document.

Netscape Navigator 4.08 and older displays the pixel resolution (size; width x height) on the title bar, where the HTML title is typically displayed. Microsoft Internet Explorer displays the name of the file on the title bar, but not the size.

Because the image displayed in Figure 5-8 is a single image file, rather than an HTML document, no <TITLE> tag exists for display on the title bar.

Anchors that Automatically Address Outgoing E-mail

You can also create anchors that perform the following actions:

1. automatically launch a user's e-mail application;

2. automatically open a new outgoing message;

3. automatically address the outgoing message to a specific e-mail address.

This type of anchor, known as a MAILTO link, is unique in that it is only different from a standard anchor in two ways:

- the `mailto:` prefix is attached to the HREF attribute value

- the HREF value is not a Web page URL, but instead an e-mail address

The MAILTO anchor allows you to create links within Web pages that fully automate the process of a user sending an e-mail message to a specific address. This process is very automated and very user friendly.

Syntax

The syntax of the MAILTO anchor is as follows. Note, in the second example, that the e-mail address is purposefully displayed to the user. This syntactical style is preferred by some Webmasters because it allows users to notice and write down an e-mail address.

- Send us your `<A HREF=mailto:feedback@ibm.com>`<u>feedback</u>`</A>` regarding our products and services.

- Send questions, comments, complaints, or general feedback to `<A HREF=mailto:feedback@ibm.com>`<u>feedback@ibm.com</u>`</A>`.

Common Uses

MAILTO anchors can be employed to solicit feedback from users regarding products and services, opinions regarding your Web site, complaints, suggestions, and overall comments.

When combined with e-mail autoresponders (described in DDC's *Using the Internet in Business*), MAILTO links can create a fully automated customer response system that functions 24 hours a day, seven days a week.

Exercise 5-5: Creating a MAILTO Anchor

In this exercise, you will create a MAILTO anchor that, when clicked, will automatically launch the user's e-mail application, open a new outgoing message, and address the message to a specific e-mail address.

1. Switch applications to your text editor.

2. Add the bold script (as shown below) to the text on your screen:

```
Your opinions and feedback are important to us. Don't hesitate to send
us a message at <A HREF=mailto:feedback@ibm.com>feedback@ibm.com</A>
informing us of what we're doing right, what we're doing wrong, or new
products and services that you would like to see.
```

3. Save the HTML document.

4. Switch applications to your Web browser.

5. Reload the Web page.

6. Scroll to the section of the Web page that features the text displayed in Step 2 of this exercise.

7. Click the **feedback@ibm.com** link.

 The default e-mail application on your PC should be launched and a new outgoing message should be opened that automatically displays the TO: address feedback@ibm.com.

If you completed this e-mail message and clicked the send button, the message would be sent to the address featured in the MAILTO link.

8. Return to your HTML document and create another MAILTO anchor that links to your personal e-mail address.

9. Save the HTML document, toggle over to your Web browser, and test the anchor to ensure that you scripted it correctly and it is functional.

Anchors That Link to Another Section of the Same Web Page

You can create anchors that link to another section of the same Web page. Commonly called *NAME anchors* or *internal links*, these are more complex than other types of anchors because they involve two anchor tags that work together: a referring anchor and a target anchor.

Note that the target of the referring link is not functionally an anchor because it provides no hypertext navigation functionality. It is simply a marker, or designated location, that gives the referring anchor a specific location to which to scroll the document for the user.

Involves Two Tags, Not One

NAME anchors involve two distinct tags that must be "coordinated" to operate properly. The NAME anchor tag family is comprised of the following tags:

- <u>Referring tag</u>: an anchor tag containing a reference to a text label preceded by a pound sign, such as <A HREF=#horse>.

- <u>Destination tag</u>: the anchor destination location must be marked by the NAME attribute (to the Anchor tag) and the identical text label as in the referring tag, *sans the pound sign*, such as <A NAME=horse>.

Syntax

The syntax of a NAME anchor is as follows:

```
<A HREF="#horse">Horse Info</A><P>

<A HREF="#dog">Dog Info</A><P>

_____


<A NAME="horse">Horse Info<P>

horse text appears here. . .


<A NAME="dog">Dog Info<P>

dog info appears here. . .
```

DDC Publishing • www.ddcpub.com

Common Uses

Internal anchors are commonly used in longer Web pages or Web pages that are segmented into different sections. NAME anchors can be used to create an index at the top of a large, segmented Web page. Each link in the index, when clicked, automatically scrolls to a specific section of the page.

It should be noted that NAME anchors can refer to NAME tags in *other* HTML documents. Thus, you can make a name anchor in one Web page point at an exact location in a different Web page. This is especially convenient if your Web pages are text-heavy and require a substantial amount of scrolling.

"Normal hypertext links do not of themselves imply that the document linked to is part of, is endorsed by, or endorses, or has related ownership or distribution terms as the document linked from. However, embedding material by reference (sometimes called an embedding form of hypertext link) causes the embedded material to become a part of the embedding document."

— *Tim Berners-Lee, Director, W3C, 1997*

Exercise 5-6: Creating NAME Anchors

In this exercise, you will create several NAME anchors that refer to different areas of the same HTML document. Because the document in which the anchors will be placed is long and text-heavy, these NAME anchors will enable quick location of desired information.

1. From your Web browser, open NAME_ANCHOR.HTM from the HTML-1 folder.

2. Scroll down the page. Note the length and content of the page. As currently formatted, this page is confusing and difficult to navigate.

3. Toggle over to Notepad.

4. Open the document NAME_ANCHOR.HTM from the HTML-1 folder.

5. Insert the following script below the horizontal rule:

```
<HR SIZE=8 WIDTH=80%><P>

<CENTER>
<FONT COLOR=red SIZE=+2
FACE=arial,verdana><B>Index</B></FONT><BR>

<A HREF=#dogs>Dogs</A> | <A HREF=#erie>Lake Erie</A> | <A
HREF=#texas>Texas</A> | <A HREF=#horses>Horses</A> | <A
HREF=#michigan>Lake Michigan</A><BR>

<A HREF=#ohio>Ohio</A> | <A HREF=#hogs>Hogs</A> | <A
HREF=#superior>Lake Superior</A> | <A HREF=#georgia>Georgia</A> |
<A HREF=#cats>Cats</A> | <A HREF=#ontario>Lake Ontario</A> | <A
HREF=#virginia>Virginia</A><P>
</CENTER>
```

6. Save the file.

7. Add the following script to each section of the document as follows:

```
<A NAME=dogs></A><FONT SIZE=+2 FACE=arial,verdana
COLOR=navy><B>Dogs</B></FONT><P>

dog text here. . .

<A NAME=erie></A><FONT SIZE=+2 FACE=arial,verdana
COLOR=navy><B>Lake Erie</B></FONT><P>

<A NAME=texas></A><FONT COLOR=navy FACE=arial,verdana
SIZE=+2><B>Texas</B></FONT><P>
```

8. Continue to add the `<A NAME=name>` opening and closing tags to each section header for the remainder of the document.

9. Save the document.

10. Toggle over to your Web browser. Reload the Web page.

 The index appears at the top of the page, as shown in Figure 5-9.

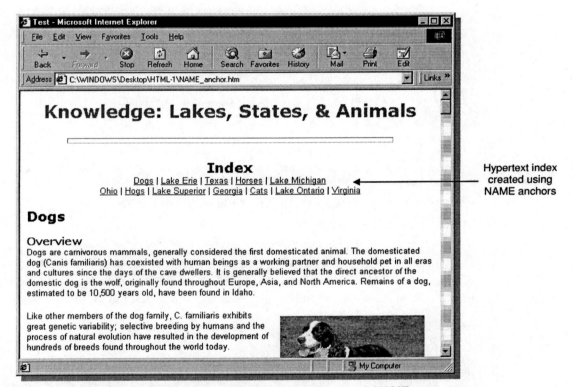

Hypertext index created using NAME anchors

Figure 5-9: Index composed of NAME anchors which refer to <A NAME=text> tags

11. In the index section at the top of the page, click the hyperlink labeled **Georgia**. The page will automatically scroll to the section of the document that contains the NAME anchor for *georgia*.

12. Return to the top of the page by clicking the **Back** button or pressing <CTRL + HOME>.

13. Test all of the hyperlinks in the index. If any links are not functional, return to the HTML document in Notepad and fix any errors. Continue until all links are functional.

Exercise 5-7: Adding "Return to Top" NAME Anchors

In this exercise, you will add NAME anchors to each section of the file you worked with in the last exercise. You will add one NAME anchor for each section of the document (in other words, for each <A NAME=*name*> tag). These NAME anchors will be identical and allow the user to conveniently return to the top of the document to access different links from the index.

1. Toggle over to Notepad. Open NAME_ANCHOR.HTM if necessary.

2. Type the following script that appears in bold:

```
<A NAME=index></A><FONT COLOR=red SIZE=+2
FACE=arial,verdana><B>Index</B></FONT><BR>
```

 This anchor will serve as the destination of the HREF anchors that you will add in the following steps of this exercise.

```
. . .breeds become established, they are promoted from a
miscellaneous class to official status.<P>
```

```
<A HREF=#index><B>Return to Index</B></A><P>
```

```
<HR ALIGN=left WIDTH=75% SIZE=7><P>
```

3. Copy the text <A HREF=#index><B>Return to Index</B></A><P> to the clipboard (<CTRL + C>) and paste it (<CTRL + V>) into each section in the same location as in the above example (just after the article text but before the horizontal rule).

4. Save the document.

5. Toggle over to your Web browser.

6. Reload the Web page.

7. Click one of the links in the index section.

8. Scroll to the bottom of the section and click the **Return to Index** link.

 You are returned to the top of the page. Test all of the **Return to Index** links in the document. Fix any links that are not functional.

Lesson 5 Summary

► The Anchor tag, `<A>`, is used to create a hyperlink from one Web page to another.

► Anchors may be either text (any block size) or images. Text anchors are blue and underlined. Image anchors have a blue border. You can remove the blue outline from an image anchor by using the `BORDER=0` attribute in the `<IMG>` tag.

► When anchors have been visited by a user, their color changes from blue to purple/fuchsia.

► Anchors can link to other Web pages at the same Web site or to a Web page at a different Web site. There are four different types of anchors: 1) standard anchors that link to another Web page, 2) anchors that download binary files from Web servers or FTP servers, 3) MAILTO anchors that automatically send e-mail messages, and 4) NAME anchors that link to a different section of the same Web page.

► Standard anchors are the most common type of anchor and involve the Anchor tag (`<A>`) and the HREF attribute. You must know the exact URL address of a Web page to which you are referring. This URL address is the value of the HREF attribute.

► There are two types of anchors that download files from servers: 1) anchors that download files from Web servers using the `http://` transfer protocol and anchors that download files from FTP servers using the `ftp://` transfer protocol. This type of anchor can download *any* type of binary file.

► MAILTO anchors can allow you or your organization to solicit feedback from visitors to your Web site. MAILTO anchors are used to gather general feedback, complaints, comments, customer testimonials, etc. Technically speaking, MAILTO anchors do three things when clicked: 1) automatically launch a user's default e-mail application, 2) automatically open a new outgoing e-mail message, and 3) automatically specify the TO e-mail address of your choice.

► NAME anchors allow you to create links between one section of a document and other sections of the same document. Often called "internal" links, NAME anchors are especially beneficial as a navigation aid in larger text documents that are segmented into distinct sections.

► NAME anchors actually involve two separate anchors, a referring anchor that features a pound sign (#) preceding a text label, and a target anchor (`<A NAME=text label>`) that marks the spot to which the Web page should be scrolled when the referring anchor is clicked by the user.

Lesson 5 Quiz

Matching

___ 1. different actions, such as link or download   a. NAME

___ 2. involves referring and destination tag set   b. pound sign

___ 3. anchor that links to an exact page location   c. hyperlinks

___ 4. HREF value for downloading files via FTP   d. internal link

___ 5. part of a referring NAME tag   e. MAILTO

___ 6. anchor that launches outgoing e-mail   f. ftp://

Fill in the Blank

7. Hyperlinks can be presented to users in two formats: _____ _____ or _____ _____ .

8. Anchors that automatically launch and address outgoing e-mail require the _____ value to the HREF attribute.

9. NAME anchors involve a referring tag and a _____ tag.

10. Anchors that download a file can use one of two attributes: HREF or _____ .

11. Image anchors, by default, feature a _____ _____ .

True or False?

T / F   12. NAME anchors involve use of a # with the NAME attribute value.

T / F   13. Anchor tags feature a required attribute.

T / F   14. NAME anchors are also known as *internal* links.

T / F   15. Anchors that download files do not require the HREF attribute.

T / F   16. Pound signs only have to be used in referring NAME anchors to accommodate older Web browsers.

Lesson 6
HTML 4.0 Tips
& Tricks

Lesson Topics

▶
 and <P> Attributes

▶ Forcing a New Browser Window

▶ <META> Tag

▶ Ordered List START Attribute

▶ Lesson 6 Summary

 and <P> Attributes

The Break tag, <BR>, and the Paragraph tag, <P>, are probably the two most frequently used tags within the HTML language. While the functionality and role of these two tags is very straightforward, new functionality has been added that can assist you in your page layout.

<BR CLEAR=all>

Aligning inline images and text (especially text broken into sections or paragraphs) in a particular manner has always been a frustrating endeavor. CLEAR, a new attribute to the <BR> tag, allows you to manipulate the position of text surrounding an inline image.

The value set of the CLEAR attribute is shown below:

```
<BR CLEAR=all|left|right|none>
```

The CLEAR attribute is used to position text past inline images on either margin, as you learned in Exercise 4-4. CLEAR=left moves the text after the line break past any inline images on the left margin; CLEAR=right does the same thing with inline images on the right.

An example of the effect of the CLEAR=all attribute setting is shown in Figure 6-1.

Figure 6-1: Effect of CLEAR: left page features <BR> tag; right page features <BR CLEAR=all>

DDC Publishing • www.ddcpub.com

A more practical demonstration of the utility provided by the CLEAR attribute is if you desire to position a block of text adjacent to an image, but have all following text fall *below* the image. Figure 6-2 presents an example of this.

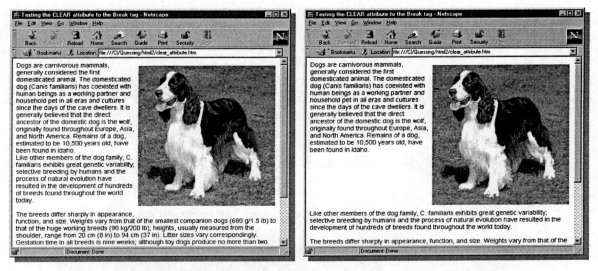

Figure 6-2: Left page uses the plain <BR> tag; right page uses <BR CLEAR=all>

You could not accomplish this effect with the <BR> tag without the CLEAR attribute or by using the <P> tag.

<P ALIGN=right>

The <P> tag now features an ALIGN attribute that can be used to align text blocks.

The value set of the ALIGN attribute is shown below:

```
<P ALIGN=left|center|right|justify>
```

Because left is the default of the <P> tag if it has no ALIGN attribute, using ALIGN=left is a waste of effort. The justify attribute value formats text in a manner that is commonly called "full justification" or "fully justified." This means the text lines up flush with both the left and right margins.

An example of the various effects of the different <P> tag values is shown in Figure 6-3.

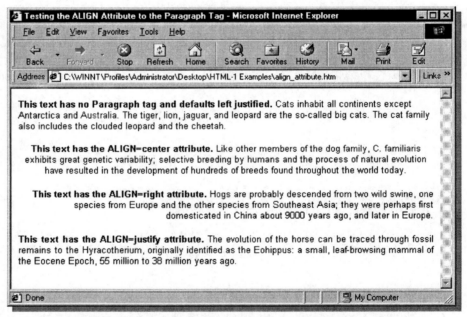

Figure 6-3: Paragraphs justified left (default), center, right, and full

Exercise 6-1: Justifying Web Page Text With the <P> Tag

In this exercise, you will justify blocks of text using the ALIGN attribute to the <P> tag.

1. Toggle over to Notepad.

2. Open the document JUSTIFY_TEXT.HTM from the HTML-1 folder.

3. Add the following script that appears in bold:

```
<HTML>

<HEAD>
<TITLE>Using ALIGN to Justify Web Page Text</TITLE>
</HEAD>

<BODY><P>

<B>This text has no Paragraph tag and defaults left
justified.</B> Cats inhabit all continents except Antarctica and
Australia. The tiger, lion, jaguar, and leopard are the so-called
big cats. The cat family also includes the clouded leopard and
the cheetah.

<P ALIGN=center><B>This text has the ALIGN=center attribute.</B>
Like other members of the dog family, C. familiaris exhibits
great genetic variability; selective breeding by humans and the
process of natural evolution have resulted in the development of
hundreds of breeds found throughout the world today.

<P ALIGN=right><B>This text has the ALIGN=right attribute.</B>
Hogs are probably descended from two wild swine, one species from
Europe and the other species from Southeast Asia; they were
perhaps first domesticated in China about 9000 years ago, and
later in Europe.

<P ALIGN=justify><B>This text has the ALIGN=justify
attribute.</B> The evolution of the horse can be traced through
fossil remains to the Hyracotherium, originally identified as the
Eohippus: a small, leaf-browsing mammal of the Eocene Epoch, 55
million to 38 million years ago.

</BODY>
</HTML>
```

4. Save the document.

5. Toggle over to your Web browser.

6. Open the document JUSTIFY_TEXT.HTM from the HTML-1 folder.

 The Web page text is now justified according to the value sets of the ALIGN attributes placed in the <P> tag, as shown in Figure 6-4.

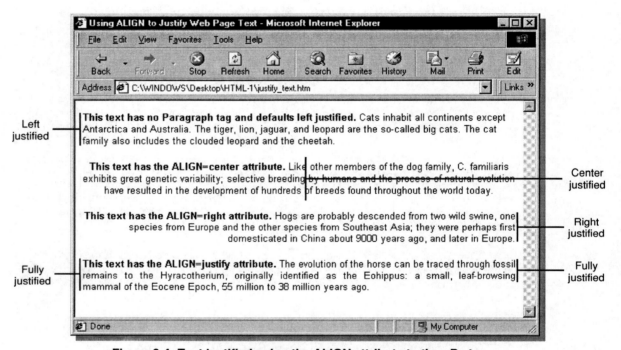

Figure 6-4: Text justified using the ALIGN attribute to the <P> tag

Forcing a New Browser Window

You learned in the last lesson how to script basic anchor tags to create hyperlinks from one Web page to another. While this basic functionality is at the heart of the navigational scheme of the Web, it can be enhanced with several subtle but powerful methods.

Keep Users at Your Site

Using a simple attribute to the Anchor tag, you can force a referred Web page to display in a new browser window. This has the effect of providing the user with two overlapping browser windows on his or her desktop, thus preserving the referring Web page from which the user accessed the link.

When done browsing the content on the "secondary" browser window, the user simply closes the window, making the original window active. You have probably accessed hyperlinks of this type in the past.

This is a powerful method by which you can keep users at your site while they temporarily explore the contents of Web pages *outside* of your site. While linking to outside content increases the overall utility of your Web site, it risks sending a visitor to another Web site and having them never return to yours. This can decrease your Web site traffic, your business, and your overall return on your Web presence investment.

The TARGET Attribute

The attribute that allows an Anchor tag to display referenced Web pages in different browser windows is TARGET. The TARGET attribute, which is used frequently when creating hyperlinks between different frames on the same Web page, has many different attributes. For our purposes, only one attribute is necessary: _blank.

This syntax of the TARGET attribute is shown below:

```
<A HREF=http://www.ddcpub.com TARGET=_blank>
```

Different browsers provide different levels of "overlap" between the referring browser window and the destination window. Netscape Navigator 3.0, for example, provides little or no offset (possibly making the user perceive that there is only one browser window). Navigator 4.0 provides a substantial amount of overlap, making it easy for a user to perceive that two windows are open.

An example of a new browser window opened by the `TARGET=_blank` attribute is shown in Figure 6-5.

Referring window containing Anchor tag with TARGET attribute

New window automatically generated by TARGET attribute

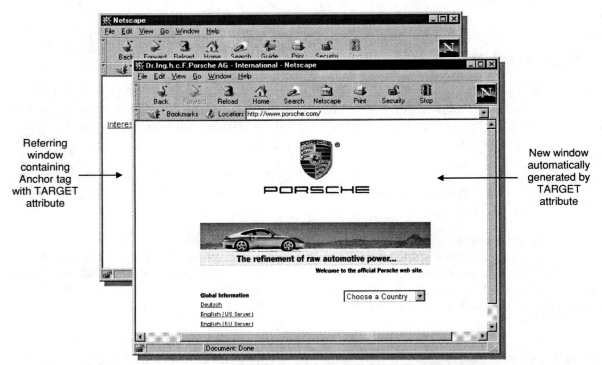

Figure 6-5: New browser window opened with TARGET=_blank attribute

DDC Publishing • www.ddcpub.com

Exercise 6-2: Generating a New Browser Window

In this exercise, you will create an Anchor tag that automatically generates a new browser window in which the content of the referred Web page is displayed.

1. Toggle over to Notepad and open a new document.

2. Type the following script:

```
<HTML>

<HEAD>
<TITLE>Using TARGET to Automatically Open a New Browser
Window</TITLE>
</HEAD>

<BODY>

<FONT SIZE=+2 COLOR=navy><B>TARGET Anchor</B></FONT><BR>

<A HREF=http://www.verio.com TARGET=_blank>Want to learn about a
national Internet Service Provider?</A><P>

<HR WIDTH=70% SIZE=6><P>

<FONT SIZE=+2 COLOR=navy><B>Regular Anchor</B></FONT><BR>

<A HREF=http://www.verio.com>Want to learn more about a national
Internet Service Provider?</A><P>

</BODY>
</HTML>
```

3. Save the document as TARGET_ANCHOR.HTM to the HTML-1 folder.

4. Toggle over to your Web browser.

5. Open the file TARGET_ANCHOR.HTM from the HTML-1 folder.

6. Click the **Want to learn about a national Internet Service Provider?** anchor below the **TARGET Anchor** section.

 A new browser window appears and the content of the Web page located at www.verio.com is displayed in the new browser window, as shown in Figure 6-6 on the following page.

Figure 6-6: New browser window (foreground) created using the TARGET attribute

7. Close the new browser window.

8. Click the **<u>Want to learn more about a national Internet Service Provider?</u>** anchor below the **Regular Anchor** section.

The Web page located at `www.verio.com` is displayed in the same browser window in which the referring anchor was clicked.

<META> Tag

The <META> tag can be used for many advanced functions in HTML. Some of the most useful functions of the <META> tag are:

- helping search engines properly index your pages and users find your pages when conducting search engine queries;

- automatically pushing a new Web page to a user (without the user clicking a hyperlink);

- providing a copyright and date for each Web page on your site;

- providing an e-mail address for the publisher or author of a Web page;

- specifying a description for a Web page that is used by search engines to identify your page within a database (for purposes of including on a query hit list).

<META> Tag Characteristics

<META> tags have a relatively unique syntax. This syntax often confuses those not familiar with <META> because of the wide variety of applications of this tag. The following syntactical rules apply to <META> tags:

- <META> tags always appear between the opening and closing <HEAD> tags;

- <META> is an empty tag;

- <META> is unique in that it has <u>two</u> required attributes; these two attributes are NAME <u>or</u> HTTP-EQUIV and CONTENT. The value of the NAME or HTTP-EQUIV attribute describes the *type* of information provided by the <META> tag. The CONTENT attribute value provides the actual information;

- multiple <META> tags can appear between the opening and closing <HEAD> tags of an HTML document.

An example of a <META> tag that automatically refreshes a Web page with a different page:

```
<META HTTP-EQUIV="refresh" CONTENT="http://www.ddcpub.com">
```

An example of a <META> tag that provides keywords to a search engine for the purpose of indexing and relevancy to user queries is as follows:

```
<META NAME="keywords" CONTENT="bicycles,bicycle
equipment,bicycle helmets,mountain bikes,French
racers,bicycle clothes,bicycle shoes,bicycle accessories">
```

Table 6-1 outlines the functions of the <META> tag as defined according to two attributes (HTTP-EQUIV and NAME) and their values.

<META> Attribute	Value	Details
HTTP-EQUIV	expires	Date: indicates the date the content "expires," often used to indicate to a search engine or other type of database when to delete the old document and index new data.
HTTP-EQUIV	reply-to	E-mail Address: indicates the e-mail address of the publisher or author.
HTTP-EQUIV	resource-type	Category of resource: indicates the type of information contained in the Web page. Common values are: ■ document ■ catalog ■ bibliography ■ news release
HTTP-EQUIV	distribution	Scope: indicates the range or scope of the Web page's distribution or application. Common values are: ■ global ■ domestic ■ local ■ private
HTTP-EQUIV	copyright	Organization & Date: indicates the copyright holder and date.
HTTP-EQUIV	refresh	Time & URL: forces a new Web page to be loaded or the current page to be reloaded after a specific number of seconds.
NAME	keywords	Keywords: provide a comma-separated list of keywords to be used by some search engines (AltaVista, Northern Light) when indexing your page.
NAME	description	Text String: this text will show up on a hit list (search results) instead of the first few lines of text from the Web page. Note that not all search engines support this feature of the <META> tag.
NAME	creation_date	Date: the date on which the HTML document was created (this is not the date of last revision).

Table 6-1: <META> tag attributes and attribute values

Search Engine Indexing by Keyword

Among the most useful applications of <META> is the ability to tag your Web pages with a list of specific keywords. These keywords can then be used by search engines to index your pages in a database. This improves the relevancy of results when users query a search engine using one of the keywords with which one of your pages is tagged.

For example, suppose your company is the Deluxe Bicycle Company. You could tag your pages with keywords that pertain to your business and are likely to be submitted to a search engine by a user when they are seeking information regarding the types of products you sell.

 Although many books and courses show the value of the CONTENT attribute as keywords separated by spaces, the official HTML 4.0 Specification dictates that this list be separated by commas with no spaces, as follows.

- Syntax: <META NAME="keywords" CONTENT="*keyword1, keyword2,keyword3...*">

- Example: <META NAME="keywords" CONTENT="bicycles,bicycle parts,bicycle helmets,bicycle apparel,bicycle parts">

Search Engine Hit List Descriptions

You can add <META> tag information that provides a description of a Web page. Search engines that support this function display this information on the hit list if your page is located during a search.

Because this functionality has only recently been available, search engines have defaulted to displaying the first few lines of text from a Web page in the description of a hit on a hit list.

If the first few sentences from a Web page do not sufficiently describe the content of the page, a user may choose a different link from a hit list or not visit your site. By providing an accurate description of your site in a <META> tag, you can increase the traffic to your site.

- Syntax: <META NAME="description" CONTENT="*description text*">

- Example: <META NAME="description" CONTENT="DDC publishes Internet courseware and training materials. Our complete catalog of courses is available on our Web site.">

Forcing a New HTML Page to be Loaded

Using <META>, you can force a Web page to be automatically reloaded or a new Web page to be loaded. This application of the <META> tag allows you to specify the exact number of seconds that a page is displayed to a user prior to the new page loading.

This function is useful for Web sites that provide dynamic information, such as current events, weather data, sports scores, stock market indicators, etc. Using this function, you can automatically revise the content of the user's browser window without he or she having to manually reload the page.

This feature is also used for "banner screens," which are slick, graphical screens that a user first sees when visiting a Web site. Such screens provide no hyperlinks and no real content, but serve to set a tone and convey a marketing theme for the entire Web site.

- <u>Syntax</u>: <META HTTP-EQUIV="refresh" CONTENT="*time (seconds)*;URL=*URL*">

- <u>Example</u>: <META HTTP-EQUIV="refresh" CONTENT="5; URL=http://www.ibm.com">

 If you simply want to refresh the current page, the syntax is CONTENT=*time*, where time is the number of seconds to elapse between refreshes.

Indicating a Copyright Holder & Date

Widespread unauthorized use of images and content available via Web sites has created a legal need to protect online intellectual property. Copyright notices are one way of declaring ownership of intellectual property and helping to expedite legal action if properties are misappropriated by unauthorized parties.

While it is recommended, when applicable, that organizations declare a copyright of their materials within the body of a Web page, in clear view of site visitors, you can also index this information within a special <META> tag.

- <u>Syntax</u>: <META HTTP-EQUIV="copyright" CONTENT= "*Organization owning copyright. - year*">

- <u>Example</u>: <META HTTP-EQUIV="copyright" CONTENT= "DDC Publishing - 2000">

Exercise 6-3: Adding <META> Tag Information to a Web Page

In this exercise, you will add various types of <META> tag information to an HTML document.

1. Toggle over to Notepad.

2. Open META.HTM from the HTML-1 folder.

3. Add the following script that appears in bold between the opening and closing <HEAD> tags:

```
<HEAD>
<TITLE>Using the META Tag</TITLE>
<META HTTP-EQUIV="refresh"
CONTENT="5;URL=http://www.porsche.com">
<META HTTP-EQUIV="description" CONTENT="This is the banner screen
for the Sports Car Enthusiast Web Site.">
<META NAME="creation_date" CONTENT="December 4, 2000">
<META NAME="keywords" CONTENT="porsche,sports cars,
cars,automobiles,corvette,lotus,spider,ferrari,911,turbo,
boxster">
</HEAD>
```

4. Save the file.

5. Toggle over to your Web browser.

6. Open the file META.HTM from the HTML-1 folder.

The temporary page appears and, after five seconds, automatically launches another Web page.

Note that the <META> information is not directly visible to a user; it functions to provide information to search engines and other databases that index your Web pages.

Ordered List START Attribute

You can change the start of an ordered list using the START attribute. This is helpful if you wish to insert non-list text blocks into a list. What would appear to a user to be the continuation of a list is actually a different list that happens to begin its numbering scheme where the previous list stopped.

The syntax of the START attribute is as follows:

```
<OL START=number>
```

 The value of the START attribute can be any integer from -2,147,483,647 to 2,147,483,648.

An example of using the START attribute on an ordered list is shown in Figure 6-7.

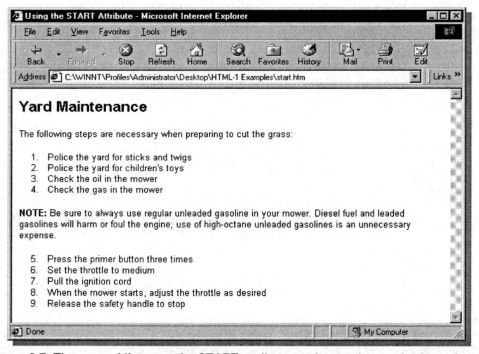

Figure 6-7: The second list uses the START attribute to change the numbering scheme

Exercise 6-4: Using START to Change an Ordered List Numbering Scheme

In this exercise, you will use the START attribute to the <OL> tag to change the numbering scheme of a number list.

1. Toggle over to Notepad.

2. Open the file START.HTM from the HTML-1 folder.

3. Add the following script that appears in bold:

```
The following steps are necessary when preparing to cut the
grass:

<OL>
<LI>Police the yard for sticks and twigs
<LI>Police the yard for children's toys
<LI>Check the oil in the mower
<LI>Check the gas in the mower
</OL>

<B>NOTE:</B> Be sure to always use regular unleaded gasoline in
your mower. Diesel fuel and leaded gasoline will harm or foul the
engine; use of high-octane unleaded gasoline is an unnecessary
expense.<P>

<OL START=5>
<LI>Press the primer button three times
<LI>Set the throttle to medium
<LI>Pull the ignition cord
<LI>When the mower starts, adjust the throttle as desired
<LI>Release the safety handle to stop
</OL>
```

4. Save the file.

5. Toggle over to your Web browser.

6. Open the file START.HTM from the HTML-1 folder.

 The second ordered list now begins at number 5, creating the effect of a single list annotated by text, instead of two different lists. Your browser should appear identical to Figure 6-7 on the previous page.

Lesson 6 Summary

▶ NAME anchors actually involve two separate but related anchors. The first anchor is a standard Anchor tag that refers to a name preceded by a pound sign (<A HREF=#porsche>). This tag refers to a NAME anchor. The NAME anchor, the second tag, is also an Anchor tag with a NAME attribute. In this example, the NAME anchor would appears as <A NAME=porsche>.

▶ The Break tag, <BR>, and the Paragraph tag, <P>, both offer enhanced functionality under HTML 4.0.
 now offers the CLEAR attribute. CLEAR can have values of all, left, right, or none and allow you to control how text breaks around an inline image. <P> now offers an ALIGN attribute, which has values of left, center, right, and justify. With the ALIGN attribute, the <P> tag can now control the alignment of text on a page.

▶ Using the TARGET attribute to the Anchor tag, you can have a hypertext anchor automatically open a referred Web page in a separate browser window. This has the effect of keeping a user at your site because the original browser window containing your Web page (and the referring hyperlink) does not change. The syntax of such a tag would appear as <A HREF=http://www.ddcpub.com TARGET=_blank>.

▶ The <META> tag performs many different functions in a Web page and for a Web site. The <META> tag can be formatted with two different attributes and over nine attribute values. Using <META>, you can help ensure that your Web pages are better indexed in a search engine's database (using keywords), provide a copyright notice, and provide a site or page description.

Lesson 6 Quiz

Matching

___ 1. refers to a NAME anchor   a. #horse

___ 2. new attribute for the <P> tag   b. CLEAR

___ 3. internal link   c. _blank

___ 4. new attribute for the <BR> tag   d. <META>

___ 5. displays a page in a new browser window   e. ALIGN

___ 6. specifies keywords for search engines   f. NAME anchor

Fill in the Blank

7. The _____ tag performs many different functions. It has two attributes and over nine attribute values.

8. _____ are a unique type of frame that are new to HTML 4.0.

9. _____ , also known as "internal" links, are a special kind of anchor.

10. You can apply the CLEAR attribute to the _____ tag to control how text wraps around inline images.

True or False?

T / F   11. Microsoft IE 5 does not support inline frames, but Netscape does.

T / F   12. You cannot create NAME anchors that link *directly* to an inline frame.

T / F   13. The <META> tag can be used to identify the author/publisher of a Web page.

T / F   14. The CLEAR attribute to the <P> tag allows you to control text justification.

T / F   15. Fully justified text is aligned flush on both the left and right margins.

T / F   16. The <META> tag is unique in that it has three required attributes.

(This page intentionally left blank)

DDC Publishing • www.ddcpub.com

Lesson 7
Course Review

Creating a Complex Web Page

The purpose of this exercise is to apply the skills you have learned from this course. Remember when completing the following exercise that Web pages are best when approached with a sense of creativity. Proper use of white space and an eye for page design and layout are critical to good Web pages.

Exercise 7-1: Creating a Complex Web Page

1. Create a new HTML document and save it as REVIEW.HTM in the HTML-1 directory.

2. Script a paragraph of text. Format some text as bold, some as italic, and some as underlined. Format one word with multiple text formatting (bold *and* italic *and* underline). Be careful to use proper tag nesting conventions.

3. Insert at least three different character entities throughout the paragraph you scripted in the previous step.

4. Insert horizontal rules between different areas of the page. Use different attributes on every horizontal rule.

5. Create an ordered list with at least four elements.

6. Create an unordered list with at least five elements.

7. Insert an image (from the HTML-1 directory) and align it on the right side of the page.

8. Insert a text anchor that links to LINKTO.HTM.

9. Specify a background pattern. If the pattern is dark, change the color of the text to maintain contrast between it and the background.

10. Create an image anchor that links to LINKTO.HTM.

11. Without using the <UL> tag, create a bullet list using the image BULLET.GIF.

12. Create a MAILTO anchor that links to the e-mail address `feedback@ibm.com`.

13. Create a NAME anchor that links to a different section of the page.

14. Create a link that downloads the file REVIEW_IMAGE.JPG from `www.quessing.com`.

*"Miriam! He's asking for help with his HTML homework.
What the heck is he talking about?!"*

Part 2:
HTML 4.0 Intermediate
Mastering Web Frames and Tables

Part 2 Description

Welcome to *HTML 4.0 Intermediate*, the second part in DDC's *Mastering HTML* Series. This section provides students with a continuation of DDC's *HTML 4.0 Fundamentals*, an introductory-level HTML course.

This section provides an in-depth review of frames and the mechanisms required to create both links between frames and Web site navigation bars. Tables are also examined in depth, including nesting tables within tables, embedding lists in tables, creating page columns with tables, and spanning table rows and columns.

Part 2 Objectives

This course was developed for Webmasters, HTML scripters, and anyone publishing Web pages and Web sites. This course utilizes lecture material, hands-on exercises, and lesson-specific quizzes to teach:

- Overview of frames

- Formatting frames

- Combining frame rows and columns

- Creating links between frames

- Using inline frames

- Overview of tables

- Using tables to create a two-column page layout

- Advanced table features and formatting

- Embedding lists within tables

- Nesting tables within tables

Lesson 8
Introduction
to Frames

Lesson Topics

▶ What are Frames?

▶ Anatomy of Frames

▶ <FRAMESET> Tag

▶ <FRAME> Tag

▶ Lesson 8 Summary

What are Frames?

A *frame* is an HTML page layout convention that enables Web pages to be divided into a series of rectangular sections, similar to boxes. Frames are very flexible in their application and configuration.

You can control the following features of frames:

- whether a frame displays borders;

- how or if a frame displays scroll bars (never display or automatically display when necessary based on user browser size configuration) ;

- various levels of margin white space within the frame;

- whether frame borders are movable.

Display Multiple HTML Documents on a Single Page

The most significant aspect of a multiple-frame HTML page is that *each frame displays a separate HTML document*. Clicking on a hyperlink in a document displayed in one frame can cause the contents of that or a different frame to change. You may find this useful if you want to ensure that a table of contents, navigation bar, or some other element remains on the user's screen as he or she browses from page to page.

Although frames have been in use since they were introduced with Netscape Navigator 2.0 in January 1996, they have not been officially supported by the HTML Specification until version 4.0 (April 1998). Today frames are supported by all major Web browsers, including:

- Netscape Navigator 2.0 and its more recent versions;

- Microsoft Internet Explorer 2.1 and its more recent versions;

- Opera (all versions).

Navigation Bars

A common application of frames is a navigation bar, often called a "nav bar," along the left or right side of a Web page. Because most sites want to provide this nav bar on all pages of a Web site, the HTML document containing the nav bar need be created only once and then referred to from the nav bar frame of every page of the site. The "content" of the site is contained in the opposite frame of the page and changes according to links the user clicks in the nav bar or within the body of the content frame.

In Lesson 10: *Linking Frames*, you will learn to create frames that contain anchors that, when clicked, change not their own contents but the contents of other frames on the page. In this manner, you can create nav bars and other sophisticated navigation schemes on a Web site.

Exercise 8-1: Observing Different Frame Configurations

In this exercise, you will view Web pages displaying frames in different configurations.

1. Click once in the URL field, type the following address, and press <ENTER>:

   ➢ **www.familycenteredcare.org**

 The homepage is downloaded and displayed. Note the layout of the frames, as shown in Figure 8-1. These frames are "invisible" in that there is no visible border between them.

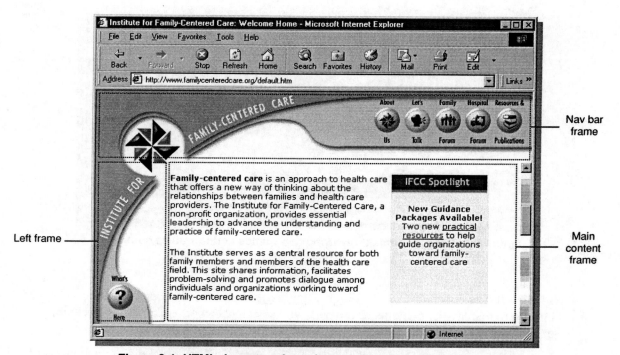

Figure 8-1: HTML document featuring two frames configured as rows

2. After it has completed downloading, scroll down the page. Note that, because these are invisible frames, they cannot manually be resized using your mouse.

3. The top and left frames do not scroll, but the content frame does. This page has been formatted with borderless frames (which you will learn to create later in this course).

4. In the top frame, click the **About Us** link. The *About Us* page will appear. Note that this page features the same basic frame layout, but with different frame sizes. The left frame is more narrow, but the top frame is slightly taller.

5. On the *About Us* page, in the top frame, click the **Resources** link. The Resource page will be downloaded and displayed in the main content frame.

6. Access **www.utm.edu/~phertzel/migration.htm**. The Shorebird Migration Pages site is downloaded and displayed, as shown in Figure 8-2. Note that the layout of the frames is nearly identical to the previous Web site, except that the left frame can be scrolled.

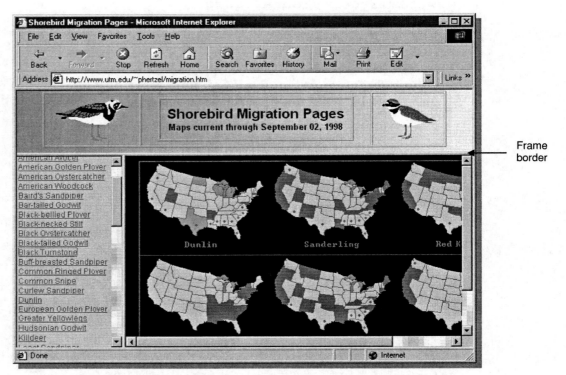

Figure 8-2: HTML document featuring two frames configured as columns

7. In the left frame, scroll down to **Black Turnstone** and click. The content frame will change to display the contents of the page you selected. All other frames will remain unchanged.

8. In the left frame, click **Curlew Sandpiper**. The page displayed in the content frame will change.

9. Position your mouse pointer over the frame border between the top and main content frames. Your mouse pointer will change to a double-headed arrow.

10. Drag the border down, expanding the size of the top frame and decreasing the size of the bottom two frames.

11. Drag the border between the left frame and the main content frame to the right. Drag it back to its original position.

12. Visit **www.calfnews.com**.

This frame layout is very similar to the previous site you visited, except that there is no border between the frames. Even though you can scroll the left nav bar frame, it has no border and cannot be resized. Like the previous site, you can scroll both the left frame and the main content frame.

13. Scroll down the page. Click one of the links in the left frame to change the content of the main frame.

14. Visit **www.global-dental.com**.

 This frame layout is similar to the previous two. Differences include the fact that the left frame extends to the top of the page and only the main content frame can be scrolled. Like the last two sites you have visited, frame borders are not visible.

15. Visit **www.barbecue-store.com**.

 This frame layout is different in that it lacks a top frame and is composed of only two frames, both of which can be scrolled. The left frame acts as a nav bar and the right frame is the content frame.

Is there a border between the frames, and can it be resized?

16. Visit **www.gear.com**. This is a two-frame layout. Unlike other sites you have visited, the bottom frame acts as a nav bar.

17. Click any link in the bottom frame. The contents of the main frame will change.

18. Visit **www.yha.org.uk**.

19. Click any of the links in the top frame. The contents of the main frame will change. What is similar and different about this site in relation to the others you have visited in this exercise?

20. Visit **www.backpackers.com.au**. This site is very similar to the previous site. Click any link in the top nav bar frame.

Anatomy of Frames

An HTML document featuring frames—while it appears to be a "single page" to a user—actually consists of several HTML documents carefully woven together. While you can have an unlimited number of frames in an HTML document, it is strongly recommended that you include only a few (2-5).

Sometimes unique applications of frames justify more than five frames per page, but this typically results in a confusing and unintuitive interface that overwhelms users with too much information on a single page.

Master Frame & Slave Frame Documents

Two types of documents comprise a frames page:

- master frame document: this HTML document specifies the size and position of the frames on the page;

- slave frame documents: separate HTML documents containing frame contents.

As shown in Figure 8-3, MASTER.HTM is the master frame document containing the code that specifies the layout, size, and position of three frames, comprised of content from the slave frame documents (SLAVE1.HTM, SLAVE2.HTM, and SLAVE3.HTM).

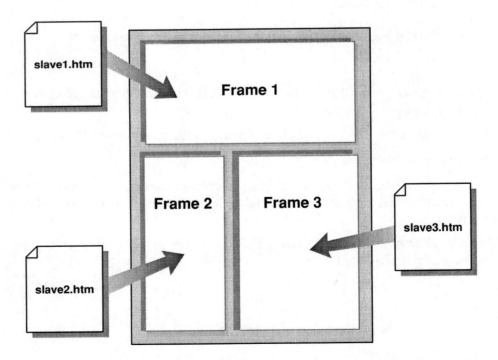

Figure 8-3: Master frame document and slave frame documents

DDC Publishing • www.ddcpub.com

<FRAMESET> Tag

Frames instruct a user's browser how to display frames within an HTML document in a structure called a frameset. The master frame document contains a **<FRAMESET>** tag set. The <FRAMESET> tag structure *replaces* the <BODY> tag set.

An HTML document with a <BODY> section cannot contain a <FRAMESET> section (sometimes called a *container*) and vice versa.

If you create an HTML document with both a <BODY> section and a <FRAMESET> container, a browser will ignore the frame structure and *none of the content of the frames will be displayed*. Instead, only the content of the <BODY> section will be shown.

<FRAMESET> is a non-empty tag with several attributes. The syntax and placement of the <FRAMESET> tag set is shown in the example below.

```
<HTML>

<HEAD>
<TITLE>Simple Frame Layout</TITLE>
</HEAD>

<FRAMESET COLS="50%,25%,25%">
<FRAME SRC=slave1.htm>
<FRAME SRC=slave2.htm>
<FRAME SRC=slave3.htm>
</FRAMESET>

</HTML>
```

COLS & ROWS Attributes

There are two major attributes of the <FRAMESET> tag:

- COLS

- ROWS

You can define any reasonable number of: 1) ROWS; 2) COLS; or 3) both ROWS and COLS, but you have to define something for at least one of these attributes. You cannot define a frameset with only one row and/or one column. A browser that encounters this type of erroneous frame will display a blank screen. Thus, the following <u>minimums</u> can be defined: 1) two rows and no columns; 2) two columns and no rows.

ROWS & COLS Values

The value of the ROWS attribute is a measure of the height of frame rows relative to 1) one another and 2) available browser screen area. The value of the COLS attribute is a measure of the width of frame columns relative to 1) one another and 2) available browser screen area.

Both ROWS and COLS values can be expressed via one of three different value types:

- percentages;
- pixels;
- relative scale values (sometimes called *relative ratios*).

These value types are detailed in Table 8-1. Note that the comma-separated value ranges have no space before or after the comma and *must be enclosed in quotation marks*.

Value Type	Syntax Example	Comment
Percentages	Numbers with percentages: COLS= "50%,25%,25%"	Recommended; easy to use
Pixels	Straight numbers: ROWS="240,100,140"	Not recommended due to variance in user video
Relative Scale Values	Numbers with asterisks: COLS="1*,2*,3*"	Recommended; not as intuitive as percentages

Table 8-1: COLS and ROWS attributes value types and syntax

Defining the Number of Rows or Columns

The number of rows or columns in a frames page is determined by the number of values defined for the ROWS or COLS attributes, respectively.

For example, <FRAMESET ROWS="25%,50%,25%"> defines a frameset with *three* rows (count the comma-separated values). This example specifies the top row as 25% of the height of the browser content area, the second as 50%, and the third as 25% (counting left to right).

Rows Commingling with Columns

You can combine the ROWS and COLS attributes in a single opening <FRAMESET> tag in order to create more sophisticated frame configurations.

Be sure to place quotation marks around the entire value set of a ROWS or COLS attribute. Without these, the row or column is not properly displayed.

1) Percentages

The example below creates three frames arranged as rows; the top row consuming 25% of the screen height, the middle taking 50%, and the bottom taking 25%. If the user resized his or her browser on their screen, the frames in this example would adjust accordingly (because the space they share had decreased or increased).

```
<FRAMESET COLS="25%,50%,25%">
```

If you miscalculate and your percentages do not add up to 100%, your frames will still display properly. Web browsers scale these percentages up or down proportionately to equal a total of 100%.

2) Pixels

It is recommended that you abstain from using absolute values (pixels) when defining ROWS and COLS sizes in frame sets. This is due to the fact that users who download your HTML documents containing frames will have an extremely wide variety of video configurations—both hardware and software—on their PCs.

Imagine the difference in the way a Web page is displayed between a 14" monitor configured at 640 x 480 pixels of resolution and a 21" monitor at 1280 x 1024 pixels of resolution. It is safer practice to define the size of frameset ROWS and COLS using relative values, such as: 1) percentages or 2) relative scale values (asterisks).

3) Relative Scale Values (*relative ratios*)

The third ROWS and COLS value type is a relative scale value (often called a proportional value). Relative scale values are denoted with asterisks, as shown in the following example:

```
<FRAMESET ROWS="1*,2*,3*">
```

The above example defines three ROWS. Simply count the numeric values to determine the common denominator of the fraction used to proportionally scale these rows. *If an asterisk appears with no number, the value defaults to 1.* Thus, the above example specifies a common denominator of 6. The first row will be allocated 1/6 of the available screen space the second row will receive 2/6 (or 1/3), and the third will receive 3/6 (1/2) of the screen space.

<FRAME> Tag

The <FRAME> tag is inserted within the <FRAMESET> opening and closing tags. The <FRAME> tag has one necessary attribute, SRC, the value of which refers to the HTML document that appears within the frame.

The <FRAME> tag is an empty tag; its basic syntax is shown in Figure 8-4.

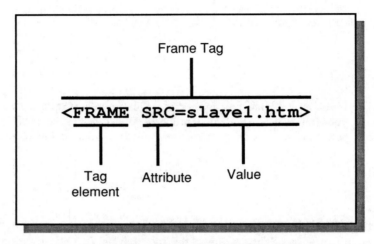

Figure 8-4: Syntax of the <FRAME> tag

You must include one <FRAME> tag per frame that is to appear in your HTML document. Also, the number of rows or columns (or both) to which you refer in the opening <FRAMESET> tag must equal the number of <FRAME> tags listed between the opening and closing <FRAMESET> tags.

An example of use of the <FRAME> tag is shown below (this example assumes a Web page comprised of four frames configured as rows).

```
<FRAMESET ROWS="25%,25%,25%,25%">
<FRAME SRC=slave1.htm>
<FRAME SRC=slave2.htm>
<FRAME SRC=slave3.htm>
<FRAME SRC=slave4.htm>
</FRAMESET>
```

The example on the previous page loads SLAVE1.HTM into the first frame, SLAVE2.HTM into the second frame, SLAVE3.HTM into the third, and SLAVE4.HTM into the fourth. The page layout would resemble Figure 8-5.

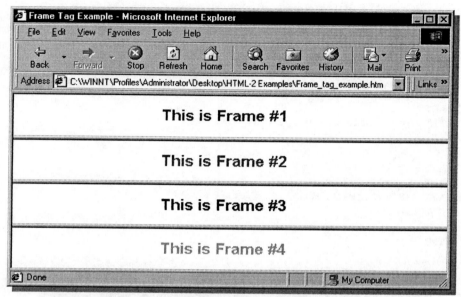

Figure 8-5: Four frames configured as rows (each with size of 25%)

By simply changing the ROWS attribute in the opening <FRAMESET> tag of the master frame document to COLS, the overall layout of the page changes dramatically and the page layout looks like Figure 8-6.

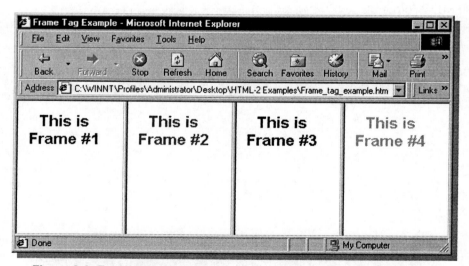

Figure 8-6: Four frames configured as columns (each with size of 25%)

Exercise 8-2: Creating a Simple Frames Layout

In this exercise, you will create a simple frames-enabled Web page comprised of rows.

1. Launch MS Notepad. A new file will automatically appear.
2. Type the following script:

```
<HTML>

<HEAD>
<TITLE>My Brothers Daryl</TITLE>
</HEAD>

<FRAMESET COLS="50%,50%">
<FRAME SRC=daryl.htm>
<FRAME SRC=daryl2.htm>
</FRAMESET>

</HTML>
```

3. Save the HTML document as MASTER1.HTM in the HTML-2 directory on your Desktop (or drive C:).
4. Open the file DARYL.HTM from the HTML-2 folder. Format this file as an HTML document, inserting all the necessary tags (<HTML>, <HEAD>, <BODY>, etc.), and then save your changes.
5. Open the file DARYL2.HTM from the HTML-2 folder. Add the same HTML tags as above and save your changes.
6. Toggle (<ALT + TAB>) to your Web browser and open MASTER1.HTM from the HTML-2 folder.

 The master frame document is displayed in your browser, along with the frame content provided by the two slave frame documents, as shown in Figure 8-7 on the following page.

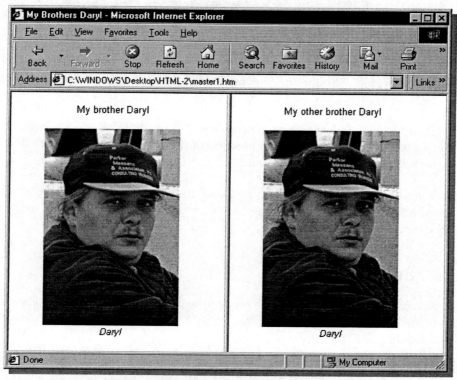

Figure 8-7: Web page displaying simple frames configuration

7. Toggle back to Notepad (<ALT + TAB>).

8. Reopen the file MASTER1.HTM. In the opening <FRAMESET> tag, change COLS to ROWS and save the file (<ALT + F>, <S> is a shortcut).

9. Toggle back to your Web browser. Refresh the Web page (<F5> in IE).[17]

 The Web page appears with the slave frames now configured as rows (not the optimal layout for these particular slave frame HTML documents).

10. Toggle back to Notepad. Change the ROWS attribute back to COLS. Save the file.

---

[17] There is a bug in Navigator 4.0*x* that does not properly refresh changes made to a master frames document using either the **Reload** button on the toolbar or the <CTRL + R> keyboard shortcut. You must reopen the file using **File ▶ Open Page** and click the **Open** button. Note that you can correctly refresh changes made to slave frames documents using **Reload** or <CTRL + R>; thus, if you change the content of a slave frame document referred to by a master frame document, Navigator's refresh (reload) function works properly.

Lesson 8 Summary

▶ Frames enable you to divide a Web page into a series of independent sections, each of which displays a separate HTML document.

▶ There are two types of frames documents in HTML: master frame documents and slave frame documents.

▶ Each frames-enabled page you create consists of several HTML documents: 1) a master document that specifies the size and position of the frames and 2) separate documents containing the contents for each frame.

▶ Frames are flexible in their application and configuration; an HTML scripter can decide if they show borders, are scrollable, and are movable. You can also control the amount of white space inside a frame.

▶ Frames are supported by Netscape Navigator 2.0, its later versions, Microsoft Internet Explorer 2.1, and its later versions.

▶ One popular application of frames is the application of a navigation bar (known as a "nav bar") to an entire Web site as an aid in quickly locating information. This is especially helpful at large Web sites.

▶ A master frame document determines the configuration and layout of frames on a Web page. The master frame document refers to other HTML documents (called slaves), the content of which is displayed according to the instructions in the master frame document.

▶ Frames are created with a frameset. A frameset replaces the Body section of a Web page (created with the <BODY> tag). The <FRAMESET> tag, a non-empty tag set, creates the frameset.

▶ Within the <FRAMESET> tag, one <FRAME> tag must exist for each frame in the set. The SRC attribute of the <FRAME> tag specifies which HTML document should be loaded into that frame.

▶ The COLS and ROWS attributes to the <FRAMESET> tag determine the number of and relative size of frame columns and rows, respectively.

▶ You can determine the size of a row or column using values denoted as percentages, pixels, or relative scale values. Use of pixels is not recommended because as an absolute value, they will not look as you intend on some video configurations.

▶ <FRAME> tags are embedded between the opening and closing <FRAMESET> tags in the master frame document and refer to slave documents (similar to how <IMG SRC=dog.gif> refers to an image file to be displayed in an HTML document).

Lesson 8 Quiz

Matching

___ 1. created by a narrow frame with links   a. pixels

___ 2. element that creates rows and columns   b. master

___ 3. also known as a frame container   c. <FRAMESET>

___ 4. frame that refers to content frames   d. frameset

___ 5. how to specify an absolute column value   e. nav bar

___ 6. HTML document referred to by a frame   f. slave

Fill in the Blank

7. The format of a _____ or _____ value in a <FRAMESET> tag determines the number of rows or columns in a frameset.

8. A frames page is comprised of two types of frames files: standard HTML documents that serve as slaves and _____ .

9. You can define the size of frame rows or columns using pixels, percentages, or _____ .

10. _____ have become a popular means of providing a user with a navigation menu that is always at his/her fingertips.

True or False?

T / F   11. The number of ROWS attributes in a <FRAMESET> tag determines the number of rows in a frames page.

T / F   12. Frames are supported by Netscape Navigator 2.0 and more recent and Microsoft Internet Explorer 2.1 and more recent.

T / F   13. The <FRAMESET> tag must be contained inside the <BODY>.

T / F   14. <FRAME> tags refer to standard HTML documents.

T / F   15. <FRAME> must be nested inside the <FRAMESET> container when using IE 3.0, but not in other browsers.

(This page intentionally left blank)

DDC Publishing • www.ddcpub.com

Lesson 9
Advanced Frame Layout

Lesson Topics

▶ Combining Rows & Columns

▶ Modifying Frame Appearance & Functionality

▶ HTML Extensions for Frames

▶ <NOFRAMES> Tag

▶ Lesson 9 Summary

Combining Rows & Columns

Typically, the frame layout you desire will involve a combination of rows and columns. This is usually the case with more sophisticated page layouts or layouts involving a nav bar (you will create such a page in Lesson 10: *Linking Frames*).

There are three methods by which you can combine rows and columns:

1. combining ROWS and COLS attributes in a single <FRAMESET> tag;

2. nesting <FRAMESET> tag sets;

3. referring to a master frame document from a <FRAME> tag.

It is important that you recognize the difference between these three methods to choose the approach that works best for you.

These methods are compared in Table 9-1.

Method	Pros	Cons
Combining ROWS and COLS attributes	■ Most straightforward of the three methods ■ Requires the least number of files of the three methods (making Web site file management easier)	■ Does not allow for more complex frame configurations, such as row spanning and column spanning ■ Browsers sometimes do not properly interpret certain ROWS and COLS configurations
Nesting Frame Sets	■ Allows complex frame configurations, such as row and column spanning ■ Fewer files to manage than when referring a master frame document to another master frame document	N/A
Referring a master frame document to another master frame document	Allows the most sophisticated and complex frame layouts and configurations	Increases the number of files required to create the frames, making Web site file management a greater burden

Table 9-1: Three methods by which you can combine frame rows and columns

ROWS + COLS in a Single <FRAMESET> Tag

You can combine a ROWS attribute (and value set) with a COLS attribute in a single <FRAMESET> tag. The syntax for combining rows and columns via multiple attributes in the <FRAMESET> tag is shown in Figure 9-1.

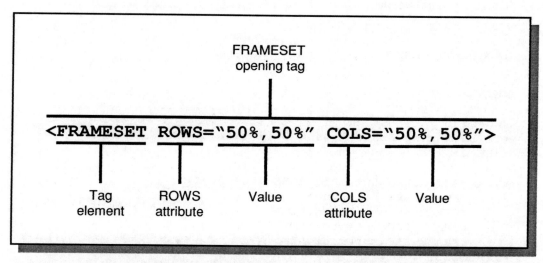

Figure 9-1: Syntax for combining columns and rows with multiple <FRAMESET> attributes

You can specify the arrangement of the frames in the user's browser. When listing the <FRAME> tags between the opening and closing <FRAMESET> tags, use this rule: the <FRAME> tags are listed in the order they occur in the HTML script going from left to right, top to bottom (in that order).

Don't Add; Multiply

If you specify X number rows and Y number columns, you must then include X times Y number of <FRAME> tags within the <FRAMESET>. Be careful not to make the mistake of *adding* the number of rows and columns.

Thus, if you specified three ROWS attribute values and three COLS attribute values, you would have to include nine <FRAME> tags (3 x 3) within the <FRAMESET> (not 6).

Exercise 9-1: Combining ROWS & COLS

In this exercise, you will combine rows and columns using a single frame set and combining ROWS and COLS attributes in the opening <FRAMESET> tag.

1. Toggle over to Notepad.

2. Open a new document (**File ▶ New**).

3. Type the following text:

```
<HTML>

<HEAD>
<TITLE>Mixing Frame Rows & Columns</TITLE>
</HEAD>

<FRAMESET COLS="50%,50%" ROWS="50%,50%">
     <FRAME SRC=erie.htm>
     <FRAME SRC=michigan.htm>
     <FRAME SRC=ontario.htm>
     <FRAME SRC=superior.htm>
</FRAMESET>

</HTML>
```

4. Save the file as GREAT_LAKES.HTM in the HTML-2 directory.

5. Toggle over to your Web browser and open GREAT_LAKES.HTM.

The page is split into four equally-sized frames, as shown in Figure 9-2 on the following page. Note that scroll bars automatically appear in those frames that do not display all of their contents. Scroll bars inform the user that additional content is available for their review. In an exercise later in this Lesson, you will learn to control this default functionality.

Note how the order of the <FRAME> tags corresponds to the arrangement of the frames in the browser (left to right, top to bottom, in that order).

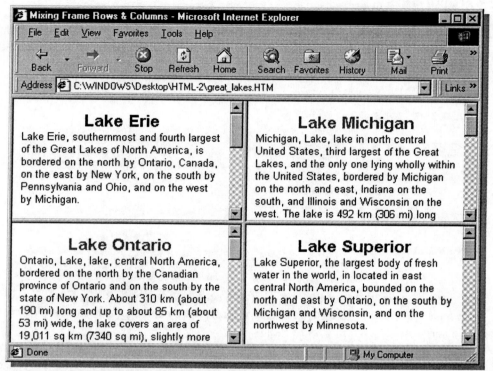

Figure 9-2: Result of combining ROWS and COLS attributes in a single <FRAMESET>

 You can rearrange the frames simply by reordering the <FRAME> tags in the master frame document (GREAT_LAKES.HTM).

Nesting Frame Sets

An alternative to using a single <FRAMESET> tag is nesting <FRAMESET> tags within one another. This allows for more complex and sophisticated frame layouts than you could achieve by combining ROWS and COLS attributes within a single frame set.

```
<FRAMESET COLS="25%,75%">

    <FRAME SRC=slave1.htm>

    <FRAMESET ROWS="50%,50%">
        <FRAME SRC=slave2a.htm>
        <FRAME SRC=slave2b.htm>
    </FRAMESET>

</FRAMESET>
```

In the above example, think of the nested frame set as simply another <FRAME>. This will help you ensure that your script is properly interpreted by the user's browser. The results of the above script are shown in Figure 9-3.

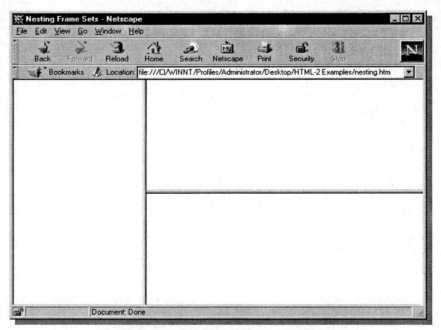

Figure 9-3: An example of a nested frame set

In the opening "outside" frame set, two columns are specified. The first column will display SLAVE1.HTM. The second column will display whatever slave frame documents are referred to by the embedded frame set.

Exercise 9-2: Combining Rows & Columns Using Nesting

In this exercise, you will combine frame rows and columns by nesting a frame set within another frame set.

1. Toggle over to Notepad. If necessary, open MASTER1.HTM from the HTML-2 folder.

2. Add the following script that appears in bold to the document:

```
<HTML>

<HEAD>
<TITLE>My Brothers Daryl</TITLE>
</HEAD>

<FRAMESET ROWS="15%,85%">

    <FRAME SRC=relatives.htm>

    <FRAMESET COLS="50%,50%">
        <FRAME SRC=daryl.htm>
        <FRAME SRC=daryl2.htm>
    </FRAMESET>

</FRAMESET>

</HTML>
```

3. Save the document.

4. Now you need to create the slave document RELATIVES.HTM. In Notepad, select **File ▶ New**. Type the following script:

```
<HTML>

<HEAD>
<TITLE>My Relatives in San Francisco</TITLE>
</HEAD>

<BODY BGCOLOR=blue>

<CENTER>
<FONT COLOR=white SIZE=+3><B>My Relatives in San
Francisco</B></FONT>
</CENTER>

</BODY>
</HTML>
```

5. Save the file as RELATIVES.HTM in the HTML-2 directory.

6. Toggle over to your Web browser. Reload the page (remember that in Navigator 4.0*x* you cannot refresh a frames page but must instead reopen the page).

 The page is downloaded and displayed, as shown in Figure 9-4.

Figure 9-4: Combining rows and columns by nesting <FRAMESET> containers

7. Place your mouse pointer on the border between the left and right frames. Drag the frame border to the left. Now drag it to the right.

8. Move the horizontal frame border between the top row and the bottom columns. Later in this lesson you will learn to modify various characteristics of frame borders.

Exercise 9-3: Referring a Master Frame Document to Another Master Frame

In this exercise, you will combine rows and columns in a frame document by referring to a master frame document from another master frame document. You do this by specifying the "slave" master frame document name from one of the <FRAME> tags in the frameset of the "master" master frame document. While this may sound confusing, it will become clear after you have completed this exercise.

1. Toggle over to Notepad.

2. Open a new document (**File ▶ New**).

3. Type the following script:

```
<HTML>

<HEAD>
<TITLE>Referring Master Frame Documents</TITLE>
</HEAD>

<FRAMESET ROWS="20%,60%,20%">
     <FRAME SRC=header.htm>
     <FRAME SRC=porsche.htm>
     <FRAME SRC=footer.htm>
</FRAMESET>

</HTML>
```

4. Save the file as REFERRING.HTM in the HTML-2 directory.

5. Open a new document in Notepad.

6. Type the following script:

```
<HTML>

<HEAD>
<TITLE>"Referred to" Master Frame Document</TITLE>
</HEAD>

<FRAMESET COLS="35%,65%">
     <FRAME SRC=porsche_pic.htm>
     <FRAME SRC=porsche_text.htm>
</FRAMESET>

</HTML>
```

7. Save the file as PORSCHE.HTM in the HTML-2 directory.

 HEADER.HTM, FOOTER.HTM, PORSCHE_PIC.HTM, and PORSCHE_TEXT.HTM have already been created for you and reside in the HTML-2 folder on your Desktop. For the purpose of this exercise, you do not need to create these files.

8. Toggle over to your Web browser.

9. Open REFERRING.HTM from the HTML-2 folder on you Desktop.

 The page is downloaded and displayed, as shown in Figure 9-5. Note the four frames of the page.

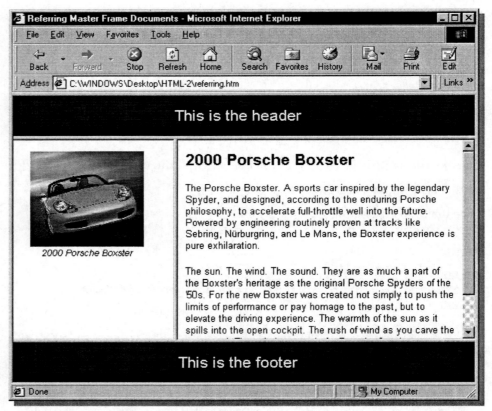

Figure 9-5: Referring to a master frame document from a master frame document

Modifying Frame Appearance & Functionality

There are many ways in which you can modify the appearance and functionality of frames within Web pages. Frame characteristics that you can control include:

- the appearance of scroll bars;

- the user's ability to resize a frame;

- amount of white space within frames;

- the appearance of frame borders.

All of the attributes to the <FRAME> tag that allow you control the above functions, in addition to other characteristics of frames, are listed in Table 9-2.

Attribute	Values	Description
FRAMEBORDER	■ YES (default) ■ NO	■ YES inserts a 3-D border around the frame. ■ NO specifies the exclusion of any border around the frame.
MARGINHEIGHT	pixels (numeric)	Controls the spacing between the top and bottom of a frame and its contents.
MARGINWIDTH	pixels (numeric)	Controls the spacing between the left and right sides of a frame and its contents.
NAME[18]	text string	Specifies a target name when establishing links between frames.
NORESIZE	*Null value set*	Adding this attribute prevents visitors from re-sizing the frame.
SCROLLING	■ YES ■ NO ■ AUTO (default)	Determines whether a scrollbar is displayed alongside a frame. AUTO, the default value, indicates that scrollbar(s) will be displayed only if frame contents extend beyond its boundaries (which depends on the user video configuration).
SRC	URL	■ Inserts the URL of the slave source file in the master frame document. ■ The only necessary <FRAME> attribute.

Table 9-2: <FRAME> tag attributes

---

[18] You will work with the NAME attribute in Lesson 10: *Linking Frames.*

Exercise 9-4: Controlling Frame Scrolling & Resizing

In this exercise, you will control the appearance of frame scroll bars and a user's ability to manually resize a frame with his or her mouse.

1. Toggle over to Notepad.

2. Make the following edits that appear in bold to MASTER1.HTM in HTML-2:

```
<FRAMESET COLS="50%,50%">
        <FRAME SRC=daryl.htm>
        <FRAME SRC=about_daryl.htm>
</FRAMESET>
```

3. Save the document, toggle over to your Web browser, and open MASTER1.HTM.

 The page now appears with a text block in the right frame. Configure your browser window so you have a scroll bar in the right frame but not in the other frames, as shown in Figure 9-6.

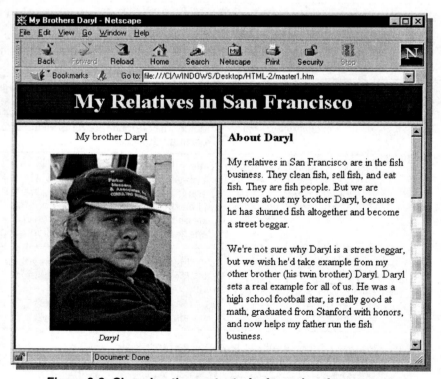

Figure 9-6: Changing the content of a frame in a frames page

4. Place your mouse pointer on the vertical border between the left and right frames and move the frame. This is the default behavior of frames.

5. Shorten your browser window.

Scroll bars automatically appear within the left and top frames when the browser window is sized too small to display all of the frame contents, as shown in Figure 9-7.

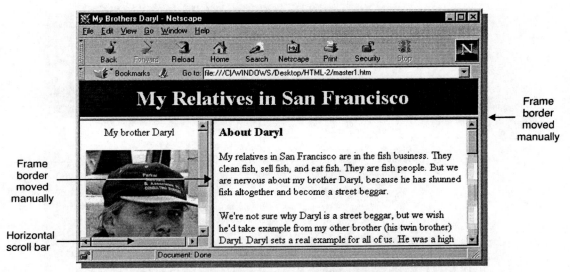

Figure 9-7: Frames resized manually and automatic scroll bars (defaults)

6. Toggle back to Notepad.

7. Make the following edits (that appear in bold) to your HTML document:

```
<FRAME SCROLLING=no NORESIZE SRC=relatives.htm>

    <FRAMESET COLS="50%,50%">
        <FRAME NORESIZE SCROLLING=no SRC=daryl.htm>
        <FRAME NORESIZE SRC=about_daryl.htm>
    </FRAMESET>
```

8. Save the HTML document. Toggle over to your Web browser. Reload the Web page.

9. Attempt to manually move the frame borders. Note that you no longer see the double arrows that previous allowed you to move the borders.

The frame borders do not move when you attempt to manually move them with your mouse. Scroll bars do not appear on the top or left frame, regardless of the size of the browser window, as shown in Figure 9-8.

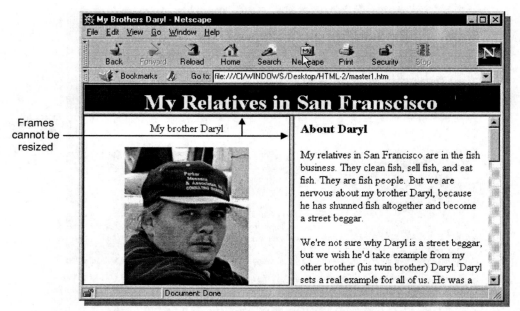

Figure 9-8: Result of <FRAME NORESIZE SCROLLING=no>

HTML Extensions for Frames

There are several useful HTML extensions available for frames. You should remember from DDC's *HTML 4.0 Fundamentals* course that extensions are tags and attributes that are not part of the official HTML 4.0 Specification (as maintained by the World Wide Web Consortium) but which have been introduced and advocated by third party organizations, typically Microsoft or Netscape.

Browser Support

All attributes listed in Table 9-3 are supported by both Microsoft IE 3.0 and more recent and Netscape Navigator 3.0 and more recent. Thus, you can use these attributes with a relatively high level of confidence.[19] Seriously consider the intended audience of your HTML documents and their likely browser version before using any of these extensions.

Attribute	Tag	Values	Description
BORDER	`<FRAMESET>`	pixels (numeric) Default=5	Specifies the thickness of all frame borders on a page.
BORDERCOLOR	■ `<FRAMESET>` ■ `<FRAME>`	■ RGB hexadecimal color value ■ 16 basic named colors	Specifies the color of all frame borders on a page (when used with the `<FRAMESET>` tag) or the borders for a particular frame (when used with the `<FRAME>` tag). Remember: all browsers recognize all RGB hex codes, but it is only safe to use the 16 basic English color names.
FRAMEBORDER	`<FRAMESET>`	■ YES ■ NO	Controls the inclusion of a frame border on *every* frame on a page. This attribute is available for the `<FRAME>` tag as part of the official HTML 4.0 Specification.

Table 9-3: HTML extensions for frames

[19] Use of tags, attributes, and character references new to the HTML Specification or introduced by Microsoft or Netscape is not recommended unless they are supported by *both* the current and previous versions of Microsoft Internet Explorer *and* Netscape Navigator/Communicator.

BORDER Attribute

The BORDER attribute to the <FRAMESET> tag allows you to specify the thickness of all frame borders in a Web page. The value of BORDER is defined as a numeric measure of pixels.

The default value of BORDER is five pixels.

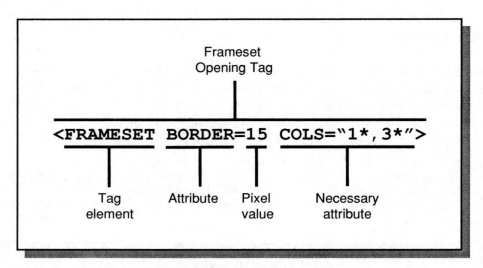

Figure 9-9: BORDER attribute syntax

 BORDER=0 can be used to eliminate the borders around *all* frames in a Web page.

However, this effect can also be accomplished by specifying a zero value to the FRAMEBORDER attribute for each <FRAME> tag. Because of the redundancy of using the FRAMEBORDER=0 tag on *each* <FRAME> tag in a master frame document, you may wish to use <FRAMESET BORDER=0...> instead.

BORDERCOLOR Attribute

Although an HTML extension (and thus not an official part of the HTML 4.0 Specification), the BORDER attribute to the <FRAMESET> tag allows you to specify the thickness of all frame borders in a Web page.

Value Set

The value of BORDERCOLOR is either: 1) an English color code or 2) an RGB hex color code. There is no default value for BORDERCOLOR.

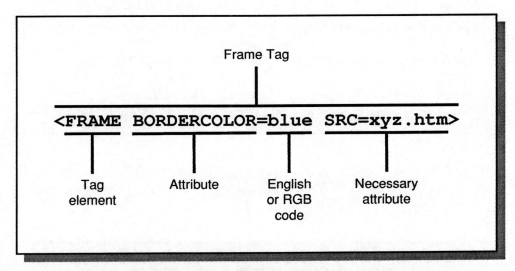

Figure 9-10: BORDERCOLOR attribute syntax

While all browsers support all RGB hexadecimal color codes (such as #00FF00), not all browsers recognize all English color names. Therefore, it is recommended that you limit yourself to the sixteen English color names, as listed in Table 9-4, that are recognized by all major browsers.

Aqua	Black	Blue	Fuchsia
Gray	Green	Lime	Maroon
Navy	Olive	Purple	Red
Silver	Teal	White	Yellow

Table 9-4: Sixteen "browser-safe" color designations

FRAMEBORDER Attribute

The FRAMEBORDER attribute can be confusing because it is both a part of the official HTML 4.0 Specification and also an HTML extension. How, you may ask, can this attribute possess characteristics that are seemingly mutually exclusive?

You may remember from DDC's *HTML 4.0 Fundamentals* that the same term can act as the name for different attributes to different HTML tags (a good example of this is the ALIGN attribute, used differently and with different value sets with tables, images, and horizontal rules).

Thus, FRAMEBORDER is:

- part of the HTML 4.0 Specification with respect to the <FRAME> tag

- an HTML extension when applied to the <FRAMESET> tag

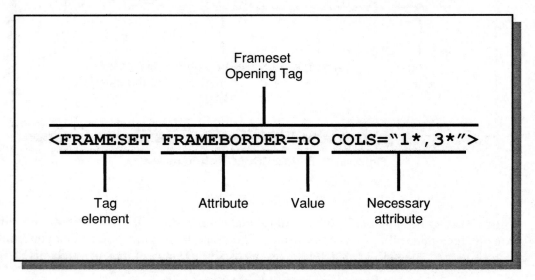

Figure 9-11: FRAMEBORDER attribute syntax

 The default value of FRAMEBORDER, when applied to either <FRAME> or <FRAMESET>, is YES. However, because the overall default behavior of a frame is to display borders, you need only use the FRAMEBORDER attribute if you wish to *not* display frame borders.

Exercise 9-5: Manipulating Frame Borders

In this exercise, you will control the thickness of frame borders using the BORDER attribute to the <FRAMESET> tag.

1. Open BORDERS.HTM in the HTML-2 folder in your browser. Note the appearance of the borders.

2. Toggle over to Notepad. Open BORDERS.HTM and add the following script that appears in bold:

   ```
   <FRAMESET BORDER=15 ROWS="1*,3*">
   ```

3. Save your changes and toggle over to your Web browser.

4. Reload BORDERS.HTM in your Web browser.

 All frame borders on the page increase in thickness (to 15 pixels), as shown in Figure 9-12.

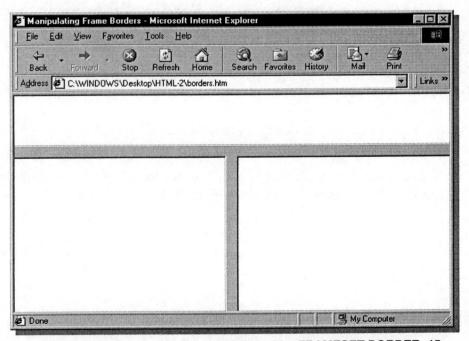

Figure 9-12: Frame borders made thicker with <FRAMESET BORDER=15>

5. Toggle back to BORDERS.HTM. Change the value of the BORDER attribute to 25 pixels.

6. Save your changes and toggle back to your Web browser.

7. Reload the HTML document. The borders should appear as in Figure 9-13.

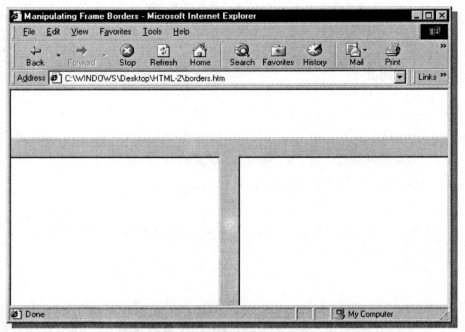

Figure 9-13: <FRAMESET BORDER=25>

8. Toggle back to BORDERS.HTM and add the following script that appears in bold:

```
<FRAMESET BORDER=10 BORDERCOLOR=navy ROWS="1*,3*">
```

9. Save your changes and toggle back to your Web browser. Reload the HTML document. The borders should appear as in Figure 9-14 on the following page.

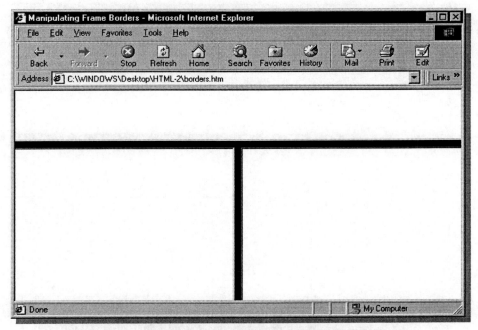

Figure 9-14: <FRAMESET BORDER=10 BORDERCOLOR=navy>

10. Toggle back to BORDERS.HTM. Remove the BORDERCOLOR attribute from the opening <FRAMESET> tag.

11. Add the following script that appears in bold:

```
<FRAMESET BORDER=10 ROWS="1*,3*">

     <FRAME BORDERCOLOR=red>

     <FRAMESET COLS="*,*">
          <FRAME>
          <FRAME>
```

12. Save your changes and toggle back to your Web browser. Reload the Web page.

The horizontal border is now red, while the vertical border reverts to default gray, as shown in Figure 9-15 on the following page.

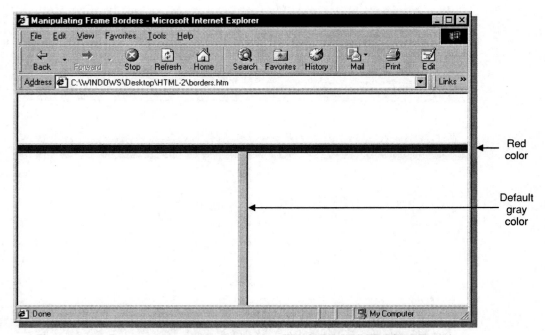

Figure 9-15: Frame color manipulated via <FRAME BORDERCOLOR=red>

13. Toggle back to BORDERS.HTM.

14. Add the following script that appears in bold:

```
<FRAMESET BORDER=10 ROWS="1*,3*">

     <FRAME BORDERCOLOR=red>

     <FRAMESET COLS="*,*">
          <FRAME BORDERCOLOR=green>
          <FRAME>
```

15. Save your changes and toggle back to your Web browser. Reload the Web page.

The vertical frame border is displayed in green, while the horizontal frame border continues to be displayed in red.

By applying the BORDERCOLOR attribute at the <FRAME> level, you can more finely control the colors of borders and mix frame colors in a single page.

DDC Publishing • www.ddcpub.com

Exercise 9-6: Turning Off Frame Borders

In this exercise, you will configure a FRAMESET to hide frame borders.

1. In your Web browser, open MASTER1.HTM. Note the default appearance of the borders.

2. Toggle over to Notepad and open MASTER1.HTM.

3. Add the following script that appears in bold:

    ```
    <FRAMESET FRAMEBORDER=no ROWS="15%,85%">
    ```

4. Save your changes and toggle over to your Web browser. Reload the Web page.

 The frame borders of all frames on the page are no longer visible, as shown in Figure 9-16. You can create aesthetically appealing page effects by combining background colors with borderless frames.

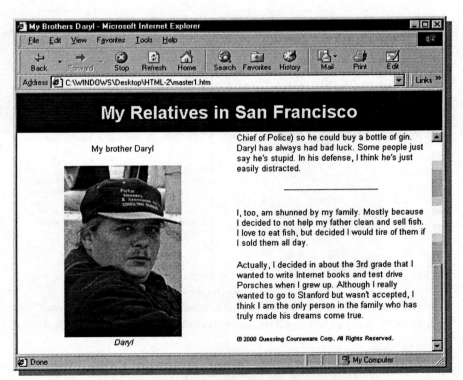

Figure 9-16: Page with <FRAMESET FRAMEBORDER=no>

5. Toggle back to Notepad and remove the FRAMEBORDER attribute from the opening <FRAMESET> tag.

6. Add the script that appears below in bold:

```
<FRAMESET COLS="50%,50%">
    <FRAME NORESIZE SCROLLING=no FRAMEBORDER=no SRC=daryl.htm>
    <FRAME NORESIZE SRC=about_daryl.htm>
</FRAMESET>
```

7. Save your changes and toggle over to your Web browser. Reload the Web page.

 The frame borders of the lower left frame are no longer visible, as shown in Figure 9-17.

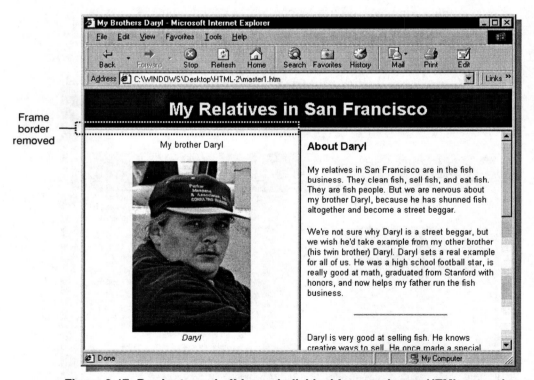

Figure 9-17: Border turned off for an individual frame using an HTML extension

 <FRAME FRAMEBORDER=no> works in Internet Explorer 4 and 5, but not in Netscape Navigator. In Navigator, the border will remain visible.

Exercise 9-7: Adding Margin Space to Frames

In this exercise, you will add margin space to frames by using the `MARGINHEIGHT` and `MARGINWIDTH` attributes to the `<FRAME>` tag.

1. Toggle over to Notepad (with MASTER1.HTM open).

2. Remove the `FRAMEBORDER` attribute from the `<FRAME>` tag.

3. Add the script that appears below in bold:

```
<FRAME MARGINHEIGHT=15 SCROLLING=no NORESIZE SRC=relatives.htm>

<FRAMESET COLS="50%,50%">
   <FRAME MARGINHEIGHT=35 NORESIZE SCROLLING=no SRC=daryl.htm>
   <FRAME MARGINHEIGHT=35 NORESIZE SRC=about_daryl.htm>
</FRAMESET>
```

4. Save your HTML document. Toggle over to your Web browser. Reload the Web page.

 The frames now appear with more white space at the top and bottom, as shown in Figure 9-18. Text in the right frame touches the border.

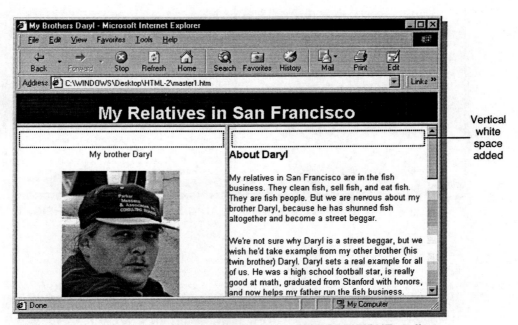

Figure 9-18: Vertical white space added with the MARGINHEIGHT attribute

5. Toggle over to Notepad.

6. Add the script that appears below in bold:

```
<FRAMESET COLS="50%,50%">
        <FRAME MARGINHEIGHT=35 NORESIZE SCROLLING=no SRC=daryl.htm>
        <FRAME MARGINHEIGHT=35 MARGINWIDTH=30 NORESIZE
        SRC=about_daryl.htm>
</FRAMESET>
```

7. Save your HTML document. Toggle over to your Web browser. Reload the Web page.

 The right frame now appears with a wider margin (more white space) between the text and the left and right frame borders, as shown in Figure 9-19.

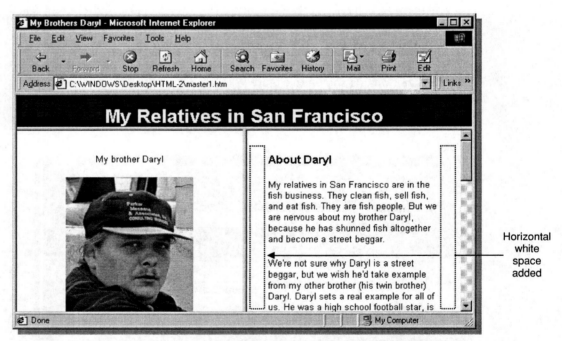

Figure 9-19: White space added via MARGINWIDTH and MARGINHEIGHT

<NOFRAMES> Tag

Although the majority of Web browser users have frames-enabled browsers, you may desire to accommodate those who are using browsers not capable of displaying frames (NCSA Mosaic, versions of Navigator prior to 2.0, and versions of Microsoft IE prior to 2.1). To do this, simply nest alternate HTML code between the opening and closing <NOFRAMES> tags.

 Place the <NOFRAMES> tag set *after* the closing </FRAMESET> tag but *before* the closing </HTML> tag.

An example using the <NOFRAMES> tag to offer a non-frames version of your page follows:

```
<FRAMESET ROWS="*, 3*">
    <FRAME SRC=slave1.htm>
    <FRAMESET COLS="100, *">
          <FRAME SRC=slave2.htm>
          <FRAME SRC=slave3.htm>
</FRAMESET>

<NOFRAMES>
    <!-- alternate HTML code goes here -->
</NOFRAMES>

</HTML>
```

Recognizing Non-Frames Browsers

It is important to notify users of non-frames enabled browsers of the fact that your site contains frames and, thus, requires a frames-enabled browser for proper viewing. You can accomplish this by inserting a simple text message between the opening and closing <NOFRAMES> tags that informs users that your site requires a frames-enabled browser.

An example using the <NOFRAMES> tag to identify non-frames enabled browsers follows:

```
<FRAMESET COLS="1*,4*">
        <FRAME SRC=slave1.htm>
        <FRAME SRC=slave2.htm>
</FRAMESET>

<NOFRAMES>
    Your browser is not capable of viewing frames; this Web site
    requires a frames-enabled browser.
</NOFRAMES>
```

Exercise 9-8: Notifying Non-Frames Enabled Browsers of Your Status

In this exercise, you will add script to a frames-enabled HTML document that notifies Web browsers not capable of viewing frames that they will not be able to view the content of your site.

1. Toggle over to Notepad.

2. Add the following script to MASTER1.HTM after the closing </FRAMESET> tag but before the closing </HTML> tag:

```
<NOFRAMES>
     This Web site requires a frames-enabled browser. Your browser
     is not capable of viewing frames. To view this site, please
     upgrade to a browser such as Netscape Navigator, Netscape
     Communicator, or Microsoft Internet Explorer.
</NOFRAMES>
```

3. Save the HTML document and toggle over to your Web browser.

4. Reload the Web page in your browser.

You should notice no difference in the appearance of the Web page. Because you are using a frames-enabled browser, the content between the opening and closing <NOFRAMES> tags is not displayed.

If you were using a browser not capable of viewing frames, this content would be displayed (and the content between the <FRAMESET> tags would be ignored).

This is because frames-enabled browsers, such as Microsoft Internet Explorer and Netscape Navigator/Communicator, are programmed to ignore the content of the <NOFRAMES> tags.

Lesson 9 Summary

▶ You can use a variety of attributes to precisely configure the layout and appearance of frames and frame content.

▶ You can mix columns and rows in a single page.

▶ There are three methods by which you can mix columns and rows in a page: 1) nesting a FRAMESET within a FRAMESET; 2) mixing ROWS and COLS attributes in a single <FRAMESET> opening tag; and 3) referring to a master frame document from a <FRAME> tag.

▶ Other attributes that can be added to the <FRAME> tag are SCROLLING, NORESIZE, MARGINHEIGHT, and MARGINWIDTH.

▶ Other attributes that can be added to the <FRAMESET> tag are BORDERS, and FRAMEBORDERS.

▶ You can rearrange the frames in a frames page simply be reordering the <FRAME> tags in a master frame document.

▶ BORDER, BORDERCOLOR, and FRAMEBORDER are all extensions to HTML and not part of the official HTML 4.0 Specification. However, all of these attributes are supported by Netscape Navigator 3.0 and more recent and Microsoft Internet Explorer 3.0 and more recent, so you can safely apply these attributes to your frames.

▶ Netscape Navigator and Microsoft Internet Explorer display frame borders differently.

▶ All browsers recognize and properly interpret all RGB color codes. However, not all browsers recognize all English color names. To be safe, you should only use the 16 English color codes that are recognized by all major browsers.

▶ To accommodate Web users who are not using a frames-enabled browser, you should: 1) include alternate HTML code between the <NOFRAMES> tags or 2) notify users that your page contains frames, that their browser is not capable of viewing frames, and that they must upgrade their browser to one that is frames-capable.

▶ The tag used to display a message to users of non-frames enabled browsers (that will not be displayed to users of frames-enabled browsers) is the <NOFRAMES> tag. <NOFRAMES> is a non-empty tag set.

Lesson 9 Quiz

Matching

_____ 1. displayed alongside a frame   a. `<FRAMETAG>`

_____ 2. must exist for each frame in a set   b. `BORDER`

_____ 3. prevents visitors from re-sizing the frame   c. `NORESIZE`

_____ 4. width may be specified   d. `SCROLLING`

_____ 5. border surrounding the frame   e. pixel

Fill in the Blank

6. An _____ is used to describe the relative size of multiple columns or rows in the same set.

7. If your master frameset will be laid out primarily in columns, you will want to use the _____ attribute of the frameset tag to specify the width of each column.

8. Within the _____ tag, one _____ tag must exist for each frame in the set.

9. To accommodate visitors to your site who are not using a frames-enabled browser, nest alternate HTML code in between the _____ and _____.

10. _____ is one of three HTML extensions covered in this Lesson.

True or False?

_T / F_   11. Column widths may be specified in pixels or as a percentage of the width of the window.

_T / F_   12. Clicking on a hyperlink in a document displayed in one frame can cause the contents of that or a different frame to change.

_T / F_   13. Microsoft's frames standard enables Web developers to divide their Web pages into a series of frames.

_T / F_   14. Navigator and Internet Explorer display frame borders almost identically.

_T / F_   15. `<NOFRAMES>` is interpreted properly by IE, but not by Navigator.

Lesson 10
Linking Frames

Lesson Topics

▶ Linking Frames Overview

▶ Reserved TARGET Values

▶ Navigation Bars

▶ Creating a Nav Bar

▶ Inline Frames

▶ Lesson 10 Summary

Linking Frames Overview

In Lesson 9: *Advanced Frame Layout*, you learned to create both simple and complex frame configurations. All of the frames you have created, however, work relatively independently. Although they share the same page and typically contain related subject matter, they are not *dynamic*. In other words, the manner in which a user interacts with one frame does not affect the contents of another frame.

Nav Bars & Navigation Structures

By linking frames, you can create even more sophisticated page and site layouts, such as a nav bar, a table of contents, or an online catalog. In this manner, you can use frames to control the manner in which a user navigates your entire Web site.

You already know how to create hyperlinks using the Anchor tag (<A>). To link frames, you simply have to learn some new attributes to tags you already understand. As you begin to harness the more powerful aspects of HTML, much of the new power of the scripting language comes from new attributes to "old" tags.

NAME & TARGET

There are two new attributes you need to learn in order to create a basic link between two frames. The first is NAME, which is an attribute to the <FRAME> tag that provides a unique identifier to a slave frame document. The second is TARGET, which is an attribute to the <A> tag. Basically, the TARGET attribute tells the Anchor tag *where* (in what frame) to display an HTML document.

- NAME: attribute to the <FRAME> tag; provides a unique identifier to a frame so that an Anchor tag can link to it.

- TARGET: attribute to the <A> tag; instructs the Anchor tag to display the file to which it links in a particular frame (by identifying a NAME reference within a <FRAME> tag).

The script for a simple link in one frame that loads a different HTML document into a *different* frame is as follows:

1. Script in frame that changes:

   ```
   <FRAME SRC=slave1.htm NAME=changeme>
   ```

2. Script in frame which contains a hyperlink that changes the above frame:

   ```
   <A HREF=slave2.htm TARGET=changeme>Click here to view more
   information</A>
   ```

Exercise 10-1: Creating a Simple Link Between Frames

In this exercise, you will create a simple link between two frames in a single page.

1. Open a new file in Notepad.
2. Type the following script:

```
<HTML>

<HEAD>
<TITLE>Explore the Great Lakes</TITLE>
</HEAD>

<FRAMESET ROWS="*,2*">

        <FRAMESET COLS="3*,2*">
                <FRAME SRC=title.htm NAME=title>
                <FRAME SRC=index.htm NAME=index>
        </FRAMESET>

        <FRAME SRC=erie.htm NAME=main>

</FRAMESET>

<NOFRAMES>

<H3>Welcome to the "Exploring the Great Lakes" Web Site</H3>

You need a frames-compatible browser, such as Netscape 2.0 and
above, to view this site.

</NOFRAMES>

</HTML>
```

3. Save the file as MASTERLINK.HTM in the HTML-2 folder.

4. Open a new file in Notepad. Type the following script:

```
<HTML>

<HEAD>
</HEAD>

<BODY BGCOLOR=blue>

<CENTER>

<FONT SIZE=+3 COLOR=white>Exploring the Great Lakes</FONT><BR>

</CENTER>

</BODY>
</HTML>
```

5. Save the file as TITLE.HTM in the HTML-2 folder.

6. Open a new file in Notepad. Type the following script:

```
<HTML>

<HEAD>
<TITLE>Hyperlink Navigation</TITLE>
</HEAD>

<BODY>

<CENTER>

<A HREF=erie.htm TARGET=main>Lake Erie Info</A><BR>
<A HREF=erie.jpg TARGET=main>Lake Erie Photo</A><P>

<A HREF=michigan.htm TARGET=main>Lake Michigan Info</A><BR>
<A HREF=michigan.jpg TARGET=main>Lake Michigan Photo</A><P>

<A HREF=superior.htm TARGET=main>Lake Superior Info</A><BR>
<A HREF=superior.jpg TARGET=main>Lake Superior Photo</A><P>

</CENTER>

</BODY>
</HTML>
```

7. Save the document as INDEX.HTM in the HTML-2 folder.

8. Toggle over to your Web browser.

9. Open the file MASTERLINK.HTM from the HTML-2 folder.

 A three frame page is downloaded and displayed, as shown in Figure 10-1.

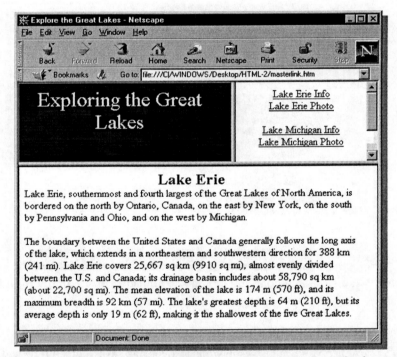

Figure 10-1: Example of frames linking to other frames in a single page

10. In the upper right frame, click the **Lake Michigan Info** hyperlink.

 The contents of the main (lowest) frame change to display the content of the MICHIGAN.HTM document.

11. In the upper right frame, click the **Lake Erie Photo** hyperlink.

The contents of the main frame change to display the file ERIE.JPG, as shown in Figure 10-2. Note that this is not an HTML document, but rather a stand-alone image file.

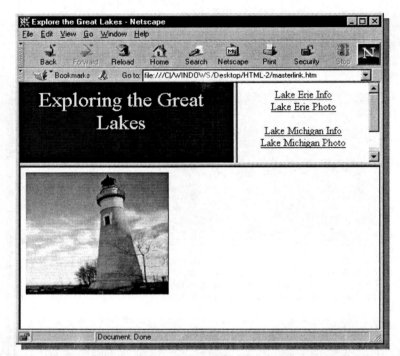

Figure 10-2: Main frame contents changed by clicking link in upper right frame

When you want to display images, you can save yourself time and effort by displaying the raw image file (instead of embedding the image file in an HTML document).

Referring directly to an image file, however, does not allow you to format the image by adding a caption or centering the image.

12. Click all of the other links in the upper right frame to ensure that they function properly. If any of the links do not work, open INDEX.HTM, find the problem, and fix it. Retest any links after you repair them.

<BASE> Tag

You can greatly simplify the script involved in the Anchor tags in a referring frame. Using the <BASE> tag allows you to specify the target of all Anchor tags in the page with a single TARGET attribute.

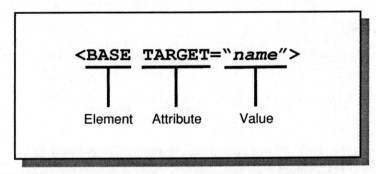

Figure 10-3: Syntax of the <BASE> tag when used to specify a frame hyperlink target

An example of a referring frame with the <BASE> tag and TARGET attribute follows:

```
<HTML>

<BASE TARGET="name">

<HEAD>
<TITLE>Your Page Title</TITLE>
</HEAD>

<BODY>
```

If both a hyperlink (Anchor tag) with a TARGET attribute and a <BASE> tag with a TARGET attribute are present in the same referring frame, the Anchor tag TARGET takes precedent.

In other words, if all Anchor tags have their own TARGET attributes, any TARGET contained in the <BASE> tag will be ignored.

Exercise 10-2: Simplifying a TARGET with Multiple Hyperlinks

In this exercise, you will simplify the INDEX.HTM page by omitting the individual TARGET attributes in the Anchor tags and replacing them with a single TARGET attribute at the beginning of the HTML document.

1. Toggle over to Notepad.

2. Open INDEX.HTM.

3. Remove the TARGET attributes from each of the Anchor tags <A HREF=erie.htm TARGET=main>.

4. Type the following script that appears in bold:

```
<HTML>

<BASE TARGET=main>

<HEAD>
<TITLE>Hyperlink Navigation</TITLE>
</HEAD>
```

5. Save INDEX.HTM.

6. Toggle over to your Web browser.

7. Reload **MASTERLINK.HTM** in your Web browser.

8. Click any link in the upper right frame.

 The frames should function exactly as in the previous exercise; the purpose of this exercise was to illustrate that you can save yourself considerable time and effort by placing a single TARGET attribute in a <BASE> tag above the <HEAD>, instead of a TARGET attribute in each of the anchors that refers to the target frame.

Reserved TARGET Values

Four reserved TARGET attribute values (sometimes called *reserved implicit frame names*) can be used to create specific results when a user clicks a hyperlink in a frame.

You can use these reserved TARGET values to:

- load the results of a hyperlink into a new, unnamed window;

- load the content into the calling frame (in which the anchor itself resides);

- load content called by an anchor into a parent frame set;

- load content called by an anchor into a "top level" frame set.

Table 10-1 displays these four reserved TARGET values.

Attribute Value	Function
_blank	Loads the HTML document (or file, as in the case of an image) specified in the Anchor tag into a new, unnamed window. This will completely wipe out the current frame set in the browser window.
_self	Loads the HTML document (or file) into the calling (referring) frame. This is the default if no NAME or TARGET attributes are used in the frame set.
_parent	Loads the HTML document into the calling frame's parent frameset window.
_top	Loads the HTML document into the calling frame's top level frame set.

Table 10-1: The four implicit reserved frame names (TARGET attribute values)

 You can use the _blank value with any hyperlink anchor; it does not have to be a frames page or a link from one frame to another frame. In this manner, you can offer a link on your Web site that refers to a page on another Web site without pushing the user away from your site.

When the user clicks the link, a new window will appear on his or her desktop, in addition to the window displaying the referring anchor. When the user is done viewing the new page, he or she can close out of the window, exposing the original page containing the calling anchor on your site.

Exercise 10-3: Using Reserved TARGET Values

In this exercise, you will use two of the reserved TARGET values to link from one frame to another.

1. Toggle over to Notepad.
2. Open INDEX.HTM (if necessary).
3. Add the following script that appears in bold:

```
<HTML>

<BASE TARGET="_blank">

<HEAD>
<TITLE>Hyperlink Navigation</TITLE>
```

4. Save the HTML document.
5. Toggle over to your Web browser.
6. Reload MASTERLINK.HTM.
7. In the upper right frame, click any of the hyperlinks.

 The target of the calling hyperlink is opened in a new window that overlaps the existing window.

8. Toggle back to Notepad.
9. Add the following script that appears in bold:

```
<HTML>

<BASE TARGET="_self">

<HEAD>
<TITLE>Hyperlink Navigation</TITLE>
```

10. Save the HTML document.

11. Toggle over to your Web browser.

12. Reload the Web page.

13. In the upper right frame, click any of the hyperlinks.

 The target of the calling hyperlink is opened in the upper right frame, the frame from which it was called, as shown in Figure 10-4.

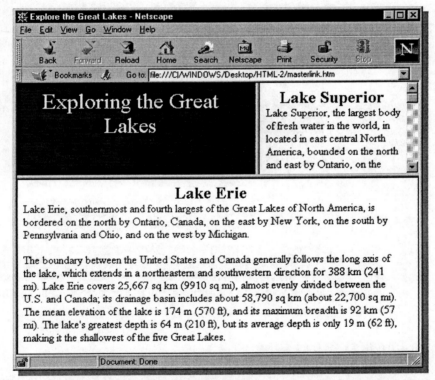

Figure 10-4: Hyperlink displays referred document in same frame via TARGET="_self"

14. On the toolbar, click the **Back** button. The frame will display its previous contents.

15. In the upper right frame, click another hyperlink. The contents of the frame will change to display the target HTML document.

Navigation Bars

A functional application of links between frames is that of a navigation bar, or "nav bar." Nav bars, which are typically available from each page of a Web site, are narrow strips of the page partitioned off through the use of two or three frames, as shown in Figure 10-5.

The nav bar, which can appear on the left, right, top, or bottom of the page (most commonly in the left frame), acts as a convenient index to the contents of the entire site. The nav bar also prevents a visitor to your site from becoming lost or confused, especially on large sites.

Figure 10-5: An example of a Web site featuring a nav bar created with linked frames

Link to Main Content Areas Only

The nav bar should be a "top level" overview of the main content areas of the site. It should accomplish two major goals: 1) provide access to the major topic areas of your Web site and 2) provide a quick and convenient visual synopsis of the contents of your site to all visitors.

The following general rules should be observed when adding a nav bar to your Web site:

- the nav bar should not provide links to *too many* topic areas; it should truly be access to only the top level subject areas of your site (6-12 links);

- the nav bar should not provide links to *too few* areas; it should give the user a brief, but comprehensive, glimpse of the contents of your site;

- the nav bar should appear on every page of your site;

- the nav bar should contain text hyperlinks that are clearly understood (not ambiguous icons or confusing graphics).

Exercise 10-4: Surveying Nav Bar Examples on the Web

In this exercise, you will view examples of actual nav bars integrated into Web sites using HTML frames.

1. Click once in your Web browser's **URL** field, type the following address, and press <ENTER>:

   ➢ **www.familycenteredcare.org**

 A Web page that is composed of three frames is downloaded and displayed. The top frame acts as a nav bar. The left frame integrates with the top to create a smooth, attractive appearance. The bottom frame is the content frame, as shown in Figure 10-6.

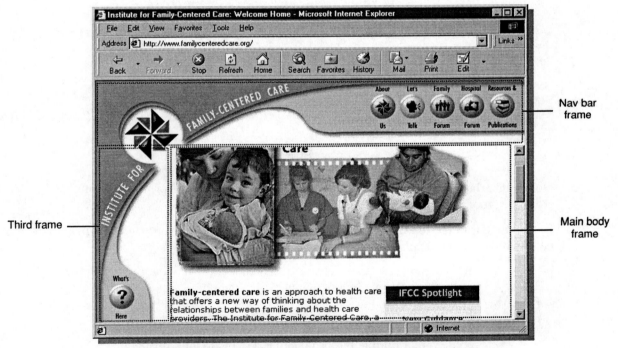

Figure 10-6: Example of nav bar at top of page that does not change

2. At the top of the nav bar, click the **About Us** hyperlink.

A new page, featuring a new frameset, is downloaded and displayed. Note that the nav bar in the top frame is different for the new page.

3. On the toolbar, click the **Back** button.

4. On the nav bar, click the **Family Forum** hyperlink.

A new page is downloaded and displayed. The content area changes completely.

Note the seamlessness of the frames. The author(s) of this site employed the FRAMEBORDER=0 and BORDER=0 attributes in the <FRAMESET> opening tag.

5. Click once in the **URL** field, type the following address, and press <ENTER>:

➢ **www.finalbell.com**

The home page will be downloaded and displayed.

6. Notice that the page is split into three frames, very similar to the previous example. However, the left frame features a scroll bar.

7. In the nav bar in the top frame, click the **BUSINESS** hyperlink. The *Business* page will be downloaded and displayed.

Although a new frameset was downloaded, the nav bar did not move, expand, or change in any manner, as shown in

Figure 10-7 on the following page. This is a standard nav bar containing multiple hyperlinks that download and display pages in the content frame using the TARGET and NAME attributes.

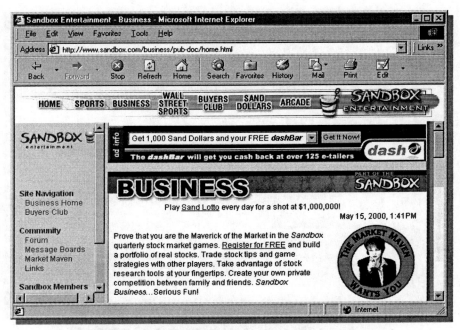

Figure 10-7: Page accessed via an anchor (link) on the nav bar

8. Click a different link on the nav bar to download and display a different HTML document in the content frame.

9. Click once in the **URL** field, type the following address, and press <ENTER>:

➢ **www.aetcorp.net**

The AET Corporation home page is downloaded and displayed. The home page does not feature frames or nav bars, but the subpages do.

10. On the home page, click the **products** hyperlink. Another page will be downloaded that displays three frames, one of which is a nav bar.

11. In the left frame nav bar, click the **training** hyperlink.

A new page is downloaded and displayed in the content frame, as shown in

Figure 10-8 on the following page. The nav bar does not change.

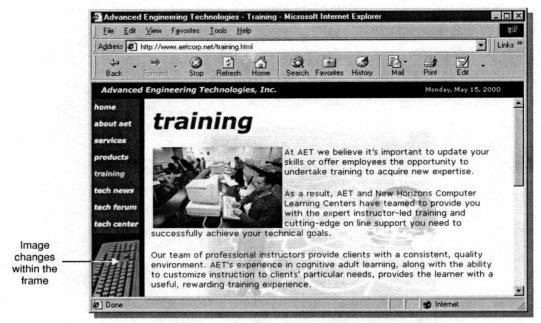

Image changes within the frame

Figure 10-8: Nav bar configured as left frame

12. In the nav bar, click the **tech news** hyperlink.

The contents of the main frame change to display the new page that is downloaded. The top frame does not change. The bottom of the left nav bar frame switches to a new image.

13. In the nav bar, click the **Services** hyperlink. This will download and display a new HTML document in the main content frame and change the image at the bottom of the nav bar.

14. Click other links in the nav bar, noting the different images that appear at the bottom of the nav bar frame.

15. If time permits, visit **www.tsrc.net/newhome.nsf**. Use the nav bars in the top and right frames to view different Web pages on this site.

16. What is different about this site from the others you visited in this exercise?

Creating a Nav Bar

Before you add a nav bar to an existing Web site or create a new site that will feature one, you should think about the consequences it will have on your site. Remember that the nav bar should appear on every page of the site (or nearly every page).

In the following set of exercises, you will create a set of Web pages, each of which is laid out as a three frame page. Each frame will serve a different purpose as listed below:

- <u>top frame</u>: a masthead, displaying the name of a fictitious organization;

- <u>left frame</u>: the nav bar;

- <u>right frame</u>: the content frame and the target of any HTML documents referred to by anchors in the nav bar.

Plan Your Page Layout

You should first plan the layout of your page using no references to actual slave frame files. This will allow you to determine the exact layout of the masthead frame, the nav bar frame, and the content frame.

The frames layout on the pages you will create in the following exercises is shown in Figure 10-9.

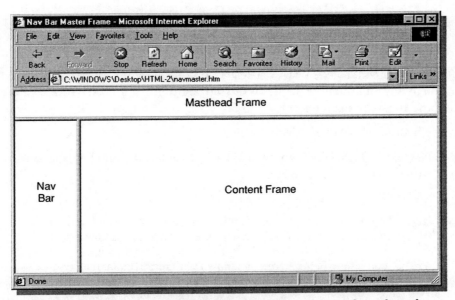

Figure 10-9: Layout of a Web site incorporating a frames-based nav bar

Exercise 10-5: Laying Out the Frame Document

In this exercise, you will create the master frame document for a Web site that incorporates a nav bar on each page of the site.

1. Toggle over to Notepad.

2. Open a new document in Notepad.

3. Type the following script:

```
<HTML>

<HEAD>
<TITLE>Nav Bar Master Frame</TITLE>
</HEAD>

<FRAMESET ROWS="15%,85%">

        <FRAME SCROLLING=no NORESIZE>

        <FRAMESET COLS="15%,85%">
             <FRAME NORESIZE>
             <FRAME NAME=master NORESIZE>
        </FRAMESET>

</FRAMESET>

</HTML>
```

4. Save the document as NAVMASTER.HTM in the HTML-2 folder. Note that this document does not include the necessary attribute SRC for each <FRAME> tag. You will add these in a later exercise.

5. Toggle over to your Web browser.

6. Open NAVMASTER.HTM from the HTML-2 folder. It should appear similar to Figure 10-9 on the previous page.

A unique characteristic of both Microsoft IE 5.0x and Netscape Navigator 4.0x is that both will properly interpret and display a frames document lacking SRC attributes. The result is a frames page containing blank frames, as shown in Figure 10-9 on the previous page.

This feature is helpful when planning the layout of a frames-based page or experimenting with frames.

Exercise 10-6: Creating the Nav Bar Slave Document

In this exercise, you will create the nav bar slave document. This document allows easy navigation because it contains the frame content visible on every page of the Web site.

1. Toggle over to Notepad.

2. Open a new document in Notepad.

3. Type the following script:

```
<HTML>
<HEAD>
</HEAD>
<BODY>
<CENTER>
<A HREF=about_dogs.htm TARGET="master"><B>Dog Info</B></A><P>
<HR WIDTH=40% SIZE=6><P>
<A HREF=about_hogs.htm TARGET="master"><B>Hog Info</B></A><P>
<HR WIDTH=40% SIZE=6><P>
<A HREF=about_cats.htm TARGET="master"><B>Cat Info</B></A><P>
<HR WIDTH=40% SIZE=6><P>
<A HREF=about_horses.htm TARGET="master"><B>Horse Info</B></A><P>
</CENTER>
</BODY>
</HTML>
```

4. Save the document as NAV_BAR.HTM in the HTML-2 folder.

Exercise 10-7: Creating the Masthead Slave Document

In this exercise, you will create the masthead slave document that will be visible from each page of the Web site.

1. Open a new document in Notepad.

2. Type the following script:

```
<HTML>

<HEAD>
</HEAD>

<BODY BGCOLOR=navy>

<CENTER>
<FONT FACE=arial COLOR=white SIZE=+3>The Animal Information
Site</FONT>
</CENTER>

</BODY>

</HTML>
```

3. Save the document as MASTHEAD.HTM in the HTML-2 folder.

Exercise 10-8: Creating the "Blank" Content Document

In this exercise, you will create the "blank" content slave document that will occupy the content frame until the user clicks one of the hyperlinks in the nav bar (left frame).

1. Open a new document in Notepad.

2. Type the following script:

```
<HTML>

<HEAD>
</HEAD>

<A NAME="master"></A>

<FONT SIZE=+2 COLOR=navy>Want to learn more about animals? Click
the links in the left column....</FONT>

</HTML>
```

3. Save the document as ABOUT_ANIMALS.HTM in the HTML-2 folder.

Exercise 10-9: Viewing the Master Frame Document

In this exercise, you will view the master frame document. The documents referred to by the hyperlinks in the nav bar have already been created for you.

1. In Notepad, open NAVMASTER.HTM from the HTML-2 folder.

2. Add the script that appears in bold:

```
<FRAMESET ROWS="15%,85%">

        <FRAME SRC=masthead.htm SCROLLING=no NORESIZE>

        <FRAMESET COLS="15%,85%">
                <FRAME SRC=nav_bar.htm NORESIZE>
                <FRAME SRC=about_animals.htm NAME="master" NORESIZE>
```

3. Save the file. Toggle over to your Web browser and open the NAVMASTER.HTM.

4. Click any of the hyperlinks in the nav bar (left frame).

 The right frame (content frame) changes to display the document referred to by the hyperlink you clicked in the nav bar, as shown in Figure 10-10.

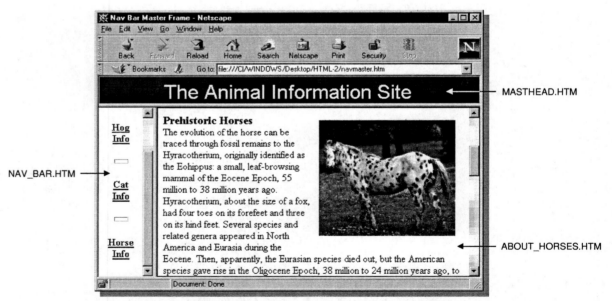

Figure 10-10: Master frame document displaying all slave documents

5. Click other links in the nav bar and notice the content change in the right frame. This is accomplished via TARGET and NAME attributes.

Inline Frames

Inline frames (<IFRAME>) are a new and unique type of Web page frame. Sometimes called "floating frames," these page elements provide a "window" in a page through which a user can view another Web page. Although not in common usage, this type of frame offers utility and flexibility that will make it increasingly popular.

Flexible & Unique

Unlike conventional frames, inline frames are not relegated to the edge of a Web page. Whereas conventional frames split an entire Web page into a minimum of two frames, inline frames allow a minimum of one frame. Another benefit of inline frames is flexibility. Inline frames can be any size and located nearly anywhere on a page. Figure 10-11 displays an example of an inline frame.

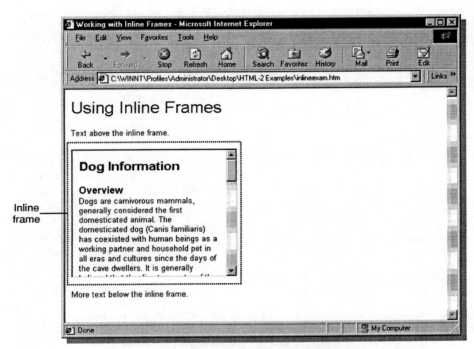

Figure 10-11: An inline frame

<IFRAME> Characteristics

- <IFRAME> tag is non-empty;

- <IFRAME> has nine attributes;

- You can include any type of data within an inline frame, including inline images and stylized (formatted) text.

Not Supported by Netscape

The biggest drawback of inline frames is that they are not currently supported by Netscape Navigator (as of version 4.08, which is a component of Netscape Communicator 4.5). Inline frames are, however, part of the official HTML 4.0 Specification as published by the W3C. It is ironic, given Netscape's leadership role in establishing and promoting HTML standards, that it does not support this new type of frame.

Unless you are scripting pages for an intranet on which all users have Microsoft Internet Explorer 4.0 or more recent (which does support inline frames), you should refrain from using inline frames. In the near future, when both major browsers support inline frames, it will be safe to use them on "public" external Web sites.

Attributes & Values

Table 10-2 outlines the attributes and their associated values for the <IFRAME> tag.

Attribute	Values	Comment
ALIGN	left | center | right | top | middle | bottom	Text flows around an inline frame, regardless of its location.
FRAMEBORDER	1 | 0	1 = on; 0 = off 1 is the default. Thus, only use this attribute if you desire to turn the frame border OFF.
HEIGHT	number | %	number = # of pixels; % = % of browser window
WIDTH	number | %	number = # of pixels; % = % of browser window
MARGINHEIGHT	number | %	number = # of pixels; % = % of browser window
MARGINWIDTH	number | %	number = # of pixels; % = % of browser window
NAME	text string	This provides a target name for the frame.
SCROLLING	yes | no	It is typically unwise to turn scrolling off because you have no control over a user's video configuration and browser size.
SRC	URL	SRC functions here identically to its use with standard frames.

Table 10-2: <IFRAME> attributes and attribute values

Exercise 10-10: Using and Manipulating Inline Frames

In this exercise, you will place an inline frame in a Web page and manipulate the frame using a variety of attributes.

If you are using Netscape Navigator, you should skip this exercise as Navigator does not currently recognize inline frames. If you have Microsoft Internet Explorer on your PC, launch it and complete this exercise.

1. Switch to Notepad.

2. Open the file INLINE_FRAME.HTM in the HTML-2 folder.

3. Add the following script that appears in bold:

```
<HTML>

<HEAD>
<TITLE>Working with Inline Frames</TITLE>
</HEAD>

<BODY>

<FONT SIZE=+2 COLOR=blue>The 50 United States</FONT>.<P>

To know about America, you have to study the states and their
history.<P>

<IFRAME SRC=ohio.htm WIDTH=50% HEIGHT=240>
</IFRAME><P><BR><P>

For maps of thousands of locations in the United States, consult
the <A HREF=http://www.mapquest.com>MapQuest Web site</A>.

</BODY>
</HTML>
```

4. Save the file.

5. Toggle over to Internet Explorer.

6. Open the file INLINE_FRAME.HTM in the HTML-2 folder.

The page is downloaded and displayed, as shown in Figure 10-12.

Note the default alignment of the frame (left) and the default appearance of the frame border and scroll bar (because the content of the frame exceeds its viewable area).

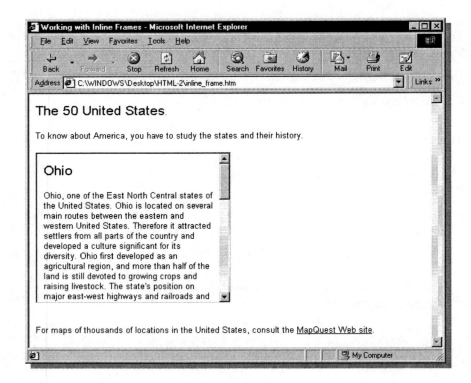

Figure 10-12: Inline frame displaying scrollable information

7. Toggle over to Notepad.

8. Add the following script that appears in bold:

```
<IFRAME SRC=texas.htm WIDTH=50% HEIGHT=240 ALIGN=right>
```

9. Save the document.

10. Toggle over to Internet Explorer and refresh the Web page (<F5>).

The updated page is downloaded and displayed, as shown in Figure 10-13. Note the right alignment of the frame and the new frame content.

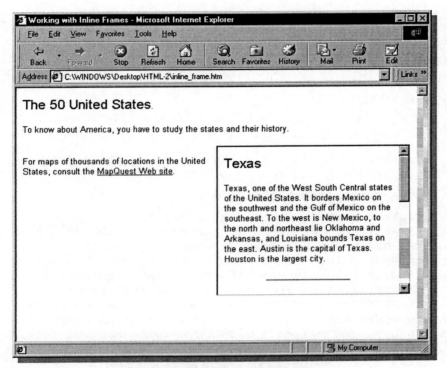

Figure 10-13: Inline frame aligned right

Exercise 10-11: Linking to an Inline Frame

In this exercise, you will create links to an inline frame using the TARGET and NAME attributes (just like you did in Lesson 8: *Introduction to Frames*). If you are using Netscape Navigator, you should skip this exercise as Navigator does not currently recognize inline frames. If you have Microsoft Internet Explorer on your PC, launch it and complete this exercise.

1. Toggle over to Notepad.

2. Add the bold text that appears below and delete the text shown in bold strikethrough in INLINE_FRAME.HTM:

   ```
   <FONT SIZE=+2 COLOR=blue>The 50 United States</FONT>.<P>

   To know about America, you have to study the states and their
   history.<P>

   Select a state from the list:<P>

   <UL TYPE=square>
   <LI><A HREF=ohio.htm TARGET="state">Ohio</A>
   <LI><A HREF=texas.htm TARGET="state">Texas</A>
   <LI><A HREF=colorado.htm TARGET="state">Colorado</A>
   <LI><A HREF=virginia.htm TARGET="state">Virginia</A>
   <LI><A HREF=florida.htm TARGET="state">Florida</A>
   <LI><A HREF=tennessee.htm TARGET="state">Tennessee</A>
   <LI><A HREF=california.htm TARGET="state">California</A>
   <LI><A HREF=new_mexico.htm TARGET="state">New Mexico</A>
   <LI><A HREF=georgia.htm TARGET="state">Georgia</A>
   </UL><P>

   <IFRAME SRC=texas.htm NAME="state" WIDTH=50% HEIGHT=240
   ALIGN=right>
   </IFRAME><P><BR><P>

   For maps of thousands of locations in the United States, consult
   the <A HREF=http://www.mapquest.com>MapQuest Web site</A>.
   ```

3. Save the file.

4. Toggle over to Internet Explorer.

5. Reload the Web page.

 Consult the HTML 4.0 Specification for additional attributes for list tags.

The updated page is downloaded and displayed.

Note the additional hyperlinks added in Step 2. Also note that the inline frame is currently empty.

6. Click the hyperlink labeled **Ohio**.

 The inline frame now displays the content of the OHIO.HTM document, as shown in Figure 10-14.

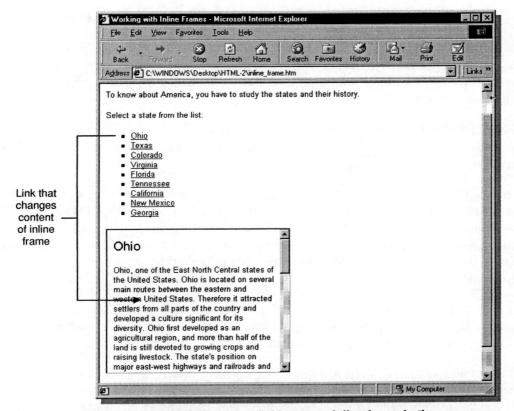

Figure 10-14: TARGET anchor linking to an inline frame in the same page

7. Click the hyperlink labeled **Virginia**. Note how the content changes in the inline frame. This is an example of combining an inline frame with a TARGET anchor (and NAME attribute within the inline frame opening tag).

8. Click the other hyperlinks to ensure that all of your links are functional. You should always test *all* links in a page.

Lesson 10 Summary

▶ You can create hypertext anchors between frames in a frames-enabled Web page. In this manner, you can make your frames pages dynamic and interactive among each other.

▶ You can use links between frames to create nav bars, tables of content, and online catalogs.

▶ The NAME and TARGET attributes allow you to create links between frames.

▶ The NAME attribute is placed inside the <FRAME> tag and provides a unique identifier for it so that an Anchor tag (in a different frame or different Web page) can refer (link) to it.

▶ The TARGET attribute is placed inside the Anchor tag and instructs the Anchor tag to display the file to which it links in a particular frame (by identifying a NAME reference within a <FRAME> tag).

▶ TARGET attributes can also be used to display a page in a new browser window.

▶ You can greatly simplify the script involved in the Anchor tags in a referring frame by using the <BASE> tag. The syntax <BASE TARGET=name> allows you to place a single <BASE> tag within a referring frame and avoid placing TARGET attributes on each <FRAME> tag.

▶ If both a hyperlink (Anchor tag) with a TARGET attribute and a <BASE> tag with a TARGET attribute are present in the same referring frame, the Anchor tag TARGET takes precedent.

▶ There are four reserved TARGET values (_blank, _self, _parent, and _top) that you can use to create unique effects when a user activates an anchor (by clicking). The most popular of these effects is loading a referred Web page into a completely new browser window (thus preserving the referring page and window). This helps prevent you from "losing" users from your Web site when you refer them to a resource that is outside of your site.

▶ Before actually scripting a nav bar master frame document, you should carefully plan the layout and contents of the nav bar page frames. This will save you time and frustration and will allow you to create a better navigation scheme for your entire site.

▶ Inline frames, new to HTML 4.0, allow a frame to be precisely configured as a single "window" within a Web page that is of the exact width, height, and location on the page that you desire. Inline frames now allow you to include as few as *one* frame on a page (standard frames allow as few as *two* frames on a page). Netscape Navigator 4.0x does not support inline frames, so you should use this new feature carefully.

Lesson 10 Quiz

Matching

___ 1. placed in the <FRAME> tag   a. _blank

___ 2. opens a new Web browser window   b. _self

___ 3. placed in the <A> tag   c. inline frame

___ 4. frames-based hyperlink system   d. SRC

___ 5. unnecessary attribute (because default) e. TARGET

___ 6. allows as few as one frame on a page   f. nav bar

Fill in the Blank

7. In an HTML document containing <FRAMESET>, each <FRAME> tag requires a unique _____ attribute that identifies it.

8. You can determine the location of inline frames using MARGINHEIGHT, MARGINWIDTH, and _____ .

9. If most of the links within an _____ document are pointing to the same TARGET, typing the TARGET attribute over and over again is needlessly repetitive.

10. Three reserved TARGET attributes are: _____ , _____ , and _____ .

True or False?

T / F 11. The BORDERCOLOR attribute can be added to a <FRAME> or <FRAMESET> to change the color of an individual frame.

T / F 12. If both a hyperlink (Anchor tag) with a TARGET attribute and a <BASE> tag with a TARGET attribute are present in the same referring frame, the Anchor tag TARGET takes precedent.

T / F 13. There are no special values that can be assigned to the TARGET attribute within an <A> tag.

T / F 14. TARGET attributes can be used to display a page in a new window.

T / F 15. Inline frames are not supported by Netscape Navigator 4.0x.

(This page intentionally left blank)

Lesson 11
Introduction to Tables

Lesson Topics

► HTML Tables

► Table Tag <TABLE>

► Creating Page Columns with Tables

► Lesson 11 Summary

HTML Tables

HTML tables are one of the more powerful and functional features of HTML. Tables were not a part of the original HTML specification. To create a table-like arrangement of data in an HTML document, it used to be necessary to use the <PRE> tag. This often provided mediocre or undesired results.

A Family of Tags

As with the list tags (<OL> and <UL>), tables are comprised of a family of tags. Due to the number of tags, HTML tables can be confusing and cumbersome to create, especially for novice HTML authors. With practice, the creation and editing of HTML tables can become a quick, efficient process.

As you will learn in the remaining Lessons of this course, tables can support sophisticated formatting and allow you to layout a Web page in ways not possible with other HTML conventions. You can:

- embed tables within tables (called *nesting*);

- span table cells across rows or columns;

- insert image or text hyperlinks within a table cell.

A sample HTML table is displayed in Figure 11-1.

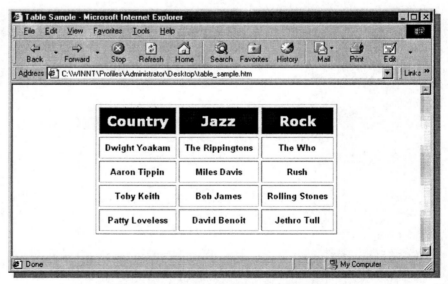

Figure 11-1: Example of an HTML table

Table Tag <TABLE>

The <TABLE> tag, a non-empty tag, is the basis for any HTML table. Two associated tags, <TR> and <TD> (shown in Table 11-1), control the layout and appearance of a table.

Tag	Description
<TR>	■ Specifies a table row ■ Non-empty tag
<TD>	■ Specifies a table cell ■ Officially a non-empty tag, but can be used as an empty tag in major browsers

Table 11-1: The <TABLE> tag family

The above tags and their corresponding attributes are shown in Table 11-2.

Tag	Attribute	Value Range	Function
<TABLE>	BORDER	1-100 pixels	Specifies a visible border and its thickness. Can be used with no value to specify a thin border. If this attribute is omitted, no visible border or gridlines will appear.
<TABLE>	BORDERCOLOR	Colors & RGB codes	Specifies the color of the outside border (not gridlines).
<TABLE>	CELLPADDING	1-100 pixels[20]	Specifies amount of spacing *inside* table cells.
<TABLE>	CELLSPACING	1-100 pixels	Specifies amount of spacing *between* table cells.
<TABLE>	WIDTH	1-100%	Specifies the width of the table relative to the width of the Web page.
<TR>, <TD>	ALIGN	left, center, right	Specifies the horizontal alignment of text within a row or individual cell.
<TR>, <TD>	BGCOLOR	Colors & RGB codes	Specifies a fill color for rows or cells.

Table 11-2: Common HTML table attributes

---

[20] For best appearance, the **CELLPADDING** and **CELLSPACING** values should not exceed 20.

Exercise 11-1: Creating a Basic Table

In this exercise, you will create a basic table consisting of three rows and four columns. Text inside the table cells will be default justified; the table itself will be default justified left.

1. Switch applications to your text editor.

2. Open the file AUTOS_TABLE.HTM from the HTML-2 folder.

3. Add the bold script (as shown below) to the text on your screen:

```
<FONT SIZE=+2 COLOR=blue>Automobiles of the World</FONT><P>

<TABLE BORDER=3>

<TR>
<TD><B>American</B></TD>
<TD><B>German</B></TD>
<TD><B>Japanese</B></TD>
<TD><B>British</B></TD>
</TR>

<TR>
<TD>Ford</TD>
<TD>Porsche</TD>
<TD>Toyota</TD>
<TD>Jaguar</TD>
</TR>

<TR>
<TD>Saturn</TD>
<TD>BMW</TD>
<TD>Acura</TD>
<TD>Rolls Royce</TD>
</TR>

<TR>
<TD>Chrysler</TD>
<TD>Audi</TD>
<TD>Mitsubishi</TD>
<TD>Land Rover</TD>
</TR>

</TABLE><P>
```

4. Save the HTML document.

5. Switch applications to your Web browser.

6. Reload the Web page.

7. Compare the screen that is displayed in your Web browser with Figure 11-2. If they are not nearly identical, repeat the steps of this exercise, taking care to accurately type the script in Step 2.

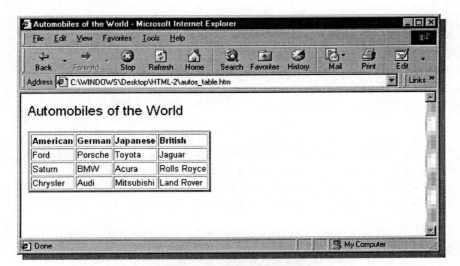

Figure 11-2: Basic HTML table

 Tables can be horizontally centered on a page using the <CENTER> tag. Remember that <CENTER> is a non-empty tag.

Exercise 11-2: Using Basic Formatting and Adding Color to a Table

In this exercise, you will align data within table cells and add color to table cells and rows. The tags and attributes, such as <FONT>, FACE, and COLOR, are a review of what you learned in DDC's *HTML 4.0 Fundamentals* regarding text formatting.

1. Switch applications to your text editor, and open AUTOS_TABLE.HTM, if necessary.
2. Edit the <TABLE> tag script from the previous exercise, adding the bold script (as shown below):

```
<CENTER>
<FONT SIZE=+2 COLOR=blue>Automobiles of the World</FONT><P>

<TABLE BORDER=8 CELLSPACING=10 BORDERCOLOR=black>

<TR BGCOLOR=gray ALIGN=center>
<TD><B><FONT FACE=arial COLOR=white>American</FONT></B></TD>
<TD><B><FONT FACE=arial COLOR=white>German</FONT></B></TD>
<TD><B><FONT FACE=arial COLOR=white>Japanese</FONT></B></TD>
<TD><B><FONT FACE=arial COLOR=white>British</FONT></B></TD>
</TR>

<TR ALIGN=center>
<TD BGCOLOR=yellow>Ford</TD>
<TD BGCOLOR=pink>Porsche</TD>
<TD BGCOLOR=brown><FONT COLOR=white>Toyota</FONT></TD>
<TD BGCOLOR=green><FONT COLOR=white>Jaguar</FONT></TD>
</TR>

<TR ALIGN=center>
<TD BGCOLOR=yellow>Saturn</TD>
<TD BGCOLOR=pink>BMW</TD>
<TD BGCOLOR=brown><FONT COLOR=white>Acura</FONT></TD>
<TD BGCOLOR=green><FONT COLOR=white>Rolls Royce</FONT></TD>
</TR>

<TR ALIGN=center>
<TD BGCOLOR=yellow>Chrysler</TD>
<TD BGCOLOR=pink>Audi</TD>
<TD BGCOLOR=brown><FONT COLOR=white>Mitsubishi</FONT></TD>
<TD BGCOLOR=green><FONT COLOR=white>Land Rover</FONT></TD>
</TR>

</TABLE>
</CENTER><P>
```

3. Save the HTML document.

4. Switch applications to your Web browser.

5. Reload the Web page.

6. Compare the two tables you just created. Note the effect of the attributes and text formatting you used. Your tables should appear similar to Figure 11-3. If not, repeat the steps of this exercise, taking care to accurately type the script in Step 2.

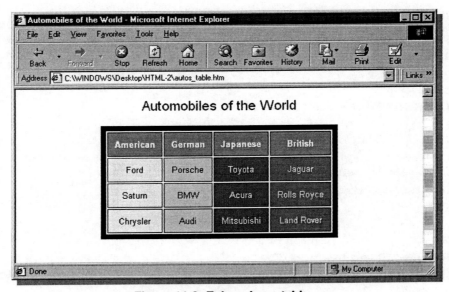

Figure 11-3: Enhancing a table

7. In the opening <TABLE> tag, change the attribute CELLSPACING to CELLPADDING. Keep the value at **10**. How does this change your table? Change the value to **20**. What change does this make? What effect is created if you use both attributes? Experiment with the CELLSPACING and CELLPADDING attributes as time permits.

BORDERCOLOR and BGCOLOR (when applied to tables) are not part of the official HTML 3.2 or 4.0 Specifications. They are examples of HTML extensions, but are recognized by both Netscape Navigator and Microsoft Internet Explorer. Because these two browsers comprise 99% of the browser market, you can apply these two attributes to tables with confidence.

Exercise 11-3: Embedding Images in a Table

In this exercise, you will embed two images in a table with adjacent descriptive text in a manner that creates an attractive, artistic effect.

1. Switch applications to your text editor.

2. Open the file IMAGES_TABLE.HTM.

3. Add the bold script (as shown below) to the text on your screen:

```
<H3>Inserting Images in a Table</H3>

<CENTER>
<TABLE WIDTH=50% BORDER=3 CELLPADDING=5>

<TR>
<TD>"On the road of life, what comes around the next corner is often
uncertain...."</TD>
<TD><IMG SRC=road.jpg></TD>
</TR>

<TR>
<TD><IMG SRC=wild.jpg></TD>
<TD ALIGN=right>"Hey, buddy...can you point me toward a good country bar
in Nashville?"</TD>
</TR>

</TABLE>
</CENTER><P>
```

4. Save the HTML document.

5. Switch applications to your Web browser.

6. Reload the Web page.

7. Note the alignment of the text. Compare the table you just created with Figure 11-4. They should appear nearly identical. If they are not, repeat the steps of this exercise, taking care to accurately type the script in Step 3.

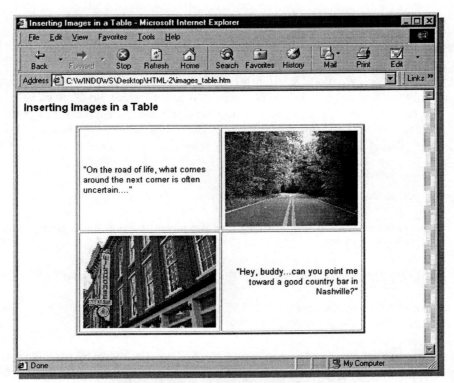

Figure 11-4: Inserting images into a table

 The use of left and right text alignment can be particularly visually appealing when used as captions for images in tables, as in Figure 11-4 above.

 A table scripted without the BORDER attribute will display the cell data arranged in rows and columns, but without a visible border. Remember to use the BORDER attribute in the <TABLE> tag if you desire a visible border.

Creating Page Columns with Tables

You will often have a need to add more structure to a Web page. HTML contains relatively few page layout conventions. Those that HTML does offer, such as <BR>, <P>, and <HR>, are relatively simple and lack sophisticated attributes.

Add Page Structure with Two Column Tables

One of the simplest ways to add substantial structure to a page is to insert the entire contents of the page into an "invisible" table. The purpose is not to create a pattern of cells established by rows and columns, as is typical when using tables. Rather, the desire is to create a two or three column page (three column pages are also known as "newspaper layout"). Such layouts can be accomplished easily with a two or three column table comprised of two or three cells, respectively.

The advantages of inserting Web page content into a two column table are:

- taking advantage of the right margin of the page, an area that is traditionally "waste land" in HTML;

- making your pages more compact, thus requiring visitors to scroll less;

- substantially improving the aesthetic appeal of your pages.

Compare the two Web pages shown in Figure 11-5. They are identical with the exception that the content of the right page has been inserted into a simple two column table. Note that the table-enhanced page has no BORDER attribute and a CELLPADDING=10 attribute to create necessary white space between the two columns.

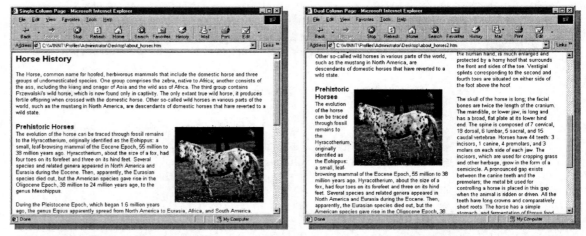

Figure 11-5: Left page is normal layout; right page has been embedded into a two column table

Exercise 11-4: Creating Page Columns with a Borderless Table

In this exercise, you will embed the content of the Web page you created in a previous exercise in a simple two-column table. Because this exercise involves inline frames, you need to use the Internet Explorer Web browser to properly complete this exercise.

This particular page, which first displays a large amount of white space on the right margin, will change dramatically in appearance, filling the right side of the page with content. This gives the page a more refined, professional appearance and requires less scrolling.

1. Toggle over to Notepad.

2. Open INLINE_FRAME.HTM from the HTML-2 folder.

3. Add the following script that appears in bold:

```
<FONT SIZE=+2 COLOR=blue>The 50 United States</FONT>.<P>

<TABLE CELLPADDING=10>
<TR>
<TD>
To know about America, you have to study the states and their
history.<P>

Select a state from the list:<P>

<UL TYPE=square>
<LI><A HREF=ohio.htm TARGET="state">Ohio</A>
<LI><A HREF=texas.htm TARGET="state">Texas</A>
<LI><A HREF=colorado.htm TARGET="state">Colorado</A>
<LI><A HREF=virginia.htm TARGET="state">Virginia</A>
<LI><A HREF=florida.htm TARGET="state">Florida</A>
<LI><A HREF=tennessee.htm TARGET="state">Tennessee</A>
<LI><A HREF=california.htm TARGET="state">California</A>
<LI><A HREF=new_mexico.htm TARGET="state">New Mexico</A>
<LI><A HREF=georgia.htm TARGET="state">Georgia</A>
</UL><P>
</TD>

<TD>
<IFRAME NAME="state" WIDTH=50% HEIGHT=240>
</IFRAME><P><BR><P>
For maps of thousands of locations in the United States, consult the <A
HREF=http://www.mapquest.com>MapQuest Web site</A>.
</TD>
</TR>
</TABLE>
</BODY>
```

4. Save the file.

5. Toggle over to Internet Explorer.

6. Open INLINE_FRAME.HTM if necessary. Examine the page as it now appears, without a table and in a single column.

7. Refresh the page. Click any of the hyperlinks to load a document into the inline frame.

 The updated page is downloaded and displayed, as shown in Figure 11-6.

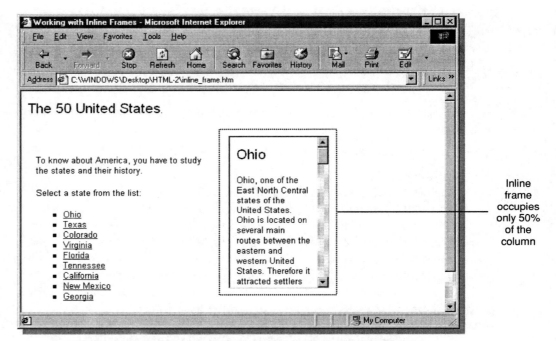

Figure 11-6: Page content inserted into a two column table

 Note the dual-column layout. Also note how the inline frame seems cut in half. Because of the WIDTH=50% attribute on the inline frame, it is now occupying only 50 percent of the width of the table cell (whereas previously, without a table, it was occupying 50 percent of the entire page width).

8. Toggle back to Notepad.

9. Change the following script that appears in bold:

`<IFRAME NAME="state" WIDTH=100% HEIGHT=240>`

10. Save the document.
11. Toggle over to Internet Explorer.
12. Refresh the page. Click any of the hyperlinks to load a document into the inline frame.

 The updated page is downloaded and displayed, as shown in Figure 11-7.

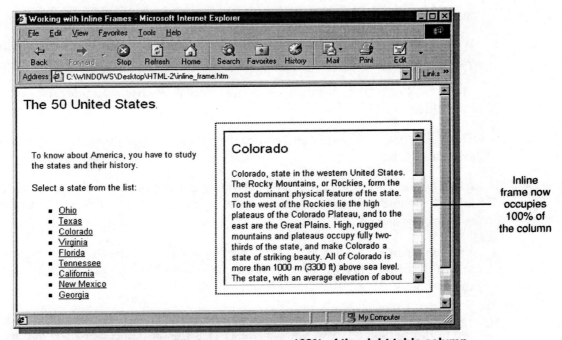

Figure 11-7: Inline frame modified to now occupy 100% of the right table column

 The inline frame now occupies 100 percent of the right column of the table, providing the page with a much more natural and refined appearance. This is a good example of how you often have to edit and clean up your script in order to properly accommodate the new two column layout.

Lesson 11 Summary

▶ HTML tables allow text and images to be structured into rows and columns in Web pages.

▶ The most basic table must include the <TABLE> tag, the <TR> tag, and the <TD> tag. <TABLE> is a non-empty tag. <TR> and <TD> are also non-empty tags, but both major Web browsers support the use of only an opening <TD> tag when creating table cells.

▶ Text inside table cells can be formatted with any attribute available to standard body text outside of a table. Bold, italic, underline, superscript, and subscript formatting are all applicable. Alignment formatting is also available via table tag attributes.

▶ Tables can be centered on a Web page using the <CENTER> tag. <CENTER> is a non-empty tag.

▶ By default, tables have no visible border. The BORDER attribute must be used to create a visible frame around a table. An attribute value of between 6 and 12 (BORDER=10) is recommended. For the thinnest possible border, do not specify a value.

▶ When used, the table tag attributes CELLPADDING and CELLSPACING provide versatility and aesthetic appeal to a table's appearance.

▶ The CELLPADDING attribute specifies the amount of spacing *inside* table cells (makes cells fatter).

▶ The CELLSPACING attribute specifies the amount of spacing *between* table cells (makes gridlines thicker).

▶ Although not part of the official HTML 4.0 Specification, color can be added to individual table cells or to an entire row using the BGCOLOR attribute. You can use many color names and all RGB codes.

▶ You can change the color of a table border by using the BORDERCOLOR attribute (not part of the official HTML 4.0 Specification) in the <TABLE> tag. You can use many color names (16 "browser-safe" colors) and all RGB codes.

▶ You can create page columns with "invisible" tables (tables with no border). Using either two or three column tables, you can create pages with sophisticated layout not typical of Web pages. Creating columns with tables can also help you use the right margin white space that is often wasted. This makes your Web page appear more like a printed publication and typically requires users to scroll less.

DDC Publishing • www.ddcpub.com

Lesson 11 Quiz

Matching

___ 1. type of table for page columns

___ 2. adds outline and gridlines to table

___ 3. used for table justification

___ 4. HTML extension for tables

___ 5. amount of spacing *between* table cells

___ 6. table display default

a. BGCOLOR

b. no border

c. "invisible"

d. CELLSPACING

e. <CENTER>

f. BORDER

Fill in the Blank

7. The _____ attribute specifies the amount of spacing inside table cells.

8. The _____ tag, which stands for "table definition," specifies table cells.

9. Embedding a table within another table is called _____ .

10. The <TD> tag is officially a _____ tag, but both major Web browsers properly interpret a table if only the opening <TD> tag is used.

11. The <TR> tag is used to create table _____ and stands for _____ .

True or False?

T / F 12. Tables can only be right aligned using an HTML extension introduced by Microsoft for Internet Explorer.

T / F 13. Tables can be given a WIDTH attribute value of up to 120%.

T / F 14. The BORDERCOLOR attribute is *not* an HTML extension.

T / F 15. The table BORDER attribute can be between 1-100 pixels.

T / F 16. <TABLE> is a non-empty tag.

T / F 17. CELLSPACING increases the space *inside* a table cell.

(This page intentionally left blank)

Lesson 12
Formatting
Tables

Lesson Topics

▶ Advanced Table Formatting

▶ Cell Spanning

▶ Rules & Frames

▶ Lesson 12 Summary

Advanced Table Formatting

In Lesson 4: *Introduction to Tables*, you learned how to script and apply tables to Web pages. You even learned some advanced features, such as adding color to table cells and alignment of data within cells. In this Lesson, you will learn how to apply advanced formatting to tables, including:

- spanning cells across columns;

- spanning columns across rows;

- combining row and column spanning;

- formatting cell rules and frames (collectively called gridlines).

Review of Formatting Attributes

As you know, two table attributes, CELLPADDING and CELLSPACING, allow you to substantially change the appearance of a table. These attributes are compared in Figure 12-1.

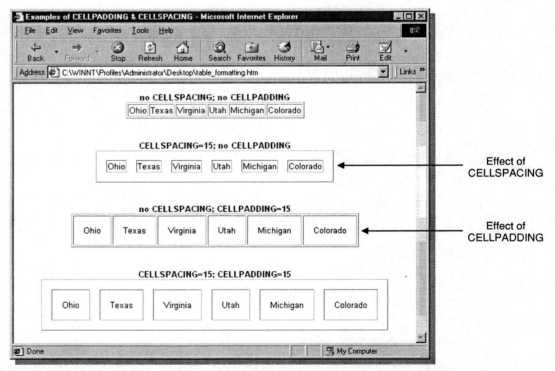

Figure 12-1: Same table with different CELLPADDING and CELLSPACING values

The default of a table is to display no border. The tables in this example were all given a default BORDER attribute (equal to 2-3 pixels in most browsers).

Table Tags & Attributes

Table 12-1 lists the most important and widely used table tags.

Tag	Attribute	Attribute Values	Comment
`<TABLE>`	BORDER	number (pixels)	Default is no border. This attribute can be used with no value (most browsers will use a 2-3 pixel border).
`<TABLE>`	BORDERCOLOR	RGB code or English color name	An HTML extension. Navigator displays the outside border in color; IE displays the border and all gridlines in color.
`<TABLE>`	RULES	none, groups, rows, cols, all	New to HTML 4.0. In IE 4.0, if you combine BORDER=x with RULES=none, you can achieve a unique effect.
`<TABLE>`	ALIGN	left, right, center	Default is left justification.
`<TABLE>`	WIDTH	number (pixels) or % (of browser window)	Default is columns that are wide enough to accommodate text or image data.
`<TABLE>`	CELLPADDING	number (pixels)	Adds space *inside* cells.
`<TABLE>`	CELLSPACING	number (pixels)	Adds space *between* cells (by making gridlines thicker).
`<TR>`	ALIGN	left, right, justify	Aligns the content of each cell within the row; this is more economical than placing ALIGN attributes in all `<TD>` tags.
`<TR>`	VALIGN	top, middle, bottom	If you add a large amount of CELLSPACING, use `<TR VALIGN=middle>`.
`<TD>`	ROWSPAN	number (of rows to span)	N/A
`<TD>`	COLSPAN	number (of columns to span)	N/A
`<TD>`, `<TR>`	BGCOLOR	RGB code or English color name	Fill color for cell or row.
`<CAPTION>`	ALIGN	top, bottom, left, right	Indicates where the caption is located *relative to the table*.

Table 12-1: HTML 4.0 table tags, attributes, and attribute values

Exercise 12-1: Reviewing Table Formatting

In this exercise, you will create a simple table and manipulate its formatting.

1. Toggle over to your Web browser.

2. Open TABLE_REVIEW.HTM from the HTML-2 folder.

 The page is downloaded and displayed, as shown in Figure 12-2. The table has no formatting; it is only plain <TD> and <TR> tags.

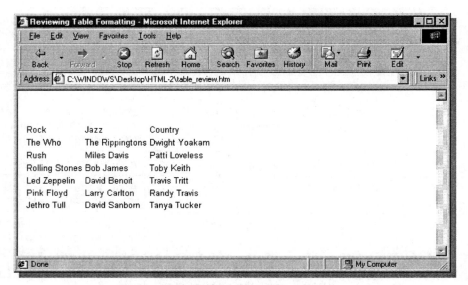

Figure 12-2: Table with no formatting

3. Toggle over to Notepad.

4. Open TABLE_REVIEW.HTM from the HTML-2 folder.

5. Center the table and add a border. Give the border a thickness of your choice.

6. Increase the space inside the cells.

7. Vertically center the text inside the cells.

8. Make the header row text larger and bold. Make the header cells navy and the text white.

9. Horizontally center the text in every cell.

10. Increase the thickness of the gridlines for the entire table.

11. Make the text "Rolling Stones" a hyperlink that refers to www.stones.com.

12. Make the text "The Rippingtons" a hyperlink that refers to www.rippingtons.com.

13. Make the text "Randy Travis" a hyperlink that refers to www.randy-travis.com.

14. Make every cell except the header row have a fill color of gray.

15. The text in the header row is already bold and white; make the text in the other row cells bold and white but do not change the font size. When you are finished, your table should appear similar to Figure 12-3.

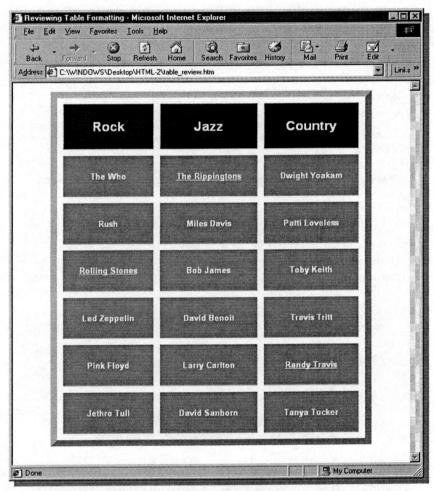

Figure 12-3: How your table should appear when you are finished

 This is the level of proficiency that you should have before completing the remainder of this Lesson. If you do not feel confident in your ability to create richly formatted tables like the one above, you should return to Lesson 4: *Introduction to Tables*, and spend more time formatting tables.

Cell Spanning

One of the easiest ways to create sophisticated table layouts is to merge rows and columns. Officially called *spanning* (because a cell must be *spanned*, or stretched, over a specific number of columns or rows), this allows you to create asymmetrical tables that accommodate images, graphics, or large blocks of data.

Cell spanning can also be used to create decorative header rows or header columns.

The two attributes involved in cell spanning are COLSPAN and ROWSPAN, both of which work with the <TD> tag, as shown in Table 12-2.

Attribute	Tag	Value
COLSPAN	<TD>	number (of cells)
ROWSPAN	<TD>	number (of cells)

Table 12-2: COLSPAN and ROWSPAN attribute characteristics

Cell spanning—when used in conjunction with other attributes, such as text formatting and cell coloring—can enhance a table, improve its appearance, and make it much easier for a user to quickly comprehend the significance of the data presented, as shown in Figure 12-4.

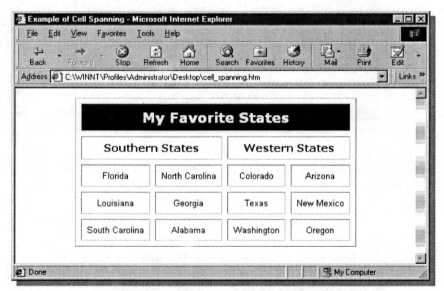

Figure 12-4: Examples of cell spanning

Exercise 12-2: Spanning Cells Across Columns

In this exercise, you will span cells across columns using the COLSPAN attribute in the <TD> tag.

1. Toggle over to Notepad. Open a new document.
2. Type the following script:

```
<HTML>

<HEAD>
<TITLE>Cell Spanning</TITLE>
</HEAD>

<BODY>

<P><BR><P>

<CENTER>

<TABLE BORDER CELLSPACING=5 CELLPADDING=10>

<TR>
<TD ALIGN=center BGCOLOR=navy COLSPAN=4><FONT SIZE=+2
COLOR=white><B>Cities of the World</B></FONT></TD>
</TR>

<TR>
<TD ALIGN=center BGCOLOR=yellow COLSPAN=2><B><FONT SIZE=+1
COLOR=navy>American Cities</FONT></B>
<TD ALIGN=center BGCOLOR=yellow COLSPAN=2><B><FONT SIZE=+1
COLOR=navy>European Cities</FONT></B>
</TR>

<TR ALIGN=center>
<TD><B>Seattle</B>
<TD><B>Cleveland</B>
<TD><B>London</B>
<TD><B>Paris</B>
</TR>

<TR ALIGN=center>
<TD><B>Houston</B>
<TD><B>Boston</B>
<TD><B>Geneva</B>
<TD><B>Madrid</B>
</TR>

<TR ALIGN=center>
<TD><B>Chicago</B>
<TD><B>Atlanta</B>
```

```
<TD><B>Brussels</B>
<TD><B>Munich</B>

</TABLE>
</CENTER>

</BODY>
</HTML>
```

3. Save the document as CELL_SPANNING.HTM in the HTML-2 folder.

4. Toggle over to your Web browser.

5. Open CELL_SPANNING.HTM from the HTML-2 folder.

 The page is downloaded and displayed, as shown in Figure 12-5.

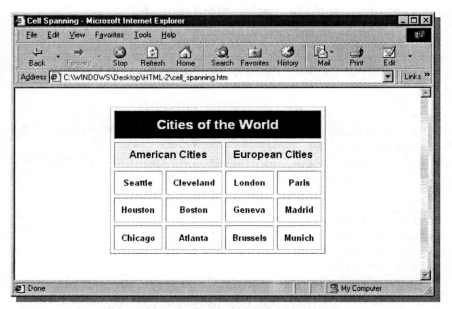

Figure 12-5: Cells spanned over columns

Exercise 12-3: Building a Table from Scratch

In this exercise, you will create a table to match a model presented to you. You should be able to complete this exercise with no difficulties. If you have problems completing this exercise, review Lesson 4: *Introduction to Tables* prior to completing the remaining sections of this Lesson.

1. In Notepad, open a new document.

2. Script a table that matches the one shown in Figure 12-6. Note the alignment of cell data, the formatting of tables rules, and the colors used.

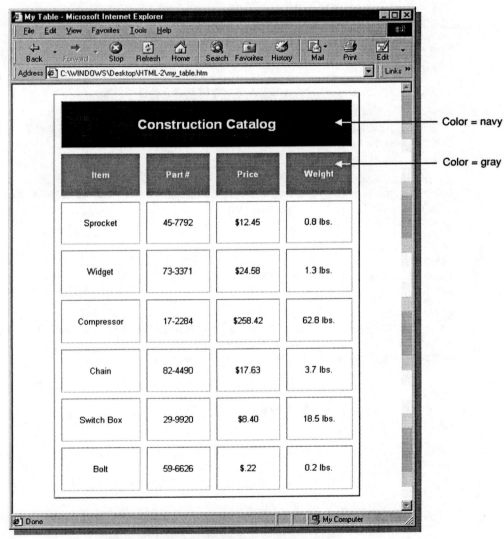

Figure 12-6: Build this table on your own

Exercise 12-4: Spanning Cells Across Rows

In this exercise, you will span cells across rows using the ROWSPAN attribute in the <TD> tag.

1. Toggle over to Notepad. Open a new document.
2. Type the following script:

```
<HTML>

<HEAD>
<TITLE>Cell Spanning</TITLE>
</HEAD>

<BODY>

<P><BR><P>

<CENTER>

<TABLE BORDER CELLSPACING=5 CELLPADDING=10>

<TR>
<TD ALIGN=center BGCOLOR=navy COLSPAN=2><FONT SIZE=+2
COLOR=white><B>My Exercise Log</B></FONT>
</TR>

<TR>
<TD ALIGN=center BGCOLOR=yellow ROWSPAN=2><B><FONT SIZE=+1
COLOR=navy>Week 1</FONT></B>
<TD><B>Ran 12 miles</B>
</TR>

<TR>
<TD><B>Biked 25 miles</B>
</TR>

<TR>
<TD ALIGN=center BGCOLOR=yellow ROWSPAN=2><B><FONT SIZE=+1
COLOR=navy>Week 2</FONT></B>
<TD><B>Ran 16 miles</B>
</TR>

<TR>
<TD><B>Biked 32 miles</B>
</TR>
```

```
<TR>
<TD ALIGN=center BGCOLOR=yellow ROWSPAN=3><B><FONT SIZE=+1
COLOR=navy>Week 3</FONT></B>
<TD><B>Ran 17 miles</B>
</TR>

<TR>
<TD><B>Biked 34 miles</B>
</TR>

<TR>
<TD><B>Swam 2 miles</B>
</TR>

<TR>
<TD ALIGN=center BGCOLOR=yellow ROWSPAN=4><B><FONT SIZE=+1
COLOR=navy>Week 4</FONT></B>
<TD><B>Ran 18 miles</B>
</TR>

<TR>
<TD><B>Biked 35 miles</B>
</TR>

<TR>
<TD><B>Swam 3 miles</B>
</TR>

<TR>
<TD><B>Lifted weights for 1 hour</B>
</TR>

</TABLE>
</CENTER>

</BODY>
</HTML>
```

3. Save the file as CELL_SPANNING2.HTM in the HTML-2 folder.

4. Toggle over to your Web browser.

5. Open CELL_SPANNING2.HTM in the HTML-2 folder.

The page is downloaded and displayed, as shown in Figure 12-7.

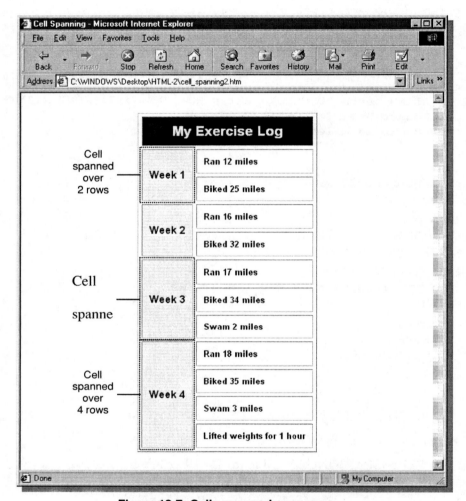

Figure 12-7: Cells spanned over rows

Exercise 12-5: Combining Row and Column Spanning

In this exercise, you will combine both row and column spanning using both the ROWSPAN and COLSPAN attributes to the <TD> tag.

To give you a better understanding of the "position" of cells relative to the <TR> and <TD> tags that are placed in the HTML document, the cells in this exercise contain a numbering scheme. Cell 1-3 is in row 1, column 3. Likewise, cell 3-2 would appear in row 3, column 2.

1. Toggle over to Notepad. Open a new document.
2. Type the following script:

```
<HTML>

<HEAD>
<TITLE>Spanning Cells Over Both Rows & Columns</TITLE>
</HEAD>

<BODY>

<P><BR><P>

<CENTER>
<TABLE BORDER CELLPADDING=10 WIDTH=80%>

<TR ALIGN=center>
<TD COLSPAN=2 ROWSPAN=2><B>Cell 1-1</B>
<TD><B>Cell 1-3</B>
</TR>

<TR ALIGN=center>
<TD><B>Cell 2-3</B>
</TR>

<TR ALIGN=center>
<TD><B>Cell 3-1</B>
<TD><B>Cell 3-2</B>
<TD><B>Cell 3-3</B>
</TR>

</TABLE>
</CENTER>

</BODY>
</HTML>
```

3. Save the file as CELL_SPANNING3.HTM in the HTML-2 folder.

4. Toggle over to your Web browser.

5. Open CELL_SPANNING3.HTM from the HTML-2 folder.

 The page is downloaded and displayed, as shown in Figure 12-8.

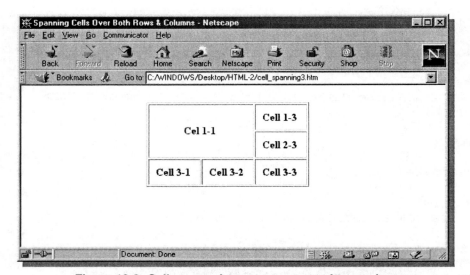

Figure 12-8: Cell spanned over two rows and two columns

Rules & Frames

HTML 4.0 allows you to control the display of the rules and frames (border segments) of a table. With previous versions of HTML, you only had the option of a border surrounding the entire table or no border.

Non-Cell Table Elements

Typically, a Webmaster's focus is on table cells and their contents. It is important to recognize, however, that there are, technically, three non-cell elements that compose a table:

- border (BORDER attribute)

- frames (FRAME attribute)

- rules (RULES attribute)

These elements are illustrated in Figure 12-9.

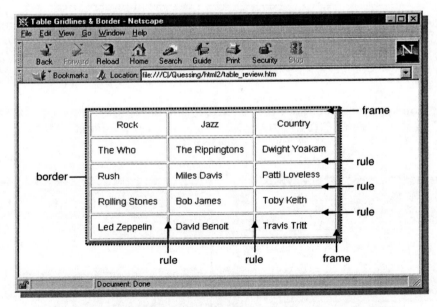

Figure 12-9: The difference between a table border and gridlines

 Netscape Navigator 4.08 and older versions do not recognize the RULES and FRAME attributes.

RULES Attribute

HTML 4.0 allows you to selectively add gridlines to a table using the RULES attribute to the
<TABLE> tag. RULES has five values, as detailed in Table 12-3.

```
<TABLE RULES=none|groups|rows|cols|all>
```

With HTML 4.0 you can, for the first time, display a table with a border but no gridlines.
Also, you can display only horizontal gridlines or only vertical gridlines.

RULES Attribute Value	Result
none	No rules. *This is the default value.*
rows	Rules will appear between rows only.
cols	Rules will appear between columns only.
all	Rules will appear between all rows and columns.

Table 12-3: RULES attribute values and their effects

RULES Examples

Two common applications of the RULES attribute are the display of only horizontal
(RULES=rows) or vertical (RULES=cols) rules, as shown in Figure 12-10.

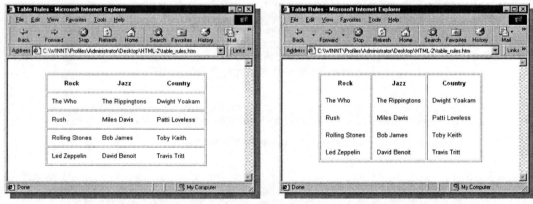

Figure 12-10: Table with RULES=rows (left) and with RULES=cols (right)

Exercise 12-6: Using the RULES Attribute

In this exercise, you will add the RULES attribute to the <TABLE> tag and experiment with different values to create different display effects in a table. Remember that Netscape Navigator 4.08 and previous versions do not recognize the RULES attribute.

1. In your Web browser, open TABLE_RULES.HTM from the HTML-2 folder.

 The page is downloaded and displayed. The table has no border and displays no rules, as shown in Figure 12-11.

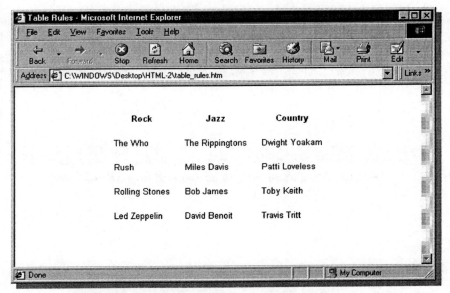

Figure 12-11: Table with no border and no rules

2. Toggle over to Notepad.

3. Open TABLE_RULES.HTM.

4. Add the following script that appears in bold:

```
<CENTER>
<TABLE RULES=all CELLPADDING=10>

<TR ALIGN=center>
```

5. Save the file. Toggle over to your Web browser. Reload the page.

 The page is downloaded and displayed. The table has no border but displays all rules, as shown in Figure 12-12.

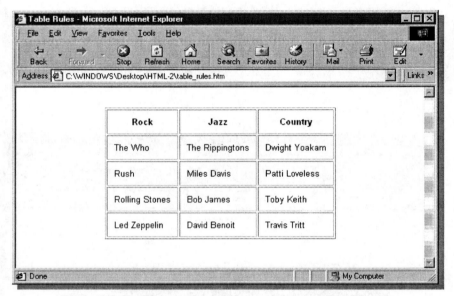

Figure 12-12: Table with no border and rules (RULES=all)

6. Toggle over to Notepad.

7. Change the following script that appears in bold:

```
<CENTER>
<TABLE RULES=rows CELLPADDING=10>
<TR ALIGN=center>
```

8. Save the file. Toggle over to your Web browser and reload the page.

DDC Publishing • www.ddcpub.com

The page is downloaded and displayed. The table has no border and displays rules on only rows, as shown in Figure 12-13.

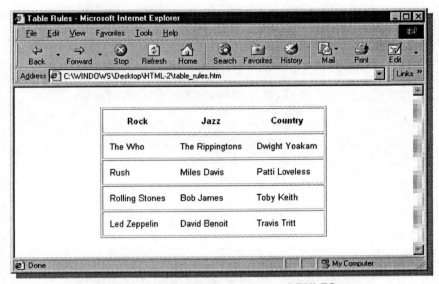

Rock	Jazz	Country
The Who	The Rippingtons	Dwight Yoakam
Rush	Miles Davis	Patti Loveless
Rolling Stones	Bob James	Toby Keith
Led Zeppelin	David Benoit	Travis Tritt

Figure 12-13: Table with no border and RULES=rows

9. Toggle over to Notepad.

10. Change the following script that appears in bold:

```
<CENTER>
<TABLE RULES=cols CELLPADDING=10

<TR ALIGN=center>
```

11. Save the file. Toggle over to your Web browser and reload the page.

 The table is displayed with only vertical rules.

12. Toggle over to Notepad.

13. Change the following script that appears in bold:

```
<CENTER>
<TABLE BORDER RULES=none CELLPADDING=10>

<TR ALIGN=center>
```

14. Save the file. Toggle over to your Web browser and reload the page.

The page is downloaded and displayed. The table has a border but no gridlines, as shown in Figure 12-14.

This effect can be produced easier with the FRAMES attribute, as you will see in the next section.

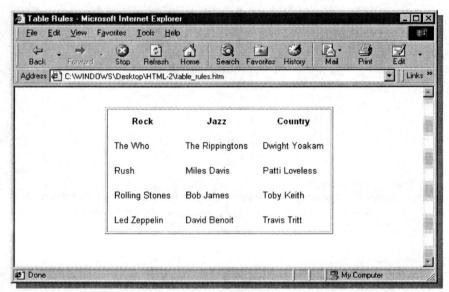

Figure 12-14: Table with a border but no rules (RULES=none)

FRAME Attribute

The FRAME attribute allows you to selectively add individual border elements (table sides). FRAME has five values, as detailed in Table 12-4.

```
<TABLE FRAME=above|below|hsides|lhs|rhs|vsides|box>
```

With HTML 4.0 you can, for the first time, display a table with a border but no gridlines. Also, you can display only horizontal gridlines or only vertical gridlines.

FRAME Attribute Value	Result
above	top side only
below	bottom side only
hsides	top and bottom sides only
vsides	right and left sides only
lhs	left-hand side only
rhs	right-hand side only
box	all four sides.

Table 12-4: FRAME attribute values and their effects

FRAME Examples

Two common applications of the FRAME attribute are the display of only horizontal (FRAME=hsides) or vertical (FRAME=vsides) rules, as shown in Figure 12-15.

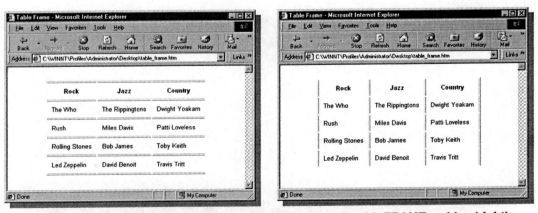

Figure 12-15: Table with FRAME=hsides (left) and table with FRAME=vsides (right)

Exercise 12-7: Using the FRAME Attribute

In this exercise, you will add the FRAME attribute to the <TABLE> tag and experiment with different values to create different display effects in a table. Netscape Navigator 4.06 and previous versions do not recognize the FRAME attribute.

1. In your Web browser, open TABLE_FRAMES.HTM from the HTML-2 folder.

 The page is downloaded and displayed. The table has no border, rules, or frames.

2. Toggle over to Notepad.

3. Open TABLE_FRAMES.HTM.

4. Add the following script that appears in bold:

```
<CENTER>
<TABLE FRAME=hsides CELLPADDING=10>
<TR ALIGN=center>
```

5. Save the file.

6. Toggle over to your Web browser.

7. Reload the page.

 The page is downloaded and displayed. The table has no border but displays horizontal frames, as shown in Figure 12-16 on the following page.

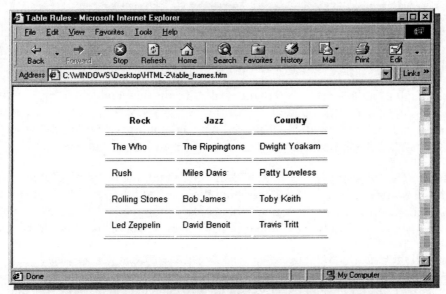

Figure 12-16: Table with no border and horizontal frames (FRAME=hsides)

8. Toggle over to Notepad.

9. Change the following script that appears in bold:

```
<CENTER>
<TABLE FRAME=vsides CELLPADDING=10>
<TR ALIGN=center>
```

10. Save the file.

11. Toggle over to your Web browser.

12. Reload the page.

 The page is downloaded and displayed. The table has no border but displays vertical frames.

13. Experiment with different FRAME values as time permits. Remember that Netscape Navigator does not currently recognize the RULES or FRAME attribute.

Lesson 12 Summary

▶ Advanced table formatting features include spanning cells across columns, spanning cells across rows, combining row and column spanning, and formatting cell rules and frames (collectively called gridlines).

▶ The default of a table is to display no border. To display a table border, you must use the BORDER attribute in the opening <TABLE> tag. A value for the BORDER attribute can be omitted and the border will be displayed with a default pixel width (2-4 pixels in major browsers). BORDER attribute values can range from 1 to 100 pixels.

▶ Cell spanning allows you to "stretch" a cell over multiple rows or columns. The ROWSPAN attribute spans a cell over multiple rows and the COLSPAN attribute spans a cell over multiple columns. Both attributes work with the <TD> tag. The value set of these attributes is simply the number of rows over which the cell should be spanned.

▶ Non-cell table formatting attributes are BORDER, RULES, and FRAME.

▶ Header text placed in spanned cells can greatly enhance the organization and logic of a table while also contributing to the formatting and attractiveness of the table.

▶ Both COLSPAN and ROWSPAN are attributes to the <TD> tag. Do not make the mistake of placing these attributes in the <TR> tag.

▶ Rules and frames are two formatting features of tables that are new to HTML 4.0. Rules and frames are added with the RULES and FRAME attributes, respectively, to the <TABLE> tag.

▶ Rules can be adjusted to display gridlines between rows only, between columns only, or between all rows and all columns. By specifying <TABLE BORDER RULES=none>, you can format a table with only an outside border and no "internal" (between cells) gridlines.

▶ The FRAME attribute has a larger value set than the RULES attribute. You can display frames within a table on the top side of cells only, on the bottom side of cells only, on the top and bottom sides only, on the right and left sides only, on the left-hand side only, on the right-hand side only, or on all four sides.

Lesson 12 Quiz

Matching

____ 1. adds a border and gridlines to a table   a. spanning

____ 2. ROWSPAN applies to this tag   b. rows

____ 3. value to the FRAME attribute   c. <TD>

____ 4. larger value set than RULES   d. FRAME

____ 5. stretching cells over multiple columns   e. BORDER

____ 6. value to the RULES attribute   f. hsides

Fill in the Blank

7. The rules and frames within a table are collectively called _____ .

8. The default of a table is to display no _____ .

9. You can change the color of a cell, row, or column using the _____ attribute.

10. The value of the COLSPAN attribute specifies the number of _____ .

11. The three non-cell table elements are _____ , _____ , and _____ .

True or False?

T / F   12. Using RULES=large, you can make the gridlines of a table thicker.

T / F   13. You can span a table cell over *both* multiple rows and multiple columns simultaneously.

T / F   14. Table borders are measured in pixels.

T / F   15. The values to the FRAME attribute are above, below, hsides, vsides, lhs, rhs, and boxers.

(This page intentionally left blank)

DDC Publishing • www.ddcpub.com

Lesson 13
Nesting &
Embedding
Tables

Lesson Topics

▶ Nesting & Embedding Data in Table Cells

▶ Embedding a List in a Table

▶ Nesting a Table within a Table

▶ Lesson 13 Summary

Nesting & Embedding Data in Table Cells

Sooner or later, you will find a need to precisely define the layout of data within a single table cell. However, there are no tags or attributes that allow you to do this.

It is possible to create sophisticated page layouts by embedding and nesting data in individual table cells. As you learned in Lesson 11: *Introduction to Tables*, you can embed inline images in table cells. In this Lesson, you will learn two new techniques:

- embedding an ordered or unordered list within a table cell;
- nesting a table within a table cell of another table

Embedding Lists in Table Cells

You learned how to create ordered and unordered lists in DDC's *HTML 4.0 Fundamentals* course. In this course, you have learned how to create sophisticated tables. The combination of these two features allows you to create richly formatted Web pages.

Nesting Tables within Tables

It is the hidden capabilities—such as embedding a table of any level of complexity within any cell of another table—that allow you to create truly sophisticated and attractive Web pages with tables.

Figure 13-1 displays an example of multiple tables and lists embedded in a single table.

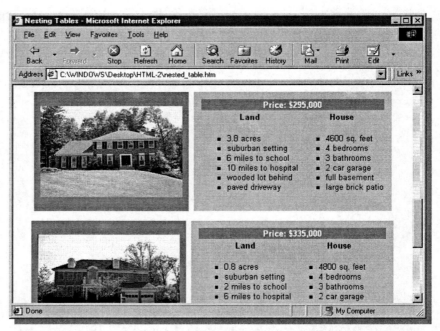

Figure 13-1: Result of nesting and embedding multiple tables and lists

Embedding a List in a Table

One method of organizing data within a table cell is to embed an ordered or unordered list. You learned about lists in DDC's *HTML 4.0 Fundamentals*. You can embed one or more lists in a single table cell or within multiple table cells.

Formatting Embedded Lists

You can apply all available list and text formatting techniques to a list that is embedded within a table.

Alignment

One of the most common problems regarding embedded lists is alignment or *justification*. If you are centering the contents of a table cell in which you are embedding a list, the list will probably not be formatted in the manner you desire. List items and bullets (or numbers) are typically left justified, at least in relation to one another.

There are two solutions to the problem of list alignment within table cells:

- left align contents of table cell;

- embed the list in an "invisible" table (one with no border) which is, in turn, nested within the primary table.

In an upcoming section of this Lesson, you will gain hands-on experience in changing the justification of an embedded list by embedding it within a table that is nested within another table.

Borders

When embedding a list or lists in a table, it is sometimes effective to not add a border to the table (by not adding a BORDER attribute to the opening <TABLE> tag). Such instances are good opportunities to experiment with or use the RULES or FRAME attribute you learned about in the previous Lesson.

Table Nesting Can Solve Problems

As you will see in the next section of this Lesson, you can solve many potential formatting problems associated with embedding a list in a table by simply embedding the list in an "invisible" table that is then nested within the master table that is recognized by a user on the Web page.

Exercise 13-1: Embedding a List in a Table Cell

In this exercise, you will take one of the tables you created in the last section and embed a list in it. You will then manipulate the list and change the alignment of table cells to improve the appearance of the list.

1. Toggle over to Notepad.

2. Open CELL_SPANNING3.HTM from the HTML-2 folder.

3. Select **File ▶ Save As** and name the file TABLE_LIST.HTM in the HTML-2 folder.

4. Insert the following script that appears in bold:

```
<TR ALIGN=center>
<TD COLSPAN=2 ROWSPAN=2><B>Cell 1-1</B>
<UL TYPE=square>
<LI>turtle
<LI>Corvette
<LI>Rolling Stones
<LI>vacation
<LI>evaporation
<LI>farm
<LI>transistor
</UL>
<TD><B>Cell 1-3</B>
</TR>
```

5. Save the file.

6. Toggle over to your Web browser and load the file TABLE_LIST.HTM.

The page is downloaded and displayed, as shown in Figure 13-2 on the following page.

Note that the bullet list is center justified because of the ALIGN=center attribute in the opening <TR> tag.

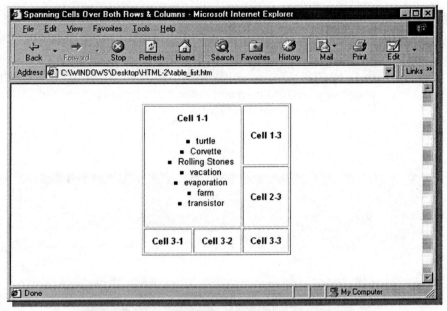

Figure 13-2: Unordered list embedded in a table cell

7. Toggle over to Notepad.

8. Remove or add the following script that appears in bold:

```
<TR ALIGN=center>
<TD COLSPAN=2 ROWSPAN=2><B>Cell 1-1</B>
<UL TYPE=square>
<LI>turtle
<LI>Corvette
<LI>Rolling Stones
<LI>vacation
<LI>evaporation
<LI>farm
<LI>transistor
</UL>
<TD ALIGN=center><B>Cell 1-3</B>
</TR>
```

9. Save the file.

10. Toggle over to your Web browser.

11. Reload the page.

The page is downloaded and displayed, as shown in Figure 13-3.

Note that the bullet list is now left justified because you removed the ALIGN=center attribute from the <TR> tag. Because you added an ALIGN attribute to the <TD> tag, you were able to maintain the center justification of Cell 1-3.

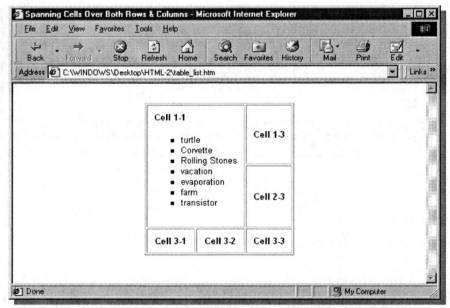

Figure 13-3: List items left justified (default) for clean appearance

12. Change the list to an ordered list.

13. Change the list back to an unordered list with square bullets.

14. Save the file as TABLE_NESTING.HTM in the HTML-2 folder.

Nesting a Table within a Table

Although it is not common knowledge, you can nest any type of table within any cell of another table.

When working with nested tables, there are two table references based on the relationship of the tables:

- <u>master table</u>: the table into which another table is nested;

- <u>slave table</u>: table that is nested within the cell of another table.

Formatting Nested Tables

It is possible to apply rich formatting to nested tables. All types of text and table formatting can be applied to text or tables nested within another table.

Borders

Sometimes, a master table is not given a border but the nested table (slave table) is. Sometimes, both tables are borderless to give them a more "natural" appearance (you will create a table like this in an upcoming exercise). Often, the table that is embedded is not given a BORDER, RULES, or FRAME attribute so a user does not perceive that it is a table.

Creating Columns in Cells

Nested tables allow you to present data in multiple columns within a single "cell" of a table. The data is not really in a single cell, but rather in a nested table and in multiple columns (with no border). The viewer of such a table would perceive the data to be arranged within a table cell, unaware of the nested table.

Browser Support

Table nesting is supported by all major browsers and offers you the opportunity to add an additional level of complexity to the arrangement of data on a page. Both Netscape Navigator/Communicator and Microsoft Internet Explorer have supported tables for several versions.

Exercise 13-2: Nesting a Table within a Table

In this exercise, you will embed a table within a cell of another table to enhance the format of the master table. You will not add a border, rules, or frames to the slave table, thus keeping it "invisible." This will create the effect of a complex data layout within the master table.

1. In Notepad, open TABLE_NESTING.HTM from the HTML-2 folder.

2. Add the following script that appears in bold:

```
<TABLE BORDER CELLPADDING=10 WIDTH=80%>

<TR>
<TD COLSPAN=2 ROWSPAN=2><B>Cell 1-1</B>

<CENTER>
<TABLE>
<TR>
<TD>
<UL TYPE=square>
<LI>turtle
<LI>Corvette
<LI>Rolling Stones
<LI>vacation
<LI>evaporation
<LI>farm
<LI>transistor
</UL>
</TD>
</TR>
</TABLE>
</CENTER>

<TD ALIGN=center><B>Cell 1-3</B>
</TR>
```

3. Save the file.

4. Toggle over to your Web browser.

5. Reload the page.

The Web page now appears with the list centered within Cell 1-1 of the table, as shown in Figure 13-4 on the following page.

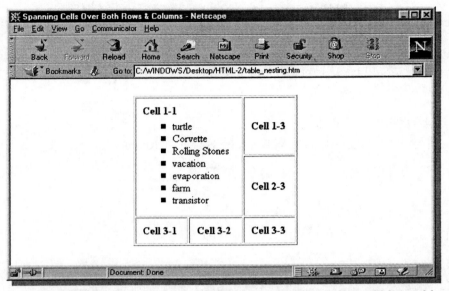

Figure 13-4: List centered within a table cell by nesting a table within a table

Sometimes it is easier to work with nested tables if you temporarily apply a border to the slave table. If you desire the nested slave table to not have a border, remember to remove the BORDER attribute from the nested table prior to finishing your scripting or uploading the HTML page to a server.

6. Toggle over to Notepad.

7. Add the BORDER attribute with no value to the opening table tag of the slave table.

8. Save the file.

9. Toggle over to your Web browser.

10. Reload the page.

The slave table now appears with a border to help you format and align it within the master table.

11. Reformat and align the slave table as you desire. Toggle over to your Web browser to view the changes you have made.

12. When you are finished, remove the slave table border and view the table in your browser.

Exercise 13-3: Nesting Multiple Tables and Lists within a Single Table

In this exercise, you will nest six tables within a single table. You will also embed lists, apply cell spanning, apply background colors, and format text.

1. Toggle over to Notepad.

2. Open NESTED_TABLE.HTM from the HTML-2 folder.

3. Add the following script that appears in bold:

```
<TABLE CELLPADDING=10 CELLSPACING=8>
<TR>
<TD BGCOLOR=gray><IMG SRC=house1.jpg></TD>
<TD BGCOLOR=silver>
<TABLE>
<TR>
<TD COLSPAN=2 BGCOLOR=gray ALIGN=center><B><FONT
COLOR=white>Price: $319,000</FONT></B></TD>
</TR>
<TR>
<TD>
<CENTER><B>Land</B></CENTER>
<UL TYPE=square>
<LI>4.3 acres
<LI>rural setting
<LI>8 miles to school
<LI>12 miles to hospital
<LI>wooded lot behind
<LI>beautiful landscaping
</UL>
</TD>
<TD>
<CENTER><B>House</B></CENTER>
<UL TYPE=square>
<LI>5800 sq. feet
<LI>4 bedrooms
<LI>4 bathrooms
<LI>3 car garage
<LI>full basement
<LI>formal dining room
</UL>
</TD>
</TR>
</TABLE>
</TD>
</TR>
```

4. Save the file.

5. Toggle over to your Web browser and open NESTED_TABLE.HTM.

The page is downloaded and displayed, as shown in Figure 13-5.

Note the effect of a table nested inside a table. A combination of nesting, background colors, text formatting, embedded lists, and text alignment forms an attractive page that provides information that is easy to read.

6. Scroll to the bottom of the page.

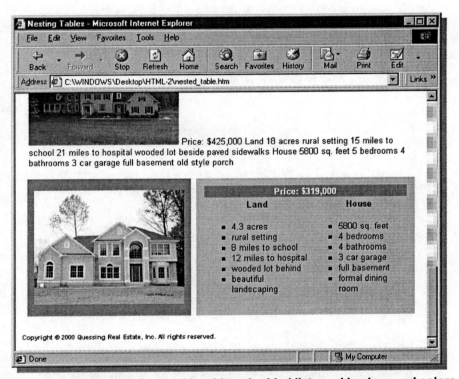

Figure 13-5: Table nested in a table with embedded lists and background colors

7. Toggle back to Notepad.

8. Add the necessary table tags, other HTML tags and attributes to the information for the five remaining homes, nesting the tables as you did in Step 3.

9. Save the file. Toggle over to your Web browser and reload the Web page.

 Your page should appear similar Figure 13-6.

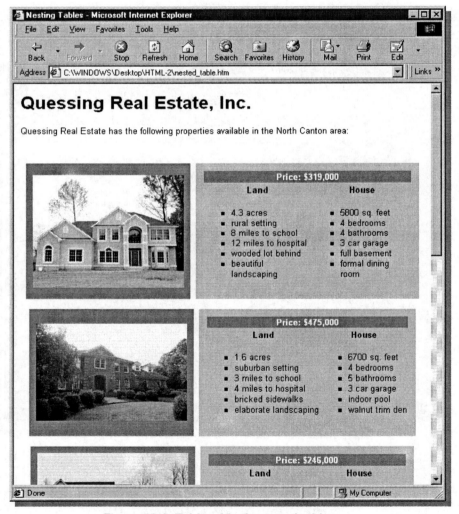

Figure 13-6: Table with six nested tables

Lesson 13 Summary

▶ Two ways to arrange data in a table cell are: 1) embedding an ordered or unordered list and 2) nesting a table. You can combine these features to create richly formatted data, such as embedding a list in a table that is, in turn, nested in another table.

▶ A table into which another table is nested is called a *master* table.

▶ A table that is nested into another table is called a *slave*.

▶ One common problem associated with embedding a list in a table is justification (alignment). You can solve this problem by embedding the list in an "invisible" table (one with no border or gridlines) that is, in turn, nested within another master table. The master table is the one that is visible to the user. The list appears to be embedded directly in the master table.

▶ There are two solutions to the problem of list alignment within table cells: 1) left align content of table cells and 2) embed the list in an invisible table which is, in turn, nested within the master table.

▶ "Master" and "slave" relational terminology is also used to denote nested framesets with HTML frames (as you learned earlier in this course).

▶ Sometimes, a master table is not given a border but the nested (slave table) is. Sometimes, both tables are borderless to give them a more "natural" appearance.

▶ Often, the table that is embedded is not given a BORDER, RULES, or FRAME attribute so a user does not perceive that it is a table.

Lesson 13 Quiz

Matching

___ 1. alignment

a. slave

___ 2. table in which another is nested

b. nesting

___ 3. inserting a list in a table cell

c. master

___ 4. table that is nested in another table

d. alignment

___ 5. inserting a table within a table

e. embedding

___ 6. potential problem with embedded lists

f. justification

Fill in the Blank

7. The two types of tables, as relates to nesting, are _____ and _____ .

8. There are two solutions to the problem of list alignment within table cells: 1) _____ align content in table cells and 2) embed the list in an "_____" table which is, in turn, nested within the master table.

9. _____ tables allow you to present data in multiple columns within a single "cell" of a table. The data is not really in a single cell.

10. By default, a table is justified _____ .

True or False?

T / F   11. There are four attributes associated with embedded lists.

T / F   12. Nesting tables typically involves only HTML 4.0 tags.

T / F   13. To properly embed a list in a table, you may find it necessary to use proprietary HTML tags (HTML extensions).

T / F   14. Like inline frames, table nesting is not supported by all major browsers.

T / F   15. You cannot nest a table within a table within a table.

"Consult my Web site."

Part 3:
HTML 4.0 Advanced
Forms, Image Maps, and Style Sheets

"I have a dream for the World Wide Web and it has two parts. In the first, the Web becomes a much more powerful means for collaboration between people. I have always imagined the information space as something to which everyone has immediate and intuitive access, and not just to browse, but to create. Furthermore, the dream of people-to-people communication through shared knowledge must be possible for groups of all sizes, interacting electronically with as much ease as they do in person. In the second part of the dream, collaborations extend to computers. Machines become capable of analyzing all the data on the Web—the content, links, and transactions between people and computers."

— Tim Berners-Lee, 1999

Part 3 Description

Welcome to *HTML 4.0 Advanced*, DDC's third part in the *Mastering HTML* series. This course is based on the official HTML 4.01 Specification, released on December 24, 1999 by the World Wide Web Consortium (W3C®). This section is a continuation of DDC's *HTML 4.0 Fundamentals* and *HTML 4.0 Intermediate* courses.

In *HTML 4.0 Advanced*, you will find an in-depth review of forms, image maps, and cascading style sheets. An *HTML 4.0 Advanced Tips & Tricks* Lesson is also included to "fill in the gaps" and to provide students with real-world direction for dealing with scripting problems. The Lesson also suggests techniques for creating impressive effects on Web pages.

Course Objectives

This course was developed for Webmasters, HTML scripters, and anyone publishing Web pages and Web sites. This course utilizes lecture material, hands-on exercises, and lesson-specific quizzes to teach:

- Introduction to forms
- Different form elements
- Client-side image maps
- Embedded fonts
- HTML validators and link checkers
- Web page watermarks
- Cascading style sheets

Follow-up Courses

- DDC's *Web Publishing with Acrobat 4.0*
- DDC's *Mastering JavaScript* Series (2 days)
- DDC's *Mastering VBScript* (2 days)
- DDC's *Creating Web Graphics* (Paint Shop Pro 6 and Photoshop 5.5 versions)
- DDC's *CGI/Perl Fundamentals* (2 days)

Part 3 Setup

DDC's *HTML 4.0 Advanced* requires some PC configuration and setup. Five primary elements are required. Those marked with an "*" are bundled on the Student Files CD-ROM.

Necessary Software

1. Web browser (Microsoft Internet Explorer 5.0 or Netscape Navigator / Communicator 4.0*x*)

2. Text editor (MS Notepad recommended)

3. Student files*

4. LiveImage image map software*

5. Basic graphics application

   ▪ Paint Shop Pro (www.jasc.com)

   ▪ LView Pro (www.lview.com)

   ▪ Adobe Photoshop (www.adobe.com)

Installing / Launching Software

Three software applications are required to take or teach this course:

   ▪ A Web browser (Netscape Navigator 4.0*x* or higher or Microsoft Internet Explorer (IE) 5.0*x* or higher).

     Navigator can be downloaded from the Netscape Web site at www.netscape.com; Microsoft IE can be downloaded from Microsoft's Web site at www.microsoft.com/ie.

   ▪ A text editor (Microsoft Windows Notepad recommended). Notepad can be launched in Windows 98/2000 and Windows NT from the **Start** button on the Task bar (choose **Programs** ▶ **Accessories** ▶ **Notepad**).

   ▪ LiveImage image map software. The install file, LIVEIMG129INST.EXE, is provided on the Student File CD-ROM in the IMAGE MAP SOFTWARE folder. Note: the free LiveImage evaluation copy is operational for only 14 days from the date of install. You must purchase and register your copy

Lesson 14
Introduction to HTML Forms

Lesson Topics

▶ Forms Overview

▶ Forms Code Syntax

▶ Form Field Types

▶ Lesson 14 Summary

Forms Overview

A *form* is not a single HTML element. Rather, it is a collection of data input fields designed to provide an interface by which a Web user can input data, select from among options, or provide personal data. Forms can be simple, complex, short, long, or composed of many different types of fields, as you will learn in this Lesson.

Forms perform two basic roles on the Web:

- gather and upload data from users to an e-mail account

- gather and upload data to a CGI program residing on a Web server[21]

Important for E-commerce

Forms are an increasingly important element in e-commerce Web sites. As business-to-consumer and business-to-business commerce becomes the main function of the Internet's World Wide Web, the commonality and popularity of forms will continue to increase.

An example of a form is shown in Figure 14-1.

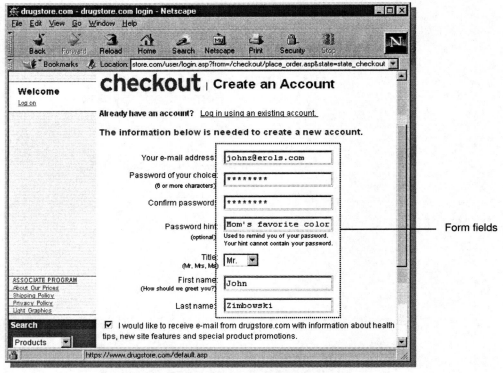

Figure 14-1: Example of an HTML form

---

[21] For more information regarding CGI and Perl, see DDC's two-day *CGI/Perl Fundamentals* course.

Form Functionality

The functionality of forms is two-fold. In this course, you will learn what is necessary to create a form interface at the user (client) level. But this is only half the equation; the other half occurs at the server level. When a user fills in a form and uploads it, a server takes the submitted data and performs some function.

Name-Value Pairs

Data is transferred from an HTML document at the client level to either a CGI program or e-mail account at the server level in *name-value pairs*, as shown in Figure 14-2.

- <u>Value</u>: the variable data being entered by the user (such as their name, address, credit card number, etc.).

- <u>Name</u>: the label used to identify the value, which you determined when you create the form.

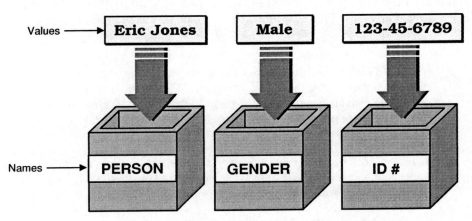

Figure 14-2: Example of name-value pairs in HTML forms

The form field name is simply an identification for the value data which allows the CGI program on a server to separate and differentiate the various values that are being uploaded by the user. This allows the CGI program to "understand" the data it is receiving and properly process it.

 <u>Important</u>: *no two values can share the same name.* Each value within a single form must have a unique name. This will become clearer as you progress through this Lesson and create your own forms.

CGI Programs

The server-level programs that receive data submitted from forms (the data submittal process is also called *posting*) and that process it in some manner can be written in one of many programming or scripting languages, including:

- Perl

- C

- C++

- TCL

- AppleScript

- any other Common Gateway Interface (CGI) language[22]

CGI programs are most commonly written in Perl. You will learn more about CGI programs in Lesson 15: *Advanced Form Functions*.

You do not necessarily have to write your own CGI programs to handle the output of the forms you create. Many Web hosting vendors provide generic CGI programs to their customers free of charge. There are also many freeware and public domain CGI programs available on the Web.

In a corporate or government agency environment, you may have programmers on staff who are available to help you develop CGI programs that work with and process your forms.

---

[22] See DDC's *CGI/Perl Fundamentals* course for more information on writing CGI/Perl scripts.

Forms Code Syntax

The syntax for an HTML form is similar to that of a table; it is a collection of carefully arranged empty and non-empty tag sets and required attributes.

<FORM> Tag

The <FORM> tag is a non-empty tag (non-empty tags are also called *containers*). One interesting characteristic of forms is that any HTML elements can be placed within the form container, including images, tables, and floating frames. You will nest a table in a form in Lesson 15: *Advanced Form Functions*.

Two Necessary Attributes

The <FORM> tag has two necessary attributes:

- ACTION (<FORM **ACTION=mailto:carlp@xyz.com** METHOD=post)

- METHOD (<FORM ACTION=mailto:carlp@xyz.com **METHOD=post**)

ACTION and METHOD are described in more detail in Table 14-1.

<FORM> Tag Attribute	Values
ACTION	■ The URL of a CGI program that accepts the content of the form uploaded from the client browser. Example: ACTION=/cgi-bin/email.cgi ■ Also can be an e-mail address using the ACTION=mailto:username@domain.com syntax.
METHOD	■ get: officially deprecated in the W3C HTML 4.0 Specification; therefore, very uncommon. ■ post: the default METHOD value. Thus, you will always specify a METHOD value of post, such as METHOD=post.

Table 14-1: ACTION and METHOD: the two necessary <FORM> tag attributes

As you will learn in Lesson 2: *Advanced Form Functions*, you can e-mail the output of a form to multiple e-mail addresses and even specify carbon copies and blind carbon copies.

`<INPUT>` Tag

`<INPUT>` is the most common tag within the `<FORM>` container. `<INPUT>` specifies the type of form element being created. `<INPUT>` is used with the following types of form elements (also called *form field types*):

- text fields
- checkboxes
- radio buttons
- password fields

Three Required Attributes

The `<INPUT>` tag has three required attributes:

- TYPE (`<INPUT `**`TYPE=text`**` NAME=first_name>`)
- NAME (`<INPUT TYPE=text `**`NAME=first_name`**`>`)
- VALUE[23] (`<INPUT TYPE=radio NAME=job `**`VALUE=exec`**`>`)

Required attributes of the `<INPUT>` tag are described in more detail in Table 14-2.

`<INPUT>` Attribute	Attribute Values / Description
TYPE	<ul><li>TYPE=text</li><li>TYPE=password</li><li>TYPE=checkbox</li><li>TYPE=radio</li><li>TYPE=button</li></ul>
NAME	<ul><li>Any unique identifier of your choice</li><li>Same NAME value for all radio buttons or checkboxes in a single group</li></ul>
VALUE	Used only with checkboxes and radio buttons. Each radio button or checkbox must have its own value (but they share the same NAME value).

Table 14-2: <INPUT> tag required attributes

---

[23] The VALUE attribute is used only with checkboxes and radio buttons.

List Boxes & Text Areas: The Exceptions

There are two major exceptions to the standard rules of form syntax. Neither involves the `<INPUT>` tag; instead, each has its own tag set to form its own container:

- list boxes (also called *selection boxes* or *selections*)

- text areas (similar to text fields to a user, but very different from a script syntax perspective)

NAME = Required Attribute

All form fields have the required attribute of NAME. Despite their unique tag syntax, list boxes and text areas are no exception, as shown in Table 14-3.

Form Field Type	Tag Syntax	Tag Attributes

List Box	`<SELECT NAME=bandwidth>`
	`<OPTION>33.6 Kbps`
	`<OPTION>56.6 Kbps`
	`<OPTION>cable modem`
	`<OPTION>DSL`
	`<OPTION>T-1`
	`<OPTION>T-3`
	`</SELECT>`
		■ SIZE: turns a "pop up" list into a scrollable list. SIZE sets the number of list items that are displayed (SIZE=5 would display five list items).
		
		■ MULTIPLE: allows multiple selections to be made in a single list box (MULTIPLE=5). User selects a contiguous block using <SHIFT> and non-contiguous list items using <CTRL>.

Text Area	`<TEXTAREA NAME=comments`
	`ROWS=5 COLS=65>`
	`</TEXTAREA>`
		■ ROWS: necessary attribute that defines the height of the text area field, as defined in text rows.
		
		ROWS=6 would display six rows of text. A user can input more than six rows, but additional text must be scrolled to be viewed.
		
		■ COLS: necessary attribute that defines the width of the text area field, as defined in characters.
		
		COLS=65 would display a text area that is 65 characters wide.

Table 14-3: List box and text area characteristics

Putting It All Together

As you can see, one HTML form can be very different from another. You may need to create a very basic form with only a couple of text fields, or you may need to create dozens of fields and use each type of field multiple times.

The code for a prototypical form involving each type of form field is displayed below. The corresponding interpretation by a browser is shown in Figure 14-3 on the following page.

```
<H3>Open a New Account with Us</H3>
<FORM ACTION=mailto:webmaster@corp.com ENCTYPE=text/plain METHOD=post>
First Name: <INPUT TYPE=text NAME=first_name><BR>
Last Name: <INPUT TYPE=text NAME=last_name><P>
Address: <INPUT TYPE=text NAME=address><BR>
City: <INPUT TYPE=text NAME=address><BR>
State: <SELECT NAME=state>
        <OPTION>Alabama
        <OPTION>Alaska
        <OPTION>Arizona
        <OPTION>Arkansas
        <OPTION>California
        <OPTION>Colorado
            </SELECT><BR>

<!-- this list should obviously contain 50 <OPTION> tags, one for each
state; for this example, only the first six states are used -->

ZIP Code: <INPUT TYPE=text NAME=zip><P>
Credit Card:<BR>
<INPUT TYPE=radio NAME=cardtype VALUE=Visa> Visa<BR>
<INPUT TYPE=radio NAME=cardtype VALUE=Mastercard> Mastercard<BR>
<INPUT TYPE=radio NAME=cardtype VALUE=Amex> American Express<P>

Credit Card #: <INPUT TYPE=password NAME=cardnum><P>
Your Hobbies:<BR>
<INPUT TYPE=checkbox NAME=hobby VALUE=running> Running<BR>
<INPUT TYPE=checkbox NAME=hobby VALUE=stamps> Stamp Collecting<BR>
<INPUT TYPE=checkbox NAME=hobby VALUE=chess> Chess<BR>
<INPUT TYPE=checkbox NAME=hobby VALUE=twister> Twister<P>
We welcome your comments and feedback:<BR>
<TEXTAREA ROWS=4 COLS=65> </TEXTAREA><P>

<INPUT TYPE=submit> <INPUT TYPE=reset>

</FORM>
```

The browser interpretation of the form code on the previous page is shown in Figure 14-3.

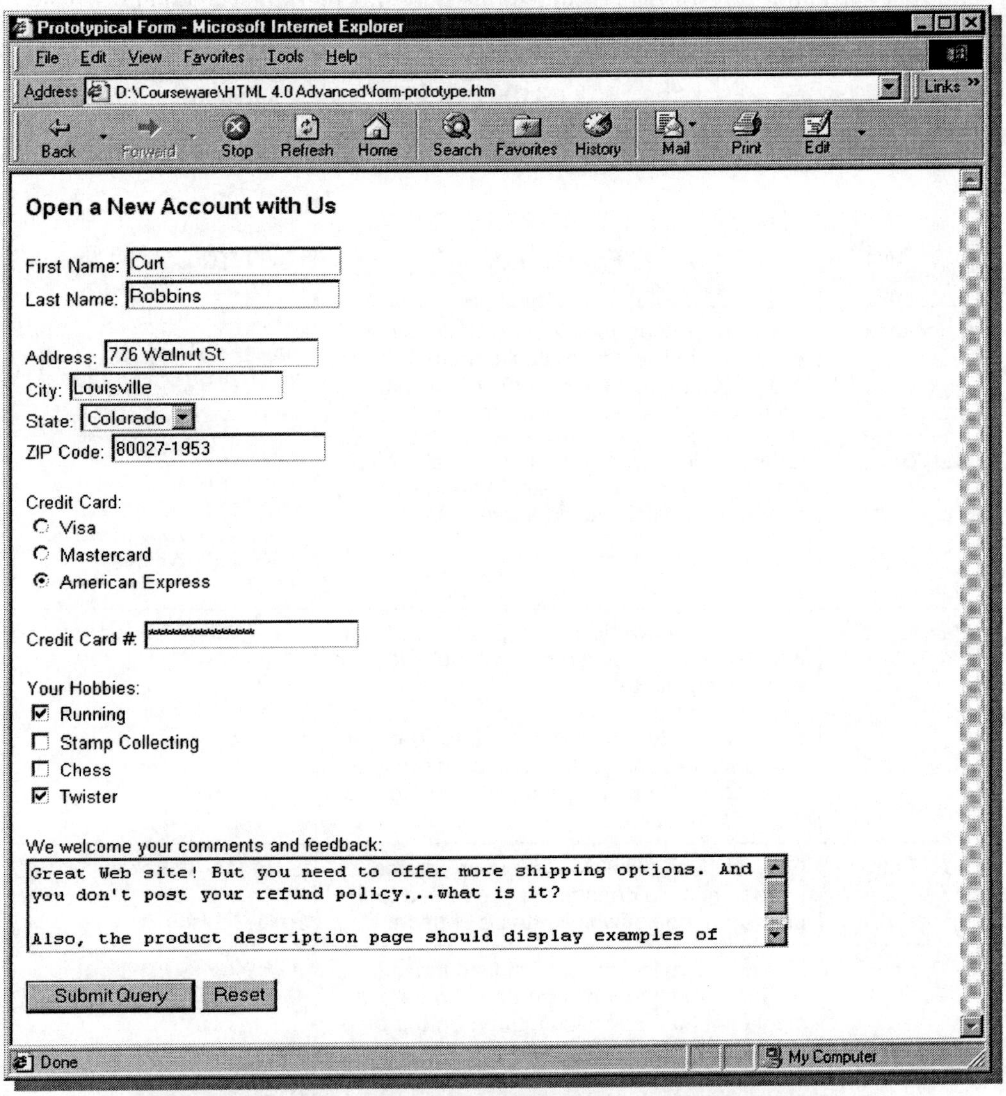

Figure 14-3: HTML form code interpreted by a Web browser (IE 5)

In the code on the previous page, the `<OPTION>` tags do not have `VALUE` attributes. While `VALUE` attributes are not prohibited and are part of the W3C HTML 4.0 Specification, both MS Internet Explorer and Netscape Navigator/Communicator do not require them.

Form Field Types

Forms are comprised of fields. There are six basic types of fields. Each field type is designed to capture a particular type of data or to capture data in a particular manner.

Table 14-4 lists all six form field types and provides a basic description. Note that each form field is created using the <INPUT> tag with a different TYPE attribute, with the exception of list boxes and text areas.

Form Field Type	Function	HTML Tag Syntax
Checkbox	Offer non-exclusive selection choices to a user. In other words, multiple options are presented to the user and they can choose none, one, or all of the options.	`<INPUT TYPE=checkbox NAME=sports VALUE=baseball>`
List Box	Offer multiple options to a user in a vertical list; the user chooses a single answer. More technically, this is called a *select list*.	`<SELECT NAME=state>` `<OPTION>Alabama` `<OPTION>Alaska` `<OPTION>Arizona` `<OPTION>Arkansas` `</SELECT>`
Password	Identical to a text field, except all data input into the field is displayed in asterisks for security purposes. If you are collecting sensitive data, such as social security number, credit card number, bank account number, etc., you should use a password field.	`<INPUT TYPE=password NAME=creditcard>`
Radio Button	Offer exclusive options to a user. In other words, multiple options are presented to the user, only *one* of which can be chosen.	`<INPUT TYPE=radio NAME=agegroup VALUE=teen>`
Text	The most basic type of form field that allows a user to input any alphanumeric data in a single line of a specific length (number of characters). You can limit the amount of text that can be typed in the text field and also determine the width of the text field as displayed in the user's browser. Similar to a text area field, but designed to accommodate much smaller text blocks.	`<INPUT TYPE=text NAME=first_name>`
Text Area	A text field designed to accommodate a relatively large amount of alphanumeric information on multiple lines. Like a text field, you can define the size of a text area.	`<TEXTAREA NAME=comments ROWS=5 COLS=65> </TEXTAREA>`

Table 14-4: Types of HTML form fields

Text Fields

Text fields are the most common type of form fields and also the easiest to script. Text fields are typically used to request brief answers or personal data from a user, such as their name or address.

Characteristics

- Any alphanumeric data can be entered into a text field.

- The width of a text field can be specified using the SIZE attribute; the value is measured in characters (example: SIZE=30).

- The maximum number of characters that can be input into a text field—regardless of its width (as determined by the SIZE attribute)—can be specified using the MAXLENGTH attribute (example: MAXLENGTH=25).

- Most browsers will display a text field as 20 characters wide if you do not use the SIZE attribute.

Example

What is your name? `Curt Robbins`

Figure 14-4: Example of a text field

Code

What is your name? **`<INPUT TYPE=text NAME=name SIZE=30>`**

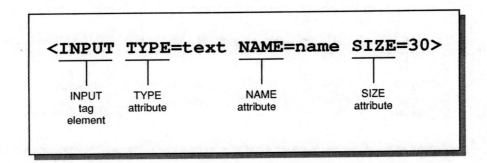

Password Fields

Password fields are very similar to text fields. The difference is that password fields do not display what a user types into them. Instead, a password field displays only asterisks. This serves the purpose of security. If a user is inputting her social security number or a credit card number into a form field, anyone looking over her shoulder will see only asterisks.

Characteristics

- Any alphanumeric data can be entered into a password field.

- The width of a text field can be specified using the SIZE attribute; the value is measured in characters (example: SIZE=30).

- The maximum number of characters that can be input into a text field— regardless of its width (as determined by the SIZE attribute)—can be specified using the MAXLENGTH attribute (example: MAXLENGTH=25).

- This is visual security; no encryption whatsoever is used when the data is uploaded (unless a security scheme, such as SSL, is being employed).

Example

What is your credit card number? `****************`

Figure 14-5: Example of a password field

Code

```
What is your credit card number? <INPUT TYPE=password
NAME=name SIZE=18>
```

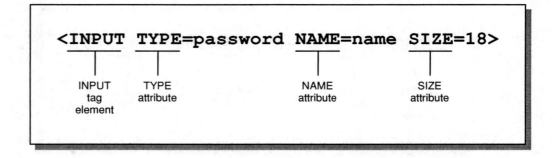

Checkboxes

Checkboxes are used to capture non-exclusive data. *What?* In plain English, checkboxes allow a user to choose from multiple options. The user can choose any number of the available checkbox options (none, one, all, etc.). Thus, checkboxes involve a non-exclusive logic, where no single option is exclusive.

Characteristics

- Checkboxes are only identified to users according to the text that is adjacent to each checkbox. Thus, you must script the data in plain body text that identifies each checkbox for the user.

- Checkboxes require an additional <INPUT> tag attribute: VALUE. All checkboxes in a single group have the same NAME value, but each checkbox is individually identified within the form using the VALUE attribute.

- Only checkbox and radio button form field types require the VALUE attribute.

- Each checkbox can be selected (checked) or unselected (not checked).

Example

Favorite Exercise
☑ Running
☑ Bicycling
☐ Aerobics
☑ Swimming
☐ Watching TV

Figure 14-6: Example of checkboxes

Code

```
Favorite Exercise<BR>
<INPUT TYPE=checkbox NAME=sports VALUE=run> Running<BR>
<INPUT TYPE=checkbox NAME=sports VALUE=cycle> Bicycling<BR>
<INPUT TYPE=checkbox NAME=sports VALUE=aerobics> Aerobics<BR>
<INPUT TYPE=checkbox NAME=sports VALUE=swim> Swimming<BR>
<INPUT TYPE=checkbox NAME=sports VALUE=tv> Watching TV<BR>
```

Radio Buttons

Radio buttons are very similar to checkboxes. Visually, radio buttons appear as circles (whereas checkboxes are displayed as squares). Logically, radio buttons are exclusive. If you create a group of radio buttons and present six options, the user can select only one answer.

Characteristics

- Radio buttons are only identified to users according to the text that is adjacent to each radio button. Thus, you must script the data in plain body text that identifies each radio button for the user.

- Radio buttons require an additional <INPUT> tag attribute: VALUE. All radio buttons in a single group have the same NAME value, but each radio button is individually identified within the form via the VALUE attribute.

- You can use an unlimited number of radio buttons in a single group or in a form.

- Only one radio button in a single group can be selected.

Example

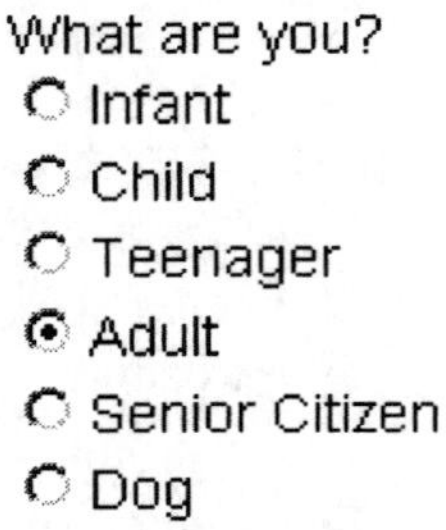

What are you?
O Infant
O Child
O Teenager
⊙ Adult
O Senior Citizen
O Dog

Figure 14-7: Example of radio buttons

Code

```
What are you?<P>
<INPUT TYPE=radio NAME=name VALUE=infant> Infant<BR>
<INPUT TYPE=radio NAME=name VALUE=child> Child<BR>
<INPUT TYPE=radio NAME=name VALUE=teenager> Teenager<BR>
<INPUT TYPE=radio NAME=name VALUE=adult> Adult<BR>
<INPUT TYPE=radio NAME=name VALUE=senior> Senior Citizen<BR>
<INPUT TYPE=radio NAME=name VALUE=arf> Dog<BR>
```

Text Areas

A text area field is similar in appearance and function to a text field, but the HTML code behind it is very different. Whereas a text field is designed for a single line of text, a text area is designed for a much larger volume of text, such as a paragraph or even several paragraphs. You determine how big and how much text a text area field will accommodate.

Characteristics

- A text area is not sized with a SIZE attribute; rather, it is sized using ROWS and COLS attributes (similar to HTML tables).

- A text area is a container; in other words, it involves an opening and closing <TEXTAREA> tag set (unlike the empty <INPUT> tag for text, password, checkbox, and radio button fields).

- Vertical and horizontal scroll bars automatically appear; they are greyed out until a user types more information than is visible in the text area.

- Text typed into a text area field automatically word-wraps in Internet Explorer, but does not in Netscape Navigator (in which it bleeds off the field).

Example

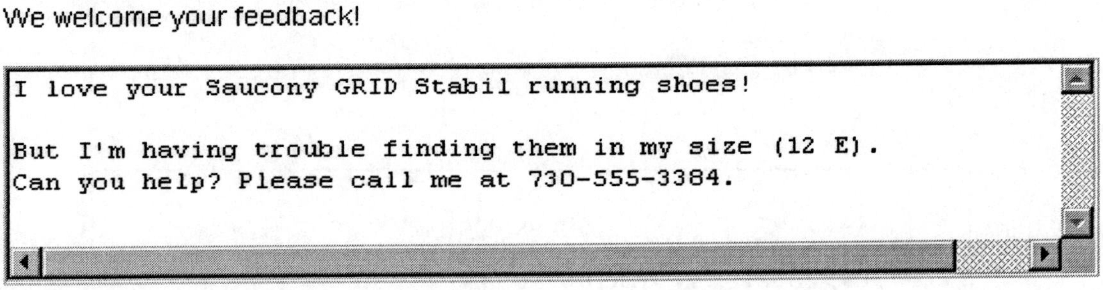

We welcome your feedback!

```
I love your Saucony GRID Stabil running shoes!

But I'm having trouble finding them in my size (12 E).
Can you help? Please call me at 730-555-3384.
```

Figure 14-8: Example of a text area field

Code

```
We welcome your feedback!<P>
<TEXTAREA NAME=comments ROWS=5 COLS=65> </TEXTAREA>
```

List Boxes

A list box, also called a *selection list*, *selection box*, or simply a *menu*, is identical in logic to radio buttons; it presents a list of options and only one option can be chosen by the user. The difference—other than appearance—between list boxes and radio buttons is that list boxes are designed to provide many more options without taking more screen space.

A list box allows you to present a user with dozens or even hundreds of options in the same space as a basic text field; something not practical using radio buttons.

Characteristics

- The select tag is a container (non-empty tag set); thus, you must use both the opening and closing <SELECT> tags to create a list box.

- Similar to an ordered or unordered list in HTML, you must use <OPTION> tags within the <SELECT> tags in order to create a list box.

Example

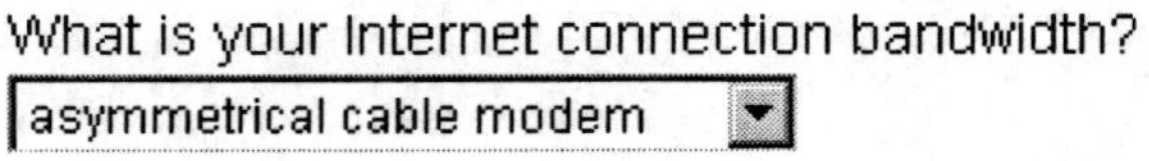

What is your Internet connection bandwidth?

asymmetrical cable modem ▼

Figure 14-9: Example of a list box

Code

```
What is your Internet connection bandwidth?<P>
<SELECT name=bandwidth>
<OPTION>28.8 Kbps dialup modem
<OPTION>33.6 Kbps dialup modem
<OPTION>56.6 Kbps dialup modem
<OPTION>64 Kbps ISDN
<OPTION>128 Kbps ISDN
<OPTION SELECTED>asymmetrical cable modem
<OPTION>symmetrical cable modem
<OPTION>cable modem (unsure of type)
<OPTION>DSL
<OPTION>T-1
<OPTION>T-3
<OPTION>None of your business!
</SELECT>
```

Submit & Reset Buttons

Regardless of the simplicity or complexity of your form, a mechanism must exist that allows a user to upload data to an e-mail address or CGI program on a server.

This is the role of the *Submit* and *Reset* buttons. Created by using the now-familiar <INPUT> tag, the Submit and Reset buttons are easy and straightforward to create. By default, the faces of the Submit and Reset buttons read "Submit Query" and "Reset," respectively. This can be changed, as you will learn in Lesson 15: *Advanced Form Functions*.

Characteristics

- The Submit button executes the actions specified by the values of the attributes in the opening <FORM> tag.

  Thus, assume your opening <FORM> tag appeared as follows:

  ```
  <FORM ACTION=mailto:webmaster@company.com METHOD=post>
  ```

  The contents of the form fields would be uploaded via e-mail to the address webmaster@company.com. If the ACTION value was the URL of a CGI program, the form field contents would be uploaded to the CGI program.

- The Reset button is very simple in function; it simply clears the contents of the form fields. Thus, a user *populates* the form fields and the Reset button *de-populates* them.

- Unlike most other form fields involving the <INPUT> tag, Submit and Reset buttons do not take the NAME attribute.

Example

Figure 14-10: Example of Submit and Reset buttons

Code

```
<INPUT TYPE=submit> <INPUT TYPE=reset>
```

Exercise 14-1: Creating a Basic Form

In this exercise, you will script a form containing a text field, a password field, and a selection of checkboxes.

1. Launch your Web browser (Netscape Navigator/Communicator or Microsoft Internet Explorer).

2. Launch Microsoft Notepad (or the plain text editor of your choice).

3. Using Notepad, open FIRST-FORM.HTM in the HTML-3 folder on your Desktop,.

4. Replace "STEP 1" with the following code (substitute the e-mail address of the computer on which you are working for the text "your e-mail address"):

```
<FORM ACTION=mailto:your e-mail address ENCTYPE=text/plain
METHOD=post>
```

 ENCTYPE formats the output of a form to make it more readable in an e-mail client application. You will learn more about ENCTYPE in Lesson 2.

5. Replace "STEP 2" with the following code:

```
<INPUT TYPE=text NAME=name>
```

6. Replace "STEP 3" with the following code:

```
<INPUT TYPE=checkbox NAME=sport VALUE=run> Running<BR>
<INPUT TYPE=checkbox NAME=sport VALUE=cycle> Bicycling<BR>
<INPUT TYPE=checkbox NAME=sport VALUE=aerobics> Aerobics<BR>
<INPUT TYPE=checkbox NAME=sport VALUE=swim> Swimming<BR>
<INPUT TYPE=checkbox NAME=sport VALUE=TV> Watching TV<P>
```

7. Replace "STEP 4" with the following code:

```
<INPUT TYPE=radio NAME=whatru VALUE=infant>Infant<BR>
<INPUT TYPE=radio NAME=whatru VALUE=child>Child<BR>
<INPUT TYPE=radio NAME=whatru VALUE=teenager>Teenager<BR>
<INPUT TYPE=radio NAME=whatru VALUE=adult>Adult<BR>
<INPUT TYPE=radio NAME=whatru VALUE=senior>Senior Citizen<BR>
<INPUT TYPE=radio NAME=whatru VALUE=arf>Dog<P>
```

8. Save your changes to FIRST-FORM.HTM.

9. Toggle over to your Web browser (<ATL + TAB>).

10. Open FIRST-FORM.HTM in your Web browser:

   ▶ In IE 5, select <CTRL + O>, click **Browse**, open the HTML-3 folder on your Desktop, and double-click FIRST-FORM.HTM.

or

   ▶ In Navigator, select <CTRL + O>, click **Choose File**, open the HTML-3 folder on your Desktop, and double-click FIRST-FORM.HTM.

 Your browser should display the page, as shown in Figure 14-11.

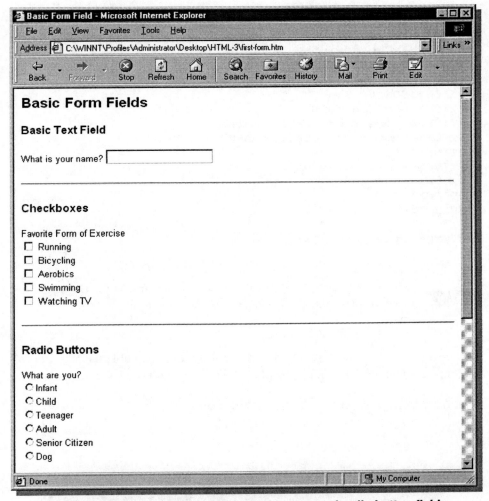

Figure 14-11: Form featuring text, checkboxes, and radio button fields

Exercise 14-2: Creating Password Fields, Text Areas, and List Boxes

In this exercise, you will enhance the form you created in the previous exercise by adding a password field, a text area, and a list box. You will also add Submit and Reset buttons to enable users to upload the contents of the form fields to your e-mail account.

1. Be sure FIRST-FORM.HTM is open in both your text editor and your Web browser.

2. In your text editor, replace "STEP 5" with the following code:

```
<INPUT TYPE=password NAME=cardnum>
```

3. Replace "STEP 6" with the following code:

```
<TEXTAREA NAME=feedback ROWS=5 COLS=65> </TEXTAREA>
```

4. Replace "STEP 7" with the following code:

```
<SELECT NAME=bandwidth>
<OPTION>28.8 Kbps dialup modem
<OPTION SELECTED>56.6 Kbps dialup modem
<OPTION>ISDN 64 Kbps
<OPTION>ISDN 128 Kbps
<OPTION>asymmetrical cable modem
<OPTION>symmetrical cable modem
<OPTION>DSL
<OPTION>satellite
<OPTION>T-1
<OPTION>T-3
</SELECT>

<HR WIDTH=15% ALIGN=left SIZE=5><P>
```

 Inserting the SELECTED attribute in a particular <OPTION> tag will display that option when a user views the form.

5. You now need to create the Submit and Reset buttons to enable users to upload form field contents or clear all form fields. Replace "STEP 8" with the following code:

```
<INPUT TYPE=submit> <INPUT TYPE=reset>
```

6. Replace "STEP 9" with the following code:

```
</FORM>
```

7. Save FIRST-FORM.HTM.

8. Toggle over to your Web browser.

9. Reload the Web page (<CTRL + R>).

 The form fields you added in the preceding steps of this exercise should appear, as shown in Figure 14-12.

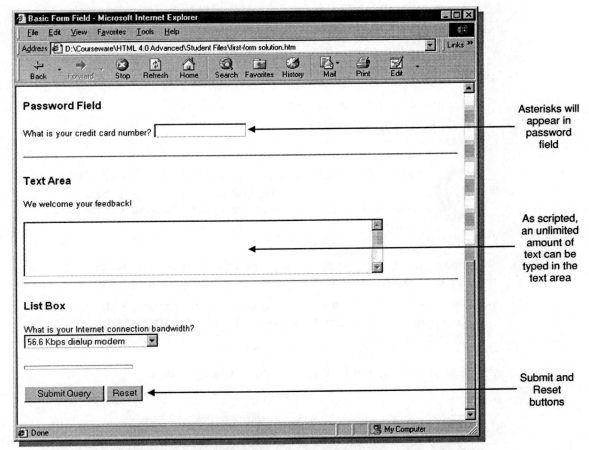

Figure 14-12: Completed form, including Submit and Reset buttons at bottom

Exercise 14-3: Testing Your Form

In this exercise, you will test your form by populating each field and uploading it. You should always thoroughly test your form to ensure that it functions properly. You want to identify and repair any errors before your form goes live online. Allowing users to identify and inform you of errors is unprofessional.

1. In your Web browser, open FIRST-FORM.HTM (if necessary).

2. At the top of the form, in the basic text field, type your name.

3. Press <TAB> to advance to the next form field. The first checkbox will appear with a marquee around it, denoting that it is the active field.

4. On your keyboard, press the space bar. The Running checkbox will be selected.

5. Press <TAB> three times to activate the Swimming checkbox. Press the spacebar.

6. Scroll down to the radio buttons section and click **Adult**.

7. Click **Senior Citizen**.

The Senior Citizen radio button will be selected while the Adult radio button will be deselected. <u>Remember</u>: radio buttons are exclusive; only one in a single group can be selected.

8. In the password field, type any 15-digit number. If you coded the password <INPUT> tag correctly, nobody around you should be able to read the numbers you type.

9. In the text area field, type the following text: **Nice form. But why am I giving you my credit card number? Is this legal?!**

10. In the list box, select **symmetrical cable modem**.

11. At the bottom of the field, click the **Submit Query** button.

The contents of the form fields will be uploaded via e-mail to your e-mail account.

If an alert box appears asking you to save passwords or warning you that the data you are uploading is not encrypted, do not save passwords and choose whatever option continues the upload of your form data.

12. If you have an e-mail account and e-mail software on the computer on which you are working, launch your e-mail software and download all new messages.

You should have an incoming e-mail message that appears similar to Figure 14-13. <u>Note</u>: the heading information (date, from, subject, etc.) will vary from the example shown below).

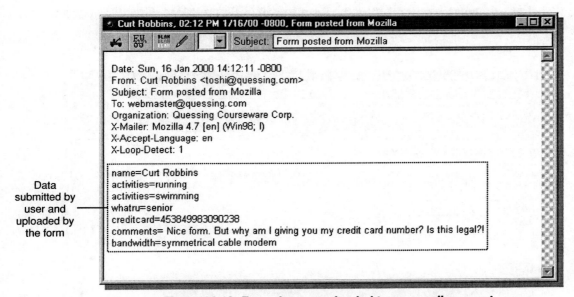

Data submitted by user and uploaded by the form

Figure 14-13: Form data as uploaded to an e-mail account

 List boxes are most useful when there are many choices to be made. If there are only a few choices, then either checkboxes or radio buttons are typically a more logical choice, providing a more streamlined, intuitive interface for users.

Exercise 14-4: Going Solo—Scripting an HTML Form on Your Own

In this exercise, you will create an HTML form on your own that contains text fields, a password field, radio buttons, checkboxes, list boxes, and a text area.

1. Using the HTML form knowledge you have gained from previous exercises, script an HTML document that will result in the form shown in Figure 14-14. Give the page an HTML title of "My First Solo Form."

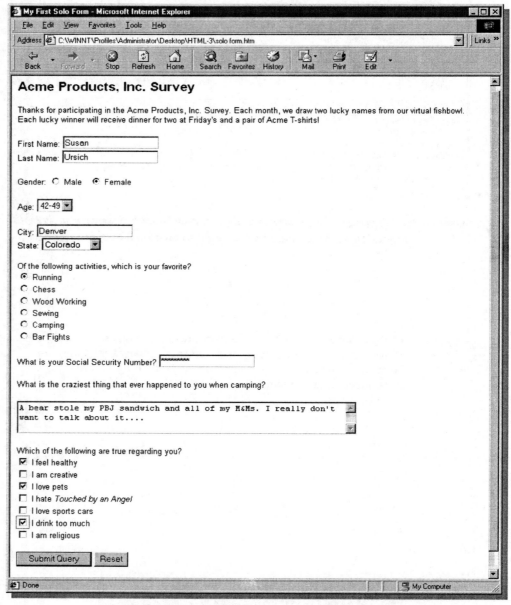

Figure 14-14: Your first challenge—create this form

2. Make the ACTION of the form to send an e-mail message to your personal e-mail account.

3. Make the **Age** field a list box with the following OPTIONS values: 18-25, 26-33, 34-41, 42-49, 50-57, 58-65, 66-73, 74-81, 82-89, 90-97.

4. For the **State** list box, include all 50 states in the U.S. Do not use abbreviations.

To save you time, you can open the file STATES.TXT in the HTML-3 folder on your Desktop.

Hint: copy the text from the file STATES.TXT into the Windows clipboard (<CTRL + C>) and paste it into your form. Then script one <OPTION> tag left adjacent of Alabama. Copy this tag to the clipboard and paste it 49 times left adjacent of each state name.

5. When you are finished, save the file as SOLO FORM.HTM and save it to the HTML-3 folder on your Desktop.

6. Open and view the completed page in your Web browser. Compare it to Figure 14-14 on the previous page. How well do they compare?

7. There will probably be minor errors. Return to your text editor and fix these problems. Check the document in your Web browser to ensure that the problems have been fixed properly.

If you are participating in an instructor-led environment and get confused or have trouble, ask your instructor for assistance.

Lesson 14 Summary

▶ A form is not a single HTML element. Rather, it is a collection of data input fields designed to provide an interface by which a Web user can input data, selecting from among options or providing personal information. Forms perform two basic roles on the Web: 1) gather and upload data from users to an e-mail account and 2) gather and upload data to a CGI program residing on a Web server.

▶ Data is transferred from an HTML document at the client level to either a CGI program or e-mail account at the server level in name-value pairs. The "value" is the variable data being entered by the user; the "name" is used to identify the value.

▶ Forms have a relatively sophisticated and strict syntax that is composed of a family of tags, containers (tag sets), and attributes (many of which are necessary). The overriding container is formed by the opening and closing <FORM> tags. <FORM> has two necessary attributes: ACTION and METHOD.

▶ The most common tag inside the <FORM> container is the <INPUT> tag. <INPUT> determines the type of form field being created. All types of form fields are created using the <INPUT> tag, with the exception of list boxes and text areas.

▶ Text fields are the most common type of form field. HTML syntax is: <INPUT TYPE=text NAME=first_name>.

▶ Password fields are similar to text fields. The only difference is that the text entered by a user in a password field is displayed as asterisks. This is because password fields are used to collect confidential information, such as credit card numbers and social security numbers. HTML syntax is: <INPUT TYPE=password NAME=ssn>.

▶ Checkboxes capture *non-exclusive* data. In other words, a user can choose any number of checkboxes within a single group (none, any, or all). HTML syntax is: <INPUT TYPE=checkbox NAME=fave_sports VALUE=football>. Checkboxes, like radio buttons, have an additional necessary attribute of VALUE.

▶ Radio buttons capture *exclusive* data. Thus, they provide options to a user where only one answer from among the options is logical. Examples are: age group, income level, race, etc. HTML syntax is: <INPUT TYPE=radio NAME=job_type VALUE=exec>.

▶ Text areas are like text fields on steroids. They have multiple lines and can be as wide as the page. They are designed to accept a large amount of alphanumeric data. The HTML syntax is: <TEXTAREA NAME=comments ROWS=5 COLS=65> </TEXTAREA>.

▶ List boxes are similar in logic to radio buttons in that they provide a list of options, only one of which can be selected. The HTML syntax is: <SELECT NAME=state> <OPTION>item 1<OPTION>item 2<OPTION>item 3<OPTION>item 4</SELECT>.

▶ The data populating form fields is uploaded to a CGI program or e-mail account by the user via the Submit button. There is also a Reset button, which simply clears all fields in a form. HTML syntax is: <INPUT TYPE=submit> and <INPUT TYPE=reset>.

Lesson 14 Quiz

Matching

___ 1. does not require the `<INPUT>` tag

___ 2. required attribute by all `<INPUT>` tags

___ 3. basic text field

___ 4. upload form data

___ 5. list box

a. `<SELECT>`

b. `TYPE=submit`

c. `text area`

d. `NAME`

e. `TYPE=text`

Fill in the Blank

6. The number of items in a list box is determined by the number of _____ tags placed between the opening and closing `<SELECT>` tags.

7. Credit card numbers and social security numbers should be collected using _____ fields.

8. In a group of checkboxes, the value of each `NAME` field is the same, but the value of each _____ field must be different (to differentiate the various checkboxes).

9. If you want populated form data to be uploaded to the `bubba@corp.com` e-mail account, you must script `ACTION=`_____ .

True or False?

T / F 10. A password field has a limit of 16 characters (because credit card numbers do not exceed this).

T / F 11. `<OPTION>` tags do not require a `VALUE` attribute, but they do require adjacent body text.

T / F 12. `<TEXTAREA>` is a container (non-empty tag set).

T / F 13. The `TYPE` attribute value for a checkbox is "check."

T / F 14. Text area fields are typically used for free-form comments or feedback.

T / F 15. All radio buttons in a single group must have the same `NAME` value.

(This page intentionally left blank)

DDC Publishing • www.ddcpub.com

Lesson 15
Advanced Form Functions

Lesson Topics

▶ HTML Form Review

▶ Supplemental Field Attributes

▶ Embedding Tables in Forms

▶ Forms Tips & Tricks

▶ Posting Forms to CGI Programs

▶ Lesson 9 Summary

HTML Form Review

Lesson 14: *Introduction to HTML Forms* provided you with a solid knowledge of and practice creating forms. In this Lesson, you will extend your knowledge by using special attributes to modify the appearance or functionality of form fields. You will also mix different HTML elements, such as forms and tables, and forms and images.

Test Your Forms Knowledge

Before you move on to this Lesson, you need to test what you learned in the previous Lesson. Complete the quiz below.

1. What are the two types of form fields that do not rely on the <INPUT> tag?

    _____

2. Script the code for a list box that presents a user with the following options: High School Grad, Some College, College Grad, Post Graduate Work, Masters Degree, Ph.D., M.D.

3. True or False: when creating list boxes, adding VALUE attributes to the <OPTION> tags will cause the user's browser to misinterpret the code and ruin the entire form.

4. True or False: there is a limit of 12 items in a group of checkboxes.

5. By default, what is the limit to the amount of text a user can type into a text area field?

6. Script the code for a password field that accepts a credit card number.

7. Script the code for the form element that allows a user to upload a populated form.

8. What is the <FORM> attribute that determines the specific action taken when a user clicks the Submit button? _____

9. Radio buttons denote an exclusive selection logic; their cousins, _____ , involve a non-exclusive logic in which the user can choose multiple or even all options.

10. Radio buttons and check boxes require the _____ attribute to the <INPUT> tag; other form fields do not.

Supplemental Field Attributes

You already know about the necessary (required) form tag attributes, such as NAME and—for checkboxes and radio buttons—VALUE.

However, there are also many useful and powerful supplemental attributes that can help you customize your form fields to best suit a particular application or user preferences.

Text & Password Fields

Text and password fields, defined by the TYPE=text and TYPE=password attributes to the <INPUT> tag, have two supplemental attributes, as shown in Table 15-1.

Attribute	Value Set
SIZE	Any positive integer. Translates into the width of the text field in characters. Example: `<INPUT TYPE=password NAME=creditcard SIZE=16>`
MAXLENGTH	Any positive integer. Limits the number of characters that a user can input into the field, regardless of the SIZE which has been specified. Example: `<INPUT TYPE=text NAME=zip MAXLENGTH=10>`

Table 15-1: Text and password field supplemental attributes

Characteristics

Remember the following characteristics of both SIZE and MAXLENGTH:

- The values of SIZE and MAXLENGTH do not have to equal each other.

- The value of MAXLENGTH does not have to be less than the value of SIZE.

- You can use either or both of these supplemental attributes when scripting a text field or a password field.

- Although not technically required, it is recommended that you always specify a MAXLENGTH value that is less than the SIZE value.

Exercise 15-1: Using the SIZE and MAXLENGTH Attributes

In this exercise, you will use the `SIZE` and `MAXLENGTH` attributes with both a text field and a password field.

1. Launch Notepad (or the ASCII text editor of your choice) and open SIZE_AND_MAXLENGTH.HTM from the HTML-3 folder on your Desktop.

2. Toggle over to your Web browser and open SIZE_AND_MAXLENGTH.HTM.

3. Toggle back to Notepad and add the following code that appears in bold:

```
First name: <INPUT TYPE=text NAME=first_name SIZE=10><BR>
Last name: <INPUT TYPE=text NAME=last_name SIZE=15><BR>
Address: <INPUT TYPE=text NAME=address SIZE=20><BR>
City: <INPUT TYPE=text NAME=city SIZE=15><BR>
State:       <SELECT NAME=state>
             <OPTION>New York
             <OPTION>Ohio
             <OPTION>Pennsylvania
             <OPTION>Maryland
             <OPTION>West Virginia
             <OPTION>Connecticut
             <OPTION>New Jersey
             </SELECT><BR>
Zip+4 Code: <INPUT TYPE=text NAME=zip MAXLENGTH=10 SIZE=11><P>

<HR WIDTH=50% ALIGN=left SIZE=6><P>

Social Security #: <INPUT TYPE=password NAME=ssn MAXLENGTH=11
SIZE=12><P>
```

4. Save the changes you have made to SIZE_AND_MAXLENGTH.HTM.

5. Toggle over to your Web browser. Note the change in the lengths of the text fields as you press <CTRL + R> to reload the Web page.

The lengths of the fields change according to the changes you made in Step 3.

6. Click once in the **Zip+4** field and type all nine characters of your zip code. Separate the first five characters and the +4 section by a hyphen. Note that you cannot type more text (the `MAXLENGTH` attribute prevents it).

7. Press <TAB> to advance to the **Social Security #** field and type your social security number, using hyphens where appropriate. <u>Note</u>: the contents of a password field will always appear as asterisks for security purposes.

8. Try to type an additional number in the **Social Security #** field. You cannot due to the value of the MAXLENGTH attribute. Depending on the configuration of your computer, you may hear an audible alert each time you attempt to type a character that exceeds the limit set by MAXLENGTH.

 Note that the SIZE attribute values have been set to one character more than the value of the MAXLENGTH fields. This is solely for aesthetic purposes.

<u>Remember</u>: there is no technical relationship between the SIZE and MAXLENGTH values. They can be set to any positive integer independently.

 The page in your browser should appear similar to Figure 15-1.

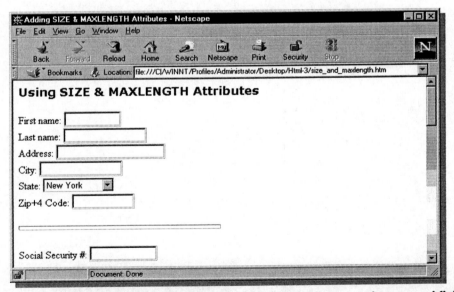

Figure 15-1: Using SIZE and MAXLENGTH to restrict input in text and password fields

Checkboxes & Radio Buttons

Checkboxes and radio buttons have a unique supplemental attribute with which you can create more specialized forms for particular applications and topics.

This supplemental attribute is described in Table 15-2.

Attribute	Value Set
CHECKED	None. By adding CHECKED to the <INPUT> tag, the checkbox or radio button will be preselected (with no user action). The user can still deselect or reselect the field. Example: <INPUT TYPE=radio NAME=age VALUE=teen **CHECKED**>

Table 15-2: Checkbox and radio button CHECKED attribute

"At its heart, HTML is about structure. Author are given a set of tools to mark the purpose and intent of each piece of text within a Web page. It's then up to the browser to decide how to display the content to the end user. By working with structure separately from appearance, HTML comes closer to achieving true independence from the proprietary demand of specific browsers."

— *Rick Darnell, Internet Writer, 1998*

DDC Publishing • www.ddcpub.com

Exercise 15-2: Using the CHECKED Attribute

In this exercise, you will apply the CHECKED attribute to both a set of checkboxes and a set of radio buttons.

1. In your Web browser, open CHECKED.HTM from the HTML-3 folder.

2. Toggle over to your text editor and open CHECKED.HTM.

3. Add the following code that appears in bold:

```
<FONT FACE=verdana COLOR=green SIZE=3><B>Favorite Form of
Exercise</B></FONT><P>

<INPUT TYPE=checkbox NAME=sport VALUE=run CHECKED> Running<BR>
<INPUT TYPE=checkbox NAME=sport VALUE=cycle> Bicycling<BR>
<INPUT TYPE=checkbox NAME=sport VALUE=aerobics> Aerobics<BR>
<INPUT TYPE=checkbox NAME=sport VALUE=swim> Swimming<BR>
<INPUT TYPE=checkbox NAME=sport VALUE=TV CHECKED> Watching TV<P>

<HR WIDTH=40% SIZE=6 ALIGN=left><P>

<FONT FACE=verdana COLOR=green SIZE=3><B>What are
you?</B></FONT><P>

<INPUT TYPE=radio NAME=whatru VALUE=infant> Infant<BR>
<INPUT TYPE=radio NAME=whatru VALUE=child> Child<BR>
<INPUT TYPE=radio NAME=whatru VALUE=teenager> Teenager<BR>
<INPUT TYPE=radio NAME=whatru VALUE=adult CHECKED> Adult<BR>
<INPUT TYPE=radio NAME=whatru VALUE=senior> Senior Citizen<BR>
<INPUT TYPE=radio NAME=whatru VALUE=arf> Dog<P>
```

4. Save your changes to CHECKED.HTM.

5. Toggle over to your Web browser and reload the page.

The page should appear similar to

Figure 15-2 on the following page.

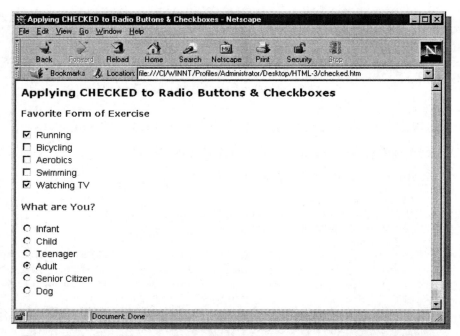

Figure 15-2: Checkboxes and radio buttons preselected using CHECKED

6. In the **Favorite Form of Exercise** section, click the checkbox adjacent to **Running**. It will become deselected.

7. Click the checkbox adjacent to **Watching TV**. It will become deselected.

8. Click the checkbox adjacent to **Swimming**. It will become selected.

9. In the **What are You** section, click **Dog**. The **Adult** radio button is deselected and the **Dog** radio button is selected.

As you can see, CHECKED only preselects options in radio button and checkbox groups. It does not in any way limit the user's choices from among the options.

DDC Publishing • www.ddcpub.com

List Boxes

List boxes have two supplemental attributes that can significantly change the appearance and functionality of the pulldown menu. Both supplemental attributes are described in Table 15-3.

Attribute	Value Set
SIZE	Any positive integer. Turns a "pop up" list into a scrollable list. A value of between 3 and 10 is typically best. Example: `<SELECT NAME=state SIZE=6>`
MULTIPLE	None. Simply add MULTIPLE to the opening `<SELECT>` tag. This will allow the user to select multiple items from the list box. MULTIPLE should be used in conjunction with SIZE. Example: `<SELECT NAME=state SIZE=6 MULTIPLE>`
SELECTED	None. Simply add SELECTED to any `<OPTION>` tag and that particular option will be displayed. In default list boxes that are displayed as one line that "pop up," the selected item is simply displayed in the unclicked window. When used in conjunction with SIZE, the selected option is highlighted. Example: `<OPTION SELECTED>Colorado`

Table 15-3: List box supplemental attributes

Examples of MULTIPLE & SIZE

Figure 15-3: <SELECT SIZE=6 MULTIPLE>: contiguous block (left); discontiguous block (right)

 A good example of a need to turn a pop up list into a scrollable list is a long list, such as all 50 states in the United States. Many browsers are not capable of displaying a list box of this size or they display it poorly.

Exercise 15-3: Using the SIZE and MULTIPLE Attributes

In this exercise, you will apply the SIZE and MULTIPLE attributes to a <SELECT> tag to create a list box that: 1) converts a pop up list to a scrollable list, displaying multiple options simultaneously, and 2) allows the user to select multiple list items in either contiguous or discontiguous groups.

1. In your Web browser, open SIZE_AND_MULTIPLE.HTM. The list box will appear with all defaults. (No supplemental attributes are being used with either the <SELECT> tag or the <OPTION> tag.)

2. Toggle over to Notepad and open SIZE_AND_MULTIPLE.HTM.

3. Add the code that appears below in bold:

```
What is your Internet connection bandwidth?<P>

<SELECT SIZE=4 NAME=bandwidth>
<OPTION>28.8 Kbps dialup modem
<OPTION>56.6 Kbps dialup modem
<OPTION>ISDN 64 Kbps
<OPTION>ISDN 128 Kbps
<OPTION>asymmetrical cable modem
<OPTION>symmetrical cable modem
<OPTION>DSL
<OPTION>satellite
<OPTION>T-1
<OPTION>T-3
</SELECT>
```

4. Save the file.

5. Toggle over to your Web browser and reload the page.

The list box should display four rows of data, as shown in Figure 15-4 on the following page.

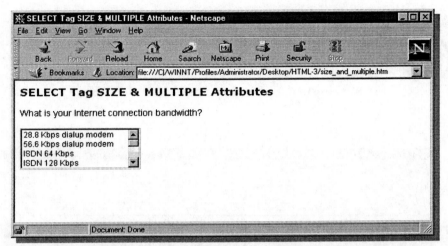

Figure 15-4: List box now displays four rows of data via the SIZE=4 attribute

6. In the list box, click the **56.6 Kbps dialup modem** list item.

7. Press and hold <CTRL> on your keyboard and click **ISDN 128 Kbps**.

 The 56.6 Kbps dialup modem list item is deselected and the ISDN 128 Kbps item is selected. By default, a user cannot choose more than one item from a list box, even if the box appearance has been modified using the SIZE attribute.

8. Toggle back to Notepad.

9. Change the value of the SIZE attribute from **4** to **7**. Add the following code to the opening <SELECT> tag:

MULTIPLE

10. Save the file.

11. Toggle over to your Web browser and reload the page.

12. Click the **56.6 Kbps dialup modem** list item. Hold <CTRL> on your keyboard and click **ISDN 128 Kbps**. Continue holding <CTRL> and click **DSL**. Release <CTRL>.

All three list items are selected, as shown in Figure 15-5.

When you use the MULTIPLE attribute, a user can select any or all items in a list box by using <CTRL> or <SHIFT>.

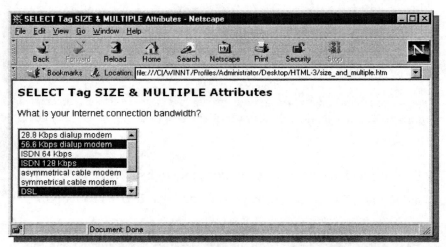

Figure 15-5: Any or all list items can be selected via the MULTIPLE attribute

13. In the list box, click **56.6 Kbps dialup modem**. Because you did not hold <CTRL> or <SHIFT>, the list item is selected while all other list items are deselected.

14. Press and hold <SHIFT> and click **symmetrical cable modem**. This will select all list items *between* the first and last items clicked, inclusive.

Many users are not aware that they have the option of choosing multiple items from a list box. Instructions describing the use of <CTRL> to select discontiguous items and <SHIFT> to select contiguous blocks may be helpful in your Web pages (especially if your target market is non-technical users).

Exercise 15-4: Using the SELECTED Attribute

In this exercise, you will apply the SELECTED attributes to a <SELECT> tag to prioritize one of the list items (options) to be displayed by default.

1. In your Web browser, open SELECTED.HTM from the HTML-3 folder on your Desktop.

 A list box appears that displays seven list items, none of which are selected (this is the default for a list of any size).

 Based on what you learned thus far and the characteristics of this list box, what supplemental attribute and value have been inserted into the opening <SELECT> tag?

2. In Notepad, open SELECTED.HTM.

3. Add the SELECTED attribute to the <OPTION> tag adjacent to **Football**.

4. Save the HTML document in Notepad, toggle over to your Web browser, and reload the Web page.

 The list box now appears with the Football list item preselected, as shown in Figure 15-6.

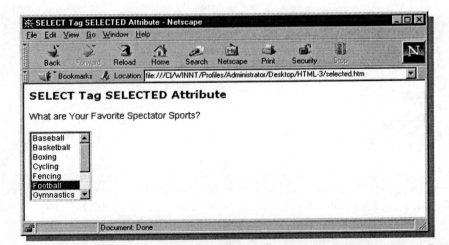

Figure 15-6: List box item preselected using the <OPTION SELECTED> attribute

5. Hold <CTRL> and click the **Baseball** list item.

The Baseball item is selected and the Football item is deselected. This is proof that the MULTIPLE attribute has not been added to the <SELECT> tag.

6. Toggle back to Notepad.

7. Add the MULTIPLE attribute to the opening <SELECT> tag. <u>Remember</u>: MULTIPLE has no value.

8. Remove the SELECTED attribute from the **Football** <OPTION> tag and add it to the **Running** list item <OPTION> tag. <u>Remember</u>: SELECTED has no value.

9. Save the HTML document, toggle over to your Web browser, and reload the page.

10. Scroll down to the bottom of the list.

The list appears with the Running list item preselected. Note that the list did *not* automatically scroll down to display the selected list item.

11. Hold <CTRL> and click **Football**. Both the preselected **Running** item and **Football** will be selected (because you added MULTIPLE in Step 7), as shown in Figure 15-7.

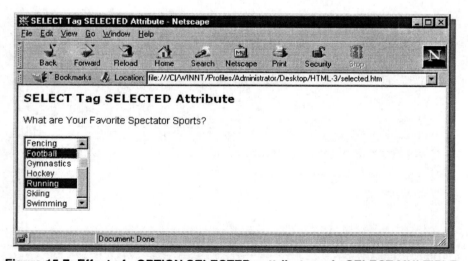

Figure 15-7: Effect of <OPTION SELECTED> attribute and <SELECT MULTIPLE>

Text Area Text

Text areas allow you to display text within the text area field. There is no special attribute or tag for this. Remember that <TEXTAREA> is a container.

To insert text into the text area field, you simply type it between the opening and closing <TEXTAREA> tags. Thus, any text that appears inside the text area container will appear inside the text area field. Note that this text can be modified by users.

Example of Modifiable Text

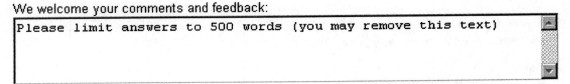

Figure 15-8: Example of modifiable text inserted into a text area field

READONLY

There is a supplemental attribute supported by the <TEXTAREA> tag, but it is not universally supported by all major browsers. This attribute, READONLY, is described in Table 15-4.

Attribute	Value Set
READONLY	Makes all text in the text area read-only, so a user cannot delete or modify the text or add new text. Not allowing a user to add new text somewhat defeats the purpose of a text area. Supported by Internet Explorer 5.0; *not supported* by Netscape Navigator/Communicator 4.x. Example: `<TEXTAREA ROWS=5 COLS=70 READONLY>This text cannot be changed</TEXTAREA>`

Table 15-4: <TEXTAREA> READONLY attribute

 READONLY can be applied to any <INPUT> tag. Thus, one application of READONLY could be the creation of online "sample" forms in which you do not want to receive input from a user.

Non-Web examples are published by insurance companies and hospitals, with large watermarks across them to denote they are samples.

Exercise 15-5: Adding Modifiable Text to a Text Area Field

In this exercise, you will add modifiable text to a text area field that provides additional instructions or direction to any user of your form.

1. In your Web browser, open TEXTAREA.HTM. Note the appearance of the text area field.

2. In Notepad, open TEXTAREA.HTM.

3. Add the following code that appears in bold:

```
<TEXTAREA NAME=comments ROWS=5 COLS=65>Please limit answers to
500 words (you may remove this text)</TEXTAREA>
```

4. Save the HTML document.

5. Toggle over to your Web browser and reload the Web page.

The text area field will now display the text you typed between the opening and closing <TEXTAREA> tags in Step 3 (known as the text area container), as shown in Figure 15-9.

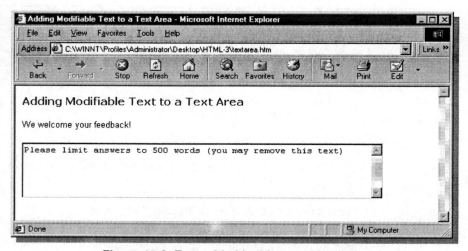

Figure 15-9: Text added inside text area field

Exercise 15-6: Adding READONLY Text to a Text Area Field

In this exercise, you will add READONLY text to a text area field. This text cannot be modified by a user, nor can additional text be added to the text area field. For this reason, the READONLY attribute is rarely added to the <TEXTAREA> tag.

1. In your Web browser, open TEXTAREA-2.HTM. Note the appearance of the text area.

2. In Notepad, open TEXTAREA-2.HTM.

3. Add the following code to the opening <TEXTAREA> tag: **READONLY**.

4. Change the text between the opening and closing <TEXTAREA> tags to read "**—This text *cannot* be altered—**".

5. Save the HTML document.

6. Toggle over to your Web browser and reload the Web page.

7. Attempt to select the text in the text area field. Attempt to type additional text in the field.

 The text inside the text area field cannot be altered and no additional text can be added, as shown in Figure 15-10.

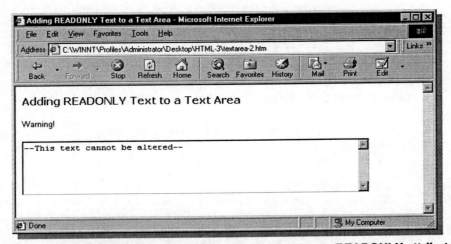

Figure 15-10: Text area field with unmodifiable text due to READONLY attribute

 READONLY is not properly interpreted by Netscape Navigator/Communicator. Therefore, this attribute works only with Microsoft Internet Explorer or any fully compliant HTML 4.0 browser.

Submit & Reset Buttons

You may have already wished you could change the text that is displayed on the Submit and Reset buttons. "Submit Query" is not logical for many applications. You may also have noticed that other Web sites display the Submit and Reset buttons with customized text.

You can, in fact, modify the text displayed on the face of the Submit and Reset buttons to the text of your choice. As you will see later in this Lesson, you can also substitute graphics for the buttons while retaining full functionality.

Example

Figure 15-11: Customized Submit and Reset button faces

The supplemental attribute that creates this effect is VALUE, as described in Table 15-5.

Attribute	Value Set
VALUE	Changes the text that is displayed on the face of the Submit or Reset buttons. The value of VALUE is case sensitive. Example: `<INPUT TYPE=submit VALUE=`**`Upload Survey`**`>`

Table 15-5: VALUE attribute to the Submit and Reset <INPUT> tags

DDC's *Mastering HTML 4.0* Series does not follow the official HTML 4.0 Specification with regard to attribute values, which the official Specification states should always be enclosed in quotation marks (exam: `TYPE="radio"`).

Going back several versions, both Netscape Navigator/Communicator and Microsoft Internet Explorer properly interpret attribute values without the quotation marks.

<u>There is one important exception, however</u>: when the attribute value is composed of more than one word. In such cases, you must always use quotations marks around the value or only the first word will be interpreted (e.g.: `<IMG SRC=bailey.jpg ALT="our pride and joy">`).

Exercise 15-7: Customizing Submit and Reset Button Faces

In this exercise, you will customize the text displayed on the faces of the Submit and Reset buttons by using the VALUE attribute to the Submit and Reset <INPUT> tags.

1. In Notepad, open BUTTON_VALUE.HTM from the HTML-3 folder on your Desktop.

2. Scroll to the bottom of the HTML document and note the standard code for the Submit and Reset buttons.

3. Toggle over to your Web browser and open BUTTON_VALUE.HTM. Scroll to the bottom of the form and note the standard appearance of the Submit and Reset buttons.

4. Toggle over to Notepad and add the following code at the bottom of the document:

```
<INPUT TYPE=submit VALUE="Upload Application"> <INPUT TYPE=reset
VALUE="Clear Form">
```

5. Save your changes to the HTML document.

6. Toggle over to your Web browser and reload the Web page.

 The Submit and Reset buttons will now appear with the new text you specified by adding the VALUE attributes to each tag, as shown in Figure 15-12.

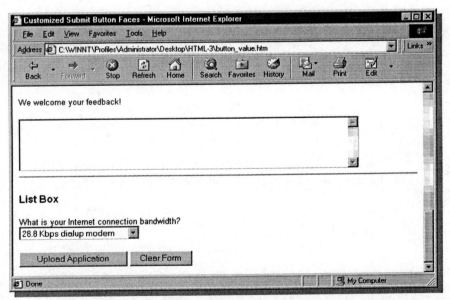

Figure 15-12: Submit and Reset buttons customized using VALUE attribute

Using an Image for the Submit Button

You already know that you can embed any HTML element into a form, including images. However, you can also use an image to replace the Submit button while retaining its functionality.

You cannot use an image in place of the Reset button. Typically, if an image is used for the Submit function, no Reset button is provided.

Many forms, regardless of whether they use an image for the Submit button, do not offer a Reset button. Note that there is no technical requirement for a Reset button; you never have to include a Reset button if you do not want one.

Process

To use an image as a Submit button, do the following:

- specify the value of the TYPE attribute as image (TYPE=image)

- add a SRC attribute, the value of which is the name of the image file referenced

- add an optional BORDER attribute and specify a value of zero (BORDER=0); this will prevent a blue border from appearing around the image.

Code

```
<INPUT TYPE=image SRC=upload_survey.gif BORDER=0>
```

You can specify a GIF, JPEG, or PNG image as the value of the SRC attribute, which is identical to the use of the <IMG> tag.

Exercise 15-8: Substituting an Image for the Submit Button

In this exercise, you will substitute a GIF image for the Submit button. Note that you cannot substitute an image for the Reset button.

1. In Notepad, open SUBMIT_IMAGE.HTM from the HTML-3 folder on your Desktop.

2. Remove the following HTML code from the bottom of the document:

    `<INPUT TYPE=submit> <INPUT TYPE=reset>.`

3. Add the following code in place of the code you removed in Step 2:

    `<INPUT TYPE=image SRC=upload_survey.gif BORDER=0>`

4. Save the HTML document.

5. Toggle over to your Web browser and open SUBMIT_IMAGE.HTM.

 The page appears with no Reset button and an image in place of the Submit button, as shown in Figure 15-13.

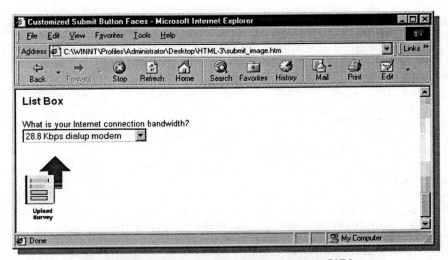

Figure 15-13: Submit button replaced with a GIF image

6. Click the **Upload Survey** image. The form will be uploaded according to the attributes in the opening <FORM> tag. Is this form going to an e-mail account or a CGI script?

Embedding Tables in Forms

You can add significant structure and order to a form by embedding tables. Figure 15-14 features an examples of the same form, with and without an embedded table.

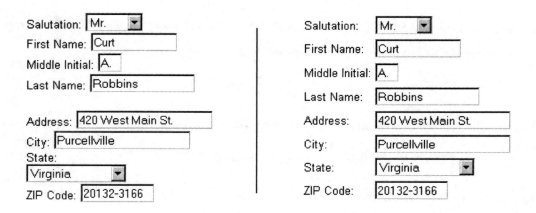

Figure 15-14: Form without a table embedded (left) and with (right)

Code

```
<FORM ACTION=mailto:webmaster@corp.com METHOD=post>
<TABLE>
<TR><TD>Salutation:</TD> <TD><SELECT NAME=title>
     <OPTION>Mr.
     <OPTION>Mrs.
     <OPTION>Ms.
     <OPTION>Dr.
     </SELECT></TD></TR>
<TR><TD>First Name:</TD> <TD><INPUT TYPE=text NAME=first_name
SIZE=12></TD></TR>
<TR><TD>Middle Initial:</TD> <TD><INPUT TYPE=text SIZE=2
NAME=mid_initial></TD></TR>
<TR><TD>Last Name:</TD> <TD><INPUT TYPE=text NAME=last_name
SIZE=15></TD></TR>
<TR><TD>Address:</TD> <TD><INPUT TYPE=text NAME=address></TD></TR>
<TR><TD>City:</TD> <TD><INPUT TYPE=text NAME=city></TD></TR>
<TR><TD>State:</TD> <TD><SELECT NAME=state>
     <OPTION>Alabama
     <OPTION>Ohio
     <OPTION>Colorado
     <OPTION>Virginia
     </SELECT></TD></TR>
<TR><TD>ZIP Code:</TD> <TD><INPUT TYPE=text SIZE=10
NAME=zip></TD></TR>
</TABLE><P>
```

One Step Further

You could take the above example one step further and right align the text labels for the form fields to give it a nice Desktop publishing effect. This is easy to accomplish; simply add ALIGN=right attributes to the opening <TD> tag of each text label.

An example of this is shown below; the code behind it follows.

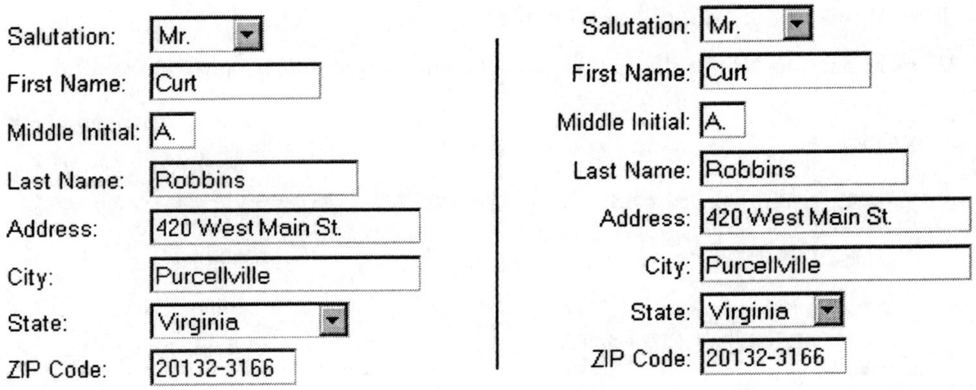

Figure 15-15: Table cells default left alignment (left) and enhanced with right alignment (right)

```
<TABLE>
<TR><TD ALIGN=right>Salutation:</TD> <TD><SELECT NAME=title>
    <OPTION>Mr.
    <OPTION>Mrs.
    <OPTION>Ms.
    <OPTION>Dr.
    </SELECT></TD></TR>
<TR><TD ALIGN=right>First Name:</TD> <TD><INPUT TYPE=text
NAME=first_name SIZE=12></TD></TR>
<TR><TD ALIGN=right>Middle Initial:</TD> <TD><INPUT TYPE=text
SIZE=2 NAME=mid_initial></TD></TR>
<TR><TD ALIGN=right>Last Name:</TD> <TD><INPUT TYPE=text
NAME=last_name SIZE=15></TD></TR>
<TR><TD ALIGN=right>Address:</TD> <TD><INPUT TYPE=text
NAME=address></TD></TR>
<TR><TD ALIGN=right>City:</TD> <TD><INPUT TYPE=text
NAME=city></TD></TR>
<TR><TD ALIGN=right>State:</TD> <TD><SELECT NAME=state>
    <OPTION>Alabama
    <OPTION>Ohio
    <OPTION>Colorado
    <OPTION>Virginia
    </SELECT></TD></TR>
<TR><TD ALIGN=right>ZIP Code:</TD> <TD><INPUT TYPE=text SIZE=10
NAME=zip></TD></TR>
</TABLE><P>
```

Exercise 15-9: Embedding a Table in a Form to Add Structure

In this exercise, you will add structure to a form by embedding a table. You will also enhance the table by right aligning the text labels in the left column.

1. In Notepad, open ADD_TABLE.HTM from the HTML-3 folder on your Desktop.

2. Toggle over to your browser and open ADD_TABLE.HTM. Note the appearance of the form fields in relation to the field labels.

3. Toggle back to Notepad and add the following code that appears in bold:

```
<TABLE>

<TR><TD ALIGN=right>Salutation:</TD> <TD><SELECT NAME=title>
     <OPTION>Mr.
     <OPTION>Mrs.
     <OPTION>Ms.
     <OPTION>Dr.
     </SELECT></TD></TR>

<TR><TD ALIGN=right>First Name:</TD> <TD><INPUT TYPE=text
NAME=first_name SIZE=12></TD></TR>

<TR><TD ALIGN=right>Middle Initial:</TD> <TD><INPUT TYPE=text
SIZE=2 NAME=middle_initial></TD></TR>

<TR><TD ALIGN=right>Last Name:</TD> <TD><INPUT TYPE=text
NAME=last_name SIZE=15></TD></TR>

<TR><TD ALIGN=right>Address:</TD> <TD><INPUT TYPE=text
NAME=address></TD></TR>

<TR><TD ALIGN=right>City:</TD> <TD><INPUT TYPE=text
NAME=city></TD></TR>

<TR><TD ALIGN=right>State:</TD> <TD><SELECT NAME=state>
     <OPTION>Alabama
     <OPTION>Ohio
     <OPTION>Colorado
     <OPTION>Virginia
     </SELECT></TD></TR>

<TR><TD ALIGN=right>ZIP Code:</TD> <TD><INPUT TYPE=text SIZE=10
NAME=zip></TD></TR>

</TABLE><P>
```

4. Save ADD_TABLE.HTM.

5. Toggle over to your Web browser and reload the page.

The form with the embedded table appears in your browser, as shown in Figure 15-16.

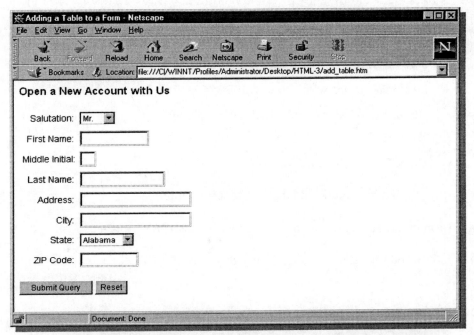

Figure 15-16: Form with an embedded table to give structure to fields

For a review of tables, see DDC's *HTML 4.0 Intermediate*.

You can also embed forms within forms. Although there is rarely a need to do this, it is important to know the capabilities of forms so you can meet any scripting or Web publishing challenge.

Enhancing Tables Embedded in Forms

You can change the color of body text in any HTML element, including forms. But to give some real graphic flair to a form, you can embed a table and color its cells.

In many respects, forms and tables are made to be co-mingled. The form shown in Figure 15-17 is the result of many different modifications to a standard form, including:

- an embedded table

  - `<TD ALIGN=right>` in the first column of rows 2 through 9

  - table cells filled with color with `BGCOLOR=blue` attribute to the `<TD>` tags

  - `CELLPADDING=6` and `CELLSPACING=6`

  - `WIDTH=75%`

  - `COLSPAN=2` for the first and last rows

- `<B>` applied to each field label in the left column

- form and table centered on the page with `<CENTER>` tag set

- Submit button face modified (using the `VALUE` attribute) and aligned right

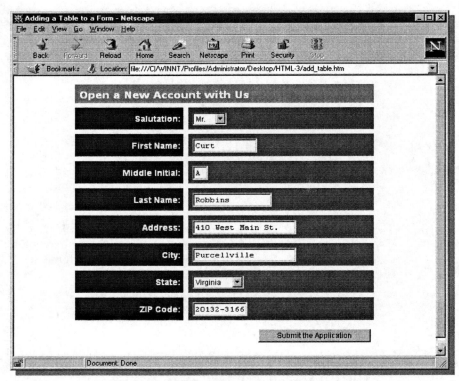

Figure 15-17: Enhanced table embedded in a form

Exercise 15-10: Enhancing a Table Embedded in a Form

In this exercise, you will enhance a table embedded in a form to give it more visual appeal. Much of this exercise should be a review of what you learned about tables in DDC's *HTML 4.0 Intermediate*.

1. In your Web browser, open TABLE-2.HTM from the HTML-3 folder on your Desktop. Note the appearance of the form fields.

2. Toggle over to Notepad and open TABLE-2.HTM.

3. Modify the following code that appears in bold:

```
<TABLE WIDTH=75% CELLSPACING=6 CELLPADDING=6>

<TR><TD BGCOLOR=gray COLSPAN=2><FONT SIZE=4 FACE=verdana
COLOR=white><B>Open a New Account with Us</B></FONT>
</TD></TR>

<TR><TD BGCOLOR=blue ALIGN=right><B><FONT COLOR=white>
Salutation:</FONT></B></TD> <TD BGCOLOR=green>

<SELECT NAME=title>
      <OPTION>Mr.
      <OPTION>Mrs.
      <OPTION>Ms.
      <OPTION>Dr.
      </SELECT></TD></TR>

<TR><TD BGCOLOR=blue ALIGN=right><B><FONT COLOR=white>First
Name:</FONT></B></TD> <TD BGCOLOR=green><INPUT TYPE=text
NAME=first_name SIZE=12></TD></TR>

<TR><TD BGCOLOR=blue ALIGN=right><B><FONT COLOR=white>Middle
Initial:</FONT></B></TD> <TD BGCOLOR=green><INPUT TYPE=text
SIZE=2 NAME=middle_initial></TD></TR>

<TR><TD BGCOLOR=blue ALIGN=right><B><FONT COLOR=white>Last
Name:</FONT></B></TD> <TD BGCOLOR=green><INPUT TYPE=text
NAME=last_name SIZE=15></TD></TR>

<TR><TD BGCOLOR=blue ALIGN=right><B><FONT COLOR=white>
Address:</FONT></B></TD> <TD BGCOLOR=green><INPUT TYPE=text
NAME=address>
</TD></TR>

<TR><TD BGCOLOR=blue ALIGN=right><B><FONT COLOR=white>
City:</FONT></B></TD> <TD BGCOLOR=green><INPUT TYPE=text
NAME=city></TD></TR>

<TR><TD BGCOLOR=blue ALIGN=right><B><FONT COLOR=white>
State:</FONT></B></TD> <TD BGCOLOR=green>
```

```
<SELECT NAME=state>
     <OPTION>Alabama
     <OPTION>Alaska
     <OPTION>Arizona
     others intentionally not listed here...
     </SELECT></TD></TR>

<TR><TD BGCOLOR=blue ALIGN=right><B><FONT COLOR=white>ZIP
Code:</FONT></B></TD> <TD BGCOLOR=green><INPUT TYPE=text SIZE=10
NAME=zip></TD></TR>

<TR><TD COLSPAN=2 ALIGN=right><INPUT VALUE="Submit the
Application" TYPE=submit></TD>
```

4. Note that the ACTION attribute in the opening <FORM> tag has no value. Specify a value that will send the output of the form to your e-mail account (replacing the "???").

5. Save the HTML file, toggle over to your Web browser, and reload the page.

The form will appear with the table enhancements, significantly increasing its graphic appeal and professionalism, as shown in Figure 15-18.

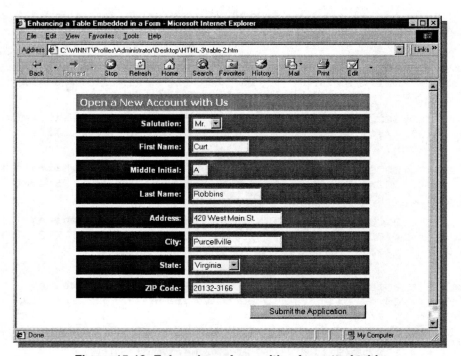

Figure 15-18: Enhancing a form with a formatted table

Forms Tips & Tricks

This section provides you with several tips and tricks that you might not otherwise know or learn for several months or even years of scripting HTML forms. As with all elements of HTML, there are special techniques that can save you significant time or give you a competitive edge over competing Web sites.

Posting a Form to Multiple E-mail Recipients

It is easy to send the output of a form to multiple e-mail accounts. You can even determine if form output is sent as a direct e-mail message or as a carbon copy.

Code

```
<FORM ACTION=mailto:person1@corp.com?cc=person2@corp.com
METHOD=post>
```

Note the question mark, "?," that separates the primary (first) e-mail recipient from the second, carbon copy recipient. Also note the "cc" denotation to signify that person2@corp.com is receiving a carbon copy message of the form content.

Three or More Recipients

It is possible to send a carbon copy and blind carbon copy to more than one e-mail account, allowing a total of three or more recipients of the posted form. Simply add the additional e-mail addresses, but do not use the "?" symbol. Instead, use the ampersand "&," as shown below:

```
<FORM ACTION=mailto:person2corp.com?cc=person2@corp.com&cc=
person2@corp.com&cc=person2@corp.com&bcc=person4@corp.com
METHOD=post>
```

Receipt of forms by multiple e-mail addresses works only in IE 4.0 and above and Netscape Navigator/Communicator 4.0 and above.

In fact, the MAILTO: protocol itself works only in version 4.0 and above of the major browsers.

Readable MAILTO Output

Many Webmasters and HTML scripters learn the hard way what is otherwise an easy trick. This trick makes the output of a form posted to an e-mail account much easier to read. It is a small <FORM> tag attribute called ENCTYPE, which stands for *Encoding Type*.

Code

```
<FORM ACTION=mailto:person1@corp.com METHOD=post ENCTYPE=text/plain>
```

The ENCTYPE attribute tells the server to separate the different form fields, making them substantially easier to read.

Figure 15-19 displays an example of form output submitted to an e-mail account in which the opening <FORM> tag did *not* have the ENCTYPE attribute.

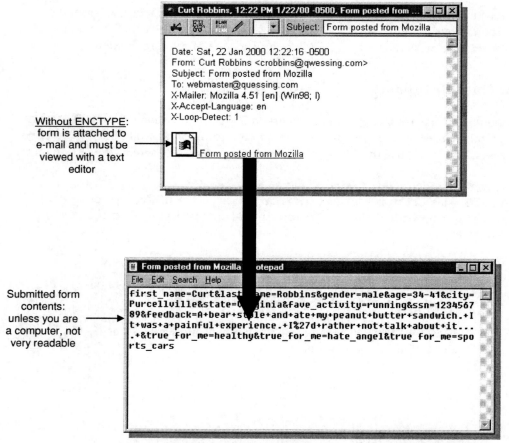

Figure 15-19: Form with <FORM> tag lacking ENCTYPE attribute

Figure 15-20 displays the exact same form with identical data populating the fields. This output, however, was submitted to an e-mail account using the ENCTYPE attribute.

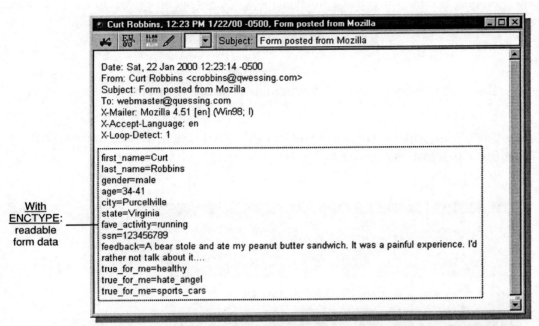

With
ENCTYPE:
readable
form data

Figure 15-20: Form output with <FORM> tag and ENCTYPE=text/plain attribute

Right Align Text in any <INPUT> Field

You will learn more about *Cascading Style Sheets*, better known as CSS, later in this course. For now, you only need to know that a small element of CSS can be applied to forms to right align the contents of any <INPUT> field.

Code

```
<INPUT TYPE=text NAME=address STYLE=text-align:right>
```

An example of a form with the contents of all <INPUT> fields right aligned using the CSS STYLE attribute is shown in Figure 15-21.

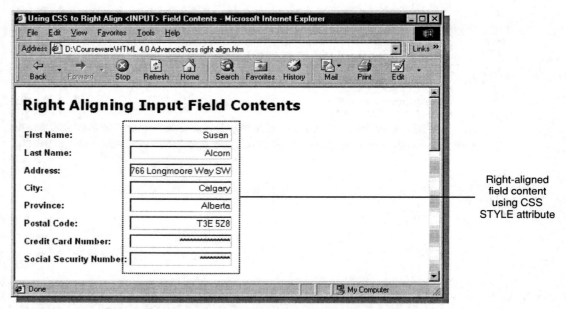

Figure 15-21: Right aligning form field contents using the CSS STYLE attribute

Posting Forms to CGI Programs

It should be noted that CGI is a complex topic and could occupy several full days of training. The purpose of this section is simply to inform you of the potential applications and basic characteristics of CGI programs that can accept output from your forms.

Note: the goal of this section is not to teach you how to write CGI programs. For an in-depth review of CGI, see DDC's two-day *CGI/Perl Fundamentals* course.

CGI Functions

As you already know, a CGI program can be written to perform almost any function or action when it receives the posted output from a form. The most common CGI program roles are:

- Database interface: a CGI program can take form output, format it, and submit it to a database for archival or action purposes. A single CGI program can submit data from a single form in various formats to multiple databases.

- User feedback: a CGI program can take form output and respond to a user in some manner by downloading an HTML document to the browser, as shown in Figure 15-22. Typically, the type and nature of the HTML document downloaded are specific to the data populating the form fields submitted.

- Perform calculations: a CGI program can take data submitted with the form and calculate it in some manner. The CGI program may or may not then download a Web page reporting the results of this calculation.

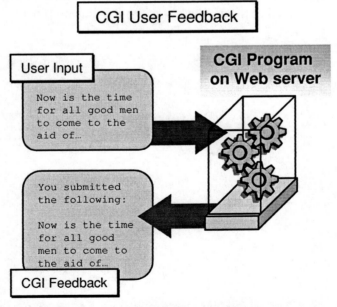

Figure 15-22: Example of CGI program that provides user feedback

<u>Example</u>: An Online Test

Sometimes, calculations are performed before the results are posted to a database (regardless of whether feedback is provided to the user). For example, assume a user takes a test online and it is administered as an HTML form.

The process is as follows:

1. User populates form fields by answering the questions.

2. User uploads the completed "test" (form).

3. The CGI program calculates which answers the user got correct and which she missed.

4. The CGI program then summarizes the details according to the desires of the programmers:

    ▪ CGI program may want to document exactly which questions were missed.

    ▪ CGI program may download to the user more questions which are pulled from a database and based on the ones the user missed.

    ▪ CGI program may only calculate the user's percentage of correct answers with no follow up action.

5. After the results are summarized, the data is transferred to a "backend" database.

6. Other applications—separate from the CGI program—may perform operations with the data after it is archived in the database, such as a reporting function or follow up action.

DDC Publishing • www.ddcpub.com

Example: User Feedback

Figure 15-23 shows an example of a simple CGI script residing on a Web server that takes data posted from a form and returns it to the user who submitted the form as a Web page.

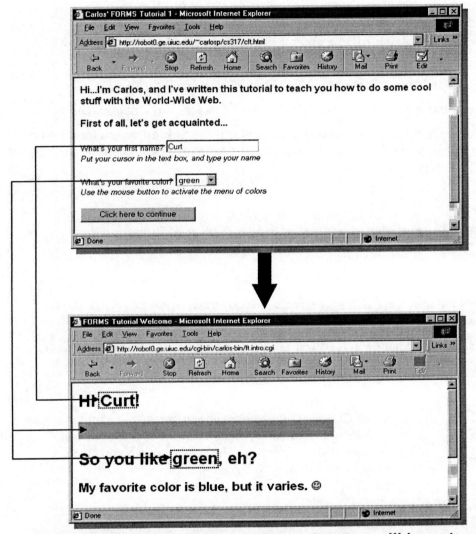

Figure 15-23: Example of a simple CGI program that returns a Web page to a user

Exercise 15-11: Using Forms that Access CGI Scripts

In this exercise, you will populate and upload multiple forms that access CGI echo scripts. This certainly does not give you the ability to write your own CGI scripts, but it does give you a better idea of the fact that forms are only part of a bigger overall system involving CGI scripts and other server-level processing mechanisms.

1. Access the following URL: **robot0.ge.uiuc.edu/~carlosp/cs317/ cft.html**.

2. In the **What's your first name?** field, type your name.

3. In the **What's your favorite color?** list box, select the color of your choice.

4. Click the **Click here to continue** button. This is the **Submit** button for the form. (Remember: you can use the VALUE attribute to change the face of the Submit button to display anything you want).

 A CGI script residing on a Web server uses the data you uploaded to populate particular fields in a customized Web page that it automatically downloads to your browser.

5. Access the following URL: **members.whro.org/~pterry/cgi-bin/ form2.shtml**.

6. Input your information in the **First Name**, **Last Name**, and **Email Add** fields.

7. Click the **Send Form** button.

 A different CGI script uses your submitted data to create a custom Web page and automatically download it to you. Note that the page also has identified the state from which you are connected to the Internet (this does not always function properly).

8. Access **www.video.ufl.edu/~yakcheez/samples/psample6.html**.

9. In the **Red, Green**, and **Blue** fields, type **22**, **33**, and **44**, respectively. Press **Compute**.

 A CGI script calculates the hexadecimal value of the combined numbers that you uploaded. Unlike the previous examples, this is a good example of a calculation performed by a CGI script.

Exercise 15-12: Posting Form Output to a CGI Script

In this exercise, you will change the ACTION value of the opening <FORM> tag to post data to a CGI script. The script, a simple echo parser, will automatically download a Web page to the user based on the content of the populated form fields.

1. In Notepad, open TEST-CGI.HTM from the HTML-3 folder on your Desktop.

2. Add the following code that appears in bold:

   ```
   <H2>Uploading to a CGI Script</H2>

   <FORM ACTION= http://sj.znet.com/~aleatory/quessing/post-query.pl
   METHOD=post>

   <H3>Basic Text Field</H3>
   ```

3. Save the file.

4. Toggle over to your Web browser and open TEST-CGI.HTM.

5. Populate the fields with your personal data. When you are done, click the **Upload to CGI Script** submit button at the bottom of the form.

 The form is submitted to a CGI script residing on a Web server at the University of Illinois. The CGI script will process the form, taking the populated content of the form fields, reformatting it in an HTML document, and downloading it to you, as shown in Figure 15-24.

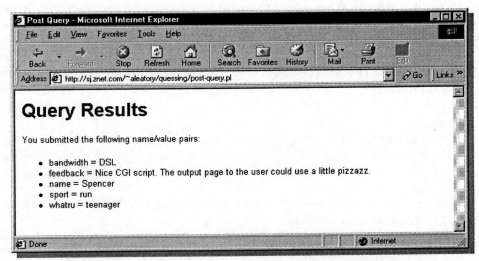

Figure 15-24: Example of output from a server-based CGI script

Lesson 15 Summary

▶ There are many supplemental attributes available to enhance and expand the functionality of your forms.

▶ The <INPUT> tag, when used with text and password form fields, offers SIZE and MAXLENGTH as supplemental attributes. SIZE can be any positive integer and translates into the width of the text field in characters. MAXLENGTH is also any positive integer and limits the number of characters that a user can input into the field. Technically, SIZE and MAXLENGTH do not affect one another.

▶ The <INPUT> tag, when used with checkboxes and radio buttons, has a supplemental attribute of CHECKED, which has no value set. CHECKED makes a checkbox or radio button preselected with no user action. The user can still deselect or reselect the field.

▶ The <SELECT> tag, used to create list boxes, has three supplemental attributes: SIZE, MULTIPLE, and SELECTED. SIZE can be any positive integer and turns a "pop up" list into a scrollable list. A SIZE value of between 3 and 10 is typically best. MULTIPLE has no value set (similar to CHECKED for radio buttons and checkboxes). It allows the user to select multiple items from the list box (using <SHIFT> or <CTRL>).

▶ SELECTED also has no value set. Unlike SIZE and MULTIPLE, SELECTED is applied to one or more <OPTION> tags within a <SELECT> container. If the list box is configured without the SIZE attribute and is a single line, the <OPTION> item tagged with the SELECTED attribute will be the only one displayed in the list box. If the list box is configured as a scroll box, any list items tagged with SELECTED will be highlighted.

▶ A rarely used supplemental attribute to the <TEXTAREA> tag is READONLY. READONLY makes all text in the text area read only, so a user cannot delete or modify the text or add new text.

▶ You can change the text that appears on the face of the Submit and Reset buttons using the VALUE attribute. When added to the <INPUT> tags, the value of VALUE will be displayed. Note: the value of VALUE is case sensitive.

▶ You can use an image in place of the Submit button. You cannot use an image in place of the Reset button. There is no technical requirement for a Reset button. To use an image in place of the Submit button, use the following HTML syntax: <INPUT TYPE=image SRC=filename.gif BORDER=0>.

▶ One way in which you can significantly enhance the visual appeal and user-friendliness of your forms is to embed HTML tables in them. Remember: you can embed any HTML element inside a <FORM> container, including frames, forms, and tables.

▶ You can post a form to multiple e-mail accounts using the MAILTO protocol to the ACTION attribute of the opening <FORM> tag.

▶ You should use ENCTYPE=text/plain in the <FORM> tags of your MAILTO forms.

Lesson 15 Quiz

Matching

___ 1. has no value set

___ 2. used with <SELECT>

___ 3. use image as Submit button

___ 4. specify the width of a password field

___ 5. preselect radio buttons and checkboxes

a. CHECKED

b. SIZE

c. SELECTED

d. SRC=filename

e. MULTIPLE

Fill in the Blank

6. When used with the <SELECT> tag, a SIZE value of between ____ and ____ is recommended.

7. A user must press either the _____ key or the _____ key in order to select multiple items in a list box (*if* the MULTIPLE attribute has been used).

8. If you do not upload a form to an e-mail account, you must submit it to a _____ program for processing.

9. The most common programming language used to write a CGI script is _____ .

True or False?

T / F   10. You can send the output of a form to multiple e-mail accounts; you can also send multiple carbon copies and blind carbon copies.

T / F   11. You should always use ENCTYPE=plain/text when sending output of a form to an e-mail account.

T / F   12. The most rarely used form attribute is READONLY.

T / F   13. SIZE allows a user to select multiple items in a list box.

T / F   14. The value of the VALUE attribute for Submit and Reset buttons is not case sensitive.

T / F   15. CGI programs can be written in nearly any language, including Perl, C++, and C.

(This page intentionally left blank)

Lesson 16
Image Maps

Lesson Topics

▶ Image Map Overview

▶ Image Map Tags

▶ Image Map Automation Software

▶ Lesson 16 Summary

Image Map Overview

Technically, image maps are just another way of providing Web users with hyperlinks. In DDC's *HTML 4.0 Fundamentals*, you learned how to create hypertext anchors that connect different HTML documents and that hyperlinks, regardless of form, are the navigational references that hold together the entire Web. Thus, you learned to create both the structure of the Web (HTML documents) and the glue that holds them together (hyperlinks).

Anatomy of an Image Map

Image maps are inline images (either photos or graphics) that offer *multiple hyperlinks* to other HTML documents or multimedia data objects. Depending on the nature of a specific image map image, the number and location of the links in the image may not be readily evident to a user. Good image maps always contain evident, intuitively placed hyperlinks.

Figure 16-1: Example of an image map (each building is a different hyperlink)

Intuitive Links

One of the secrets of a good image map is choosing an image that offers intuitive access to the links it contains. Many image maps display text labels superimposed on the image to assist users in finding and utilizing hyperlinks.

The syntax of an image map hyperlink is very different and significantly more complex than that of a text hyperlink. In function and purpose, however, image maps are identical to text hyperlinks.

Text Hyperlinks vs. Image Maps

There are three primary differences between text hyperlinks and image maps:

1. Image maps offer a dramatic departure in appearance and user interface from the conventional text-based format of a text hyperlink.

2. Image maps offer *multiple hyperlinks*, whereas text hyperlinks offer only one hyperlink.

3. From an HTML code perspective, image maps are significantly more complex.

Art + Creativity + Code

Good image maps are the result of a careful blend of art, creativity, appropriateness for your particular application, and HTML code. This course can only teach you about the code, but it is important to note that you can know more about HTML than anyone in your organization and still produce poor image maps.

The best image maps are the result of:

- Careful planning: how many links?, located where?, embedded in what type of image?, how big on the page?, what position on the page?, etc.

- Intuitive link placement: if users cannot easily discern the location of links in an image map, the links might as well not exist.

- Correct bandwidth sensitivity: you should generally use images and graphics that are not overly bandwidth intensive. This depends on your intended audience, however. An image posted to an intranet on a high-bandwidth internal network can be much bigger than one posted to an external Web server in which the majority of users connect via dialup modems.

- Visually attractive: there are many "ugly" image map examples on the Web. While they provide the intended functionality, they are unprofessional and provide a poor image for you or your organization. If you desire simple functionality, you should use text hyperlinks with the Anchor tag, as you learned in DDC's *HTML 4.0 Fundamentals*.

Exercise 16-1: Viewing Examples of Image Maps

In this exercise, you will view online examples of image maps. You will also see examples of how image maps can interface with JavaScript code and frames.

1. Launch your Web browser.

2. Access the following URL: **www.kraft.com**. The Kraft home page will be downloaded and displayed.

3. On the image map, click the **What's New** grocery bag beside the sink. This will download the *What's New* page. This is a good example of using an image map to navigate in a frames site.

4. On the toolbar, click the **Back** button.

5. On the image map, click the Cook Book link. The *Cookbook* page will be downloaded.

6. On the toolbar, click the **Back** button.

7. Access **www.cvc.org/java_script/cs_image_map.htm**.

8. On the image map, click the woman with the yellow gloves (left most person).

 The text in the Clicked Item field will change to read "Kim says ALWAYS WEAR YOUR GLOVES WHEN DISECTING A SHARK!"

9. On the image map, click the man in the middle. The **Clicked Item** field will change to display a different text string.

10. Click the right-most person in the image map and note the change in the **Clicked Item** field.

 This is a good example of how image maps, form fields, and JavaScript can be combined to create more sophisticated mechanisms on Web pages.

11. Access **dgucc.dongguk.ac.kr/dgucc/JavaScript/examples/ imagemap.htm**.

12. Click each field of the image map and note how the text changes in the **Clicked Item** field. This page integrates JavaScript and functions almost identically to the previous site.

13. Access **www.bloomington.org**. The Web site for the city of Bloomington, Minnesota will appear, as shown in Figure 16-2 on the following page.

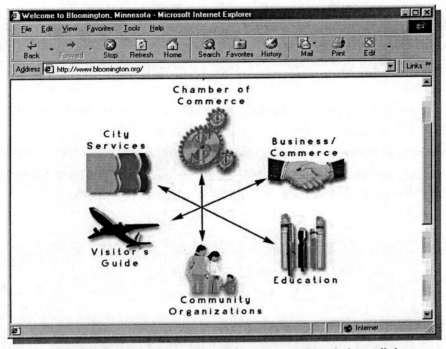

Figure 16-2: Example of an image map featuring six hyperlinks

14. Now view the source HTML code for this page. In Netscape Navigator/Communicator, select **View ▶ Page Source** (<CTRL + U>). In Internet Explorer, select **View ▶ Source**.

Netscape will launch a new browser window that displays the HTML source code of this page.

Internet Explorer will launch Notepad and display the HTML code in standard ASCII text, as shown in Figure 16-3.

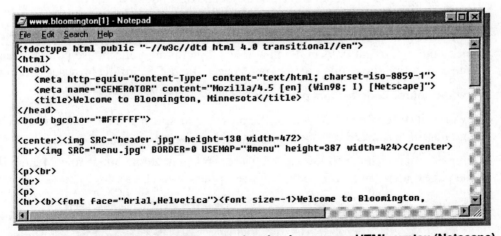

Figure 16-3: Source code for Web page showing image map HTML syntax (Netscape)

15. Examine the source code. You know enough about HTML at this point that you could teach yourself about image maps by analyzing this code and experimenting with your own image maps.

16. Close Notepad.

17. Visit **www.collegenet.com**. Locate the image map in the page. View the source code.

18. How does the source code for this image map differ from the previous image map?

19. Visit **www.tabasco.com**. A splash screen for the Tabasco Web site will appear. Click the splash screen to advance to the home page, as shown in Figure 16-4.

Figure 16-4: Example of a photo collage used for an image map

20. Identify the individual links in the image map by moving your mouse pointer around the image and noting the display in the status bar at the bottom of the browser window.

21. View the source code for this page.

22. How does it differ from the code for the previous image maps? In what way are all of the image maps the same?

23. If time permits, visit the following Web sites and analyze the image maps featured on the home pages: www.mattel.com/sitemap and www.thatpetplace.com.

Client-side vs. Server-side

Technically speaking, there are two types of image maps: server-side and client-side, as described in Table 16-1. In this Lesson, you will learn how to create client-side image maps.

Image Map Type	Description
Client-side	■ All code resides on the user's client computer and downloads as part of the HTML document. ■ Significantly faster than server-side image maps because no code has to be uploaded to a CGI script residing on a server in order to calculate and execute the coordinates of individual map areas. ■ Significantly easier to script. ■ The majority of image maps are now client-side due to their faster processing and less complex code.
Server-side	■ The first type of image map; originally, only server-side configurations were available. ■ Code resides on both the client and the server. When the user clicks a particular hyperlink area of the map: 1) a request is sent to a Web server, 2) a CGI script on the server computes the coordinates of the region, and 3) the CGI script sends instructions to the client regarding the URL that corresponds to the coordinates. ■ Requires a knowledge of CGI scripts to create.

Table 16-1: Client-side and server-side image maps

Server-side image maps are very rare today. The fact that client-side image maps are faster, significantly easier to create, and less complex has made them the choice for nearly all Webmasters. What was only a few years ago the only type of image map available is now the scorned child of HTML.

This is a good example of how quickly the pace of Internet technology advances and why you must always be alert to modifications in the official HTML Specification, trends in usage and application of HTML, and the status of browser capabilities.

Image Map Tags

The tags and attributes involved in image maps are relatively simple. The most difficult aspects regarding image maps are: 1) choosing an appropriate image and 2) scripting the coordinates of the areas of the image that will be used as various hyperlinks.

There are three tags involved in client-side image maps:

- `<MAP>`
- `<IMG>`
- `<AREA>`

<MAP> Container

`<MAP>` is a container, so you must always remember to include both an opening and closing tag. Similar to forms, an opening `<MAP>` tag must have a NAME attribute. The value of NAME can be whatever you desire.

Code

```
<IMG SRC=map_1.gif USEMAP=#divisions>

<MAP NAME=divisions>
<AREA SHAPE=rect HREF=http://www.xyz.com COORDS=202,42,297,90>
<AREA SHAPE=rect HREF=http://www.pu.com COORDS=119,97,174,152>
<AREA SHAPE=circle HREF=http://www.cnn.com COORDS=74,52,35>
<AREA SHAPE=default HREF=http://www.webmonkey.com>
</MAP>
```

Note the role of the `<IMG>` tag. To work with an image map, the `<IMG>` tag must include the USEMAP attribute. The value of USEMAP must be equal to a pound sign (#) (also called a *hash symbol*) followed by the value of the NAME attribute to the opening `<MAP>` tag.

<IMG> Tag

You are already familiar with the `<IMG>` tag for placing inline images in Web pages. Because all image maps involves images, the `<IMG>` tag must be used for all image maps.

Code

```
<IMG SRC=map_1.gif USEMAP=#states>

<MAP NAME=states>
<AREA SHAPE=circle HREF=http://www.buick.com COORDS=74,63,55>
```

<AREA> Tag

The <AREA> tag is an empty tag and is the only image map tag that appears inside the <MAP> container. Each <AREA> tag must contain three necessary attributes that specify the shape, exact coordinates, and referenced URL of its particular hyperlink area.

<AREA> Attribute	Value Set	Syntax Example
SHAPE	<ul><li>rect: any form of rectangle, including squares</li><li>circle: circles and ellipses</li><li>poly: any polygon</li><li>default: not a shape; a URL that will be activated if a user clicks inside the image map, but outside designated areas</li></ul>	\<AREA **SHAPE=rect** COORDS=202,42,297,90 HREF=http://www.xy.com>
COORDS	Depends on the SHAPE value (see Table 16-3 on the following page for more detail)	\<AREA SHAPE=rect **COORDS=202,42,297,90** HREF=http://www.xy.com>
HREF	The URL of the hyperlink referenced by the zone	\<AREA SHAPE=rect COORDS=202,42,297,90 **HREF=http://www.xy.com**>

Table 16-2: Necessary attributes to the <AREA> tag

Coordinates

The foundation of all client-side image maps is *coordinates*. All image maps contain multiple hyperlinks; therefore, each hyperlink must be defined as an area, or *zone*, within the image. These zones are defined in terms of X and Y axis coordinates, similar to geometry.

All GIF and JPEG images are rectangular. Thus, they can be plotted on a two-dimensional plane using X axis and Y axis coordinates, as shown in Figure 16-5 on the following page. Each square on the grid represents a pixel.

All images are composed of pixels. A pixel is the smallest part of an image, similar to an atom in physics. An image that is 400 pixels wide and 200 pixels tall contains a total of 80,000 pixels.

You can include multiple image maps per HTML document if you desire. The only precaution is that each image must be paired with its own <MAP> container; the value of <IMG USEMAP=#x> must be equal to the value of <MAP NAME=x>.

COORDS Value Syntax

The format of the COORDS attribute value is determined by the type of shape being used (in other words, the value of the SHAPE attribute).

In the previous section, you learned that there are four possible SHAPE values, three of which specify different geometric shapes for hyperlink objects in an image. Thus, there are three different COORDS value syntax structures, as shown in Table 16-3.

SHAPE Value	COORDS Value Syntax
SHAPE=rect	COORDS=upper_left_x,upper_left_y,lower right_x,lower_right_y
SHAPE=circle	COORDS=center_x,center_y,radius
SHAPE=poly	COORDS=first_point_x,first_point_y,second_point _x,second_point_y,…,last_point_x,last_point_y

Table 16-3: COORDS attribute value set syntax

The coordinates of the shapes in Figure 16-5 are expressed in the following HTML code:

```
<AREA SHAPE=rect COORDS=1,1,4,4>
<AREA SHAPE=poly COORDS=7,1,10,1,10,3,9,3,9,5,7,5,7,4,6,4,6,2,7,2>
<AREA SHAPE=circle COORDS=4,7,2>
```

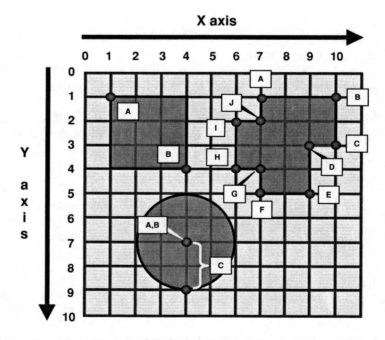

Figure 16-5: X and Y coordinates for a rectangle, a polygon, and a circle

Rules to Remember

Table 16-4 details the rules regarding COORDS value sets.

Image Map Shape	# of COORDS Values	COORDS Values Locations
Rectangle	Four	■ Upper left corner X and Y ■ Lower right corner X and Y
Circle	Three	■ X center ■ Y center ■ Radius span
Polygon	As many values as are necessary to plot its points	The order of the coordinates does not matter.
SHAPE=default	N/A	N/A

Table 16-4: Rules regarding COORDS values

SHAPE=default does not function in Internet Explorer 5.0; it is only functional in Netscape Navigator. Therefore, you should not use SHAPE=default if you are scripting to an audience of all browsers. It is safe, however, if you are creating an image map for a intranet on which all users have Netscape Navigator/Communicator.

All COORDS attribute values are separated with a comma and *no space*. Be sure to proofread your image map HTML code for this as you are conditioned by English grammar to place spaces after commas.

Geometrically speaking, rectangles are polygons (because polygons are defined as shapes with many sides). In HTML image maps, however, SHAPE=poly is used for objects with a series of short lines outlining an odd shape that cannot be encompassed by a rectangle or circle.

Exercise 16-2: Scripting Image Map Rectangles

In this exercise, you will create two image map hyperlinks using rectangular zones within an image.

<u>Note</u>: you will need a graphics application that displays the X and Y coordinates of your mouse pointer in order to complete this exercise. Paint Shop Pro, LView Pro, or Adobe Photoshop is recommended.

1. In Notepad, open IMAGE_MAP.HTM from the HTML-3 folder.

2. Launch your graphics application. You will use this to identify and plot the X and Y coordinates within the image used to script the image map hyperlink zones.

- Paint Shop Pro versions 5 and 6 display the X and Y coordinates of your mouse pointer on the left side of the status bar at the bottom of the window.

- LView Pro versions 2.1 through 2.8 display this information on the right side of the status bar at the bottom of the window.

- Adobe Photoshop versions 4.0 through 5.5 display this information on the **Info** tab, which is accessed via **Window ▶ Show Info**.

3. In your graphics application, open MAP_1.GIF from the HTML-3 folder. The image should appear as shown in Figure 16-6.

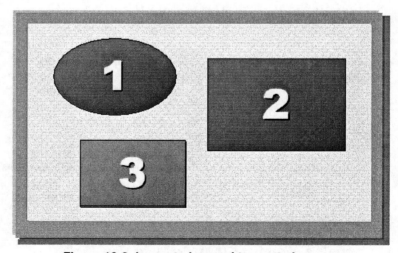

Figure 16-6: Image to be used to create image map

4. Toggle back to your text editor and type the following script that appears in bold:

```
<FONT SIZE=6 COLOR=blue FACE=verdana>My First Image Map</FONT><P>

<IMG SRC=map_1.gif USEMAP=#first>

<MAP NAME=first>
<AREA SHAPE=rect HREF=http://www.abcnews.com COORDS=
```

5. Save the HTML document.

6. Toggle over to your graphics application and place your mouse pointer in the image and move it around. Note the X and Y coordinates that change on the status bar (or, in Photoshop, in the Show Info window).

7. Carefully position your mouse pointer on the upper left corner of the #3 orange square. What are the X and Y coordinates of this position? Remember these numbers.

8. Toggle over to Notepad and enter these numbers, separated by a comma, as the value for the COORDS attribute in the <AREA> tag.

 Remember: separate each coordinate by a comma but do not use spaces following the commas.

9. Toggle over to your graphics application and position your mouse pointer on the lower right corner of the #3 orange square. Note the X and Y coordinates.

10. Toggle back to Notepad and add these numbers to the COORDS value to complete the COORDS attribute. Do not forget the closing wicket for the <AREA> tag.

11. Type the following code directly below the first <AREA> tag that you entered in the previous step:

```
<AREA SHAPE=rect HREF=http://www.cnn.com COORDS=
```

12. Toggle back to your graphics application and determine the X and Y coordinates for the upper left corner and lower right corner of the #2 red rectangle.

13. Toggle over to Notepad, add these coordinates to the unfinished COORDS attribute, and complete the <AREA> tag.

14. Add a closing <MAP> tag below the last <AREA> tag.

15. Save the HTML file.

Even though you have not yet scripted the ellipse shape in the image map, you should test hyperlinks for shapes #2 and #3 to ensure that they work properly before moving on to the ellipse.

16. Launch your Web browser and open IMAGE_MAP.HTM from the HTML-3 folder on your Desktop.

17. Move your mouse pointer over the #3 orange square but do not click. Note the status bar at the bottom of the browser window.

 The status bar, which typically indicates Document: Done (in Netscape Navigator/Communicator) and Done (in Internet Explorer), now displays the URL of the ABC News Web site.

18. Move your mouse pointer over the #2 red rectangle. Note the indication of the hyperlink reference on the status bar.

19. Click the #2 red rectangle to execute the hyperlink. If you have scripted your <AREA> tags correctly, the CNN Web site should be downloaded and displayed.

20. On the toolbar, click the **Back** button.

21. Test the #3 orange square. The ABC News Web site should be downloaded by the image map hyperlink.

22. If either of these image map hyperlinks did not function properly, review your HTML document to find the problems and fix them. Do not move on to the next exercise until you have scripted and successfully tested both image map hyperlinks.

Exercise 16-3: Scripting Image Map Circles

In this exercise, you will script an image map circle and modify the radius pixel value of the COORDS attribute to see the effect of applying SHAPE=circle to an ellipse.

1. In Notepad, be sure that IMAGE_MAP.HTM is open.

2. In your graphics application, be sure you have MAP_1.GIF open.

3. In Notepad, add a new <AREA> tag directly below the other two <AREA> tags that plots a hypertext link for the ellipse. The tag should appear similar to the code below:

```
<AREA SHAPE=circle COORDS=132,88,65 HREF=http://www.cbs.com>
```

Your first two coordinates may vary slightly from those shown above. However, use a radius value of **65** pixels for the purpose of this exercise.

4. Save the HTML document.

5. Toggle over to your Web browser and load IMAGE_MAP.HTM (if necessary).

6. Place your mouse pointer in the #1 blue ellipse and move it to the extreme left side of the image. Watching the status bar of your browser, note at what point your mouse pointer exits the hyperlink zone.

 The hyperlink zone is not as wide as the ellipse.

7. Beginning with your mouse pointer in the center of the #1 blue ellipse, move it straight up and straight down until you can determine the border of the hyperlink zone.

 Note that the hyperlink zone extends beyond the top and bottom of the blue ellipse.

8. Click within the hyperlink zone for the blue ellipse to test the new image map hyperlink. The CBS Television Web site should be downloaded and displayed.

9. Toggle over to Notepad and change the radius value of the COORDS attribute to **75**. Save the HTML document and reload the page in your Web browser. How does this affect the hyperlink zone in the blue ellipse?

10. What happens to the hyperlink zone if you change the radius value to 50? Or 80?

Exercise 16-4: Scripting Image Map Polygons and Using Default

In this exercise, you will script image map polygons and create a default hyperlink zone.

1. In Notepad, open POLYGONS.HTM from the HTML-3 folder.

2. Toggle over to your graphics application and open POLYGONS.JPG.

3. Toggle back to Notepad. Add COORDS values for blue polygon #1 to the first <AREA> tag directly below the opening <MAP> tag. When complete, the code should appear similar to the sample below:

```
<AREA SHAPE=poly HREF=http://www.salon.com
COORDS=60,30,155,31,185,116,107,169,30,115>
```

 Your individual coordinates may vary *slightly* from those shown above. The coordinates above begin with the upper left corner of the polygon; you may choose to begin with a different corner.

4. In the second <AREA> tag, add the COORDS values for red polygon #2. Carefully plot the coordinates using your graphics application. Specify an HREF value of your choice if you wish.

5. Add a third <AREA> tag for orange polygon #3. Carefully plot the coordinates using your graphics application. Set the HREF value to the Web site of your choice.

6. Save the HTML document. Toggle over to your browser and open POLYGONS.HTM. The Web page will appear with the image map, as shown in Figure 16-7.

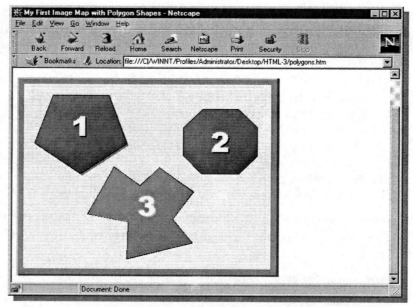

Figure 16-7: Image map featuring polygon shapes for hyperlinks

7. Without clicking, carefully move your mouse pointer over each side of each of the polygon shapes, noting when the mouse pointer changes from an arrow to a pointing hand (denoting you have come across a hyperlink).

8. As you move your mouse pointer over the polygon shapes, watch the status bar to detect when you are in a hyperlink area and to note the URL that will be activated if you click.

9. Test the hyperlink of polygon #1 by clicking it.

10. Test polygon #2 and polygon #3.

 If all three polygon images do not function properly as hyperlinks, or if the hyperlink zones are "sloppy" and do not coincide with the edge of any polygon image, return to POLYGONS.HTM and adjust the HTML code until the hyperlink zones function as intended.

11. Toggle back to Notepad.

12. Add the following code directly below the bottom <AREA> tag for polygon #3:

```
<AREA SHAPE=default HREF=http://www.w3.org>
```

13. Save the HTML document.

14. Toggle back to your browser and load the Web page.

15. Move your mouse pointer around the image map. Note the appearance of the mouse pointer and the status bar.

 The mouse pointer should appear as a pointing hand in *any* area of the image map. The status bar should indicate http://www.w3.org when the mouse is not hovering over a polygon shape.

The default value to the SHAPE attribute specifies that any area of an image map not specified by an AREA tag (for a particular shape) should reference a particular URL. In this case, the URL is for the World Wide Web Consortium (W3C), the organization that publishes the official HTML Specification.

16. Test the default value by clicking *within* the image map but *outside* any of the polygons. Your browser should access the Web site of the W3C.

 Remember: SHAPE=default functions in Netscape Navigator and Communicator, but not in Internet Explorer 5.

Exercise 16-5: Using a Photo for an Image Map

In this exercise, you will use a photo to create an image map.

1. In Notepad, open PHOTO_MAP.HTM from the HTML-3 folder.

2. In your graphics application, open FAMILY.JPG. There are 17 people featured in this photo. You will turn the face of each person into a different hyperlink.

3. Using Figure 16-8 and Table 16-5 as your guide, script an image map that uses circles, a polygon, and rectangles. Each hyperlink will refer to a different Web site.

Figure 16-8: Create an image map using this photo

#	Shape	URL	#	Shape	URL
1	Circle	www.abcnews.com	10	Circle	www.lionel.com
2	Rectangle	www.lucent.com	11	Rectangle	www.apa.org
3	Rectangle	www.skidmore.edu	12	Rectangle	www.techweb.com
4	Circle	www.rotary.org	13	Rectangle	www.sec.gov
5	Circle	www.salon.com	14	Circle	www.art.com
6	Rectangle	www.nba.com	15	Rectangle	www.reebok.com
7	Circle	www.food.com	16	Rectangle	www.mtv.com
8	Polygon	www.flowers.com	17	Rectangle	www.garden.com
9	Rectangle	www.country.com			

Table 16-5: URLs to use for image map hyperlinks

DDC Publishing • www.ddcpub.com

For person #8, in which you use a polygon, trace the outline of the woman's hat and the bottom of her face.

 Unless you spend many hours and use all polygon shapes, it is impossible to exactly cover the area of each person's face. What is important here is that you create an intuitive, easy-to-navigate image map. When the average user clicks a person's face, the hyperlink should function properly.

4. It is important to provide basic instructions with a complex image map. Add the following code directly after the closing `</MAP>` tag:

```
<B>Click any face to visit that person's favorite Web
site.</B><P>
```

5. Save the HTML document.

6. In your browser, open PHOTO_MAP.HTM. The page should appear as Figure 16-9.

Figure 16-9: Image map created with 17 hyperlinks

7. Click each face to test the image map. If any hyperlink zones do not function properly, return to the HTML document and repair them. Also, if you judge any hyperlink zones to be non-intuitive or "sloppy," fix them.

Exercise 16-6: On Your Own—A Complex Image Map

In this exercise, you will be tested on your knowledge of all three types of image map shapes (rectangles, circles, and polygons) and the default hyperlink zone.

1. In your graphics application, open ON_YOUR_OWN.JPG from the HTML-3 folder.

 The image file should appear identical to Figure 16-10.

Figure 16-10: Turn this image into an image map

2. In Notepad, open ON_YOUR_OWN.HTM.

3. Directly above the </CENTER> tag, insert an <IMG> tag and all necessary attributes for the image file ON_YOUR_OWN.JPG.

4. Below the <IMG> tag, add the opening <MAP> tag and any necessary attributes.

5. Add one <AREA> tag for each shape in the image (a total of six tags). Determine the COORDS values using your graphics application. (You must toggle back and forth between your graphics application and Notepad, as you did in the previous exercises.) Specify the HREF values of your choice.

 You could use a SHAPE=circle attribute for shape #2, but you have already learned that this will produce a "sloppy" click zone for the user. Instead, use a SHAPE=poly attribute for #2. This will enable you to create a more well-defined click zone, even though it is more work.

6. Add a seventh `<AREA>` tag to the `<MAP>` container. Specify a `SHAPE` value that will result in all areas within the image map—but outside of a numbered shape—referencing `www.accuweather.com` when clicked. (Note: this will *not* work in IE 5.0.)

7. Close the `<MAP>` container with the appropriate tag.

8. Save the HTML document.

9. Toggle over to your Web browser and open ON_YOUR_OWN.HTM.

 The Web page is displayed, as shown in Figure 16-11. There should be no blue border surrounding the image. If there is, repair your HTML document using the appropriate attribute to the `<IMG>` tag.

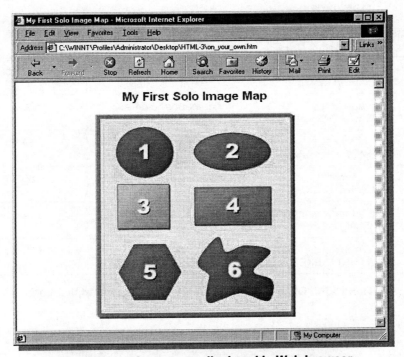

Figure 16-11: Image map displayed in Web browser

10. Move your mouse pointer around all areas of the image map. Carefully run it over the borders of each shape.

 Are the hyperlink zones accurately defined? Are there any sloppy zones?

If there are any sloppy zones or non-functional image map areas, toggle back to Notepad and repair them.

Image Map Automation Software

Even if you master scripting image maps "by hand," you will eventually want to experiment with image map software that automates the task. Image map software is especially nice for polygon shapes that can be time-consuming and cumbersome when scripted by hand.

There is much freeware, shareware, and commercial software available for creating professional image maps. The choice of which application to use is yours (or that of your employer). For this Lesson, you will use LiveImage from LiveImage Corp.[24]

Table 16-6 provides a list of popular image map applications you may wish to evaluate.

Application	URL Source	Price (USD)
Advanced Imagemap Designer (ADID18.ZIP)	www.altersoft.com	$25.00
CoffeeCup Image Mapper++ (COFFEEMAP30.ZIP)	www.coffeecup.com	$20.00
CuteMap (CUTEM11.EXE)	www.globalscape.com	$19.95
Image Mapper (IMAGEMAPPER.ZIP)	imagemapper.cjb.net	$9.95
LiveImage (LIVEIMG129INST.EXE)	www.mapthis.com	$29.95
MapEdit (MAP32DST.EXE)	www.boutell.com/mapedit	$25.00
Splash! ImageMapper (SPLASH12.ZIP)	www.gosplash.com	$14.95
WebMapper (WMINST13.EXE)	www.spinel.com	$20.00

Table 16-6: Client-side image mapping software applications

The shareware and demo versions of all image map applications listed in Table 16-6 are provided on the Student Files CD-ROM in the IMAGE MAP SOFTWARE folder.

---

[24] If you are teaching this course in an instructor-led environment, you may substitute different image map software for LiveImage to complete the hands-on exercises in the remainder of this Lesson. Note, however, that this will change the steps involved in completing the tasks in Exercise 3-7 and Exercise 3-8.

Exercise 16-7: Creating an Image Map with Automation Software

In this exercise, you will create an image map that includes circles, rectangles, and polygons using LiveImage. You must have installed the LiveImage software from the student files CD to perform this exercise (LIVEIMG129INST.EXE in the IMAGE MAP SOFTWARE folder).

Note: the LiveImage evaluation is operational for only 14 days. After this time period, you must register the software (`www.liveimage.com`).

1. Launch LiveImage (**Start ▶ Program ▶ Live Image ▶ Live Image**).

2. In the **Welcome to LiveImage!** dialog box, click **OK** and then close the Tip Window. This accepts the default to use the New Image Map Wizard to create a new image map.

3. In the **Create a new image map** dialog box that appears, click **a brand-new HTML file** radio button. This instructs LiveImage to create a new HTML document (instead of using an existing document) for the image map.

4. In the **Brand New HTML file – Step 1** dialog box, in the **Filename of new HTML file** field, type `liveimage.htm`. Save the file to the HTML-3 folder on your Desktop.

5. Click the **Next** button.

6. In the **Brand New HTML file – Step 2** dialog box, scroll to the top of the left pane and double-click **My Computer**.

7. Click the HTML-3 folder.

8. In the right pane, select OFFICE_PHOTO.JPG and click **Next**.

9. In the **Brand New HTML file – Step 3** dialog box, in the **Image Map title** field, insert an underscore between "office" and "photo" (because the image map title cannot contain spaces).

10. Click the **Finish** button.

The image OFFICE_PHOTO.JPG will be opened in LiveImage, as shown in Figure 16-12 on the following page. You are now ready to begin creating hyperlink zones in the image.

If necessary, extend the LiveImage window so that the complete photo is displayed.

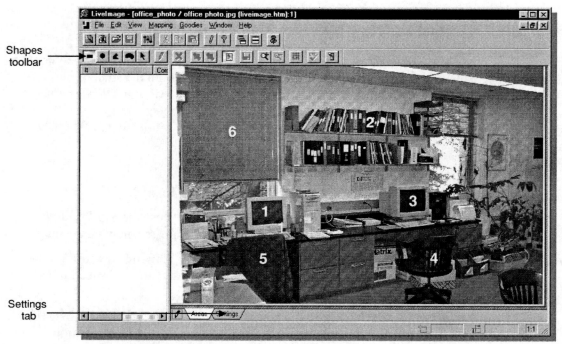

Shapes toolbar

Settings tab

Figure 16-12: Image opened in LiveImage to create an image map

11. On the Shapes toolbar, click the **Define Rectangle area** tool (left most button).

12. In Area #1, drag and drop your mouse on the monitor screen area to define the hyperlink zone.

> When you release your mouse, the Area #1 Settings dialog box will appear.

13. In the **URL to activate when this are is clicked (required)** field, type `http://www.nokia.com/americas/displays` and click **OK**.

> A rectangular hyperlink zone is established in the area of the monitor screen that links to the Nokia Display Web site.

14. Drag and drop in Area #2 to encompass the entire upper bookshelf in a horizontal rectangle.

15. In the **Area #2 Settings** dialog box, specify a URL of `http://www.amazon.com`. and click **OK**.

16. Drag and drop in Area #3 to encompass the other monitor screen. Define a URL for this shape of `http://www.nectech.com/monitors`.

17. On the Shapes toolbar, click the **Define Smooth Polygon area** tool.

18. Place your mouse pointer anywhere alone the outer edge of Area #4 (chair). Hold your mouse button and drag it along the outside of the chair. Include the support stand for the chair, being careful not to release your mouse button.

 When you "connect" the lines, the shape will automatically close and the Area #4 Settings dialog box will appear. If the Area #4 Settings dialog box does not appear, simply double-click to force the shape to "close" and open the dialog box.

19. Specify a URL of `http://www.hermanmiller.com`.

20. Also using the **Define Smooth Polygon area** tool, define the outside of the sweater on the back of the other chair in Area #5. Specify a URL of `www.landsend.com`.

21. On the Shapes toolbar, click the **Define Polygon area** tool.

22. Click once in the upper right corner of Area #6 (blinds). Drag down and click again in the lower right corner of the window.

23. Move your mouse pointer over to the lower left corner of the window and click again.

24. Drag up and click as necessary to navigate around the wall trimmings and the red object. It will require approximately six to eight clicks to reach the upper left corner of the window.

25. Close the shape by moving your mouse to the point at which you started in the upper right corner of the window. If the shape does not automatically close, double-click to force it to close. Define a URL of `www.levelor.com`.

26. Select **File ▶ Save As**.

27. In the **Save the Image Map** file dialog box, choose the HTML-3 folder on your Desktop and name the file `office_photo.htm`.

 An alert box will appear that informs you that the location to which you have chosen to save the HTML file containing the image map code is the same folder that contains the referenced graphic file (OFFICE_PHOTO.JPG), as shown in Figure 16-13 on the following page.

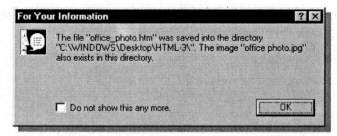

Figure 16-13: HTML document and graphic file reside in same folder

28. In the alert box, click the **OK** button.

29. At the bottom of the LiveImage window, click the **Settings** tab (as shown in Figure 16-12 earlier in this exercise).

 The Settings tab will appear, as shown in Figure 16-14.

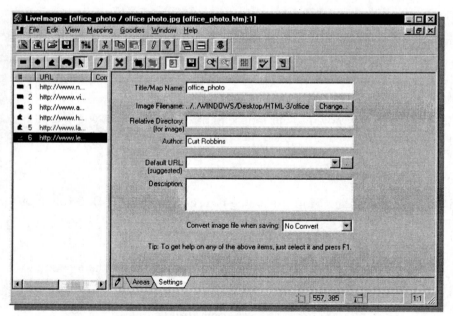

Figure 16-14: Settings tab in LiveImage

30. In the **Author** field, type your full name. Click the **Areas** tab to return to the image map.

31. On the toolbar, click the **Save** button and close out of LiveImage.

Exercise 16-8: Editing and Testing Your Image Map

In this exercise, you will edit and test the image map you created in the previous exercise using LiveImage. You will open it in your Web browser and test each hyperlink zone to ensure that everything works properly. You will then change one of the hyperlink zones to encompass a different area and point at a different Web site.

1. Launch LiveImage.

2. Open OFFICE_PHOTO.HTM from the HTML-3 folder on your Desktop (you can also use the list of most recently used files at the bottom of the **File** pulldown menu).

3. Move your mouse pointer over each of the hyperlink zones.

 Each zone displays a yellow outline when it is highlighted, as shown in Figure 16-15. A yellow pop up also appears that displays the referenced URL. This helps you to determine if the hyperlink zone is exactly where you want it and references the correct Web site.

Figure 16-15: Image map displayed in LiveImage with all hyperlink zones highlighted

4. Move your mouse pointer over the hyperlink zone of the books on the bookshelf (Area #2 from the previous exercise).

5. Drag the hyperlink area down to the bottom bookshelf (so it does *not* cover the top shelf).

6. Rectangular hyperlink zones are surrounded by eight selection handles. Place your mouse pointer on the right middle handle and drag to the left to slightly reduce the width of this zone.

7. Using the top middle handle, slightly increase the height of this zone.

8. On the toolbar, click the **Save** button. In the alert box that appears, click **OK**.

 You can turn off automatic backups by selecting **File ▶ Preferences**. In the Preference Settings dialog box, deselect the **Backup original HTML when saving** checkbox and click **OK**.

9. Place your mouse pointer on the right-most monitor and click the right mouse button.

10. On the pop-up menu that appears, select **Edit Area Info**. The **Area #3 Settings** dialog box will appear.

11. In the **Area #3 Settings** dialog box, change the referenced URL to `http://www.viewsonic.com` and click **OK**.

12. Select **Goodies ▶ Test Map** (or <CTRL + T>).

 The Test the Map dialog box appears.

13. Select the lower radio button entitled **The second (and best) way is to have** and click **OK**.

14. In the alert box that appears, click **OK**. (You can turn this feature off by clicking the **Do not show this any more** checkbox.)

 Your default browser is automatically launched and the HTML document containing the image map is opened.

Depending on your computer configuration, you will probably see a Web page containing a broken image.

LiveImage defaults to using absolute (full) URLs for hyperlinks and <IMG> tag image references. Many Webmasters prefer relative (partial) URLs because they offer more flexibility.

You are obviously only testing the image map on your local PC and—when actually creating Web pages—you would upload your HTML documents and image files to a Web server after having created and successfully tested them on your local client PC. Thus, this is a good opportunity to edit the HTML document created by LiveImage to better suit your purposes.

15. Test each of the hyperlink zones by clicking them.

16. <u>On Your Own</u>: using LiveImage, create three additional hyperlink zones within the image map. Use the shape types and reference URLs of your choice.

Lesson 16 Summary

▶ Image maps are another way of providing Web users with hyperlinks. Good image maps always contain evident, intuitive hyperlinks. Image maps offer a dramatic departure in appearance and user interface from the conventional text-based format of a text hyperlink. The major difference between text hyperlinks and image maps is that image maps offer *multiple hyperlinks* in a single image.

▶ There are two types of image maps: client-side and server-side. Server-side image maps were the first type introduced to HTML and involve client-server interaction and CGI scripts running on a Web server.

   Client-side image maps, by contrast, involve no server-side processing and, thus, operate faster. All instructions for client-side image maps are downloaded in a Web page. The relative simplicity and faster processing speed of client-side image maps has made them the image map type of choice by today's Webmasters.

▶ There are three tags involved in image maps: <MAP>, <IMG>, and <AREA>.

▶ <MAP> is a container (non-empty tag) that has one necessary attribute, NAME. The value of NAME must coincide with the value of <IMG SRC=x>. The <MAP> container must be populated by <AREA> tags, one for each shape that represents a hypertext zone in the image map.

▶ You are already familiar with the <IMG> tag from the introductory and intermediate courses in DDC's *Mastering HTML* Series. In normal use for inline images, <IMG> has one necessary attribute, SRC. The value of SRC is the path and name of the GIF or JPEG file to be displayed in the Web page. When used with image maps, <IMG> involves an additional required attribute, USEMAP. The value of USEMAP must begin with a pound sign (#) and be the same as the value of the <MAP> tag NAME attribute.

▶ The <AREA> tag is an empty tag that has three necessary attributes: SHAPE, COORDS, and HREF.

▶ SHAPE has four possible values: rect, circle, poly, and default. The rect, circle, and poly values define the three possible types of shapes for image map hyperlink zones. The default value defines all areas of an image map that are not defined by other <AREA> tags to reference a particular URL.

▶ The COORDS value is the X and Y axis coordinates of the shape specified by the SHAPE value. For a rectangle, there are four coordinates (X and Y for the upper left corner and lower right corner of the rectangle). For a circle, there are three coordinates (X and Y for the center of the circle and the pixel value of the radius). For a polygon, there is an X and Y coordinate pair for each point on the polygon. A polygon can have an unlimited number of coordinate pairs.

▶ The HREF value is the URL referenced by the hyperlink zone within the image map. The http:// transfer protocol must be included with all Web page addresses. MAILTO and FTP hyperlinks can also be specified (be sure to use the appropriate transfer protocol).

Lesson 16 Quiz

Matching

___ 1. coordinates for a circle

___ 2. <IMG> attribute

___ 3. coordinates for a rectangle

___ 4. <MAP> attribute

___ 5. server-side image maps

___ 6. most simple SHAPE value coordinates

a. 24,19,73,54

b. USEMAP

c. involves CGI

d. 4,7,2

e. rect

f. NAME

Fill in the Blank

7. The first two COORDS values for a circle are the X and Y coordinates for the center of the circle. The third coordinate is the circle's _____ .

8. There are three tags involved in image maps: _____ , _____ , _____ .

9. USEMAP is an attribute to the _____ tag.

10. When defining the value for the HREF attribute, you must always remember the transfer protocol _____ .

True or False?

T / F   11. The order of polygon COORDS values is not important.

T / F   12. Client-side image maps were the first type of image map introduced.

T / F   13. There is a total of three values to the SHAPE attribute.

T / F   14. The <MAP> tag has two necessary attributes.

T / F   15. You must always include a pound sign (#) preceding the value of the USEMAP attribute.

T / F   16. IE 5 does not properly interpret SHAPE=default.

(This page intentionally left blank)

Lesson 17
Introduction to
Cascading Style
Sheets

Lesson Topics

▶ Cascading Style Sheets

▶ Style Attribute

▶ Font & Text Properties

▶ Color & Background Properties

▶ Border Properties

▶ Lesson 17 Summary

Cascading Style Sheets Overview

Cascading Style Sheets, also known as *CSS*, provide a way for you to apply styles—such as fonts, font sizes, borders, and colors—to HTML and other online documents.

Traditionally, publishers used *style sheets* to track page elements such as typefaces and headings that they wanted to apply to books, newspapers, and other long documents. CSS is a modern Internet version of the style sheet that you can use not only with Web pages, but also with print documents.

Cascade: in the context of Cascading Style Sheets, this term means, in essence, that one style sheet can derive from, or spill over into, another. For example, a Web page may have a preferred style sheet attached, but a user can apply her favorite styles locally on her client browser.

Likewise, you can use more than one style sheet for one document to reduce labor. Rules of precedence apply in such a case.

Origin of CSS

Like HTML, CSS was developed by a committee of the World Wide Web Consortium (W3C). CSS grew out of a need to separate the *format*, or appearance, of an online document from the *content* of the document.

The early browsers displayed Web page content with limited formatting ability. For example, you could control fonts on the client (in the local browser), but not from the Web server.

<TABLE> and <FONT>

The advent of the <TABLE> tag in HTML enabled the more precise placement of design elements. The <FONT> tag added variety in the display of fonts. However, these elements did not provide enough power and flexibility. CSS allows Web designers to have significantly more control over where and how Web content is displayed.

CSS Level 1 (CSS/1) has been a World Wide Web Consortium (W3C) recommendation since December 1996 (available at www.w3.org/TR/REC-CSS1). The W3C recommended CSS Level 2 (CSS/2) in May 1998 (see www.w3.org/TR/REC-CSS2).

In this course, both CSS/1 and CSS/2 are referred to generally as CSS.

Content vs. Format

When Tim Berners-Lee invented the World Wide Web in 1989, his intent was to share simple engineering documents across the Internet. In 1990, Berners-Lee and others created an SGML[25] document type definition (DTD) called HyperText Markup Language (HTML). They also invented HyperText Transfer Protocol (HTTP), the mechanism that transports HTML and related data between clients and servers on the Internet. HTTP is a subset of another important protocol called Transmission Control Protocol/Internet Protocol (TCP/IP).

In the beginning, HTML documents had headings, paragraphs, bold, italic, underline, graphics, and so forth. However, every HTML document depended on a client, such as a browser (or other *user agent*) to apply a format to the content of the document. Once the Web began gaining popularity among businesses and consumers—rather than just among the engineering and academic communities—in about 1993, the desire arose for more control over how content was displayed.

Differences

What is the difference between content and format?

- <u>Content</u>: the actual text, graphics, and other features of document design.
- <u>Format</u>: contrary to content, refers to how those features *appear*.

CSS is important to Web page designers because it allows them to separate content and format. The ability to separate the two opens the door to applying formats more consistently across Web pages and reusing them in different contexts.

In addition, you can take the same HTML file and—by applying different style sheets—make the content of the file appear very differently. This gives much more control and power to Web programmers and designers.

Lack of Universal Browser Support

Many advanced users of HTML 4.0 today are using CSS in some form or another, although neither of the two most popular browsers fully supports CSS/2 (or even CSS/1). However, with almost universal acceptance of W3C specifications, both Netscape and Microsoft are committed to making their browsers comply with the W3C CSS recommendations.

Not all features of CSS/1 and CSS/2 are covered in these Lessons. Full coverage is left to another, more comprehensive course, available soon from DDC Publishing.

---

[25] Standard Generalized Markup Language: the precursor to HTML and XML.

Three Ways to Add Style

CSS provides three methods for applying styles to a Web page:

- STYLE attribute
- STYLE element
- external style sheets

STYLE Attribute: Inline Styles

The STYLE attribute applies to individual elements or tags whose style you want to control. A style applied through the STYLE attribute applies only to the current element and is called an *inline style*.

You cannot reuse inline styles unless you copy and move them around, which can be error prone and tedious. However, when styles are used in this way, they take precedence over a style presented through some other means, such as a separate style sheet.

Below is a simple example of the STYLE attribute centering text in a <P> tag:

```
<P STYLE="text-align: center">Warning!</P>
```

STYLE Element: Document Styles

As part of the HEAD section of an HTML document, the STYLE element provides a place for you to specify styles that can apply to all tags of a certain type within an HTML document.

For example, you can specify styles for the <H1> tag within the STYLE element, making it apply to *all* <H1> tags within the document. However, you can override a style indicated in a STYLE element by using the STYLE attribute. Using a fragment of an HTML document, below is an example of a text-centering style applied to the <H1> tag within a STYLE element:

```
<HEAD>
<TITLE>Cascading Style Sheets</TITLE>
<STYLE TYPE=text/css>
<!--

H1     {text-align: center}

-->
</STYLE>
</HEAD>
```

External Style Sheets

The third method for invoking styles in a Web page is collecting all of your styles in a separate document that can be linked to or imported into an HTML document. This allows you to reuse an external style sheet with other documents. You can also link to more than one style sheet at a time.

As a very simple example, assume the file named STYLE.CSS contains the following content:

```
/* File: STYLE.CSS */

H1      {text-align: center}
```

The first line, enclosed by /* and */, is merely a comment; the second line is an instruction stating that the text within <H1> tags should be centered. When you have a style sheet in a separate file, you can link one or more HTML documents to it with the <LINK> tag in a HEAD section, as shown below:

```
<HEAD>
<TITLE>Cascading Style Sheets</TITLE>
<LINK REL=STYLESHEET HREF=style.css TYPE=text/css>
</HEAD>
```

<u>To maximize consistency and reuse, external style sheets are the best choice for applying styles</u>. You can learn more about external styles sheets in the *Linking to an External Style Sheet* section in the following Lesson.

Style Methods Review

Below is a quick recap of what you just learned regarding style methods:

- Inline styles prescribed by the STYLE attribute apply only to *individual* elements or tags, but take precedence over document-level styles or external styles.

- Document styles specified in the STYLE element can apply to *all* elements or tags of the given type within the current document. The STYLE element allows you to reuse styles throughout a document.

- External style sheets allow you to place a collection of styles in a separate file, making it possible to reuse styles not only within a single document, but with multiple HTML documents. External styles sheets represent the <u>best method</u> for maximizing consistency and reuse of styles.

Style Attribute

The STYLE attribute is a core attribute of HTML 4.0 and provides a quick way for you to learn how to apply styles. As you know, an attribute modifies an HTML tag, often changing its appearance. The STYLE attribute allows you to change a wide variety of characteristics, or properties, of a tag. You can apply CSS style properties with the STYLE attribute or with a separate style sheet. You will learn about how to create separate style sheets in Lesson 19: *Reusing Styles*.

A core attribute in HTML 4.0 is defined in the HTML Document Type Definition (DTD) as an attribute that applies to *all* or *nearly all* HTML elements (tags).

Inline Styles

A style applied with the STYLE attribute is known as an *inline style. Inline* in this context denotes that the style is specified in the same line that the element is specified.

Best Learning Method

While using this attribute does not constitute creating a separate style sheet, it is an early step in creating one. You will be able to transfer most of what you learn about inline styles to creating external style sheets later. By first learning the STYLE attribute, however, you will learn CSS much more quickly.

Inline styles are not the preferred method for CSS; external style sheets are. However, inline styles are a preferred method for *learning* CSS.

The quickest way for you to learn inline styles is to complete some hands-on exercises. In the first exercise, you will create an HTML document called CSS.HTM. In the following exercise, you will apply your first style.

Exercise 17-1: Creating a Simple HTML File

In this exercise, you will create a simple HTML document including an instance of the <P> tag.

1. Launch your text editor.

2. With your cursor at the beginning of the document, type the following text:

```
<HTML>

<HEAD>
<TITLE>Cascading Style Sheets</TITLE>
</HEAD>
<BODY>

<P>This paragraph has no style.</P>

</BODY>
</HTML>
```

3. Select **File ▶ Save As**.

4. Save the file as CSS.HTM in the HTML-3 folder on your Desktop.

5. Launch your Web browser (because of better CSS support, Microsoft Internet Explorer 4 or later is suggested.)

6. Open the HTML document named CSS.HTM in your Web browser.

The text "This paragraph has no style" is displayed using the default Web page font (Times New Roman) in your browser, as shown in Figure 17-1 on the following page.

If your browser is not using this font, you can change it back to the default by selecting Tools ▶ Internet Options ▶ Fonts in IE or Edit ▶ Preferences ▶ Appearance ▶ Fonts in Navigator, and then selecting the Times New Roman font.

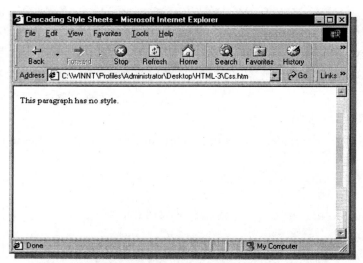

Figure 17-1: CSS.HTM displayed in your browser

Exercise 17-2: Adding a Font Property to the Style Attribute

In this exercise, you will add the STYLE attribute to the <P> tag and will apply the font-family property to the tag.

1. Switch applications to your text editor.
2. Delete the text shown in bold strikethrough and add the text shown in bold:

   <P **STYLE="font-family: Arial"**>This paragraph has **some ~~no~~** style.</P>

3. Save the HTML document.
4. Switch applications to your Web browser and reload the Web page.

 The default Web page font in your browser, Times New Roman, is changed to Arial, as shown in Figure 17-2.

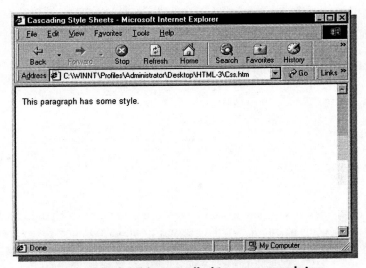

Figure 17-2: Arial font applied to a paragraph tag

Properties & Values

In the previous exercise, you added the following script to the example:

```
STYLE="font-family: Arial"
```

The value of the STYLE attribute is slightly different than some of the other attributes about which you have learned because it is broken into parts, as shown in Figure 17-3.

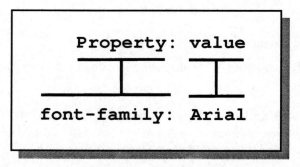

Figure 17-3: Property and value in the STYLE attribute

Two Parts to the Style Value

The two parts of the STYLE value are:

- actual property

- value of the property

The *property* describes what appearance or feature you want to change and the *value* describes how you want to change it. The property and value are always separated by a colon (:). The space between the colon and value is optional, but it certainly helps readability.

So in this example, the property is font-family and the value is Arial. Now that you understand this concept, you can experiment with properties and values as quickly as they are presented to you.

A Word About <FONT>

The <FONT> tag, while still common, is not part of the strict HTML 4.0 Specification. However, it is still alive and well in the transitional HTML 4.0 Specification. In other words, the W3C HTML committee is trying to move away from older tags, such as those from HTML 2.0 and 3.2, that are still in wide use. However, the committee is still tolerant of many of these tags.

Why Say Goodbye to <FONT>?

One way to encourage HTML scripters to move away from older, deprecated tag elements and attributes is to provide more powerful ones in the latest versions of the language. The STYLE attribute does exactly that; it provides access to a much richer set of properties than the <FONT> tag ever did.

 The term *deprecated* applies when a tag has fallen out of favor, usually because a better tag has been added to the latest specification. Nevertheless, it is still supported for backwards compatibility, though not strictly. A tag labeled *deprecated* is also likely to disappear in future versions of HTML, so it is good to move away from it.

The <FONT> tag allows you to control such things as:

- typeface with the FACE attribute

- font color with the COLOR attribute

- font size with the SIZE attribute

Font & Text Properties

While graphics are very important in Web design, the presentation of text is at the heart of what the Web is about. CSS offers a variety of properties that control fonts and text, some of which are shown in Table 17-1. With these properties, you can:

- change a font typeface

- control font size

- make text bold or italic

- justify text

Font & Text Properties	Description	Example(s)
font-family	Font or typeface	font-family: Tahoma;
font-size	Size of the font	font-size: 12pt;
font-weight	Normal or bold	font-weight: bold;
font-style	Normal, italic, or oblique	font-style: italic;
text-align	Left, center, right or justify	text-align: right;
text-indent	Indent first line	text-indent: 10pt;

Table 17-1: Font and text properties

 This Lesson is introductory. It does not document all of the font and text properties of CSS.

Font-Size Property

If you are familiar with typography, you already know the term *points*. However, point size is not the only unit of measure that you can apply to fonts. All units of measure are collectively referred to as *length units*.

 Length units apply to other CSS properties besides the `font-size` property. Other properties that use length units are `line-height`, margin properties, border properties, and so forth. For additional information, see section 6.1 of the CSS/1 Specification or 4.3.2 of the CSS/2 Specification.

Four Ps

CSS applies four length units that start with the letter *P*, as shown in Table 17-2.

Length Unit	Definition	Code Example
Point (pt)	1/72 of an inch	`font-size: 12pt;`
Pica (pc)	Equal to 12 points	`font-size: 2pc;` (equivalent to 24pt)
Pixel (px)	Units measure by pixel will vary according to the number of picture element dots (pixels) on a display, such as a computer monitor.	`font-size: 40px;`
Percentage (%)	Units divisible by 100, similar to monetary units and financial indicators. For example, a value of 120% would make the font 20% larger than normal.	`font-size: 200%;`

Table 17-2: Four CSS length units

International Standards

Perhaps you are more comfortable with common units of measure, such as:

- Inches (in)

  ```
  font-size: 0.75in; (3/4 of an inch)
  ```

- Millimeters (mm)

  ```
  font-size: 30mm;
  ```

- Centimeters (cm)

  ```
  font-size: 14cm;
  ```

Keyword Font Size Values

The `font-size` property also accepts several keywords in place of a numerical value. These keywords are shown in Table 17-3.

Absolute Keywords	Relative Keywords
xx-small	smaller
x-small	larger
small	
medium	
large	
x-large	
xx-large	

Table 17-3: Font size keywords

The browser has an internal table that keeps track of the normal font size. Absolute values scale font sizes up and down by a factor of 1.5, based on the browser's internal font size. This factoring applies as you move from one index to the next.

In other words, moving down the list of indices, if `font-size: medium` were equivalent to 10 points, then `font-size: large` would be 15 points (10 x 1.5)

The relative values increase or decrease the size of the font based on the next index value. For example, if the previous setting was `font-size: small`, then `font-size: larger` would nudge the value up to the next index (that is, to `font-size: medium`). If you issue yet another `font-size: larger`, the value is nudged up again to `font-size: large`.

Em & Ex

CSS also offers two other length units, or sizes, that are somewhat more obscure. They are *em* and *ex*:

- Em (`em`): relative to the height of the font associated with the element. In the following example, if the font associated with the element was, for instance, 12 point, then this code would result in the element being displayed in 48 point type:

  ```
  font-size: 4em;
  ```

- X-height (`ex`): relative to the height of the letter *x* of the font associated with the element. This example will make the font six times the height of the letter *x* of the font:

  ```
  font-size: 6ex;
  ```

Exercise 17-3: Adding the Font-Size Property

In this exercise, you will add the `font-size` property to the `STYLE` attribute of the `<P>` tag.

1. Switch back to your text editor.

2. Add the following text that appears in bold. Notice that a semicolon (;) separates the property-value sets.

```
<P style="font-family: Arial; font-size: 24pt">This paragraph has
some style.</P>
```

 In CSS, each property-value set in a list or series is always separated by a semicolon; however, a semicolon is not required at the end of the list.

3. Save the document.

4. Switch to your Web browser and reload the Web page.

 The text on the Web page is now significantly larger, as shown in Figure 17-4.

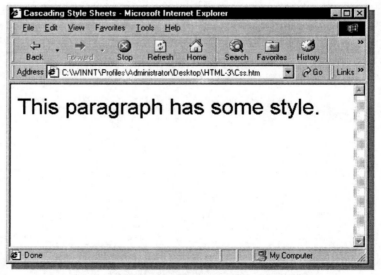

Figure 17-4: Applying the font-size property

Font-Weight Property

You can make the font appear bold with the font-weight property. By default, a font weight is normal (not bold). With CSS, you can be very specific about how you apply a bold value, as shown in Table 17-4.

Font-weight Keyword or Value	Description	Example
normal	Normal font weight (same as 400)	font-weight: normal;
100-900	Nine-value range of boldness	font-weight: 700;
bold	Bold font weight (same as 700)	font-weight: bold;
bolder	Increment to the next value in the range	font-weight: bolder;
lighter	Decrement to the previous value in the range	font-weight: lighter;

Table 17-4: CSS font weight properties

 You are not limited to one weight of bold, but you can use a range from light to dark to very dark to black.

Exercise 17-4: Adding the Font-weight Property

In this exercise, you will add several other font and text properties to the STYLE attribute.

1. Switch back to your text editor.

2. Delete the text shown in bold strikethrough and add the text shown in bold:

    ```
    <P style="font-family: Arial; font-size: 24pt 1pc; font-weight:
    bold">This paragraph has some style.</P>
    ```

3. Save the document.

4. Switch back to your Web browser and reload the page.

 The text on the refreshed Web page appears in the Arial font, bold, and one pica (12 points) in size, as shown in Figure 17-5.

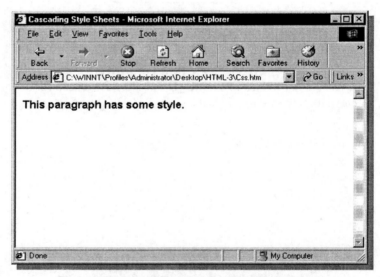

Figure 17-5: Applying the font-weight property

More About the Font-Family Property

A browser can easily render fonts that are installed locally on a user's computer. Fonts that are common on PCs include:

- Times New Roman

- Arial

- Helvetica

- Courier New

However, you can never be sure exactly which fonts are installed on computers in New York City, St. Petersburg, or Tokyo that are requesting your Web pages. This is one reason why you can specify more than one font with the font-family property. You can list them in a series so that the client browser can determine how to render fonts on your Web pages (based on those fonts available on the client computer).

Font Series

Assume that you provide a comma-separated list to the font-family property, such as:

    font-family: Verdana,Arial,Helvetica,Geneva,sans-serif;

The browser interprets this list in priority fashion. That is, it reads Verdana first, then Arial, and so forth. The browser displays the first font for which it finds a match.

The Verdana TrueType font is growing in popularity and is becoming readily available. This highly-readable font, like the Georgia TrueType font, is optimized for Web viewing

If the Verdana font is on the client computer, it will display the appropriate text in Verdana. However, if the client computer cannot find Verdana, it will display the text in Arial, and so on down the list. Finally, if the browser cannot find any of the fonts listed in font-family, it will turn to the generic font—sans-serif in this example—and use the first occurrence of this type of font it finds.

Spaces, Cases & Quotes

The `font-family` property (or any other CSS property) does not care if you use uppercase or lowercase when specifying font names, nor does it care if there is a space after the comma.

The two examples listed below are interpreted identically:

- `font-family:georgia,"times new roman",times,serif;`
- `font-family: Georgia, Times New Roman, Times, serif;`

The CSS/1 Specification states that you should use quotation marks around font names with spaces. However, if you choose to not use quotation marks when specifying a font name with spaces, the parser will typically interpret the name correctly.

 Parser: a program associated with a Web browser that examines the contents of a Web page, word-for-word or character-by-character. Each character is tested for validity and usefulness.

If a parser encounters something it dislikes or does not recognize, it merely ignores it and moves on to the next item. If you have not already noticed, Web browsers are very forgiving. However, parsers used with other programs, such as C++ and XML, are typically less tolerant of mistakes.

Generic Family Font Names

Generic font family names specify one of five kinds of fonts, as shown in Table 17-5.

The purpose of generic names is to help compensate for the unknown on client computers. In essence, this mechanism gives the browser permission to choose a font of the correct type and does not require the Web page to know what fonts are installed on a client computer.

Generic Font Names	Example
serif	Times
sans-serif	Helvetica
cursive	*ZapfChancery*
fantasy	**Playbill**
monospace	Courier, Andale Mono

Table 17-5: Generic font names

Adding Italic

You can add italic with the `font-style` property. This property takes three values:

- `normal`

- `italic`

- `oblique`

As specified by CSS, the keyword *oblique* is associated with sans serif font families, whereas *italic* is associated with serif families. Nonetheless, the Navigator and IE browsers use the term interchangeably. The other keyword for `font-style` is `normal` which, of course, turns italic off.

Exercise 17-5: Adding Style to the <H1> Tag

In this exercise, you will add an <H1> tag with a `font-family` series and pull style properties out of the <P> tag.

1. Switch back to your text editor.

2. Delete the text shown in bold strikethrough and add the text shown in bold:

   ```
   <H1 STYLE="font-family: Arial, Helvetica, sans-serif">Stylish
   Heading</H1>

   <P style="font-family: Arial; font-size: 24pt 1pc; font-weight:
   bold">This paragraph has some no style again.</P>
   ```

3. Save the document.

4. Switch back to your Web browser and reload the page.

The <H1> tag you just added appears in the upper-left corner of the browser, as shown in Figure 17-6. It is 14-point Arial bold.

You will notice that the <H1> tag is bold, even though you did not specify bold for it. This is because the tag inherited this style property from the default bold property of <H1>.

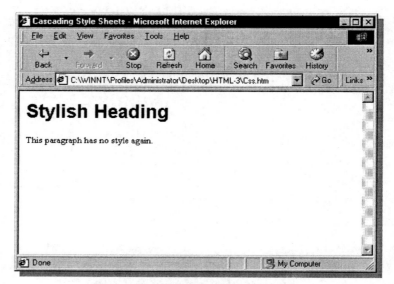

Figure 17-6: Adding <H1> with style

Exercise 17-6: Adding Italic to <H1>

In this exercise, you will add italic to the <H1> element.

1.   Switch to your text editor.

2.   Add the following text that appears in bold.

```
<H1 STYLE="font-family: Arial, Helvetica, sans-serif; font-style:
oblique">Stylish Heading</H1>
```

3.   Save the document.

4.   Switch to the browser and reload the page.

   If you are using IE 4 or above, the text in the <H1> tag is now displayed in italic, as shown in Figure 17-7.

If you are using Netscape, the text will not appear italic.

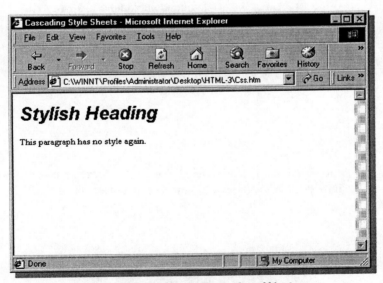

Figure 17-7: Adding italic to the <H1> tag

Aligning Text with text-align

The possible values for the `text-align` property are:

- `left`

- `center`

- `right`

- `justify`

Table 17-6 describes the `text-align` property.

text-align Property	Description
left	The initial, or default, value that produces a ragged right margin.
center	Centers text in the middle of the current text column.
right	Produces a right-justified alignment with a ragged left margin.
justify	Balances text within the current column so that left and right margin edges appear square; also known as "perfect margins."

Table 17-6: text-align properties

But what about indenting text? The `text-indent` property will be introduced in the *Indenting Text* section of Lesson 18.

Exercise 17-7: Centering Text

In this exercise, the `text-align` property will center the `<H1>` heading with the `center` keyword or value.

1. Switch back to the text editor.

2. Add the following bold text.

   ```
   <H1 STYLE="font-family: Arial, Helvetica, sans-serif; font-style:
   oblique; text-align: center">Stylish Heading</H1>
   ```

3. Save the file.

4. Switch to your browser and reload the page.

 The heading is now centered, as shown in Figure 17-8.

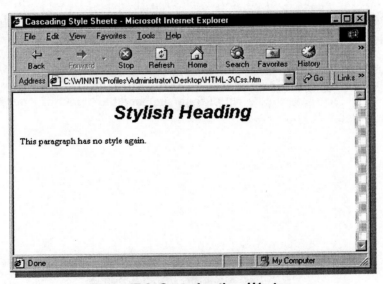

Figure 17-8: Centering the <H1> tag

Lesson 17 Summary

▶ Cascading Style Sheets (CSS) provide a way to control how HTML elements appear on a Web page. Styles include such properties as font families, font size, colors, margins, and borders, and many others. You can apply styles directly to an element or through the use of a separate style sheet.

▶ Though it is improving regularly, browser support for CSS—by both Microsoft Internet Explorer or Netscape Navigator—is not complete.

▶ The `STYLE` attribute is a core attribute in HTML 4.0 and applies to nearly all of its elements. You can specify styles using this attribute in nearly the same manner as when you use a separate style sheet.

▶ Styles are defined by properties and the values of those properties. For example, in the statement `font-size: 12pt`, `font-size` is the property and `12pt` (meaning 12 points) is the value.

▶ Font properties include: `font-family`, which sets the font face, `font-size`, which sets the size of the font, `font-weight`, which applies bold, and `font-style`, which applies italic. The `font-variant` property, which specifies small caps, is not fully supported and is not covered in this Lesson.

▶ Text properties are closely related to font properties. They include `text-align`, which justifies text or aligns it on the left, right, or center, and `text-indent`, which indents the first line of a block of text. There are several more text properties, but they are not discussed in this Lesson.

▶ Length units can be applied to several properties, such as `text-size` and `margin`. These length units include points (`pts`), pixels (`px`), picas (`pc`), inches (`in`), centimeters (`cm`), millimeters (`mm`), the height of font (`em`), and the height of letter x (`ex`). Percentage values are also valid.

Lesson 17 Quiz

Matching

___ 1. display area in a browser window

___ 2. optimized for viewing on the Web

___ 3. listed in order of preference for appearance

___ 4. a core attribute of HTML 4.0

___ 5. bold property

a. `font-weight`

b. `STYLE`

c. Verdana font

d. canvas

e. font families

Fill in the Blank

6. One pica equals _____ points.

7. The best way to reuse styles is through an _____ style sheet.

8. An _____ is relative to the height of a font.

9. You can use a `STYLE` element only in the _____ section of an HTML document.

10. You can justify text with the _____ property.

True or False?

T / F   11. A font size may be represented as a percentage of the current font size.

T / F   12. HTML parsers associated with browsers are very unforgiving.

T / F   13. Both the Microsoft Internet Explorer and Netscape Navigator browsers support all features of CSS Level 2.

T / F   14. The <FONT> tag was not deprecated in HTML 4.0.

T / F   15. A point is 1/72 of an inch.

T / F   16. A point equals 12 picas.

(This page intentionally left blank)

DDC Publishing • www.ddcpub.com

Lesson 18
CSS Color &
Background
Properties

Lesson Topics

▶ Color & Background Properties

▶ Border Properties

▶ Lesson 18 Summary

Color & Background Properties

On Web pages, color helps your users distinguish contrasts and discover beauty. People read mostly black-and-white on the pages of books because the cost of producing color on printed pages is prohibitive. But this is not so on the Web!

Color has greater presence on the Web because, understandably, it costs much less to produce it on Web pages. Naturally then, CSS offers a number of ways to present color.

Color and background properties allow you to display:

- the color of an object or text

- a Web page's background color

- background color for a tag or element

- an image as a background to a Web page

- a background image that is repeated, either along the X or Y axis

Other color and background properties, not listed here, can position a background image or determine if a background picture scrolls with Web page content.

Table 18-1 lists some of the color and background properties.

Color & Background Properties	Description	Example(s)
color	Color of text, borders, etc.	color: blue;
background-color	Background color of a tag	background-color: black;
background-image	Image to place in background of page	background-image: url(water.gif);
background-repeat	How a background image is displayed	background-repeat: repeat-y;

Table 18-1: CSS color and background properties

 These are not all of the color and background properties. A complete list will be provided in DDC's forthcoming CSS course series.

Color Property

The `color` property is similar to *foreground color* in other contexts. It adds color to a variety of HTML elements. Tags that apply directly to text, such as <P> and <B>, are ideal candidates for `color`. However, there are some elements to which you would be unlikely to apply the `color` property—
, for example, would not yield a worthwhile result. A large number of colors are available, and you can use a variety of methods to apply color information.

Browsers can render colors applied through styles faster than they can download GIF, JPG, or PNG images. This is because a client can execute the commands locally rather than waiting for data to download and display.

Thus, often you can achieve better results by producing simple color effects through styles rather than images. In other words, if you want to present a graphic with simple colored text and a color background, you might be able to do it more effectively with styles rather than an image.

You can specify colors using the following methods. Each of following examples applies the color red:

- A color name.

    `color: red;`

- A red, green, blue (RGB) triplet.

    `color: rgb(255,0,0);`

- An RGB triplet using percentages.

    `color: rgb(100%, 0%, 0%);`

- A hexadecimal value representing the RGB triplet:

    `color: #FF0000;`

Hexadecimal values are six digits (three pairs) long and are preceded by the pound (#) sign. Each pair represents an equivalent RGB value in the form #RRGGBB. For example, the FF pair is the same as 255, while 00 equals 0. If each member of the pair is identical, such as FF, you can abbreviate the hex value with a single digit. For example, #F00 will yield the same result as #FF0000.

Color Names, Hexadecimals & RGB

As a convenience, the major browsers introduced the ability to use a preset name rather than a hexadecimal or RGB numeric value to specify a color. Microsoft originally offered a short list of colors names, after which Netscape added many more. With few exceptions, both the IE and Navigator browsers now support a combined list of color names equally well.

Table 18-2 provides a sample of eight color names with equivalent numeric values.

Color Name	Hexadecimal Value	RGB Value
antiquewhite	#FAEBD7	250,235,215
cornflowerblue	#6495ED	100,149,237
gainsboro	#DCDCDC	220,220,220
lemonchiffon	#FFFACD	255,250,205
linen	#FAF0E6	250,240,230
moccasin	#FFE4B5	255,222,173
peru	#CD853F	205,133,63
wheat	#F5DEB3	238,222,179

Table 18-2: Sample color names with hexadecimal and RGB values

Many of the color names introduced by Netscape may have a familiar ring if you have ever used colors in the XWindows or Motif windowing environment on UNIX systems.

Because it is possible that your Web pages will be displayed in older browsers, it may be safest to stick with hex values for colors.

However, if your pages are available only on an intranet, or you are asking users to upgrade to the latest browsers, you can better predict what browsers are in use. You may then want to simply use color names for the sake of usability.

Exercise 18-1: Adding a Splash of Color

In this exercise, you will add color to the text in the `<H1>` tag with the CSS `color` property.

1. Switch back to your text editor.

2. Add the following text that appears in bold.

   ```
   <H1 STYLE="color: blue; font-family: Arial, Helvetica,
   sans-serif; font-style: oblique; text-align: center">Stylish
   Heading</H1>
   ```

3. Save the document.

4. Switch back to your Web browser and reload the page.

 The heading text is now blue, as shown in Figure 18-1. The color blue could also be applied in this context as `rgb(0,0,255)`, `rgb(0%,0%,100%)`, or `#0000FF`.

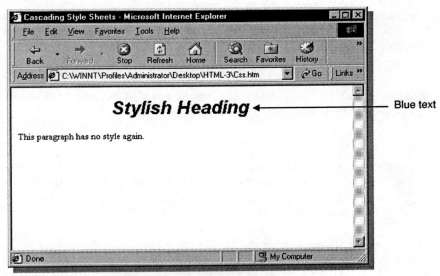

Figure 18-1: Blue heading

Background Colors & Images

The concept of adding a background color to a Web page was introduced to you in DDC's *HTML 4.0 Fundamentals* course. Before the STYLE attribute became available in HTML 3.2, the way to specify background color was with the BGCOLOR attribute to the <BODY> tag, in the following form:

```
<BODY BGCOLOR=cornflowerblue>
```

The BGCOLOR attribute of the <BODY> tag is now considered *transitional* in HTML 4.0. This means that the HTML committee at W3C has determined that, while still permissible, this tag is transitioning out of use in favor of the more powerful and flexible STYLE attribute.

Applying a Background Color Using STYLE

Now, rather than the BGCOLOR attribute, you can use the STYLE attribute with the <BODY> tag, as shown below:

```
<BODY STYLE="background-color: cornflowerblue">
```

As you can see, this takes a little more typing, but you can use this same attribute and value set in this exact form universally.

Avoid bad contrasts of text and background color. That is, do not use light-colored text on a light-colored background or dark text on a dark background. This will negatively affect the readability, usability, and even popularity of your Web pages.

Exercise 18-2: Applying a Background Color to a Web Page

In this exercise, you will learn how to apply a background to a Web page using the CSS `background-color` property.

1. Switch to the text editor.
2. Add the following text that appears in bold to the `<BODY>` tag.

   `<BODY `**`STYLE="background-color: cornflowerblue">`**

3. Save the document.
4. Switch back to the browser and reload the page.

 The background color of the Web page is now a rich blue, as shown in Figure 18-2.

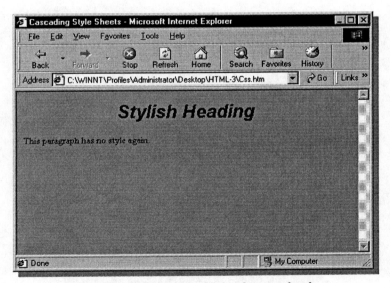

Figure 18-2: Web page with background color

Element Background Color

In a similar way, you can add a background color to a tag. In other words, instead of coloring the entire page, this background color will cover only the block area that is part of the tag.

Below is an example:

```
<P STYLE="background-color: cornflowerblue">
```

The attribute information is precisely the same as applied to the <BODY> tag, but now it applies to the <P> tag (with somewhat different results).

When you apply a background color to a tag, you will see that the color extends across the Web page. This is because of the tag's default box properties.

You will learn more about box properties in the *Border Properties* section later in this Lesson.

Exercise 18-3: Applying a Background Color to a Tag

In this exercise, you will add a background color to a <P> tag.

1. Switch to the text editor.
2. Delete the text shown in bold strikethrough and add the text shown in bold.

   ```
   <BODY STYLE="background-color: cornflowerblue">

   <P STYLE="background-color: cornflowerblue">This paragraph has no
   a little style again.</P>
   ```

3. Save the file.
4. Switch back to your browser and reload the page.

 The background of the line with the <P> tag appears in the color *cornflowerblue*, as shown in Figure 18-3.

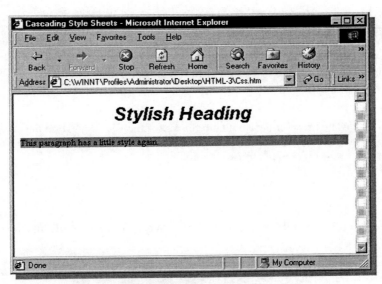

Figure 18-3: Background color for a tag

Background Images

As you probably know, you can place background images on your Web page that appear in a browser behind the text in the foreground. In earlier versions of HTML, you specified background images with the BACKGROUND attribute to the <BODY> tag, as shown below:

```
<BODY BACKGROUND=bg.gif>
```

Like the BGCOLOR attribute, the BACKGROUND attribute is *transitional* in HTML 4.0. This means that W3C has determined that this tag is transitioning out of common use and is no longer part of the official HTML 4.0 Specification (although it is still allowable). You should use the more powerful STYLE attribute.

Specifying a Background Image with the STYLE Attribute

Rather than the BACKGROUND attribute, you can now use the STYLE attribute with the <BODY> tag in this form:

```
<BODY STYLE="background-image: url(bg.gif)">
```

This form is slightly different, but is also self-explanatory. Instead of the attribute name BACKGROUND, the STYLE attribute uses the more specific background-image property name and the URL reference is enclosed in the url( ) keyword.

The browser automatically looks for the file BG.GIF in the same directory where the HTML files reside. Thus, you do not have to use a full pathname to find the file.

If you wanted to use a graphic from a different Web site, you could use a full URL, as shown below:

```
url(http://www.website.com/images/bg.gif)
```

Background-Repeat Property

You can use the background-repeat property to indicate how you want the background image to be displayed. Four values are associated with this property:

- repeat: the background image is repeated both vertically and horizontally.

- repeat-x: the image is repeated along the horizontal X axis, but only a single line.

- repeat-y: the image is repeated along the vertical Y axis, but in a single line.

- no-repeat: as you may have guessed, the image is not repeated at all, but is only displayed once.

The following exercise uses the repeat-y property value.

Exercise 18-4: Adding a Background Image to a Web Page

In this exercise, you will add a background image to your Web page and make it repeat along the Y (vertical) axis.

1. Switch to your text editor.

2. Delete the text shown in bold strikethrough and add the text shown in bold:

   ```
   <BODY STYLE="background-image: url(bg.gif); background-repeat:
   repeat-y">


   <P STYLE="">This paragraph has a little no style again.</P>
   ```

3. Save the document.

4. Switch back to your Web browser and reload the page.

 The graphic BG.GIF appears in the background of your Web page, starting in the upper-left corner (which is the default, or initial, position for background images), as shown in Figure 18-4. The image then repeats down the page along the left edge. Note how the image appears behind the paragraph text. You will get a chance to fix that in the next exercise.

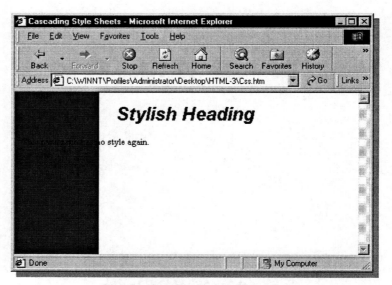

Figure 18-4: Background image

Indenting Text

As you can see in Figure 18-4 on the previous page, the background image shows up behind the lone paragraph on your Web page. Sometimes this is exactly what you want; sometimes it is not. For the purposes of this portion of the Lesson, it is *not* what you desire.

So what to do now? You can indent the text with the `text-indent` property.

Text-Indent Property

The CSS property `text-indent` indents the first line of its element based on the value you set. If you review the section *Font-Size Property*, you will see a variety of methods for specifying font sizes, such as points, picas, pixels, etc. All of those methods, collectively called *length units*, apply to `text-indent` as well.

The `text-indent` exercise that follows uses pixels as the length unit.

Exercise 18-5: Indenting Text With the text-indent Property

In this exercise, you will indent the text with the text-indent property.

1.   Switch back to your text editor.

2.   Add the text shown in bold and delete the text shown in bold strikethrough:

    ```
    <P STYLE="text-indent: 120px">This paragraph has ~~no~~ a little
    style again.</P>
    ```

3.   Save the document.

4.   Switch to the browser and reload the page.

 The text is now indented 120 pixels to the right and is positioned away from the background image, as shown in Figure 18-5.

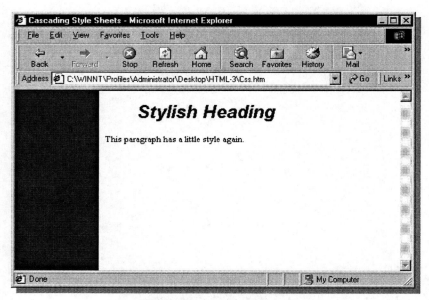

Figure 18-5: Indented text

Margins

It looks great now, but if you were to add more words to the sentence—enough that it would wrap down a line—you would be disappointed. Why? Because the second line will wrap back to the original margin.

To prevent this, it is time to learn about margin properties:

- `margin-left`: controls the *left* margin of an element.

  `margin-left: 120px;`

- `margin-right`: affects the *right* margin.

  `margin-right: 24pt;`

- `margin-top`: adjusts the margin *above* the element.

  `margin-top: 1in;`

- `margin-bottom`: handles the margin *below* it.

  `margin-bottom: 1pc;`

- `margin`: handles *all* four margins with one command.

  `margin: 1in;`

With the last example, a one inch margin is applied to all four margins (by supplying a single value). You can use the `margin` property in other ways, but that will be left to a more comprehensive DDC CSS course.

Margin properties are part of CSS *box properties*. Box properties, such as margins and borders, control the size, shape, and position of surrounding elements. The box is invisible until you apply a property to it; you can then observe its appearance. *Padding properties* are also box properties, but they are not discussed in this Lesson.

With the `margin-left` property, you will make a change to the previous exercise and apply it to the next exercise. Then, instead of simply indenting the first line, each succeeding line will have the same margin.

 Margins work from the outside in. That is, they work from the outer edge of the browser's display canvas rather than from the element out. It is just like in high school typing class: the margins are measured beginning from the outer edge of the page toward the center.

Exercise 18-6: Indenting Text With the margin-left Property

In this exercise, you will indent the `<P>` tag with the `margin-left` property.

1. Switch to the text editor.
2. Add the text shown in bold:

```
<P STYLE="text-indent: 120px">This paragraph has a little style
again. Row, row, row your boat gently down the stream; merrily,
merrily, merrily, merrily life is but a dream.</P>
```

3. Save the document.
4. Switch to your Web browser and reload the page.

 The first line of text is indented while the remaining text wraps all the way to the left margin, conflicting with the background image, as shown in Figure 18-6.

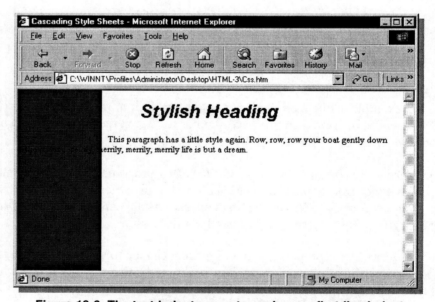

Figure 18-6: The text-indent property works as a first-line indent

5. Delete the text shown in bold strikethrough and add the text shown in bold:

    ```
    <P STYLE="~~text-indent~~margin-left: 120px">This paragraph has a
    little style again.  Row, row, row your boat…dream.</P>
    ```

6. Save the document.

7. Switch to your Web browser and reload the page.

 The margin of the entire paragraph is now 120 pixels, as shown in Figure 18-7.

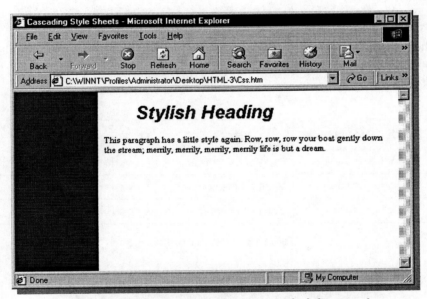

Figure 18-7: Indenting text with the margin-left property

Border Properties

In traditional graphic design and page layout, a border surrounds a graphics element. A border can emphasize or change the mood of a graphic feature. While still somewhat limited, CSS offers a number of ways to render borders using *border properties*.

Border properties, like those used with margins, are part of CSS box properties. Border properties allow you to:

- display a border around an element

- determine the style of a border, such as solid, dotted, dashed, etc.

- choose the thickness of a border line

- select a border color

Some other border properties, such as those that control top, bottom, left, and right borders individually, are not covered in this Lesson. Those demonstrated in this Lesson are listed in Table 18-3.

Border Properties	Description	Example
border-style	Style of the border	border-style: solid;
border-width	Width of the border	border-width: 3pt;
border-color	Color of the border	border-color: red;

Table 18-3: Border properties

 There are other border properties, but the three shown in Table 18-3 will suffice to introduce how CSS handles borders.

Border Styles

CSS includes a good number of border styles:

- `solid`: produces a solid border line.

- `dotted`: makes a dotted border.

- `dashed`: creates a dashed border.

- `double`: shows a double line. Though there are two lines, they and the white space between them equal the same width as a solid line.

- `groove`: displays a 3-D groove using the current value of the `border-color` property.

- `ridge`: draws a 3-D ridge using the value of the `border-color` property.

- `inset`: produces a 3-D inset using the `border-color` property value.

- `outset`: renders a 3-D outset with the current value of `border-color`.

- `none`: the default; turns the border off.

Some of the values, such as `groove` and `ridge`, are difficult to describe. The best way to learn their effects is to try them. Then you can determine if you want to use them.

Border Width

To adjust the width of a border, assign a value to the `border-width` property. Like the `font-size` property, the `border-width` property takes length units such as points, picas, pixels, and so forth. For a list of length units and examples that apply to this and other properties, see the section labeled *Font-Size Property* earlier in this Lesson.

Border Colors

The `border-color` property controls the color of the border. This property takes a value in the same way as the `color` property, such as with a color name, an RGB value, or a hexadecimal value representing an RGB value. For details and examples, see the discussion earlier in this Lesson in the *Color Property* section.

Exercise 18-7: Adding Borders to the <H1> Tag

In this exercise, you will add a border style, width, and color to the <H1> tag.

1. Switch to the editor.

2. Add the text in bold as it appears here.

```
<H1 STYLE="color: blue; font-family: Arial, Helvetica, sans-
serif; font-style: oblique; text-align: center; font-size: 14pt;
font-weight: bold; margin: .2in 2in; border-style: solid; border-
width: 3pt; border-color: blue">Stylish Heading</H1>
```

3. Save the document.

4. Switch to the browser and reload the Web page.

 A three-point wide blue border appears around the heading, as shown in Figure 18-8. The box around the <H1> tag is now made visible by the application of border properties.

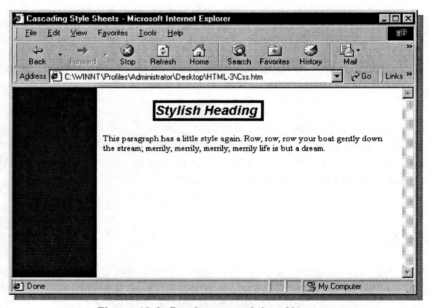

Figure 18-8: Border around the <H1> tag

Lesson 18 Summary

▶ The `color` property can apply to many elements and commonly applies to text. Color values may be specified as hexadecimal values (#RRGGBB), abbreviated hex values (#RGB), preset color names—such as `blue`, `red`, or `cornflowerblue`—and finally by inputting RGB values directly, with `rgb(255,255,255)`.

▶ It is possible to set the background color of a Web page with `background-color` and to apply background images with `background-image`.

▶ You can indent the first line of a paragraph with the `text-indent` property. You can set margins on all four sides of the display canvas using `margin` properties, starting from the outer edge and moving inward.

▶ All elements have an essentially invisible box surrounding them. This box can be controlled and even made visible by applying margin, padding, and border properties.

▶ When applied, border properties can make box properties apparent. You can control border styles, border colors, and border widths.

Lesson 18 Quiz

Matching

___ 1. property that controls element color   a. border styles

___ 2. for specifying a URL as a property value   b. RGB

___ 3. indents all lines, not just first line of text   c. color

___ 4. solid, dotted, dashed, double, groove, ridge, inset, outset   d. margins

___ 5. red, green, and blue   e. url( )

Fill in the Blank

6. The first line of a paragraph is indented by the _____ property.

7. Margins begin from the _____ edge of the display canvas.

8. The repeat property repeats a background image across both the _____ and _____ axes.

9. Elements (tags) are surrounded by an invisible _____ .

10. Box properties include margin, padding, and _____ properties.

True or False?

T / F   11. Colors specified through styles render or display faster than GIF, JPG, or PNG images.

T / F   12. FF in hexadecimal is the same as 255 in decimal.

T / F   13. Six-digit hexadecimal values may be abbreviated to three.

T / F   14. Without margins, the border of a block element like <H1> will stretch across a page.

T / F   15. RGB colors are represented in quadruplets.

Lesson 19
Reusing Styles

Lesson Topics

▶ Reusing Styles

▶ <STYLE> Element

▶ Selectors, Properties, & Values

▶ Linking to an External Style Sheet

▶ Adding Style with CLASS

▶ Lesson 19 Summary

Reusing Styles

In the previous Lesson, you learned how to apply a wide variety of styles to individual elements or tags using the STYLE attribute. For example, if you want to center a heading, such as an <H1> tag, you define it as follows:

```
<H1 STYLE="text-align: center">Reusing Styles</H1>
```

Inline Styles

This style, defined with the STYLE attribute, is called an *inline style* because it only applies to the element or tag inline with the definition of the attribute. Using this attribute was a good way to learn about style properties and values, but you cannot reuse the style information unless you copy and paste it into another tag. Copying and pasting, however, is time consuming and prone to mistakes.

Use It Again, Sam

Among the most powerful features of CSS is the ability to reuse style definitions so they apply not to only one, but to *all* tags of a particular type. This is a great way to make the appearance of a set of Web documents consistent (as well as all the pages of an entire Web site).

How do you reuse styles? First, you need to learn about the STYLE element.

The STYLE element is one of the few HTML 4.0 tags that does not support or use the core STYLE attribute. This is because the STYLE tag does not appear on a Web page. It defines how other elements appear, but does not appear itself.

`<STYLE>` Element

The `<STYLE>` element is a special HTML 4.0 tag that allows you to define the style characteristics of the tags in your HTML document. It works only inside the `<HEAD>` tag (also called the `HEAD` section) of an HTML document.

Document Styles

When you define styles in the `STYLE` element for a tag or class of tags, those styles apply to every instance of the tag or class in the document, making a style definition available for reuse. Thus, instead of defining the same style for every instance of the `<H1>` tag in a document, you need only define it once. This also means that as you use the `<H1>` tag normally, the styles will automatically appear without more work on your part.

Reuse = Reduced Maintenance

Having all of your styles in one location is a huge time saver and focuses style-related maintenance on one location in the file. In the past, you may have used the `ALIGN` attribute, for example, with every occurrence of `<H1>` to achieve the same effect. Using this document-level style method makes your styles in HTML behave more like styles in a typical word processor or editor, such as Microsoft Word or Adobe PageMaker.

HEAD Section

A `<HEAD>` element is a vital part of an HTML document. It contains descriptive information regarding the document itself, such as a document title, JavaScript code in a `<SCRIPT>` container, META tags, and now the `<STYLE>` element. Information inside the `<HEAD>` element is *about* the document and cannot be viewed by a user in the same way as normal Web page content. The style information in the `HEAD` section applies to its related file only.

`<STYLE>` Element TYPE Attribute

The `<STYLE>` tag often has a `TYPE` attribute that defines the style sheet type. It appears as follows:

```
<STYLE TYPE=text/css>
```

Content Types

If the TYPE attribute is used, it is specified as TYPE=text/css (if you are using CSS). The value of TYPE is text/css. This value is known as a *content type*. Content types describe message entities. *Message entities* are types of transmissions that are sent over the Internet. CSS style sheets are sent over the Internet as transmissions of the type *text/css*.

Content types are also called *MIME* types. MIME stands for Multipurpose Internet Mail Extensions. MIME is a standard way of labeling data for transport over the Internet. MIME-type names are sprinkled throughout HTML.

Use of the **TYPE** attribute is not mandatory because the style information in the **STYLE** element provides enough hints to the browser that it knows when it is dealing with CSS. However, it is good practice to include the **TYPE** attribute because different style languages will be possible in the future.

Commenting Styles with <!-- and -->

In the following example, you will see that the style information is enclosed in HTML comment tags. This is a precaution for the benefit of older browsers that do not know how to interpret data in the <STYLE> element.

Older browsers know what to do with tags they do not recognize—absolutely nothing—but they *may* try to render the content of unknown tags. Therefore, comments are a good idea if you know your HTML document will receive broad exposure on the Web.

Style Selector

Finally, the example that follows introduces the *selector*. A selector is a keyword that indicates the tag or class of tags that is selected for the style (<H1> in this instance). Selectors are more fully explained in the *Selectors, Properties, & Values* section later in this Lesson.

Exercise 19-1: Applying a Style to an Entire Document

In this exercise, you will create a new HTML document with a document-level style for the
<H1> tag.

1. If it is not already open, launch your text editor.
2. Select **File ▶ New** to open a new document.
3. Place the cursor at the beginning of the document and type the following text:

```
<HTML>

<HEAD>
<TITLE>Cascading Style Sheets</TITLE>
<STYLE TYPE=text/css>
<!--

H1 {text-align: center;}

-->
</STYLE>
</HEAD>
<BODY>

<H1>Document Styles</H1>

<P>Document styles allow you to reuse styles throughout a
document.</P>

<H1>Reduced Maintenance</H1>

<P>Document styles reduce maintenance.</P>

</BODY>
</HTML>
```

4. Save the file as CSS-2.HTM in the HTML-3 folder on your Desktop.
5. Switch back to your Web browser. Launch your browser if it is not already running.
6. Open CSS-2.HTM in your Web browser.

This HTML document has two instances of the <H1> tag. Both use the document text-centering style defined in the HEAD section, as shown in Figure 19-1.

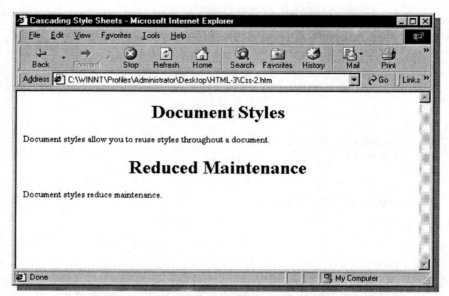

Figure 19-1: Reusing the document style for the <H1> tag

DDC Publishing • www.ddcpub.com

Selectors, Properties, & Values

The last example introduced the *selector*. A selector is a keyword that indicates the element (tag) or class of elements to which a style is applied. The keyword H1 was the selector in the previous example.

Figure 19-2 shows the relationship between selectors, properties, and values.

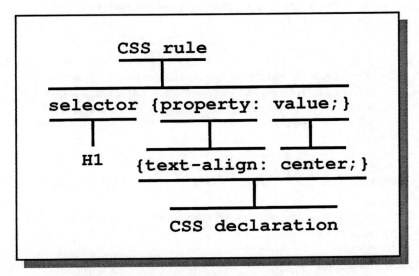

Figure 19-2: CSS selectors, properties, and values

Select a Selector for You

CSS supports a variety of selectors. However, not all selectors are fully supported by the current browsers. Table 19-1 lists some of the selectors that are available.

Selector	Description	Example
Type (tag) selector	Matches tag (element) name	`P {font-size: 12pt};`
Class selector	Matches class name	`P.small {font-size: 9pt};`
ID selector	Matches a tag (element) ID	`#ez2 {color: blue};`
Pseudo-class (dynamic)	Matches a user action	`A:hover {color: red};`
Universal selector	Matches any tag (element)	`* {font-size: 11pt};`

Table 19-1: CSS selectors

CSS Rule

As you can see in Figure 19-2 on the previous page, a CSS rule is a combination of:

- a selector

- a property and value set (one or more sets) enclosed in braces ({ })

- each property/value set is delimited by a semicolon (;)

CSS/2 provides 18 different selectors (see section 5.1 of the CSS/2 Specification, included in the HTML-3 folder on your Desktop). This course allows only enough time to describe a few.

Netscape Navigator 4 supports only type and class selectors.

CSS Declaration

The *CSS declaration* is a subset of the *CSS rule*, as shown in Figure 19-2 on the previous page. The CSS declaration consists of:

- opening brace ({)

- CSS property, followed by a colon (:)

- value that is legal for the property (space between the colon and the value is optional)

- semicolon (;) should follow each property/value set

- closing brace (})

Brace Yourself

If you are familiar with the C or Java programming languages, you will recognize braces ({ }) as a convention to organize procedures, such as functions and methods. In CSS, braces encapsulate a set of properties and values that apply to the selector.

Property

You will recall that a property, such as `text-align`, defines a characteristic of a tag. Some other properties you learned about in the previous Lesson were `font-size`, `color`, and `background-image`. The CSS experts at W3C were wise to name properties so that you could easily guess their function.

Don't Forget the Colon

Following a property keyword is the colon (:). It immediately follows the keyword, without any intervening space. Next comes the value keyword. One or more spaces can come after the colon and before the value keyword.

Property Values

Values, such as `center`, define the function of a property. For example, a `text-align` property can have `left`, `right`, `center`, or `justify` values.

Semicolon

Normally, a semicolon (;) follows each property/value pair. A semicolon is also a line delimiter in C and Java. Thus, if you are a programmer in those languages, it will not feel unnatural to terminate a line with one. However, semicolons are optional under two conditions:

- when there is only one property/value set

- after the last property/value pair in a series

Even though the semicolon is optional in some cases, it is good practice to always end a property/value pair with one. If you want to add CSS declarations later, you will not have to recover from the errors caused by a missing semicolon.

If you would like to see the type of problems this error generates, simply omit a semicolon or two in one of the exercises and watch what happens!

Exercise 19-2: Adding More Document Styles

In this exercise, you will add a font family, font size, top margin, and color to the <H1> tag. You will also add a font family and left margin to the <P> tag.

1. Switch back to the text editor.

2. Add the bold text that appears below to the HTML document.

```
<STYLE TYPE=text/css>
<!--

H1 {font-family: Verdana,Arial,Helvetica,sans-serif;
    font-size: 18pt;
    margin-top: .5in;
    color: cornflowerblue;
    text-align: center;}

P   {font-family: Book Antiqua,Times New Roman,Times,serif;
    margin-left: 50px;}

-->
</STYLE>
```

3. Save the document, switch back to your browser, and reload the Web page.

 The <H1> tags remain centered, but now have a sans serif font, a ½-inch top margin, and an attractive blue color, as shown in Figure 19-3. All <P> tags now prefer the Book Antiqua font over Times and have a 50-pixel left margin.

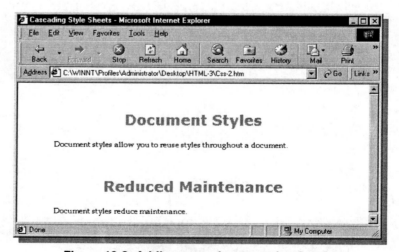

Figure 19-3: Adding more document-level styles

Linking to an External Style Sheet

Now that you know how to apply reusable styles at the document-level, you are ready to take the next step by creating a separate, external style sheet. External style sheets exist in ASCII text files that are altogether separate from HTML documents.

In fact, external style sheets are not HTML documents at all, but have a unique form. However, you may not be aware of it, but you already know the form for CSS files, as you will see in the following exercise.

Advantages of External Styles

External style sheets have several advantages over document-level or element-level styles. Using external style sheets, you can:

- reuse external style sheets with other HTML documents

- link more than one style sheet to a single HTML document

- easily establish a look and feel for an *entire* Web site from a *single* external style sheet

- reduce the time and cost of maintaining styles by placing all styles in a single repository; that is, in a separate, external document

You associate a style sheet with a Web page using the <LINK> tag, as you will learn next.

<LINK> Element

Like the <STYLE> element, the <LINK> element is part of the HEAD section of an HTML document. The syntax of <LINK> is as follows:

```
<LINK HREF=stylesheet.css TYPE=text/css REL=stylesheet>
```

As you can see, this instance of <LINK> uses several attributes.

The <LINK> element has a number of other attributes in HTML 4.0, with varying support from the major browsers.

HREF Attribute

As you already know from DDC's *HTML 4.0 Fundamentals*, the HREF attribute allows you to indicate a local (relative) URL or an absolute URL for a style sheet. This example shows a relative URL for a style sheet named STYLESHEET.CSS. The .CSS file extension is the normal extension for external CSS files.

The difference between relative and absolute URLs are as follows:

- A relative URL is one that the browser finds because of the base URL. It learns the base location either implicitly (relative to the location of the current HTML file the browser is displaying) or explicitly (from the <BASE> tag in the HEAD section).

- An absolute URL is a fully qualified URL that can reference any location on the Web (such as http://www.yoursite.com/style/stylesheet.css).

<TYPE> Attribute

Like the TYPE attribute discussed in the *<STYLE> Element TYPE Attribute* section earlier in this Lesson, the TYPE attribute of <LINK> specifies the content or media type of the style sheet (which is text/css).

 The .CSS file extension is the normal extension for external style sheet files.

REL Attribute

REL indicates the relationship between the current document and the relative document (in this case, STYLESHEET).

Other values for the REL attribute include:

- NEXT (for the next document)

- PREV (for the previous document)

- HELP (for a related help page)

In the next two exercises, you will create an external style sheet and link it to your HTML document.

Exercise 19-3: Creating an External Style Sheet

In this exercise, you will cut the contents of the STYLE element in CSS-2.HTM and paste the contents into a new file named STYLESHEET.CSS.

1. Switch back to the text editor.

2. Highlight the text that appears in bold.

```
<HTML>

<HEAD>
<TITLE>Cascading Style Sheets</TITLE>
<STYLE TYPE=text/css>
<!--

H1 {font-family: Verdana,Arial,Helvetica,sans-serif;
    font-size: 18pt;
    margin-top: .5in;
    text-align: center;
    color: cornflowerblue;}

P  {font-family: Book Antiqua,Times New Roman,Times,serif;
    margin-left: 50px;}

-->
</STYLE>
</HEAD>
<BODY>
```

3. Cut the highlighted area with **Edit ▶ Cut** in Notepad.

4. Save CSS-2.HTM.

 By removing the STYLE element from CSS-2.HTM, it no longer has document styles. However, in the next exercise, you will add a link to CSS-2.HTM that points to the same styles in an external style sheet.

5. Select **File ▶ New**.

6. Select **Edit ▶ Paste**.

7. Save the file as STYLESHEET.CSS in the HTML-3 folder.

8. Add a comment and delete the text shown in bold strikethrough:

```
<STYLE TYPE=text/css>
<!--
/* STYLESHEET.CSS */

H1 {font-family: Verdana,Arial,Helvetica,sans-serif;
    font-size: 18pt;
    margin-top: .5in;
    text-align: center;
    color: cornflowerblue;}

P  {font-family: Book Antiqua,Times New Roman,Times,serif;
    margin-left: 50px;}

-->
</STYLE>
```

9. Save STYLESHEET.CSS.

10. Switch to your Web browser.

11. Refresh CSS-2.HTM.

 You have created an external style sheet, as shown in Figure 19-4. At the same time, styles are removed from CSS-2.HTM, as shown in Figure 19-5 on the following page.

Figure 19-4: External style sheet

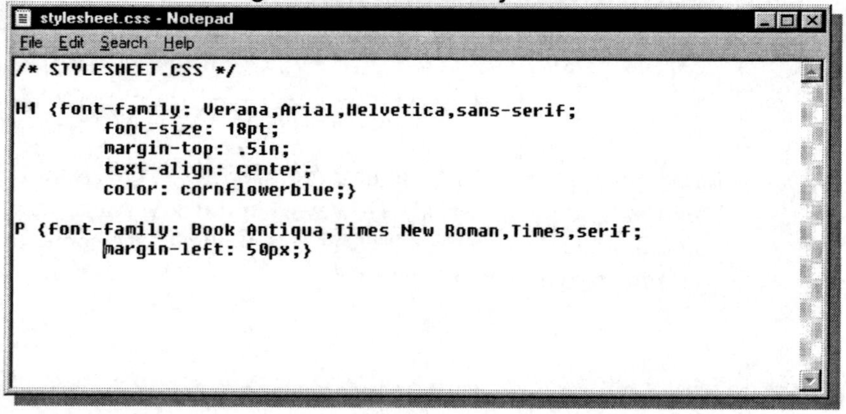

```
stylesheet.css - Notepad
File   Edit   Search   Help

/* STYLESHEET.CSS */

H1 {font-family: Verana,Arial,Helvetica,sans-serif;
        font-size: 18pt;
        margin-top: .5in;
        text-align: center;
        color: cornflowerblue;}

P {font-family: Book Antiqua,Times New Roman,Times,serif;
        margin-left: 50px;}
```

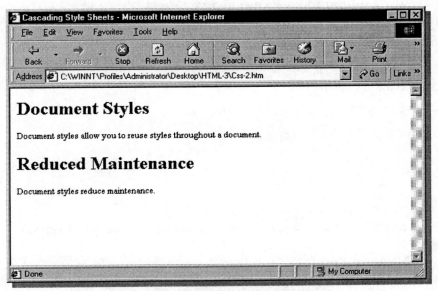

Figure 19-5: CSS-2.HTM without styles

Exercise 19-4: Linking to an External Style Sheet

In this exercise, you will add a <LINK> element to CSS-2.HTM.

1. Switch to the text editor.

2. Open CSS-2.HTM from the HTML-3 folder.

3. Add the following text that appears in bold:

```
<HTML>

<HEAD>
<TITLE>Cascading Style Sheets</TITLE>
<LINK HREF=stylesheet.css TYPE=text/css REL=stylesheet>
</HEAD>
<BODY>
```

4. Save the document.

5. Switch back to your Web browser and reload the page.

 The Web page now appears as it did in Figure 19-3, although now with external styles rather than document styles, as shown in Figure 19-6.

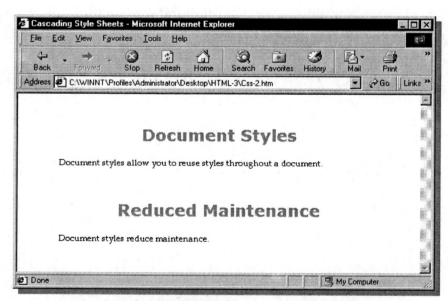

Figure 19-6: CSS-2.HTM with an external style sheet

Style by Inheritance

Elements or tags in HTML have a parent-child relationship. For example, the tag <HTML> is the root element of an HTML document; all other HTML tags are its children. Likewise, the <P> and <TABLE> tags are both children of the <BODY> tag, and the <TD> tag is a child of the <TABLE> tag.

It is not important for you to know all of the parent-child relationships for all HTML tags, but it is important to understand that this relationship exists.

DTD

The parent-child relationship of tags is established in the HTML Document Type Definition (DTD) that defines all of the elements, attributes, entities, and other notations that are part of the HTML scripting language. HTML is a subset of the Standardized General Markup Language, or SGML. The DTD concept is derived from SGML.

Styles Descend from Parent to Child

A style applied to a <BODY> tag, for example, will be inherited by its children. This means that if you apply a style—such as font-size: 12pt—to <BODY>, it will be adopted by the <P> and <TABLE> tags as well.

You can override a style inherited from a parent tag by using the STYLE attribute. For example, assume you applied a 12-point font size to <BODY>, as shown below:

```
<STYLE TYPE=text/css>
<!--
BODY {font-size: 12pt}
-->
</STYLE>
```

All child elements of <BODY> would inherit this font size. However, to set off a table stylistically with a smaller font size, you could override the inherited style with the STYLE attribute, as shown below:

```
<TABLE STYLE="font-size: 10pt">
```

@import Rule

Another way to associate a style sheet with an HTML document is with the @import rule. On the surface, this command may appear to work the same way as <LINK>, but there are some differences. Below is an example of how to use it:

```
<STYLE TYPE=text/css>
<!--

@import url(stylesheet.css)

-->
</STYLE>
```

 Netscape Navigator 4.0*x* does not yet support the @import rule, although it is likely that the forthcoming Navigator version 6 will. Until then, it is wise to use <LINK> on Web pages that are offered over the Web and may be requested by browsers that do not support @import.

<LINK> vs. @import

Compare and contrast how style sheets are associated with <LINK> and @import:

- Both are legal only in the HEAD section.

  However, @import must be included in the <STYLE> element when it is part of an HTML document (rather than an external style sheet). To cascade reliably, the @import rule in a <STYLE> element should come before any other document-level style rules.

- You can include multiple instances of both <LINK> and @import. However, the styles in the *last* instance takes precedence over earlier instances. For example, if you have two @import commands importing two different style sheets, with H1 {color:black} in the first style sheet and H1 {color:blue} in the second, the color rule in the second will take precedence over the first; <H1> text will be blue.

- An external style sheet can include @import commands, but it cannot include a <LINK> element. In other words, an HTML document can import an external style sheet that, in turn, can import yet another external style sheet. Remember that the last style rule generally takes precedence.

You can move a style up in precedence by adding the `!important` rule. Apply it as follows: `H1 {color:black !important}`. Generally, an earlier style with the `!important` rule applied will take precedence over a later rule.

Cascading Order

To recap precedence, or *cascading order*, below is a general review of how style rules prevail. These rules are listed from strongest to weakest precedence.

This is a general summary. The CSS/2 Specification spells out a variety of exceptions. Taken together, all these exceptions can be complicated and are not well-suited to these introductory CSS Lessons.

Refer to section 6 of the CSS/2 Specification for complete details. The official CSS Specification is available online at `www.w3.org/REC-CSS2/cascade.html` or in the HTML-3 folder on your Desktop.

In most cases, the following general rules for cascading order will suffice.

1. Element-level styles, applied by the `STYLE` attribute directly to an element, take first precedence.

2. Document-level styles, applied in the `<STYLE>` element, take second precedence.

3. External style sheets, associated with either `<LINK>` or `@import`, take third precedence.

4. The last external style sheet included when multiple style sheets are present, either with `<LINK>` or `@import`, takes precedence over style sheets included earlier.

5. Style sheets imported directly into HTML documents take precedence over style sheets that are imported indirectly through an external style sheet. In other words, an `@import` rule in an HTML document's `<STYLE>` element will take precedence over an `@import` rule buried in an external style sheet.

Remember: you can generally boost a style rule's precedence with the `!important` rule. Some exceptions, based on CSS rules and current browser support may apply, so experiment and analyze your results.

Exercise 19-5: Using the @import Notation

In this exercise, you will use the @import rule—rather than the <LINK> tag—to import a style sheet.

1. Switch back to your text editor and open CSS-2.HTM, if necessary.

2. Delete the text shown in bold strikethrough and add the text shown in bold:

    ```
    <HTML>

    <HEAD>
    <TITLE>Cascading Style Sheets</TITLE>
    <LINK HREF=stylesheet.css TYPE=text/css REL=stylesheet>
    <STYLE TYPE=text/css>
    <!--

    @import url(stylesheet.css);

    -->
    </STYLE>
    </HEAD>
    <BODY>
    ```

3. Save the document.

4. Switch back to your Web browser. The @import rule works only if you are using Microsoft Internet Explorer 4 or later.

5. Reload the page.

The Web page appears the same as it did in the last exercise (see Figure 19-6). The difference is that you are now using @import rather than <LINK>.

Adding Style with CLASS

Another way to associate styles is with a *class selector*. The CLASS attribute, like the STYLE attribute, is a core attribute of HTML 4.0. Think of a class selector as a container of sorts that can hold styles. The styles held in a class container can be associated with different kinds of tags.

Begin with a Period

Class selector definitions begin with a period (.). Later, you can apply styles by specifying a class selector name as the value of a CLASS attribute, without the leading period.

The following example shows how to specify a class selector in a style sheet:

```
.small {font-size: 9pt}
```

Small

Now you can use the class name *small* with a tag, as shown below:

```
<P CLASS=small>The font size for this element is 9
points.</P>
```

Early releases of Netscape Navigator 4.0x supported class selectors but needed to associate both the type (tag) selector and class selector to function properly. Because of this, .small {font-size: 9pt} would **not** work, but P.small {font-size: 9pt} would.

Fortunately, later releases of Navigator (such as version 4.7) work without the type selector.

ID Selectors

Like class selectors, ID selectors can apply styles to elements. The ID attribute is a core attribute in HTML 4.0 that specifies a unique identifier for an element.

The ID selector:

- is alphanumeric
- begins with either an uppercase or lowercase letter
- contains only letters, digits, hyphens, and periods
- identifies with a single element
- cannot (should not) be reused

ID Selector Definitions

ID selector definitions begin with a pound sign (#). When you can apply a style identified with an ID selector, you leave the pound sign off in the value of the ID attribute.

The example below shows how to use an ID selector:

```
#big {font-size: 18pt}
```

You can now use ID *big* with a tag:

```
<P ID=big>The font size for this element is 18 points.</P>
```

While section 5.9 of the CSS/2 Specification claims that "no [ID] attributes can have the same value," this is not exactly how the major browsers interpret IDs.

You can reuse an ID in different elements. However, an ID selector will work more as specified if it is also associated with a type selector, such as: H1#big {font-size: 18pt}. It is still best to use the ID selectors based on the CSS/2 Specification, rather than on what a browser might let you get away with.

Exercise 19-6: Adding Class and ID Selectors

In this exercise, you will add class and ID selectors and make other revisions to STYLESHEET.CSS. You will then make some related changes to CSS-2.HTM to better reflect the altered style sheet.

1. Switch to the text editor.

2. Open STYLESHEET.CSS from the HTML-3 folder.

3. Add the following text that appears in bold:

```
/* STYLESHEET.CSS */

H1 {font-family: Verdana,Arial,Helvetica,sans-serif;
    font-size: 18pt;
    margin-top: .5in;
    color: cornflowerblue;
    text-align: center; }

#section1   {font-size: 24pt;
             text-align: left;
             font-style: italic;}

H2 {font-family: Verdana,Arial,Helvetica,sans-serif;
    font-size: 14pt;
    margin-top: .2in;
    text-align: left;
    color: cornflowerblue;}

P   {font-family: Book Antiqua,Times New Roman,Times,serif;
     margin-left: 50px;}

.note {margin-top: 30px;
       margin-left: 150px;
       margin-right: 150px;
       margin-bottom: 40px;
       font-size: 10pt;}

B      {color: cornflowerblue;}
```

4. Save the style sheet document.

5. Open CSS-2.HTM.

6. Delete the text shown in bold strikethrough and add the text shown in bold:

```
<HTML>

<HEAD>
<TITLE>Cascading Style Sheets</TITLE>
<STYLE TYPE=text/css>
<!--

@import url(stylesheet.css);

-->
</STYLE>
<LINK HREF=stylesheet.css TYPE=text/css REL=stylesheet>
</HEAD>
<BODY>

<H1 ID=section1>Section 1</H1>

<H1>Document StylesExternal Style Sheets</H1>

<P>Document stylesExternal style sheets allow you to reuse styles
throughout a document Web site.</P>

<H12>Reduced Maintenance</H12>

<P>Document stylesExternal style sheets help reduce Web site
maintenance.</P>

<P CLASS=note><B>Note:</B> This is an exciting development! Stay
tuned to this Web page for more exciting news in the near
future.</P>

</BODY>
</HTML>
```

7. Save CSS-2.HTM.

8. Switch back to your Web browser.

9. Reload the page.

The Web page has many changes, most importantly the use of class and ID selectors, as shown in Figure 19-7 on the following page.

You also see a note format that can be reused throughout a Web site. The change back to <LINK> notation is to support Netscape Navigator.

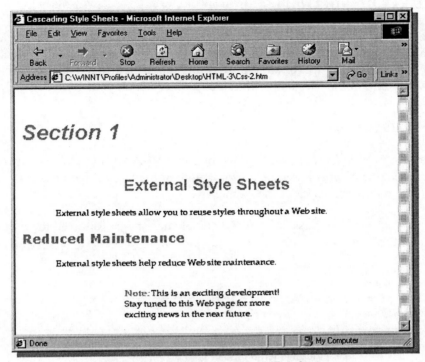

Figure 19-7: Adding class and ID selectors

Using DHTML to Create Effects

You have probably heard of *Dynamic HTML (DHTML)*. DHTML is not a standard language, such as HTML. Instead, it is a term that describes the creation of dynamic effects using HTML, CSS, and JavaScript (or another scripting language). In the next example, you will learn how to combine HTML and CSS to create an effect on your Web page.

Pseudo-Classes

CSS offers seven *pseudo-classes*, as shown in Table 19-2. Pseudo-classes allow you to alter the appearance of elements based on a user action, or to classify them based on some criteria other than the name or content of the element.

The selector for a pseudo-class is formed by an element name followed immediately by a colon (:) and the pseudo-class name (see examples in Table 19-2). <u>Pseudo-class names are case-sensitive.</u>

Pseudo-Class	Description	Example
:hover	A dynamic pseudo-class that changes when a mouse pointer hovers over the element, for example.	`A:hover {text-decoration: underline; color: red;}`
:active	A dynamic pseudo-class that changes when activated by the click of a mouse button, for example.	`A:active {color: blue;}`
:focus	A dynamic pseudo-class that changes while the element has focus, that is, it is ready to accept keyboard input, for example.	`A:focus {background-color: ivory;}`
:link	A link-related pseudo-class that controls the appearance of a link.	`A:link {text-decoration: none;}`
:visited	A link-related pseudo-class that controls the appearance of a visited link.	`A:visited {color: black;}`
:first-child	A pseudo-class that identifies an element that is the first child of another element.	`DIV > P:first-child {margin-left: 1in;}`
:lang	A pseudo-class that identifies the language of an HTML document.	`HTML:lang(de) {quotes: '«' '»' '\2039' '\203A';}`

Table 19-2: Pseudo-classes

<SPAN> Element

The <SPAN> tag is a special inline element with the sole purpose of providing a way to apply styles or scripting to inline text. Inline elements are different from block-type elements such as <P> because they only apply to text within other elements. Other examples of inline elements are <B>, <I>, and <STRONG>.

In the following exercise, you will use the A:hover selector to create an effect when you hover the mouse pointer over a link on your Web page. You will also use the <SPAN> tag.

"Historically, style control with HTML is clumsy at best and nonexistent at worst. However, with cascading style sheets, a Web designer has dramatically improved ways of working with important style elements, such as font face, font size, font weight, font style, and leading. Style controls extend beyond basic typographic functions to margins, indents, colors, graphics, and myriad other options."

— *Rick Darnell, Internet Writer, 1998*

Exercise 19-7: Using the A:hover Pseudo-class

In this exercise, you will use the <SPAN> tag and associate styles with A:hover to produce a DHTML effect.

1. Switch to the text editor.

2. Open STYLESHEET.CSS from the HTML-3 folder.

3. Add the following bold text at the end of the style sheet.

   ```
   B       {color: cornflowerblue;}

   SPAN    {font-family: Courier New,monospace;
            font-size: 13pt;}

   A       {text-decoration: none;
            color: black;}

   A:hover      {text-decoration: underline;
            color: cornflowerblue;
            background-color: gainsboro;}
   ```

4. Save the style sheet document.

5. Open CSS-2.HTM from the HTML-3 folder.

6. Add the text that is displayed in bold:

   ```
   <H2>Reduced Maintenance</H2>

   <P>External style sheets help reduce Web site maintenance.</P>

   <P>For examples of inline styles, see <A HREF=css-2.htm>
   <SPAN>CSS-2.HTM</SPAN></A>.</P>
   ```

7. Save the document.

8. Switch back to the browser and reload the Web page.

9. Move the mouse pointer over the link at CSS-2.HTM.

 You introduce several effects with this change to the Web page content. The link changes to a light blue, is underlined, and has a gray background when the mouse pointer hovers over it, as shown in Figure 19-8.

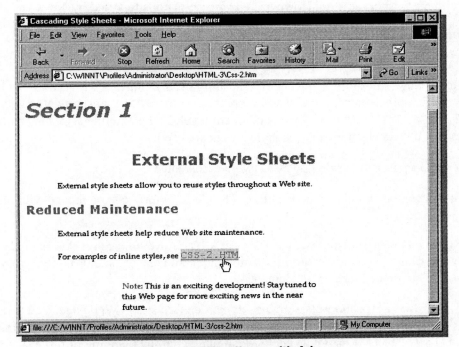

Figure 19-8: DHTML effects with A:hover

Lesson 19 Summary

▶ The ability to reuse styles is one of the most powerful features of CSS. In order to reuse styles, you must use either the STYLE element or an external style sheet.

▶ A CSS rule consists of a selector followed by a CSS declaration. A CSS declaration is encapsulated in braces ({ }) and contains one or more property/value pairs. Each property/value pair is separated by a colon, with no space between the property keyword and the colon. Each pair must be terminated by a semicolon (unless there is only one pair or after the last pair).

▶ External style sheets are linked to HTML documents with the <LINK> tag or imported with the @import rule. However, @import is not supported by Netscape Navigator 4.

▶ Elements or tags can inherit styles from parent elements. For example, a <P> element is a child of the <BODY> element, and therefore will inherit styles from it.

▶ Styles have rules of precedence (a cascading order). Starting with styles that have the strongest precedence, the cascading order is: 1) the STYLE attribute at the element level, 2) the <STYLE> element at the document level, 3) the external style sheet, and 4) the last external style sheet if multiple style sheets are used.

▶ The !important rule boosts a style's precedence.

▶ Styles can be associated with a class. The class, in turn, can be reused with one or more elements.

▶ Styles can be associated with an element's ID. However, such styles can only be used with a single element because ID's are unique and can (or should) only be associated with a single instance of an element.

▶ The A:hover pseudo-class creates dynamic effects on a Web page. The combination of HTML, CSS, and JavaScript (or another scripting language) is called Dynamic HTML or DHTML. DHTML is not a specified language, but the blending of three standards to create special effects.

Lesson 19 Quiz

Matching

___ 1. terminates a CSS declaration

___ 2. takes precedence over the \<STYLE\> tag

___ 3. tag used for document-level styles

___ 4. boosts a styles precedence

___ 5. indicates a tag or class for applying style

___ 6. encloses a CSS declaration

a. selector

b. braces ({ })

c. !important

d. semicolon (;)

e. STYLE attribute

f. STYLE tag

Fill in the Blank

7. An inline style is defined with a tag using the _____ attribute.

8. The _____ tag or @import rule associates an external style sheet with an HTML document.

9. A _____ element inherits styles from its parent element.

10. Rules of precedence are called the _____ order.

11. You can associate styles with a _____ , a container of sorts that can hold styles and be applied to different kinds of tags or elements.

True or False?

T / F   12. You can easily reuse inline styles.

T / F   13. A CSS declaration is identical to a CSS rule.

T / F   14. A style associated with an ID should only be used once.

T / F   15. A style applied at the element level has stronger precedence than a document-level style.

(This page intentionally left blank)

Lesson 20
Advanced HTML
Tips & Tricks

Lesson Topics

► Embedded Fonts

► Multiple MAILTO Addressees

► Watermarks

► HTML Validation

► Splash Screens

► Lesson 20 Summary

Embedded Fonts

Embedded fonts, also known as *downloadable fonts*, are a new and still embryonic Web technology. Unfortunately, at this stage, there are currently two competing embedded font formats and a lack of universal browser support. The W3C HTML 4.0 Specification has not yet added support for embedded fonts.

Even if you decide not to use embedded fonts in your Web pages at this time, it is important for you to understand the state of the art and be prepared to utilize embedded fonts when the technology becomes more mature and standards emerge.

Currently Best for Intranets

If you plan to use embedded fonts on an intranet, many of the shortcomings of the technology disappear. For example, if all employees on your intranet are using Microsoft Internet Explorer 4.0 or later, you could utilize one of the major embedded font technologies with a high level of success.

Pros & Cons

The current immature state of embedded font technology means there are some significant pros and cons regarding their use, as outlined in Table 20-1 below.

Embedded Font Pros	Embedded Font Cons
■ Significantly enhances the visual and aesthetic appeal of a Web page: sets your pages apart from the hundreds of millions of pages using Windows and Macintosh core fonts such as Times New Roman, Arial, Helvetica, Verdana, and Georgia. ■ Other Web authors cannot use your embedded fonts: when you embed a font, you can specify the exact Web pages (via URL) on which it will function. ■ Embedded fonts are typically displayed as anti-aliased: fonts appear smoother and more professional.	■ Poor browser support: embedded fonts do not work with Internet Explorer for the Macintosh at all. One format works best in Netscape Navigator and a different format works best in IE. Embedded fonts are best utilized on an intranet where most users have the same browser. ■ Not all fonts can be embedded: you can only use fonts that have been approved by their creators for embedding. Not all fonts are approved for embedding, but many are. ■ Anti-aliasing requires client configuration: Windows 95 requires supplemental font smoother software; Windows 98/NT require font smoothing to be turned on in the Control Panel.

Table 20-1: Embedded font pros and cons

Computer Fonts Overview

To understand embedded fonts, you first need to have a basic knowledge of the major computer font formats. There are currently three major computer font formats:

- <u>PostScript Type 1</u>: the veteran font format introduced by Adobe Systems many years ago. PostScript was intended to look best when printed, not on a computer monitor.

- <u>TrueType</u>: originally developed by Apple Computer, TrueType is now built into both the Windows and Macintosh operating systems. TrueType has superior hinting to PostScript and, therefore, produces better on-screen display.

- <u>OpenType</u>: a new format introduced by Microsoft and Adobe Systems that merges many of the features of PostScript and TrueType.

Conversion Necessary

Unfortunately, it is impossible to embed PostScript, TrueType, or OpenType fonts into a Web page in their native format. All of these fonts must be converted to one of two competing embedded font formats: *Embedded OpenType* or *TrueDoc*. Both of these embedded font formats are described in detail in the following section.

Many Options

As you have now learned, you can take any of the three computer font formats and convert them to either of two competing embedded font formats. Because neither embedded font format is universally supported by all major Web browsers, you cannot currently achieve universal interpretation of your embedded fonts by all modern browsers[26].

TrueType fonts have an advantage in that they can be converted to both TrueDoc and Embedded OpenType. TrueDoc offers the advantage of being semi-supported by both browsers.

---

[26] Modern browsers are defined as the current and last version. For example, the modern versions of Internet Explorer are currently version 5.*x* and version 4.*x*.

Embedded Font Formats

There are currently two competing embedded font technologies, as shown in Table 20-2.

Embedded Format	Fonts Supported	Browser Support
Embedded OpenType (.EOT files)	■ TrueType ■ OpenType	Internet Explorer 4 and higher
TrueDoc (.PFR files)	■ TrueType ■ PostScript Type 1	■ Navigator 4.03 and higher ■ Internet Explorer 4 and higher (Windows only)[27]

Table 20-2: Competing embedded font technologies

Embedded OpenType

Embedded OpenType, championed by Microsoft and Adobe, converts both TrueType (the most common font format) and OpenType (new, powerful, but uncommon).

You can create Embedded OpenType embedded fonts using a software utility from Microsoft called the *Web Embedding Fonts Tool* (WEFT), available as Windows freeware from `www.microsoft.com/typography/web/embedding/weft2`.

Shortcomings of Embedded OpenType:

- A lack of support for PostScript fonts

- Not supported by Netscape Navigator/Communicator

TrueDoc

TrueDoc, backed by Netscape and Bitstream, converts TrueType and PostScript. You can create TrueDoc embedded fonts using WebFont Maker ($199.00) or HexWeb Typograph ($149.00). Unlike WEFT, these programs are available for both Mac and Windows.

Shortcomings of TrueDoc:

- Software utilities used to create TrueDoc are not as robust as WEFT.

- Online font display quality is slightly decreased because TrueDoc fonts do not include the outlines and hintings of the original fonts.

---

[27] To view TrueDoc fonts in Internet Explorer (Windows only), a user must install an ActiveX control.

Multiple MAILTO Addressees

Most Webmasters are not aware of the fact that a MAILTO anchor can configure an outgoing e-mail message to be addressed to multiple recipients, including carbon copy (cc) and blind carbon copy (bcc) messages.

You learned the basic functionality of the mailto protocol (a subset to the HREF attribute of the <A> tag) in DDC's *HTML 4.0 Fundamentals*, so you already know how to use MAILTO at a basic level.

Code

```
<A HREF=mailto:bubba@xyz.com?cc=zeek@dot.gov&cc=bertha@osu.edu
&bcc=bob27@aol.com>Click to send e-mail to Bubba</A>
```

 You can include multiple primary recipients, multiple carbon copies, multiple blind carbon copies, or any combination thereof.

Prepopulated Subject Field

You can "prepopulate" the subject field of a MAILTO message. This may sound trivial on the surface, but it can provide great utility if you filter incoming e-mail messages. For example, you can have multiple e-mail anchors on a Web site that are sent to the same person (using either the same or different e-mail addresses). If the messages have prepopulated subject field content, they can easily be filtered.

Code

```
<A HREF=mailto:bubba@xyz.com&subject=Consumer%20Products
%20Division%20Sales%20Inquiry>Click to send your sales inquiry</A>
```

Characteristics

- The %20 character represents a space.

- You can use an unlimited number of words in the prepopulated subject line, but it is recommended that you keep the subject field content brief, as you should with any e-mail message.

Exercise 20-1: Creating E-mail Anchors for Multiple Recipients

In this exercise, you will create a single e-mail hypertext anchor that reconfigures a user's e-mail client software to send multiple messages, including carbon copies and blind carbon copies.

1. In Notepad, open MAILTO.HTM from the HTML-3 folder on your Desktop.

2. Add the following code that appears in bold:

    ```
    For feedback, send mail to:<P>

    <A HREF=mailto:bubba@corp.com?cc=zeek@corp.com&cc=
    jethro@osu.edu&bcc=theboss@company.com>bubba@corp.com</A>
    ```

3. Save the HTML document.

4. Toggle over to your Web browser and open MAILTO.HTM.

5. Click the **bubba@corp.com** hyperlink.

 Your default e-mail application is launched and a new outgoing message is opened. It is pre-addressed to the primary recipient Bubba with carbon copies to Zeek and Jethro and a blind carbon copy to The Boss.

6. Cancel the outgoing e-mail message and close your e-mail software.

7. Toggle back to Notepad and add the following code that appears in bold:

    ```
    <A HREF=mailto:bubba@corp.com?cc=zeek@corp.com&cc=
    jethro@osu.edu&bcc=theboss@company.com&subject=Dig%20the
    %20prepopulated%20Subject%20field,%20dude>bubba@corp.com
    </A>
    ```

8. Save the HTML document.

9. Toggle over to your Web browser and reload the Web page.

10. Click the **bubba@corp.com** link.

Your default e-mail application is launched and a new outgoing message is pre-addressed to multiple recipients and contains a prepopulated Subject field, as shown in Figure 20-1.

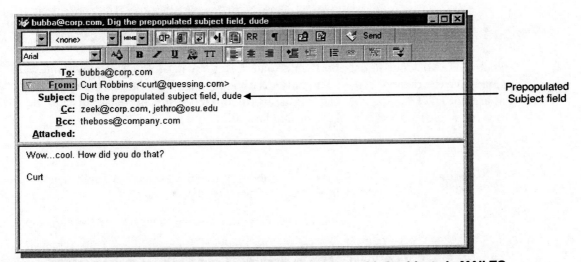

Figure 20-1: Example of a prepopulated Subject field created with &subject= in MAILTO

Watermarks

You may have used watermarks with Microsoft Word or WordPerfect documents, or perhaps when creating a PDF file using Adobe Acrobat 4.0. Watermarks are typically light grey images or "ghost images" that are used as a backdrop for other page elements, such as text, images, tables, bullet lists, etc. On Web pages, semi-transparent watermarks can be configured to hover in place, independent of the page on which they appear.

Beyond HTML: DHTML

Standard HTML does not support watermarks. But if you mix in some Dynamic HTML, you can achieve the desired effect. The only disadvantage of this solution is that Web browsers that are not DHTML capable cannot display the image as a watermark. Instead, non-DHTML browsers will display the image as a standard inline image.

- Versions 4.0 and above of Internet Explorer, for both Windows and Macintosh, are DHTML capable.

- Version 4.5 and above of Netscape Navigator are DHTML capable.

If you are scripting on an intranet for an all-IE 4.0 or above user base, you can use a proprietary solution: `<BODY BACKGROUND=imagename.gif BGPROPERTIES=fixed>`.

Choosing the Image

Probably the most important issue when choosing an image is being sure you do not choose or configure an image that will obscure the other elements on your page or distract your users.

When choosing an image for a Web page watermark, be sure to focus on the following issues:

- Do you want the image to appear to be transparent?

- Do you want the image to blend into the background? Are you also using a background color?

- What is the size of the image?

DDC Publishing • www.ddcpub.com

Code

```
<DIV ID=waterMark STYLE=position:absolute>
<A HREF=/index.html><IMG SRC=imagename.jpg WIDTH=90 HEIGHT=90
BORDER=0></A>
</DIV>

<script language-JavaScript1.2>...
```

Further detail regarding DHTML goes beyond the scope of this course. You should simply note that the above code contains DHTML. It is not typically recommended that you copy HTML or other code from outside sources without having a true understanding of its function and nuances. In this particular case, however, you can create an attractive and unusual page effect by simply copying some code and adjusting some attribute values.

Adjusting the Code

Script Variable	Value Set
markW	Measure of the width of the image in pixels
markH	Measure of the height of the image in pixels
markX	Measure of the X axis position of the image relative to the upper left corner of the page as a percentage of page width
markY	Measure of the Y axis position of the image relative to the upper left corner of the page as a percentage of page height
markRefresh	The frequency, as measured in milliseconds, with which the browser will update the watermark's position

A lower number means less delay between the page scrolling and the watermark repositioning itself; however, this places greater demand on the browser |

Table 20-3: Variables of the JavaScript code that enables a page watermark

Use the following settings for common watermark page locations:

- center = set both markX and markY to 50.

- upper left corner = set both markX and markY to 0.

- upper right corner = set markX to 100 and markY to 0.

- lower right corner = set both markX and markY to 100.

- lower left corner = set markX to 0 and markY to 100.

Exercise 20-2: Creating a Web Page Watermark

In this exercise, you will create a Web page watermark using a pre-coded script and your own image. You will customize the script variables to the characteristics of your particular image.

1. In Notepad, open WATERMARK.HTM from the HTML-3 folder.

2. About half way down the HTML document, change the following code that appears in bold:

```
<H5>Copyright &copy; 2000 Cargui Productions, LLP. All Rights
Reserved.</H5>

<DIV ID=waterMark STYLE=position:absolute>

<A HREF=/index.htm><IMG SRC=watermark.jpg WIDTH=150
HEIGHT=142></A>

</DIV>
```

3. Save the file. Change the following code that appears in bold:

```
markW = 150;        // pixels wide
markH = 142;        // pixels high
markX = 100;        // percent right
markY = 100;        // percent down
markRefresh = 10;       // milliseconds
```

4. Save the file.

5. Toggle over to your Web browser and open WATERMARK.HTM.

 The page is displayed with the watermark image in the lower right corner. Note the unattractive blue border surrounding the image.

6. Toggle over to Notepad and add the following code to the <IMG> tag between the opening and closing Anchor tag:

   BORDER=0

7. Save the HTML document.

8. Toggle back to your Web browser and reload the page.

The page now appears with the watermark in the lower right corner and without the blue border, as shown in Figure 20-2.

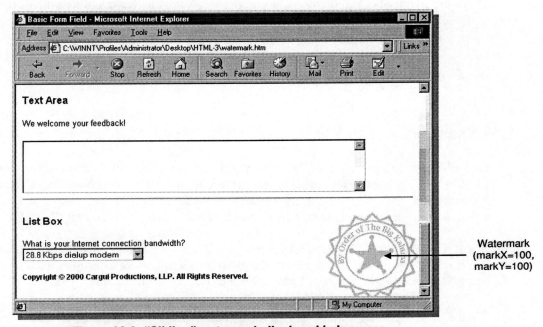

Figure 20-2: "Sliding" watermark displayed in browser

9. Scroll up and down the page. Note how the JavaScript code instructs the watermark to maintain its position relative to the browser window, regardless of the current view of the page. This gives the impression of the watermark moving up and down the page as the user scrolls.

10. Toggle over to Notepad and change the `markRefresh` value to **500**. Save the HTML document.

11. Toggle back to your browser and reload the Web page. Scroll up and down the page. Do you notice a change in the speed at which the watermark refreshes?

12. Toggle back to Notepad and change the `markRefresh` value to **5**.

13. Toggle back to your browser and reload the page. How does this affect the display of the watermark when you scroll up and down the page?

HTML Validation

Two of the biggest problems, especially on large organizational Web sites, is compliance with the HTML Specification and non-functional links. It is estimated that 5% of all links on the Web are broken (tens of millions of links, considering that the Web is comprised of *one billion* pages). Links that do not operate properly are described as *broken* or *bogus*.

There are two tools available to help you deal with the challenges of avoiding broken links and maintaining compliance with the HTML Specification:

- link checkers
- HTML validators

Link Checkers

Link checkers are software applications that run from a Web site (server-level) or on your local PC (client-level) and are relatively simply in operation. You provide a URL and a link checker tests its Anchor tags to ensure that the URLs referenced are available. Link checkers are also built into many HTML editors, such as FrontPage 2000 and HotDog Pro.

If a 404 or other error is found, the software will report it. Some link checkers offer much detail regarding broken links; others simply report a link as valid or invalid. Link checkers denoted with an asterisk (*) in Table 20-4 are bundled on the Student File CD-ROM.

Link Checker	URL	Level / Comments
NetMechanic	www.netmechanic.com	Server-level — Requires annual subscription; limited sample output available
Linkbot Pro* (NKBOTEXPRESS.EXE)	www.tetranetsoftware.com/ products/linkbot.htm	Client-level — Full Web site testing, including JavaScript, forms, Flash. Generates intuitive graphical reports
Doctor HTML	www2.imagiware.com/RxHTML	Server-level — Offers spell checking, image syntax, form structure, image analysis, table structure, document structure, and link verification
Dr. Watson	watson.addy.com	Server-level — Offers link and image verification, word counts, spell check, and search engine compatibility
URL Checker	www2.ucsc.edu/cats/sc/ services/www/urlchecker.shtml	Server-level — Very basic link checker with clean interface

Table 20-4: HTML link checkers

Exercise 20-3: Using Link Checkers

In this exercise, you will use and compare two different link checkers to identify broken links on a Web page.

1. Access the following URL using your Web browser: **watson.addy.com**.

2. Scroll down to the **URL (http://is optional)** field and type **www.amazon.com**.

3. In the checkboxes below the URL field, select **Verify regular links, Spell-check non-HTML text**, and **Check search engine compatibility**.

4. In the **Browser extensions allowed** section, select the **None** radio button.

5. Click the **Proceed with diagnosis** button.

 A server response page is downloaded and displayed, as shown in Figure 20-3. It contains hundreds of lines of code and content analysis. Even with the level of HTML standards enforcement set to Normal, note that the level of enforcement is relatively strict.

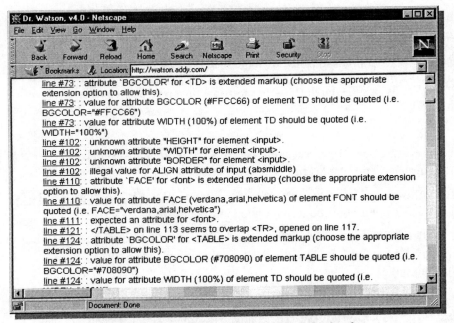

Figure 20-3: Output from an HTML link checker

6. Scroll down and browse the list. Note the nature of the analysis.

7. Click on any of the red **line #x** links (where *x* is a line number).

That particular line of the original HTML code is displayed. This is a convenient feature that allows you to compare the analysis comments with the actual code, thus helping you to decide whether a fix is necessary.

8. On your browser's toolbar, click the **Back** button.

9. Scroll down to the **Spelling Check** section. Note the nature of the spellcheck.

10. Scroll down to the **Link verifications** section.

Dr. Watson reports that the Amazon.com home page contains 110 links and that this number exceeds what it is capable of checking.

Many Web pages contain in excess of 75 or 100 links. Thus, for many Webmasters, this limitation is a major shortcoming of Dr. Watson.

11. Scroll down to the **Search engine compatibility** section. Note the comments.

12. Submit the URL of your employer's Web site. Peruse the results.

What needs to be fixed on the site? Because most Web sites change daily, weekly, or at least monthly, do you think it is wise to check a Web site with link checker software on a regular basis?

13. Access **www2.imagiware.com/RxHTML**. The *Doctor HTML Introduction* page will be downloaded and displayed.

14. In the yellow section on the left side of the page, click **Single Page Analysis**. The *Single Page Analysis* page will be downloaded and displayed.

15. In the URL field, type **www.michelangelo.com** and click the **Go!** button. A Summary Report will be downloaded and displayed, as shown in Figure 20-4 on the following page.

How does this Web site compare to Amazon.com? Remember that you are now using a different link checker, so you are not comparing apples to apples.

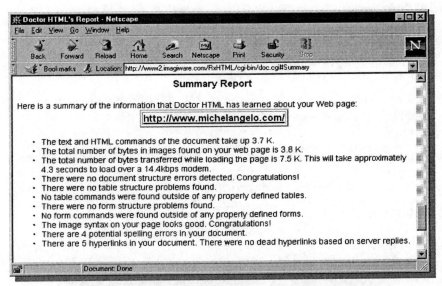

Figure 20-4: Summary Report from an HTML link checker

16. Scroll up the page to **Table Structure Analysis**. Scroll down the page, noting the **Form Structure Analysis**, **Image Analysis**, **Image Syntax**, and **Spelling Check** sections.

17. Scroll to the most important section: **Hyperlink Analysis**.

18. Return to the *Doctor HTML Single Page Analysis* page and type **www.techweb.com**. Peruse the results of the analysis of tables, forms, image syntax, spell check, and hyperlinks.

Doctor HTML limits "guests" (non-paying customers) to four visits per session to preserve performance for paying customers.

If you are serious about analyzing the link integrity and other aspects of your HTML, you should subscribe to a server-level reporting service (such as Doctor HTML) or purchase a client-level HTML analysis package (such as Linkbot Pro).

HTML Validators

HTML validators perform three primary functions:

- check for errors in your HTML code

- check to ensure compliance with the HTML 4.0 Specification (many offer user-definable compliance level configuration, allowing more or less strict compliance checking)

- check for limited non-HTML errors, such as spell checking of page content

Accept Extensions?

As you learned in DDC's *HTML 4.0 Fundamentals* and *HTML 4.0 Intermediate*, there are extensions to HTML that are not part of the official HTML Specification, but are properly interpreted by all modern versions of MS Internet Explorer and Netscape Navigator/Communicator. Only you can decide if you will stray from the official HTML Specification and include extensions.

Table 20-5 features a list of HTML validators. Validators denoted with an asterisk (*) are bundled on the Student Files CD-ROM.

HTML Validator	URL	Level / Comments
CSE HTML Validator* (CSELITE.EXE)	www.htmlvalidator.com	Client-level — Includes link checking, spell checking, and configuration for specific Web browsers; commercial and freeware versions available
WDG HTML Validator	www.htmlhelp.com/tools/ validator	Server-level — Allows validation of entire Web site
W3C HTML Validation Service	validator.w3.org	Server-level — Includes support for XHTML; from the same organization that publishes the HTML Specification; includes Weblint
Weblint* (WEBLINT-1_020.ZIP)	www.weblint.org	Client-level — Syntax and minimal style checker written in Perl; for serious techies
A Real Validator* (ARV.ZIP)	www.arealvalidator.com	Client-level — HTML syntax checker for Windows; yields true HTML validation using SGML parser

Table 20-5: HTML validators

Exercise 20-4: Using HTML Validators

In this exercise, you will use and compare two HTML validators to analyze the HTML code from a Web site.

1. Access the following URL using your Web browser: `validator.w3.org`.

2. Scroll down to the **Validate Documents on the Web** section, type `www.amazon.com` in the **Location** field, and press <ENTER>.

 The validation *Results* page is downloaded and displayed, as shown in Figure 20-5. This page also indicates any URL redirection and the type of server software used by the site.

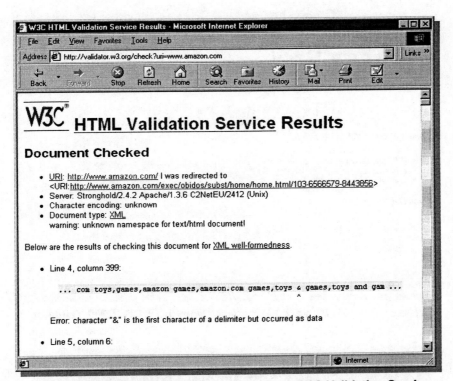

Figure 20-5: HTML validation results from the W3C Validation Service

3. Scroll down the page, noting the large number and nature of the comments.

4. On the toolbar, click the **Back** button to return to the URL submit form.

5. In the **Location** field, type the URL of your employer's Web site and press <ENTER>.

What needs to be fixed on your employer's site?

6. Check another Web site of your choice. Identify the elements of the site that you would change if you were the Webmaster.

7. Access the WDG HTML Validator at **www.htmlhelp.com/tools/validator**.

8. In the **URL** field, type **www.amazon.com** and press <ENTER>. The *Results* page will appear, as shown in Figure 20-6.

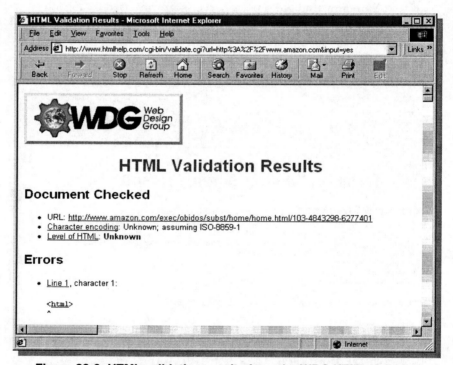

Figure 20-6: HTML validation results from the WDG HTML Validator

9. Return to the home page. Submit the URL of your employer's Web site. Analyze the results to determine what you would change if you were the Webmaster.

10. Submit other URLs to both the WDG HTML Validator and the W3C Validation Service as time permits. Analyze the results to get a better idea of the types of HTML code errors that are common in Web pages.

Splash Screens

You learned many functions of the <META> tag in DDC's *HTML 4.0 Fundamentals*. In this section, you will learn yet another application of the <META> tag: splash screens. *Splash screens* are graphic or artistic screens that display for a few seconds when you first visit a Web site's home page.

Splash screens are a combination of two attributes to the <META> tag:

- HTTP-EQUIV
- CONTENT

Correct Timing

Splash screens tap into the delicate end-user perceptional psychology that all Webmasters deal with to one extent or another. Depending on the content displayed in a particular splash screen (i.e., how long it takes the average user to digest the content), a couple of seconds too short or too long in the display could result in poor implementation. The display time until redirection to another Web page is specified via the CONTENT attribute.

Code

```
<META HTTP-EQUIV=refresh CONTENT=5;URL=www.xyz.com>

<BODY>
<IMG SRC=splash.jpg WIDTH=600 HEIGHT=400>
</BODY>
```

Implementation

When users submit the base URL of your Web site, they access either an INDEX.HTM or DEFAULT.HTM HTML document residing on your Web server (the name of which depends on the type of Web server software used). For the purposes of this course, assume your home page is called INDEX.HTM.

Depending on the nature of the splash screen, a couple of seconds too short or too long for the <META> tag CONTENT value will confuse and disorient your site visitors (if too short) or bore and drive them away (if too long).

To implement a splash screen, you would rename INDEX.HTM to INDEX2.HTM (or another name that is logical for your particular Web site). You would then name the HTML document that contains the <META> code and the <IMG> tag for the splash screen to INDEX.HTM. This will replace your regular home page as the first HTML document downloaded by visitors to your Web site.

Exercise 20-5: Creating a Splash Screen

In this exercise, you will create a splash screen that will display for five seconds and then advance to another HTML page (this second page would typically be your "real" home page). For graphic effectiveness, the background color of the image displayed on the splash screen will be purposefully matched to the background color of the Web page.

1. Launch your graphics application and open DESERT_SUN.JPG. This is the image you will use for the splash screen that automatically rolls over to your standard home page.

 You can use any HTML elements within a splash screen, including text, images, tables, forms, etc. It is simply a matter of practice that most splash screens are a professional and eye-pleasing graphic that helps brand your organization.

2. Toggle over to Notepad and open SPLASH_SCREEN.HTM.

3. Add the following code to the document that appears in bold:

```
</HEAD>

<META HTTP-EQUIV=refresh CONTENT=10;URL=index-2.htm>

<BODY BGCOLOR=#336699>

<CENTER>
<IMG SRC=desert_sun.jpg>
```

4. Save the document.

5. Toggle over to your Web browser.

6. Open SPLASH_SCREEN.HTM.

 The page will appear with a slate blue background (RGB color #336699) and the DESERT_SUN.JPG image, as shown in Figure 20-7 on the following page. The JPEG image is the only element on the page.

After 10 seconds, the page will automatically forward to another Web page (INDEX-2.HTM).

Figure 20-7: Example of a splash screen created using a <META> tag

 10 seconds is too long for this particular splash screen. It contains very little information that must be digested by a user.

7. Toggle back to Notepad and change the CONTENT attribute value from 10 to **5**.

8. Save the HTML document.

9. Toggle back to your browser. Click the **Back** button and refresh the Web page.

 The splash screen will now be displayed for five seconds before automatically downloading INDEX-2.HTM.

 Do you think five seconds is the correct amount of time? Experiment with other CONTENT values. This image might be perfect with a value of three seconds, but you will not know until you actually see it.

Lesson 20 Summary

- Embedded fonts allow a user to download a Web page that displays text in a font that is not installed on their computer.

- The disadvantages of using embedded fonts include: 1) two competing embedded font formats, 2) lack of browser support, 3) not all fonts can be embedded, and 4) no inclusion of embedded fonts in the official W3C HTML Specification. However, use of embedded fonts can still be beneficial on external Web sites and even more so on intranets. Advantages include: 1) security – other Web authors cannot use your embedded fonts, and 2) significant enhancement of the visual appeal of your pages.

- There are currently three major computer font formats: PostScript Type 1, TrueType, and OpenType. OpenType is the newcomer to the field introduced by Microsoft and Adobe Systems. OpenType merges many of the features of PostScript and TrueType.

- If you have a font that is capable of being used as an embedded font, you must first convert it to one of the two competing embedded font formats. Embedded OpenType supports TrueType and OpenType, while TrueDoc supports TrueType and PostScript.

- You can address multiple e-mail accounts, including carbon copies and blind carbon copies, in MAILTO anchors. You simply code the second e-mail address (part of the value of the HREF attribute) using ?cc= followed by the e-mail address. All other addresses should be separated with no space and &cc= or &bcc= (for carbon copies and blind carbon copies, respectively).

- You can also include a prepopulated subject field on outgoing messages automatically launched by MAILTO anchors. Simply include &subject=word1%20word2%20 word3%20word4%20 in the value of the HREF attribute. Note that the %20 character represents a space.

- You can include watermarks in your Web pages by using DHTML and JavaScript. You should carefully choose your image (size, color, etc.). Using markX, markY, and markRefresh values, you can specify the exact position of the watermark on the page and how frequently the user's browser updates the display of the watermark when the user is scrolling. Obviously it is preferable to have faster display update, but this results in more processing burden on the client computer.

- HTML validation and link checking are two very important steps that many Webmasters ignore. Especially important in larger Web sites—where broken links and incompatible HTML are more likely to occur—link checking should be conducted at least monthly and preferably weekly. The frequency of link checking depends on how often the Web site is updated.

- Using the <META> tag and two specific attributes, you can create splash screens that display for a few seconds and then automatically download another Web page. Conventional use of <META> splash screens replaces the INDEX.HTM file that acts as a home page on a Web site and refers to the intended home page from the splash screen. Be careful not to display a splash screen too briefly or for too long.

Lesson 20 Quiz

Matching

___ 1. `markX` and `markY`   a. Weblint

___ 2. `<META HTTP-EQUIV=refresh>`   b. DHTML

___ 3. represents a space in `&subject=` value   c. watermark

___ 4. HTML validator   d. splash screen

___ 5. extend HTML capability for watermarks   e. %20

Fill in the Blank

6. To position a watermark in the lower left corner of the page, you would specify a `markX` value of _____ and a `markY` value of _____ . To specify a position of upper right corner of the page, you would specify `markX` and `markY` positions of _____ and _____ , respectively.

7. The file extension for the Embedded OpenType embedded font format is _____ .

8. There are currently three major computer font formats available: _____ , _____ , and _____ . The newest format is _____ .

9. The two `<META>` tag attributes necessary when creating a splash screen are `HTTP-EQUIV` and _____ .

True or False?

T / F   10. Embedded fonts allow a Web user to view a font that is not installed on his or her local PC.

T / F   11. You can prepopulate the subject field of a `MAILTO` anchor message using `&subject=`.

T / F   12. When scripting multiple e-mail anchors in a `MAILTO` anchor, you separate all e-mail addresses with a question mark (?).

T / F   13. The TrueDoc embedded font format features files with .TDF extensions.

T / F   14. In splash screens, `CONTENT=6` means six minutes before the new URL is retrieved.

(This page intentionally left blank)

Appendices

Appendix A: HTML 4.0 Major Tags

HTML Element	Description	Attributes?
`<!-- content -- >`	Comment text (not displayed by browser and also not acting as an instruction element, such as a tag or character entity)	⊘
`<A>...</A>`	Anchor tag used with HREF and NAME to create hypertext links and MAILTO anchors	✓
`<B>...</B>`	Creates bold text	⊘
`<BLOCKQUOTE>... </BLOCKQUOTE>`	Indents text and is useful for quotes and citations	⊘
`<BODY>...</BODY>`	Establishes the body region of an HTML document	✓
` `	Creates line break (without vertical white space)	⊘
`<CAPTION>...</CAPTION>`	Creates a table caption	✓
`<CENTER>...</CENTER>`	Centers any HTML element (text, image, table, form field)	⊘
`<H1>...</H1>`	Heading Level 1 (largest relative size)	✓
`<H2>...</H2>`	Heading Level 2	✓
`<H3>...</H3>`	Heading Level 3	✓
`<H4>...</H4>`	Heading Level 4	✓
`<H5>...</H5>`	Heading Level 5	✓
`<H6>...</H6>`	Heading Level 6 (smallest relative size)	✓
`<HEAD>...</HEAD>`	Establishes the document header	⊘
`<HR>`	Creates a horizontal rule (line)	✓
`<HTML>...</HTML>`	Identifies document type as HTML	✓
`<I>...</I>`	Creates italicized text	⊘
`<IMG>`	Image tag used to insert an image	✓
`<LI>`	List item used in ordered and unordered lists	✓

HTML Element	Description	Attributes?
<OL>...</OL>	Creates an ordered list (numbered list)	✓
<P>	Creates paragraph break (line break with vertical white space)	⊘
<PRE>...</PRE>	Creates preformatted text (preserving spacing between characters and using monotype font [Courier])	✓
<STRIKE>...</STRIKE>	Creates strikethrough text (draws a horizontal line through text)	⊘
_{...}	Creates subscript text	⊘
^{...}	Creates superscript text	⊘
<TABLE>...</TABLE>	Creates an HTML table	✓
<TITLE>...</TITLE>	Specifies the document title (as appears in the title bar of the browser)	⊘
<TT>...</TT>	Formats text in a monospaced (fixed) font, typically Courier or Courier New	⊘
<U>...</U>	Creates underlined text	⊘
<UL>...</UL>	Creates an unordered list (bullet list)	✓

Reference Table A-1: HTML elements used in course

Appendix B: HTML 4.0 Character Entities

Symbol	Character Entity	Description
Æ	&AElig;	Capital AE diphthong (ligature)
Á	&Aacute;	Capital A, acute accent
Â	&Acirc;	Capital A, circumflex accent
À	&Agrave;	Capital A, grave accent
Å	&Aring;	Capital A, ring
Ã	&Atilde;	Capital A, tilde
Ä	&Auml;	Capital A, dieresis or umlaut
Ç	&Ccedil;	Capital C, cedilla
É	&Eacute;	Capital E, acute accent
Ê	&Ecirc;	Capital E, circumflex accent
È	&Egrave;	Capital E, grave accent
Ë	&Euml;	Capital E, dieresis or umlaut
Í	&Iacute;	Capital I, acute accent
Î	&Icirc;	Capital I, circumflex accent
Ì	&Igrave;	Capital I, grave accent
Ï	&Iuml;	Capital I, dieresis or umlaut
Ñ	&Ntilde;	Capital N, tilde
Ó	&Oacute;	Capital O, acute accent
Ô	&Ocirc;	Capital O, circumflex accent
Ò	&Ograve;	Capital O, grave accent
Ø	&Oslash;	Capital O, slash
Õ	&Otilde;	Capital O, tilde
Ö	&Ouml;	Capital O, dieresis or umlaut

Symbol	Character Entity	Description
Ú	&Uacute;	Capital U, acute accent
Û	&Ucirc;	Capital U, circumflex accent
Ù	&Ugrave;	Capital U, grave accent
Ü	&Uuml;	Capital U, dieresis or umlaut
Ý	&Yacute;	Capital Y, acute accent
á	&aacute;	Small a, acute accent
â	&acirc;	Small a, circumflex accent
æ	&aelig;	Small ae, diphthong (ligature)
à	&agrave;	Small a, grave accent
å	&aring;	Small a, ring
ã	&atilde;	Small a, tilde
ä	&auml;	Small a, dieresis or umlaut
ç	&ccedil;	Small c, cedilla
é	&eacute;	Small e, acute accent
ê	&ecirc;	Small e, circumflex accent
è	&egrave;	Small e, grave accent
ë	&euml;	Small e, dieresis or umlaut
í	&iacute;	Small i, acute accent
î	&icirc;	Small i, circumflex accent
ì	&igrave;	Small i, grave accent
ï	&iuml;	Small i, dieresis or umlaut
ñ	&ntilde;	Small n, tilde
ó	&oacute;	Small o, acute accent
ô	&ocirc;	Small o, circumflex accent
ò	&ograve;	Small o, grave accent

Symbol	Character Entity	Description
ø	&oslash;	Small o, slash
õ	&otilde;	Small o, tilde
ö	&ouml;	Small o, dieresis or umlaut
ß	&szlig;	Small sharp s, German (sz ligature)
ú	&uacute;	Small u, acute accent
û	&ucirc;	Small u, circumflex accent
ù	&ugrave;	Small u, grave accent
ü	&uuml;	Small u, dieresis or umlaut
ý	&yacute;	Small y, acute accent
ÿ	&yuml;	Small y, dieresis or umlaut
<	&lt;	Less than symbol
>	&gt;	Greater than symbol
&	&amp;	Ampersand symbol
"	&quot;	Double quote symbol
space		Non-breaking space
®	&reg;	Registered symbol
©	&copy;	Copyright symbol
º	&deg;	Degree symbol

Reference Table B-1: HTML 3.2 character entities

Appendix C: ANSI Character Set

The following table displays those members of the ANSI character set that may be used as HTML character entities. Note that not all of the 256 ANSI characters translate to use as a character entity; those that do begin at number 33, excluding zero through 32.

Symbol	ANSI Number	Symbol	ANSI Number	Symbol	ANSI Number
!	33	8	56	O	79
"	34	9	57	P	80
#	35	:	58	Q	81
$	36	;	59	R	82
%	37	<	60	S	83
&	38	=	61	T	84
'	39	>	62	U	85
(	40	?	63	V	86
)	41	@	64	W	87
*	42	A	65	X	88
+	43	B	66	Y	89
,	44	C	67	Z	90
-	45	D	68	[	91
.	46	E	69	\	92
/	47	F	70	]	93
0	48	G	71	^	94
1	49	H	72	_	95
2	50	I	73	`	96
3	51	J	74	a	97
4	52	K	75	b	98
5	53	L	76	c	99
6	54	M	77	d	100
7	55	N	78	e	101

Symbol	ANSI Number	Symbol	ANSI Number	Symbol	ANSI Number
f	102	„	132	¢	162
g	103	…	133	£	163
h	104	†	134	¤	164
i	105	‡	135	¥	165
j	106	ˆ	136	¦	166
k	107	‰	137	§	167
l	108	Š	138	¨	168
m	109	‹	139	©	169
n	110	Œ	140	ª	170
o	111	N/A	141	«	171
p	112	N/A	142	¬	172
q	113	N/A	143	-	173
r	114	N/A	144	®	174
s	115	'	145	‾	175
t	116	'	146	º	176
u	117	"	147	±	177
v	118	"	148	²	178
w	119	•	149	³	179
x	120	–	150	´	180
y	121	—	151	µ	181
z	122	˜	152	¶	182
{	123	™	153	·	183
|	124	š	154	¸	184
}	125	›	155	¹	185
~	126	œ	156	º	186
•	127	N/A	157	»	187
N/A	128	N/A	158	¼	188
N/A	129	Ÿ	159	½	189
‚	130	(space)	160	¾	190
ƒ	131	¡	161	¿	191

DDC Publishing • www.ddcpub.com

Symbol	ANSI Number	Symbol	ANSI Number	Symbol	ANSI Number
À	192	Ü	220	ø	248
Á	193	Ý	221	ù	249
Â	194	Þ	222	ú	250
Ã	195	ß	223	û	251
Ä	196	à	224	ü	252
Å	197	á	225	ý	253
Æ	198	â	226	þ	254
Ç	199	ã	227	ÿ	255
È	200	ä	228		
É	201	å	229		
Ê	202	æ	230		
Ë	203	ç	231		
Ì	204	è	232		
Í	205	é	233		
Î	206	ê	234		
Ï	207	ë	235		
Ð	208	ì	236		
Ñ	209	í	237		
Ò	210	î	238		
Ó	211	ï	239		
Ô	212	ð	240		
Õ	213	ñ	241		
Ö	214	ò	242		
×	215	ó	243		
Ø	216	ô	244		
Ù	217	õ	245		
Ú	218	ö	246		
Û	219	÷	247		

Reference Table C-1: The ANSI character set

Appendix D: RGB Color Codes

Color	RGB Code	Color	RGB Code
Aquamarine	#70DB93	Gray	#C0C0C0
Aquamarine (Med)	#32CD99	Gray (Dark Slate)	#2F4F4F
Black	#000000	Gray (Light)	#A8A8A8
Blue	#0000FF	Khaki	#9F9F5F
Blue (Cadet)	#5F9F9F	Magenta	#FF00FF
Blue (Corn Flower)	#42426F	Maroon	#8E236B
Blue (Dark Slate)	#6B238E	Olive	#4F4F2F
Blue (Light)	#C0D9D9	Orange	#FF7F00
Blue (Med)	#3232CD	Orchid	#DB70DB
Blue (Midnight)	#2F24F4	Pink	#BC8F8F
Blue (Navy)	#23238E	Plum	#EAADEA
Blue (Neon)	#4D4DFF	Purple (Dark)	#871F78
Blue (Sky)	#3299CC	Quartz	#D9D9F3
Brass	#B5A642	Red	#FF0000
Bronze	#8C7853	Red (Orange)	#FF2400
Brown	#A62A2A	Rose (Dusty)	#856363
Brown (Dark)	#5C4033	Salmon	#6F4242
Brown (Faded)	#F5CCB0	Scarlet	#8C1717
Chocolate (Baker's)	#5C3317	Sienna	#8E6B23
Chocolate (Semi-sweet)	#6B4226	Silver	#E6E8FA
Copper	#B87333	Sky (Summer)	#38B0DE
Copper (Dark Green)	#4A766E	Tan	#DB9370
Copper (Green)	#527F76	Tan (Dark)	#97694F
Coral	#FF7F00	Thistle	#D8BFD8
Cyan	#00FFFF	Turquoise (Dark)	#7093DB
Firebrick	#8E2323	Turquoise	#ADEAEA
Gold	#CD7F32	Violet	#4F2F4F
Gold (Bright)	#D9D919	Violet (Blue)	#9F5F9F
Gold (Old)	#CFB53B	Violet (Red)	#CC3299
Goldenrod	#DBDB70	Wheat	#D8D8BF
Goldenrod (Med)	#EAEAAE	White	#FFFFFF
Green	#00FF00	Wood (Dark)	#855E42
Green (Dark)	#2F4F2F	Wood (Light)	#E9C2A6
Green (Pale)	#8FBC8F	Wood (Med)	#A68064
Green (Yellow)	#99CC32	Yellow	#FFFF00

Reference Table D-1: RGB Colors

Appendix E: Web Server Error Codes

A system of codes exists to inform client browsers of the nature of technical problems that may occur while attempting to download Web pages.

- The 400 series of Web error codes indicates an error with the Web *client*
- The 500 series of Web error codes indicates an error with the Web *server*

Error Code	Meaning	Remedy
400 (Bad Request)	1) The Web server contacted does not recognize the requested document; 2) the document requested does not exist; 3) the client is not authorized to access the requested document	Seek the information from another source or contact the Webmaster of the site for an explanation of the error
401 (Unauthorized)	The Web server is expecting some type of encryption ID from the client and—when it does not receive it—refuses access to the client browser	Obtain authorization to access the server from the Web site's Webmaster or seek the information desired from an alternate source
403 (Forbidden)	Web site from which HTML document is being requested requires permission—at least a password	Ensure the accuracy of the password submitted or obtain password from site's Webmaster
404 (Not Found)	The Web server has been located, but the HTML document requested cannot be located	Specify a URL that is "up" one level in the server hierarchy to determine if the Web site exists
500 (Internal Error)	The Web server is unable to send the Web page or associated data due to an internal (server software) error	Seek the desired information from an alternate source or attempt the download at a later time
501 (Not Implemented)	The Web server does not support the specific feature being requested	Seek the desired information from another source
502 (Service Overloaded)	The Web server cannot process the request due to bandwidth restrictions	Seek the desired information from an alternate source or attempt the download at a later time
503 (Gateway Time-out)	The connection between the Web server and the browser has timed out, due to: 1) server problems; 2) Internet problems; or 3) browser problems	Attempt the download again. If this does not work, attempt the download at a later time, preferably when network traffic is lighter
Failed DNS Lookup	1) The IP address of the Web site could not be located by the ISP's domain name server; or 2) the server is too burdened to process the request	1) ensure that the correct URL has been provided to the client browser; 2) wait until less network traffic exists on the ISP's domain name server

Reference Table E-1: Common Web server error codes

Appendix F: HTML Editors

HTML editors, such as HotDog Pro and Microsoft FrontPage, are software applications that automate the creation and editing of HTML documents. HTML editors also format HTML documents in ASCII format by default. HTML editors serve two important functions:

- they expedite (quicken) development and editing of HTML documents

- they help ensure accuracy and validity of HTML script

Many software companies market and herald their HTML editors as software applications that enable individuals with little or no HTML knowledge to craft high-quality, high-impact Web pages. This is typically an exaggeration and more marketing than reality.

HTML editors can certainly enable HTML novices to create *rudimentary* HTML documents and fulfill the requirements of basic Web publishing. However, a person who is unfamiliar with the inherent strengths, weaknesses, and nuances of the HyperText Markup Language will typically be unable to create a robust Web-based publication. HTML editors have limited value for novice users who wish to create elaborate, high-impact Web pages.

 HTML editors are popular software applications, especially within organizations, because they theoretically allow the production of more HTML script in less time with greater accuracy.

Some popular HTML editors are listed in Reference Table F-1:

HTML Editor	URL	Comment
HotDog Pro	www.sausage.com	Shareware version available.
HoTMetaL PRO	www.softquad.com	No shareware version; "walkthrough" demo available on Web site.
HTML Assistant Pro	www.brooknorth.com	Shareware version available.
Microsoft FrontPage 2000[28]	www.microsoft.com/frontpage	No shareware version; Microsoft Office 2000 Premium includes FrontPage 2000.

Reference Table F-1: Popular HTML editor software

---

[28] For more information regarding FrontPage 2000, see DDC's *Mastering FrontPage 2000* Series.

Appendix G: Glossary

Anchor

An element in an HTML document from which a link is accessed by a user. Anchors may be either text or inline images, and provide access to various data, including other Web pages, binary files, Gopher and FTP servers, and launching E-mail client applications. Anchors also provide a method for advancing to another section of the same Web page or a specific location in a different Web page.

Animated GIF

An advanced capability of the GIF 89a image file format that allows several discrete GIF images to be archived in a single GIF image. Animated GIFs are then referenced in an HTML document for use as inline images. No special tagging or attributes are required to use an animated GIF, although advanced control functions that allow infinite or limited looping are available. Browsers capable of displaying animated GIF files automatically detect and display the animated GIF, the individual GIF images comprising the master GIF are displayed in rapid succession, creating the illusion of animation.

ANSI Character Set

A set of 256 characters, numbered from 0 to 255, established by ANSI, the American National Standards Institute. HTML scripters may use them to establish character entities. The standard HTML character entity syntax applies, but the character entity element (copy, reg, deg) is a pound sign (#) followed by the ANSI character number, such as 112 or 241. Thus, a character entity featuring an ANSI character would have a syntax of .

ASCII

The acronym for *America Standard Code for Information Interchange*. A universal, cross-platform plain text file format. The ASCII format does not support text formatting (such as bold, italic, or underline) and will not store layout information, such as margins, tabs, or embedded objects. Also known as *DOS text* or *plain text*, ASCII is the format in which an HTML document must be stored.

Attribute

An HTML element that modifies or enhances the behavior of a tag by providing additional instructions to a Web browser. Not all HTML tags have attributes. Multiple attributes may be used simultaneously with a single tag (providing they do not logically negate or interfere with each other). Netscape Communications Corporation, Microsoft, Netscape, and the W3C frequently introduce new attributes to existing HTML tags.

Body

The larger portion of the HTML document that is interpreted and displayed by a Web browser as a Web page. It can contain hypertext link anchors, inline images, content data, and multimedia objects. The Body, combined with the Head, comprises an entire HTML document.

Border

A visible rule between two frames (*see Frame*) within a single Web page; also the outside rules of a table (*see Table*).

Box properties

These properties set the size, position, and space around the boxes that surround elements. By default, the box is usually invisible, but as you apply margin, padding, or border properties, you can watch the box change its shape.

Browser

(see *Web browser*)

Canvas

See *Display canvas*.

Cascading order

Styles have a cascading order or rules of precedence. Starting with styles that have the strongest precedence, the general cascading order is: the STYLE attribute at the element level, the <STYLE> element at the document level, the external style sheet, and the last external style sheet if multiple style sheets are used. This is a general statement of precedence order; exceptions may apply.

Cascading Style Sheets (CSS)

CSS is a standard set of rules that govern how elements are displayed. CSS Level 1 has been a recommendation of the World Wide Web Consortium (W3C) since 1996, while CSS Level 2 has been a recommendation since 1998. The leading browsers are not yet in full compliance with either of these recommendations, though they are constantly improving their support. Recommendations of W3C are widely considered *the* standard for the Web.

Cells

Individual "compartments" for data that are created by the intersection of rows and columns within a table (*see Table*). Table cells can contain text, hyperlinks, and images.

Character Reference

An HTML element that begins with an ampersand (&), followed by a predefined term, and ends with a semicolon (;). For example, the copyright symbol (©), may be created with the sequence ©. The degree sign may be generated with the ° character reference. Character references may also be created using the ANSI character set. (see *ANSI Character Set*)

Child element

See *Inheritance*.

Class selector

See *Selector*.

Column

A group of adjacent cells positioned vertically within a table. Columns can also be formed by narrow, vertical frames (*see Frame*).

Content type

The CSS content type is "text/css." It is used as part of the <STYLE> and <LINK> elements. Content types describe message entities. Content types are also called *MIME types*. See *Message entity* and *Multipurpose Internet Mail Extensions (MIME) type*.

CSS

See *Cascading Style Sheets*.

DHTML

Dynamic HTML (DHTML) does not refer to a standard, specified language like HTML, but is a term that describes the creation of dynamic effects on a Web page using HTML, CSS, and JavaScript (or another scripting language).

Display canvas

Usually the display canvas is just the browser window, but it could be any surface to which CSS could be applied, even a printed piece of paper.

Document Type Definition (DTD)

HTML is an application of Standard Generalized Markup Language (SGML). As such, all elements (tags), attributes, entities, and so forth, that make up HTML are defined in something called a Document Type Definition (DTD). A browser relies on the DTD to help it determine how to display files formatted in HTML. If you would like to see the strict DTD of HTML 4.0, refer to `www.w3.org/TR/REC-html40/strict.dtd`.

DTD

See *Document Type Definition*.

Embedding

To insert or place an item or object within a different item or object. For example, ordered and unordered lists can be nested within table cells.

Empty Tag

One of two categories of HTML tag types. An empty tag is a single tag; it does not require opening and closing tags. Empty tags may have attributes. Examples of empty tags are the horizontal rules `<HR>`, paragraph breaks `<P>`, and line breaks, `<BR>`.

Form

A collection of various field types designed to collect data from a client (user) and upload it to a server. In HTML, forms are created using a family of tags and attributes and can send form content to either a POP e-mail account or to a CGI or Perl script that calculates or stores the data in some manner, possibly interacting with a backend database. Completed forms are also called *populated* forms.

Frame

One of multiple sections of a Web page that has been created using a frameset. Individual frames are either scrollable or not scrollable and may or may not display a visible border. Frames borders may be movable or not movable. A common application of frames is the creation of a nav bar for an entire Web site to aid users in navigating and locating specific information.

Frameset

All HTML code between (and including) the opening and closing `<FRAMESET>` tags. A frameset can be nested (*see Nesting*) within another frameset to create more sophisticated frame layouts.

GIF (Graphics Interchange Format)

Introduced by CompuServe in 1987 (and updated in 1989), GIF is the most common image file format found on the Internet and is one of the preferred formats for inline images. Available in both 87a and 89a formats, GIF is an inherently compressed format, meaning that GIF files require less space than non-compressed image formats (BMP). The GIF format has a maximum color depth of 256 (8 bit) and is not a lossy format. GIF 89a offers the ability to create transparent images.

Head

The Head of an HTML document is the minority of the document and contains global instructional information and other Web browser cues that are not directly displayed by the browser to a user. The Head, combined with the Body, comprises an entire HTML document.

Heading Styles

HTML 4.0 provides six heading styles—or levels—denoted with the following tag syntax: `<H1>...</H1>`. Heading Level 1 is the largest header and Heading Level 6 is the smallest. There are no absolute point sizes for Heading Levels, only a relative scale from largest to smallest.

Horizontal Rule

A horizontal line that, by default, has a width that spans the Web page. The horizontal rule is inserted with the `<HR>` tag and has many associated attributes for adjusting width, thickness, and justification.

HTML (HyperText Markup Language)

The authoring language used to develop Web pages. The standard for HTML is currently under development. The International Standards Organization ratifies and publishes the HTML standard, but many independent browser developers have added significant and numerous extensions to the HTML language.

HTTP (HyperText Transfer Protocol)

The protocol for transporting HTML documents across the Internet. HTTP requires that TCP/IP be running on both the client and server computers. HTTP is the transfer protocol used by HTML authors when scripting anchor tags that refer to documents and multimedia data that reside on Web servers.

Hypermedia

The fusion of hypertext (see *Hypertext*) and multimedia. Hypermedia is available in the form of audio, video, animation, and special image and multimedia data types on the World Wide Web. Hypermedia information is located, downloaded, and consumed in the technical framework of the Web and hypertext navigation systems, including standard Web browsers and the HTTP transfer protocol. Many high-end multimedia data formats require special Netscape Navigator or Microsoft Internet Explorer plug-ins.

Hypertext

A term coined by computer visionary Ted Nelson in 1965. Hypertext is text that contains links to other pieces of text, or to various types of media, including sound, video, animation, and images. Hypertext allows a user to navigate through an information hyperspace in a user-defined, non-linear sequence.

ID selector

See *Selector*.

Inheritance

HTML tags have a parent-child relationship. For example, the `<P>` tag is a child of the `<BODY>` tag, as `<P>` is expected to appear within `<BODY>`. Child elements automatically inherit styles from their parents. To be more precise, if a font size of 12 points is applied to `<BODY>`, `<P>` will also have a point size of 12 points, unless it is overridden by another style rule.

Inline Image

Any image displayed in a Web page by an HTML browser. Inline images are GIF or JPEG format.

Inline style

An inline style is one that applies only to the current element or tag and is specified by the `STYLE` attribute of the tag. Inline styles override or take precedence over document-level or external styles.

Internal link

Another name for a `TARGET` anchor. A `TARGET` anchor refers to a section of the same Web page, a specific section of a different Web page, or a target frame in a master frame document (*see Master frame*).

JPEG (Joint Photographic Experts Group)

JPEG is an increasingly popular image file format on the Internet. The JPEG image file format is recognized by leading Web browsers for use as inline images. JPEG can support a color depth of 16.7 million (24 bit) but is a lossy compression ratio. JPEG is rapidly gaining popularity among Web authors and publishers because it provides greater compression ratios for images and, thus, creates images that are fewer bytes in size than other image file formats, including GIF. JPEG was designed for compressing high-resolution, photographic quality images. (see *Inline image*)

Keyword

A term used by a search engine to index a Web page in a database or to retrieve a Web page from a database. Keywords can be tagged with the Meta tag to help search engine databases index Web pages.

List

There are two categories of HTML lists: ordered and unordered. Ordered lists are more commonly called numbered lists. Unordered lists are typically called bullet lists. Lists are created using the list tag family, involving either the <OL> (ordered list) or <UL> (unordered list) tag in conjunction with the <LI> (list item) tag.

Master frame

One of many files that compose a Web page divided into frames. The master frame contains the instructions for the size and placement of all "slave" frames (*see Slave frame*). The slave frames contain the actual content of the frames.

Masthead

In some pages that segment information into frames, the masthead is the top, horizontal frame that displays the name, tagline, and logo of the organization to which the site belongs. Mastheads may also display the date and a navigation bar (*see Nav bar*). The term masthead is borrowed from newspapers, which use mastheads for a similar purpose.

Message entity

A message entity is a kind of transmission that is sent over the Internet. Message entities have certain characteristics. A content type such as text/css, for example, allows a browser to know that it can expect a message entity that conforms to an expected format, that is, a CSS style sheet. See *Content type*.

Meta tag

Denoted as <META> in HTML, this tag must be placed between the opening and closing <HEAD> tags in an HTML document. This tag can perform many functions; the primary purpose of the Meta tag is to provide identification information to databases. Applications include keywords for database indexing, author/publisher information, and publication date.

Microsoft Internet Explorer (IE or MSIE)

A freeware Web browser available from Microsoft Corporation. MSIE supports JavaScript, Java, ActiveX, and many multimedia data formats via plug-ins.

MIME type

See *Multipurpose Internet Mail Extensions (MIME) type*.

Multipurpose Internet Mail Extensions (MIME) type

MIME types provide standard ways for labeling packages of data for transport over the Internet. See *Content type*.

Name anchor

Also called an "internal" link, this is a special type of hypertext anchor that refers to another anchor. The referring anchor has a `TARGET=text` attribute and the anchor that is referred to has a `NAME=text` attribute. Together, the `TARGET` and `NAME` attributes work with the Anchor tag to create anchors that refer to specific sections of HTML documents (instead of simply to a URL address). Name anchors are also used to refer anchors in one frame of a Web page to a different frame on the same Web page.

Nav bar

A section of a Web site, typically housed within a narrow frame, that provides links to all major areas of the site. Nav bar links change the content of the "content" frame—the main focus of each page on the site—using `TARGET` anchors and `NAME` attributes attached to the target frame.

Nesting

To insert or place an item or object within another item or object that is of similar or the same type. For example, in HTML, tables can be nested within other tables and framesets can be nested in other framesets (*see Frameset*).

Netscape Navigator

(`www.netscape.com`). A freeware Web browser available from Netscape Communications Corporation. Netscape Navigator supports JavaScript, Java, and many multimedia and streaming data formats via the use of plug-ins. Navigator does not support ActiveX controls.

Non-empty Tag

One of the categories of HTML tag categories. A non-empty tag set contains both an opening and closing tag. The vast majority of HTML tags are non-empty. The closing tag differs from the opening tag with the addition of a forward slash following the opening wicket (`<B>dog</B>`).

Parent element

See *Inheritance*.

PNG (Portable Network Graphics)

A new graphics file format introduced in 1998 by the W3C that, unlike JPEG (see *JPEG*) and GIF (see *GIF*) was specifically developed for the Web and HTML. PNG is well suited for both graphics and images and is intended to be a replacement for JPEG and GIF.

Precedence

See *Cascading order*.

Property

A property is a keyword that specifies a characteristic of an element. It is always immediately followed by a colon (:). Examples of properties are `text-align` and `font-size`.

Pseudo-class selector

See *Selector*.

RGB Color Code

The six-letter codes that represent three (3) pairs of hexadecimal codes across a spectrum of values for the: 1) red, 2) green, and 3) blue color attributes. In combination, these three hexadecimal code value pairs form a single color code. In HTML, RGB color codes are used to specify background colors and text colors (both unvisited and visited hypertext links).

Row

A group of adjacent cells positioned horizontally within a table. Columns can also be formed by narrow, horizontal frames (*see Frame*).

Rule

Also known as a gridline, this is the top or bottom side of a table row or the left or right side of a column. The display of rules can be controlled using the RULES attribute to the Table tag.

Script

Term used to describe the contents of an HTML document; the combination of the content of a Web page and the HTML elements (tags, tag attributes, character entities, etc.) that instruct a Web browser how to interpret and display Web page content (non-HTML text and images).

Selector

A selector is a keyword that specifies the element or class to which style properties and values apply. A tag name, for example, can be a selector, such as in H1 {text-align: center} where H1 is the selector. This is also called a type selector. A class name can also be a selector, as in H1.center {text-align: center}. where center, the class name, is the selector. Other selectors include ID selectors (#small {font-size: 9pt}), dynamic pseudo-class selectors (A:hover {color: red}), and the universal selector (* {font-size: 12pt}). See *Value*.

Slave frame

Any HTML document that is referred to by a master frame document and displays its content within a single frame of an HTML document according to instructions contained in the master frame document (*see Master frame*).

Strict

A term that refers to HTML tags and attributes that follow the strict definition of HTML 4.0. It means that the tag or attribute is part of the formal definition of the language and is not planned for phase out. To see the strict DTD, refer to www.w3.org/TR/REC-html40/strict.dtd.

Table

Grid made up of rows and columns for the purpose of presenting data in a logical and segmented order. In HTML, tables are created with the <TABLE> tag and the collection of related tags.

Tag

An HTML tag is an element that is unseen by the user but is interpreted by the browser. A tag can be either empty or non-empty. Non-empty tags act upon text enclosed in a pair of opening and closing tags. An opening tag begins with a left wicket (<) followed immediately by the tag element and any attributes (and their associated values) and ends with a right wicket (>). Closing tags differ from opening tags with the addition of a forward slash (/) between the opening wicket and the tag element. An empty tag is a single tag that resembles an opening tag in a non-empty tag set.

Target anchor

A hypertext anchor that refers to a Name anchor within the same or another HTML document. Target anchors—in combination with Name anchors—are used to create nav bars (*see Nav bar*) in frames-enhanced Web sites (*see frames*) and to refer to specific sections of the same or a different Web page.

Tiling

The process of repeating a background image in a Web page to create the illusion of a consistent, single backdrop pattern. Web browsers automatically tile image files (GIF or JPEG) that are referenced using the BACKGROUND attribute to the <BODY> tag.

Transfer protocol

A common set of data transmission technical standards for exchanging information between two computer networks or two computers. All Internet transfer protocols are subsets of TCP/IP.

Transitional

A term used in the HTML 4.0 Specification to refer to older HTML tags and attributes. It means that the tag or attribute is still permitted for use, but are on their way out. They are no longer part of the strict definition of the language. To see what the transitional DTD looks like for HTML 4.0, refer to `www.w3.org/TR/REC-html40/loose.dtd`.

Type selector

See *Selector*.

Universal selector

See *Selector*.

URL (Uniform Resource Locator)

The address of any Internet-based information resource when accessed via a Web browser. Neither IE nor Navigator require the entry of the transfer protocol `http://` as part of a Web page URL.

Value

A value, paired with a CSS property, determines how an element or class is displayed. For example, in the definition `H1 {text-align: center}`, the keyword `center` is the value. See *Property*.

Web browser

A universal Internet software application that runs on a client computer. The browser performs five basic functions: 1) locates Internet resources, 2) requests the resources from a server, 3) downloads data, 4) interprets data, and 5) displays the information to the user. Browsers can download and display information from Web servers, Gopher servers, and FTP servers.

Wicket

The commonly accepted term for the left angle bracket (<) and the right angle bracket (>) that are used to syntactically enclose HTML tag elements. Used as mathematical operators, these characters are called the "less than sign" and the "greater than sign."

World Wide Web (Web, WWW, or W3)

A global hypertext and hypermedia-based service of the Internet that is known simply as "the Web." The Web was conceived in 1990 by Tim Berners-Lee and Robert Cailliau at CERN in Geneva, Switzerland and was officially introduced to the Internet community in 1992. Today the Web is the fastest-growing service of the Internet, offering over *one billion* pages. It is estimated that 1.5 million pages are added to the Web *each day*.

Index

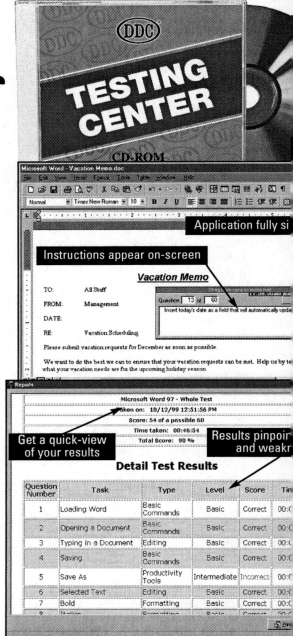

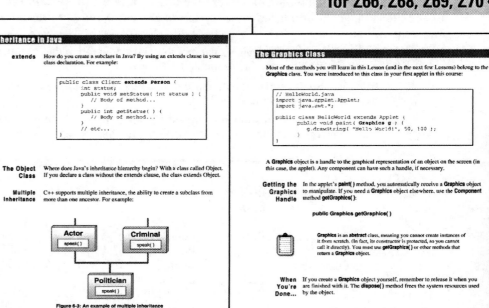

Less Surfing—More Answers—*FAST*

ese books bring helpful Internet information into focus, so you won't have to spend a lifetime surfing it. Each book provides you with practical Web sites plus these skills:

- **common e-mail systems** (like AOL, Outlook, Messenger)
- **search engines and browsing** (keywords, Yahoo, Lycos, etc.)
- **refining searches for minimizing search time** (Boolean searching, etc.)

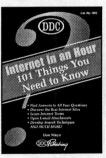  

FOR BEGINNERS
Cat. No. HR3 • ISBN 1-56243-603-1

FOR MANAGERS
Cat. No. HR2 • ISBN 1-56243-602-3

FOR SALES PEOPLE
Cat. No. HR4 • ISBN 1-56243-604-X

FOR STUDENTS
Cat. No. HR1 • ISBN 1-56243-601-5

BUSINESS COMMUNICATION & E-MAIL
Cat. No. HR6 • ISBN 1-56243-676-7

101 THINGS YOU NEED TO KNOW
Cat. No. HR5 • ISBN 1-56243-675-9

FOR SENIORS
Cat. No. HR7 • ISBN 1-56243-695-3

ENTERTAINMENT & LEISURE
Cat. No. HR8 • ISBN 1-56243-696-1

FOR SHOPPERS & BARGAIN HUNTERS
Cat. No. HR9 • ISBN 1-56243-697-X

HEALTH & MEDICAL RESOURCES
Cat. No. HR10 • ISBN 1-56243-713-5

INVESTING & PERSONAL FINANCE
Cat. No. HR11 • ISBN 1-56243-758-5

ROMANCE & RELATIONSHIPS
Cat. No. HR12 • ISBN 1-56243-772-0

$10 ea.

Preview our books online at:
http://www.ddcpub.com

DDC *Publishing* **to order call 800-528-3897 or fax 800-528-3862**

275 Madison Avenue / New York, NY 10016

#6-2K IH